Recoded City:
Co-creating Urban Futures

Thomas Ermacora + Lucy Bullivant

LONDON AND NEW YORK

First published 2016
by Routledge
2 Park Square, Milton Park, Abingdon, Oxon OX14 4RN

Simultaneously published in the USA and Canada by Routledge
711 Third Avenue, New York, NY 10017

Routledge is an imprint of the Taylor & Francis Group, an informa business

British Library Cataloguing-in-Publication Data
A catalogue record for this book is available from the British Library

Library of Congress Cataloging in Publication Data
Ermacora, Thomas.
Recoded city : co-creating urban futures /
Thomas Ermacora and Lucy Bullivant.
pages cm
Includes bibliographical references and index.
1. Urbanization. 2. City planning--Citizen participation. 3. Urban policy--Citizen participation. I. Bullivant, Lucy. II. Title.
HT361.E76 2015
307.1'216--dc23
2015005534

ISBN: 978-1-138-81979-5 (hbk)
ISBN: 978-1-138-81980-1 (pbk)
ISBN: 978-1-315-74420-9 (ebk)

Typeset in Chronicle Text
by Hoefler & Co.

Typeset in Akzidenz Grotesk
by H.Berthold type foundry

Publisher's Note:
This book has been prepared from camera-ready copy provided by the authors.

Printed in Canada

Recoded City:
Co-creating Urban Futures

Thomas Ermacora FRSA is a regeneration architect, impact entrepreneur and futures thinker, nominated for the UK Placemaking Awards 2013 and 2014. He is founder and creative director of the tactical urban design non-profit Clear Village (Clear-Village.org), delivering participatory initiatives catalyzing the recovery of neighbourhoods across Europe, as well as of the Limewharf cultural innovation hub (Limewharf.org) and Machines Rooms fab lab (MachinesRoom.org) in east London. Inspired by project work with Gehl Architects and Gehry Partners among others, and now working closely with Carmody Groarke, his observations and commitments are the reason for this book.

Lucy Bullivant PhD Hon FRIBA is a cultural historian and award-winning author, critic, exhibition curator and consultant specialising in architecture, urban design and adaptive planning. She is Adjunct Professor, Urban Design History and Theory at Syracuse University, founder and editor-in-chief of the webzine Urbanista.org, and author of many books, including *Masterplanning Futures*, published by Routledge in 2012 and winner of the Book of the Year Award at Urban Design Awards, London, 2014; and *Responsive Environments: Architecture, Art and Design* (V&AContemporary, 2006). Lucybullivant.net

Growing urbanisation, accelerating complexity and deteriorating ecosystems affecting cities and their peripheries make them the nexus of mankind's challenges and opportunities. Top-down masterplanning, conventional policymaking and green design are not delivering the systemic changes needed to secure better living conditions for the 90%. Without appropriate and scalable strategies, public health, economic vitality, political stability and environmental conservation across the globe will be significantly impacted.

New mindsets, methods, tools and technologies can create a renaissance in urban sustainability. As *Recoded City* shows, localist design strategies and interventions are already forging new stakeholder dynamics, and through various collaboration processes and sophisticated DIY approaches that make more with less, are solving problems everywhere. The burgeoning practice of participatory placemaking, which Ermacora terms 'recoding', combines bottom-up and top-down thinking. Through its ways and means of regenerating and rebalancing neighbourhoods affected by financial or social segregation, it represents a new standard for urban design.

Today's radically different placemaking landscape puts individuals and groups at the heart of urban renewal, helping to build resilience from the ground up and nurturing what we define as 'place capital' for the benefit of all. New commons for citizens, often connected to public realm improvements, counter a discriminatory market and limited public attention, and affirm an alternative model of society based on greater self-reliance.

Recoded City critically investigates participatory placemaking's topical themes, charting its historic rise in society, and exploring adaptive, inclusive practices across cultures, including future-proofing and rebuilding from disaster. The book discusses new collaborative, distributed governance and welfare models as emerging platforms of the open society, the democratisation of technology, 'wiki culture' and art as a community actor. It sheds light on issues including appropriate funding models, priorities of best practice in participatory placemaking, the nurturing of local assets, evaluation processes, and how to consider legacy.

Including 43 stories drawing on fresh research about pioneering practitioners and projects around the world, and illustrated by some 250 photographs and more than 20 custom-designed infographics, this book shows how, through innovative approaches, both social and environmental capital can be maximised and more equitable and satisfying places created.

Recoded City is for all decision-makers concerned with the public realm, the private sector, local government, social enterprises, architects, urban and landscape designers, planners, ecologists, engineers, urban geographers, artists, filmmakers and urbanists.

Contents

A B C O N M S T P

Preface
John Thackara

I write these words outside the Portakabin control room of Shambala, a summer festival staged annually in Northamptonshire, England. On the wall is the street plan of what looks like a mid-sized town. Some 15,000 people have indeed filled a vast field with tents, yurts, sound stages, composting toilets, drinking-water tanks, hot tubs, food vans, cellphone charging stations, yoga enclosures, a barber shop, an aromatherapy area, cash vending machines in a caravan and pagan circles around wood-burning stoves. Surrounding Shambala's 'downtown' core is a densely packed suburbia of tents; in these, the sleeping area per person – a mere couple of square metres – is similar to the space available to billions of people in the world's other favelas.

Most of Shambala's prosperous urban tribe will return to a world of concrete and media screens when the festivities end – but, for two thirds of the world's population, nomadism and contingency are everyday conditions of life. Most of the world's 800 million urban farmers, for example, produce food because they need it, not to be cool.[1] In megacities across the Global South, informal settlements are also filled with the pop-up retail stands, food trucks, street traders, guerilla gardening and unofficial parks that at Shambala are celebrated as fashionable novelties. In the world's refugee camps and post-disaster settlements, too, a dynamic variety of social micro-economies is emerging in which people share energy, materials, time, skill, software, space or food.

These activities depend more on social energy and trust than on fixed assets and real estate: there's an emphasis on collaboration and sharing; on person-to-person interactions; on the adaptation and reuse of materials and buildings. Such resource-light ways to meet daily life needs are usually described as poverty, or a lack of development. But in 35 years as a guest in what used to be called the 'developing' world, I've come to a startling conclusion: people who are poor in material terms are highly accomplished at the creation of value in ways that do not destroy natural and human assets.

DIY urbanism, in other words, is second nature for people who cannot depend on the resource- and energy-intensive support systems of the industrial world. This is not to trivialise the extreme challenges faced by poor people on a daily basis; but, to the extent that a regenerative economy is based on local production, human labour and natural energy, then the poor people of the world are further along the learning curve than the rest of us.

This book will help the North to catch up with the South. *Recoded City: Co-creating Urban Futures* is filled with inspiring confirmation that, when it comes to shelter and placemaking in an age of limits, a city's primary resource is the energy and motivation of its inhabitants. Shelter, we learn in the pages that follow, is more of a social process than a product-design one. From my own research I know that in Haiti after the catastrophic earthquake of 2010, for example, 90% of surviving families wanted to repair or rebuild their own dwellings, but they were often constrained from doing so by an incoming army of young architecture students over-confident in their design skills and under-equipped with social ones.

The 43 Stories in *Recoded City* (from page 107) provide welcome evidence that a transformation in socially motivated architecture is tangible. They reflect the rich variety of responsive approaches and needs in very diverse places around the world as far apart as Rwanda in Africa, Moscow in Russia, Roxbury in Boston, USA, the eastern coast of Japan, and Christchurch, New Zealand. A number of the stories in *Recoded City* are from the edges of cities rather than from their centres – which is one of the book's many strengths: the edges are where the future lies. A major emphasis today is on collaborative construction and participatory placemaking, in which the main measure of success is the capacity of a community to continue improving its place after the 'experts' have left.

For the past 150 years, the modern city and its buildings have been shaped by the ready availability of fossil fuel, and by credit. Prior to the global economic crisis of 2008, the land- and concrete-devouring real estate-industrial complex was such a huge part of the global economy that, in one way or another, it employed a third of salaried workers. Our institutions, and professional practices, too, were formed by the use of massive energy inputs to create structures, to heat and cool buildings, to move and treat water, and to grow and supply food.

How things change: by 2020, according to the Organisation for Economic Co-operation and Development (OECD), two thirds of the world's workers will be employed in a vast and growing shadow economy that's reshaping our cities even as the formal economy stagnates. From Shenzhen in China's Pearl River Delta to Odessa in the Ukraine, economic activity is emigrating from shiny glass towers into a perpetually shifting mosaic of street-level locations. This shadow economy is more fragmented, and more reliant on social networks, than the formal one – but it is no less dynamic for that. Because social practices are a key part of this urban transformation, the tasks of design are mutating. Rather than focusing on logistics infrastructures, or retail parks, the new priority is on what the Mumbai-based collective CRIT calls a city's 'transactive capacity' – the services, policies, platforms, hubs and infrastructures that are needed to help communities share, collaborate and construct.

Recoded City should help to facilitate this 'new priority' for transactive capacity and give all participatory placemakers, and those aspiring to play a role in this growing field, plenty of inspirational ideas and examples of best practice.

John Thackara - @johnthackara - is the founder and director of Doors of Perception. A writer, philosopher and event producer, he leads workshops and organises festivals at the intersection between ecological, social and societal change. He is the author of the widely read blog doorsofperception.com and of the best-selling book *In the Bubble: Designing In a Complex World.* His latest book, *How to Thrive in the Next Economy: Designing Tomorrow's World Today,* is published by Thames & Hudson in 2015.

Introduction

What comes first in your priorities for the communities you most closely identify with? Solvency, security, stability, sustainability, aesthetics, ethics, liveability, well-being, better social integration? It's hard to choose – they all matter such a lot. To actually achieve all of them, firstly, questions must be asked: who are the guardians of the public-realm spaces and environments these communities enjoy? What are their roles and are they fully capable? Are you aware of disused, dilapidated spaces in your city or neighbourhood, and do you need on-the-ground help with places acutely damaged by natural or man-made trauma? Do you see ways beyond mainstream urban design and planning practices in which needs and possibilities could be united, and have a lasting positive effect on your priorities? How could you make valuable change, representing the aspirations of those living there, actually happen on the ground?

Top-down placemaking, engineered by private firms or public-private partnerships, and generally facilitated through bureaucratic planning processes, has a limited capacity to answer valid and frequently pressing questions such as these. The results of development processes – or 'recreation', as they are sometimes termed in euphemistic marketing speak – managed this way in today's climate of weakened scope of public sector governance, are often not geared to increasing social and natural capital, as hard as these may be to comprehensively measure.[1] Schemes are all too easily formulaic and 'instant' in nature, using superficial market research geared to specific goals, rather than evolving over time with strong social infrastructure plans, and being genuinely responsive to the lives of residents and people using spaces.

To be content just with such typical commercial models, or not to imagine that valid alternatives can be forged, by failing to probe more deeply or by not taking a keener interest, is to miss a huge opportunity to understand the future of neighbourhood identities differently. The impact of places upon people's lives, and the ways in which cultural meaning resonates at a local scale, through spatial and environmentally beneficial co-creation activities, are profound.

This book is addressed as much to mayors, developers, institutional investors, philanthropists, urban entrepreneurs, and all social enterprises that have a unique influence on city making, as it is to placemaking professionals who are converging and hybridising. The input of the former group revolves around what they offer inhabitants and visitors through established and new policies, which relates directly to how far they support those who can scarcely afford commercially driven choices. These positions are not foregone conclusions, and never have been. Today's levels and structures of inequality and the history of the distribution of wealth are 'shaped by the way economic, social and political actors view what is just and what is not, as well as by the relative power of those actors and the collective choices that result', writes economist Thomas Piketty in *Capital in the Twenty-first Century.*[2]

These realities have impacted on human habitation patterns, and the resources built co-creatively at different times in history represent bulwarks against inequality which contribute to our collective heritage, but often their impact is lost or the temporary gains do not mean vicious circles are broken. Community contexts undergoing reassessment and challenges deserve more resilient growth visions, and the best way they can achieve these, and build their localities as assets in the future, is through opening up the possibilities of increased local creative agency. How this process is managed is still hypothetical, and requires further study of emerging models, that demonstrate how the digital sphere is transforming people's ability to stimulate self-organisation and enable service provision in a distributed, rather than a centralised way.

Recoded City is a book about alternative, hybrid and complementary practices of placemaking, one that has been written in an era of both overt, and less apparent, paradigm shifts impacting on many fields of public life. Participatory placemaking differs from the conventional model of urban design and planning in that, from inception, it engages citizens in processes for the co-creation of contexts in which they live or can see a future. These are relatively experimental practices both for and within communities, drawn out of a place and its particular character and conditions, not imposed on it, for which co-author Thomas Ermacora, a pioneering practitioner in this field, has coined the term 'recoding'. The philosophy and approach of 'recoding' draws metaphorically on the fields of biology and computational intelligence. These rely on generative programmes, codes such as DNA or bits, that are both inherently reactive and evolutionary in the ways they express their use of resources.

Recoded City is not intended to be encyclopedic in scope, but presents a spectrum of contexts in which the imaginations of front line local actors and activist architects, or 'recoders', have succeeded in yielding significant social and economic added development – places where traditional placemaking was either absent or incapable of answering the demands of a community. Hence the book's validity lies in opening out, as a topical prism, the promise and demonstrable value of innovative ways of questioning, thinking and acting, in a manner that is both cost-effective and hugely transformative of urban economies.

These participatory activities, while being wedded to the special qualities of particular localities, are global in reach, and are documented through fresh research of all examples analysed across the book. Taking the form of a profound investigative study of participatory placemaking processes, *Recoded City* examines the major role of such activities we observe emerging from culture to culture, over a variety of timescales from nine months to three–five years or more of iterative efforts, and positively impacting on urban communities' self-knowledge, health, wealth and resources and, consequently, their scope for self-determination.

We are not saying that participatory placemaking should be wholly bottom-up or grassroots. For projects to succeed, the involvement of a wide range of bodies is necessary, and existing institutions undergoing transformation, as well as new organisations, are a part of the landscape of co-creation that we regard as fundamental and discuss in this book. Such activities, involving a high degree of testing and prototyping, carry strong potential for cultural momentum in building human capital, both with and for local people as their own legacy, as exercises in practical dreaming that bring responsibilities of many kinds. However, while they possess considerable versatility and advantages, and scope to address myriad needs, they face many challenges in becoming more widely accepted and scaling up.

Evolutions in theory and practice commonly involve a fight for adoption between freethinkers and the incumbent power structures of the global plutocracy, wedded as they mostly are to narrow indicators of Gross National Product (a strategy for society first questioned by Robert F Kennedy in 1968) rather than to those of Gross National Happiness (a philosophy introduced by the king of Bhutan in the 1970s).[3] In the fields of urban design and planning, in direct response to recent and ongoing economic,

ecological and cultural crises, there is today a renewed challenging of the orthodoxies of the past in order to give greater recognition to the centrality of social well-being as the basis for general sustainability.

Recoded City presents a new discourse about the identity of socially sustainable urban design and planning and their relationship with city dwellers, based on a cultural-historical analysis of relational thinking in politics, philosophy, sociology, urban geography and urbanism.

The book addresses the potentials and the capacities of a range of bottom-up and DIY urban design strategies – participatory placemaking – and the wide variety of cultural contexts in which it is practised. As our cultural, historical and philosophical perspectives underline, such approaches respond to the social inadequacy of top-down processes, and seek to provide alternatives to their intervention in the public realm.

Participatory placemaking is also about taking care of the aftermath and legacy. Instead of being in thrall to the gentrifying impact of the creative class on neighbourhoods – a rising trend chronicled by such writers as Richard Florida and Charles Landry – bringing new identities that politicians and developers can capitalise on but also pricing out local people, we believe in the power of an alternative process.[4] 'Recoding' anchors and stabilises growth, and supports local relationships, respecting and rewarding communities for their creativity and staying power.

Urban 'retrofitting' and 'acupuncture', 'tactical urbanism', 'social urbanism', 'radical urbanism', 'support and infill' – and 'recoding': while these terms stem from different sources, they refer to interrelated practices that are part of questioning placemaking approaches currently taking place. Each of these strategies has powerful proponents – for example writer Justin McGuirk's recent book *Radical Cities,* on urban acupuncture, and Pedro Gadanho's Museum of Modern Art New York exhibition and book, *Uneven Growth.*[5] The vast majority address themselves specifically to the needs of the 90%. So does this book, encompassing goals for social equity as well as post-disaster strategies, through new operating systems rather than the old ones based on silo thinking.

Moreover, participatory placemaking – or 'recoding' – as a vision, regards building capacity for resilience, social equity and liveability as the proper basis for ecological policies, adoption of technologies and behavioural shifts. It possesses a more realistic vision of sustainability, encompassing applications of technology to reach carbon targets, but equally, it draws on the intelligence of societies much more widely across the board, rather than focusing on the impacts of top-down processes alone.

Accordingly, placemaking is also closely related to issues of urban governance, and our book investigates the potentials of alternative, horizontal, cross-sector approaches to neighbourhood development. It opens up questions about innovative governing methods of projects, certainly, but also of social enterprise bodies with a self-appointed remit to regenerate their locales. These are vital issues for dissection in order to strengthen communities' means for their own self-determination, whatever individual members' personal histories and capacities.

Following a number of years of professional work, and many discussions and dialogues about the future of placemaking, Thomas Ermacora initiated and directed the Recoded City project from 2010, and in late 2012 he invited Lucy Bullivant to collaborate on it. As an integrated body of new texts, including a chapter on Ermacora's 'recoding' approach and the lessons to be drawn from it, the book represents a crucible of the extensive ideas and research of both *Recoded City*'s authors, from our respective professional standpoints. Ermacora is a leading regeneration architect and digital fabrication/maker movement specialist who founded the first fab lab in London; he has directed numerous innovative participatory placemaking projects around the world, and also acts as a futurist, curator and public speaker. Lucy Bullivant is an award-winning author, curator, journalist, lecturer and consultant. Her book *Masterplanning Futures* (2012) discusses the validity of alternative masterplanning frameworks and adaptive planning tools and processes around the globe, and her earlier publications, such as *4dsocial* (2007), have evaluated responsive, digitally enabled designs co-created by participants.[6]

Recoded City's first chapter, 'The Rise of Bottom-up Placemaking', discusses the centuries of contestations and negotiations with top-down institutions and patrons of the day. The clash of values manifested by the civil rights movement and emerging age of civil society organising from the 1950s has its roots in much earlier periods of history.

Applying narrow scientific theories to urban design and planning has been shown to reduce the cultural spirit of a place, but today's grasp of complexity theory and ecological systems, if allied with values of social capital and a sufficient vision of the art of placemaking, can change that dominant and destructive model.

Today there is a renewed challenging of the orthodoxies of the past in order to give greater recognition to the centrality of social well-being.

Self-sufficiency – including merchant craftsmen and alternative utopias – has coexisted alongside imperial and state-driven plans for modernisation operating on a command and control basis, and by the law of capital. Human agency, in gaining its mandate from the emergence of rational ethics – 'reason's own plan', as Kant put it – has benefited from the Enlightenment's social contract and more recent notions of human and social capital within frameworks of liberal democracy, embracing wider contexts and emotional capacities.

History's handed-down aspirations for ideal urban orders – whether represented by the 20th-century work of Modernist planning or by the City Efficient movement – are challenged by environmental populism, as the architectural writer and critic Reyner Banham noted in 1962.[7] In calling for, and seeing the potential, of new tools appropriate to the age, *Recoded City* recalls the fierce debates of the 1960s that challenged structures of authority and neo-liberal democracy. Pioneering figures such as urban activist and author Jane Jacobs, perceiving the growing gap between experts' technocratic approaches – city as machine – and citizens' own needs, called for the city to be designed around people's needs.[8]

Applying narrow scientific theories to urban design and planning has been shown to reduce the cultural spirit of a place, but today's grasp of complexity theory and ecological systems, if allied with values of social capital and a sufficient vision of the art of placemaking, can change that dominant and destructive model. Urban design teams and individuals such as the pioneering architect Jan Gehl have worked consistently to introduce urban quality of life criteria for city building, and to make the everyday, intimately experienced life of the city statistically visible. The explosive growth of cities from the 1960s, with its accompanying problems of air and water pollution – part of the cocktail of issues confronting the futures of global cities – require intelligent adaptive planning if today's Anthropocene era is to defy its many drawbacks and the inescapable consequences of past behaviours.

Today's imperative for equitable urban renewal calls for another social contract between civil society, local government and businesses, we argue,

to overcome the gap between people's aspirations to self-governance and the ways in which urban planning legislation impacts on neighbourhoods. Building new ownership models and lines of responsibility through innovative governance is as important as achieving integrated sets of amenities. In an era in which localism, in the UK, has been promoted as part of a different relationship between citizens and state, and with the expansion of informal settlements needing ongoing support for social infrastructure and through retrofitting, this is a matter of pivotal importance.

Expanding on these priorities, the second chapter, 'Wiki Culture' (named after a term coined by Ermacora) defends the merits of an open society, a multi-faceted vision calling for governments to be accountable to their citizens, for tolerant and transparent democracy, and for the freedom of everybody to participate in the making of civil, cultural and economic life, supported by education, an independent media, public health and legislation. The ideals of the open society face Hydra-type challenges – weakened governance, market pressures, uneven globalisation, ideological fundamentalism and the overall complexity and speed at which today's issues unfold. But the evolving patterns and tools of the network society are bringing less hierarchical dynamics and capacities, radically impacting on collective abilities to create, maintain and develop new societal support systems.

Open-source productions and designs of all kinds, with their sharing-economy ethos and creative-commons intellectual property framework, are playing a transformational role in every single industry and organisational reconfiguration. With the spectacular growth and penetration of smart phones worldwide, leapfrogging infrastructural challenges, digital natives are proliferating. Uber and Airbnb challenge old models, and online tools like Brickstarter and Spacehive – Kickstarter-style services – are unprecedented options for discerning placemakers. With the Internet of Things and digital fabrication fast influencing every domain including genetics and robotics, a clash of generations and cultures is happening that will affect, if not completely redefine, the creation and the management of places.

Today's imperative for equitable urban renewal calls for another social contract between civil society, local government and businesses, we argue, to overcome the gap between people's aspirations to self-governance and the ways in which urban planning legislation impacts on neighbourhoods.

Modern material dignity is at stake in the wider emerging culture of self-organisation and DIY, rooted in alternative groups of the 1960s but also in the Arts and Crafts social thinking of the late 19th and early 20th centuries. Customisation is a key feature of co-housing and shared agricultural plots, but also improvised tinkering, participatory learning and hacking across crafts, electronics, digital open-source platforms, with growth of almost 400 fab labs globally by 2016, according to Neil Gershenfeld, director of the Center for Bits and Atoms at the Massachusetts Institute of Technology (MIT).[9] The cost- and resource-effectiveness enabled by a growing faction of makers and 'prosumer'-citizens will have an increasingly critical impact on major infrastructural and technological investments in cities and beyond, further empowering the concept of distributive ownership and authority.

This emerging cultural landscape for professionals and enthusiasts shapes an alternative economy for design and architecture, bringing the factory into any context, democratising production through systems driven by common purpose. To make headway, though, all distributed urbanism's processes call for negotiation between all collaborators in this playing field. The rise in the sharing economy demonstrates a rapidly adopted new norm, empowered by a potentially superior performing process that outdoes the hierarchical patterns of the traditional owning economy. Through crowd transaction systems, civic project finance is being reinvented; this changes placemakers' roles, making them catalysts, facilitators, and even at times campaigners, rather than designers.

'Fast Forward Now', the following chapter, registers the age of acceleration affecting and destabilising almost every aspect of knowledge creation, science and technology. The exciting hypothesis of the 'singularity' envisages a convergence between the biosphere and the technosphere as a consequence of an exponential growth in human and computational capabilities. But this shift also calls for measures to ensure that it leads to the building of ethical frameworks and platforms that both properly comprehend such rapid mutation of our surroundings, and adapt to it.

The ubiquity of technology, with its relational, interactive capacities and greater ease of access to developments and options, has challenged closed source and silo thinking. In both the developing and the developed world, new online platforms wedded to social enterprise – ranging from Ushahidi's SMS platform in Kenya to the online University of the People and the fastest growing education platform, the Khan Academy – build a host of unprecedented relations and networks, hyper-locally, across sectors. Whether at these platforms' conceptual stage or when they seek viability to help trigger local benefits, this growing phenomenon needs greater recognition and moral support by patrons.

Big data sets are hotly sought after by commercial concerns, calling for new arbitrations and pacts between institutions, progressive civil society and corporate bodies for their deployment in new social infrastructures and ostensibly more citizen-driven governance. Open-data platforms change the notion of accountability, bringing transparency and real-time data intelligence to help enable citizens to make more knowledgeable decisions. In the field of urban planning, however, 'smart city' products based on a narrow ideal of optimum functioning of cities may be cited as a new holy grail of operational empowerment, but many people are sceptical about these products' greater contribution beyond being glorified augmented domotics (home automation) or remotely controlled environments.

'Reframing Placemaking' puts the qualities of the liveability of cities centre stage. Liveability becomes increasingly essential in the face of myriad challenges – among them diminishing resources, the polarisation between urban rich and poor and the rise in climate change impacts, denied by only the most narrow-minded members of society. Mitigating the effects of climate change is not enough: the task is to adapt to today's and tomorrow's climatic reality with related strategies and action plans. The severely deracinating effects of climate change and civil disorder have brought more than a decade and a half of new-era disaster relief and place rescue strategies, allowing people and resources to recuperate, supporting social cohesion and building a pragmatic legacy based around self-determination. Through his or her duty of care in increasing numbers of transitional and precarious situations, the activist architect attempts to 'build back better'.

Correspondingly, the artist as cultural and societal facilitator has for many decades cultivated a different

relationship with an audience playing an unforeseen participatory role, and the arts have been deployed as arenas in which to discuss social and political issues. The writer and curator Nicolas Bourriaud's concept of 'relational aesthetics' proposes an open-endedness in art practices so as to enhance human networks and their social contexts. The inspiration of the methods involved has been threaded into participatory placemaking both at the level of social enterprise, and by today's brokers and arbiters of civil society, specific culture ministers and even city mayors such as Edi Rama (mayor of Tirana, Albania, for more than a decade until 2011, now prime minister of Albania), as well as by innovative artists like Theaster Gates and JR, all building new alliances between cultural expression and social mandates.

Liveability as a key influencer of urbanistic practice is replacing historic means to draw industry and workers into cities, with the desire to create desirable places in which to live and work. Diversified genres of operational processes and models of land use and resilience strategies provoke professional debates about new methods and organisational alliances across sectors. With fewer projects today getting off the ground without public support, participatory processes are coming into their own. Participatory institutions have spread globally, and there are now more than 1,500 participatory budgets around the world. Hybrid forums about city-making, which include social enterprises and citizens from all cultural and ethnic backgrounds, are growing, as they are in politics, technology and to a lesser extent, science.

Our 43 Stories are profiles of participatory placemaking projects and bodies responding to needs across all continents around the world. Each has its own particular genesis and cultural operating system, and the book discusses their inherent strengths, weaknesses, opportunities and threats. As evidence-based narratives about the work of a range of types of practitioners in various global contexts, formal and informal – in the UK, Europe, USA, South America, Africa, India and the Far East – they deal with interconnected themes of social, cultural, economic and environmental sustainability, cultural identity, food production, future-proofing and adaptive planning, including testing and prototyping.

The Stories include the recent placemaking work of leaders in the field, many responding to different kinds of extreme situations: Elemental, led by Alejandro Aravena, and its Calama PLUS plan, Chile; Toyo Ito, Mark Dytham MBE and Astrid Klein (co-founders of Klein Dytham architecture) and colleagues who founded Home for All in Japan; Michael Murphy and Alan Ricks, co-founders of MASS Design Group, with recent work in Rwanda; Teddy Cruz's projects for the San Diego-Tijuana border; and the tactical urbanism in South Africa of Urban-Think Tank, co-founded by Alfredo Brillembourg and Hubert Klumpner. *Recoded City* analyses activities for building neighbourhood-scale resilience, but also considers their impacts on a city-wide and regional level.

Each Story reveals a unique, process- and context-based approach to placemaking from which many insights and lessons can be drawn. Forums in which local needs are articulated and discussed, and working with local materials and labour, with mediatory methods and materials – such as those forged for example by the Center for Urban Pedagogy in response to many challenges of civil society and urban territories – create a legacy in terms of social, educational and professional capacities and infrastructure.

Many of the participatory processes discussed in the Stories have not completely transformed places, but have paved the way for a more profound renewal. To have real significance, liveable urbanism needs to build social capital, to reflect an egalitarian spirit of open city, and to apply inclusive planning processes that foster a greater sense of ownership and self-determination. As a non-institutionalised cultural practice, 'recoding' is more flexible and adaptive in managing crises, and better at surviving changes collectively. This is exemplified by the rapid responses of informal groups such as New York-based Operation Resilient Long Island in the wake of Hurricane Sandy. The deep-rooted impacts of social segregation and deprivation cannot be treated by rote planning textbook approaches: an acute sensitivity to social psychology and cultural diversities is as important as are formal skills in planning, design and building.

With the forging of participatory platforms of various kinds, the boundary lines between hard and soft, short-term and long-term planning are becoming more blurred. That brings adaptability and versatility. Geolocation technologies and real-time automated data capture will increase the influence and the evolution of models in the future. While many perceive these capacities as one more way in which technology is creating distance between humans and their world, boundaries are being broken by open-source, real-time, location-sensitive tools for the city developed by groups such as the SENSEable City Laboratory at MIT.

The chapter 'Recoding: the art of participatory placemaking' examines the synthesised philosophy and approach applied through Thomas Ermacora's practice of participatory placemaking, often conducted through his practice Clear Village (see page 128). He regards recoding as a field needing its own methods and metrics, analogous in some ways to the need for social and psychological sciences to emerge at the end of the 19th century. As a significantly more responsive approach to the built environment, one which gives value to the rich array of relationships and scope for social networks in the future, recoding is based on specific concepts, methodologies and practices Ermacora has developed through his work as a professional placemaker. This chapter includes advice to active and would-be placemakers that they can follow to help strengthen their own work and quality of alliances.

Ermacora practices and advocates for the continuous adaptation of a context, through the active involvement of a placemaker working in partnership with local bodies or groups, in order to create a genuine legacy they can adopt and fully implement. Through its commitment to cyclical, rather than linear or universal, processes, and to well-being and participation, recoding aims to adapt and renew different public-realm contexts into community assets with strong 'place capital', or the shared wealth of the built and natural environments, as the foundation of a more holistic approach to sustainable growth, resilience and innovation. Recoding applies a sense of guardianship of places that is vital in today's era of localism.

There are pros and cons, benefits and risks, to recoding, and individual sections of this chapter discuss and evaluate how to maximise success in this field: involving the professional and the non-professional; strategies for developing relevance and credibility; using time wisely; funding and funding solutions; evaluating the process; building a legacy and sustaining the results. The challenge presented by urban gentrification is the subject

→

Through its commitment to cyclical, rather than linear or universal, processes, and to well-being and participation, 'recoding' aims to adapt and renew different public realm contexts into community assets with strong 'place capital', or the shared wealth of the built and natural environments, as the foundation of a more holistic approach.

↓

of a final section, taking the form of a discussion between Ermacora and Dougald Hine, founder of the regeneration agency Space Makers.

'Open Society, Inequality and the Post-individualist Spirit', the penultimate core chapter, discusses aspects of the open society as an equilibratory force today. These include the impact of cyberwarfare and hacking on notions of transparency, and the effects of erosion in public trust caused by collapses in public management, considered as negative effects of an open society. Counteracting energies that bring increased distribution of authority, as well as improved accountability and authority, are in turn challenged by information totalitarianism in many guises.

The pivotal point at which the advent of social media began to make its impact is marked by their use as part of more recent waves of global insurgence, from the Arab Spring to the coalescing of the Occupy movement, and the protests at Gezi Park in Istanbul in Turkey, which directly contested the government's proposed retrogressive urban development plan. The spotlight these tremors place on tense issues of inequality affecting the 99% further underlines our priority to investigate collective intelligence's influence on society, at a time when human rights have come more severely under attack than at any point since the end of World War II, wider alliances are being forged between human and environmental rights, and people seek to influence their own well-being through democracy as opposed to relying on top-down models they increasingly mistrust.

That is not a foregone, limited model of democracy, but a 'technical democracy' – meaning one in the making, as sociologists Michel Callon, Pierre Lascoumes and Yannick Barthe put it, involving 'new actors' and exploring possible identities directly reflecting today's societal crises.[10] In such a context, the forging of new non-governmental social enterprises dedicated to community-based strategies of meta-welfare is of particular value, and of relevance to the need to foster local placemaking, governance models and hyper-local tools.

'Futures' concludes the core chapters, firstly by assessing the imperatives of the next generation of innovative placemakers and decision-makers, and the scope they will have to influence processes and localist tactics, networks and platforms, to promote social

Our priority is to investigate collective intelligence's influence on society. In today's context, the forging of new non-governmental social enterprises dedicated to community-based strategies of meta-welfare is of particular value, and of relevance to the need to foster local placemaking, governance models and hyper-local tools.

Participatory placemaking can redirect energies to a discourse about place and people's capacities to influence society's nature and value.

inclusion, well-being and future-proofing. Our global evidence shows us that participatory placemaking has the capacity to stay unique to place and time, and to cross-pollinate a great variety of processes without standardisation. We envisage many more pilot schemes attracting the interest of local parties able to help, inspired to create models addressing related issues. Some may reinterpret traditional building techniques; others adopt a greater 'Internet of Things' model with open data, gamification and voting, as already observed in various contexts.

We then consider how a scaling up of hands-on practices, by a greater number of bodies and through engaged philanthropism, can be achieved so that participatory placemaking can continue to foster a multi-modal geography of meaning and politics of belonging, with local people as partners and agents in the process. It also requires a departure from participatory placemaking's limitations of being perceived as a charitable practice, more knowledge-sharing platforms and an association of placemakers to expand the facilitation and assessment of collaborative solutions.

'Voices', the final section of *Recoded City*, includes essays evaluating participatory placemaking in relation to the mandate and duty of the architect, and the pitfalls of trying to achieve social equity; on adaptive participatory urbanism as part of slum urbanism; on the crucial role of strategic intermediaries; on locally organised projects in informal settlements; and on the work of a non-profit environmental advocacy group promoting sustainable urban ecosystems in citizen forestry.

Adopting unprecedented types of creative stewardship models in the face of exponential change aligns with complexity's logic of momentum. Participatory placemaking cannot be the whole panacea to the ills of society, but it can redirect energies to a discourse about place and people's capacities to influence society's nature and value. We join many valued peers in predicting that the power of bottom-up groundbreakers, based on collective intelligence and cooperation, will forge a whole new era of democracy and democratic practices. That process will be developed collectively, co-creatively, in ways that this book aims to facilitate, critically document and celebrate for their courage and intelligence.

The megatrends of DIY resourcefulness, digital ubiquity and bio-regionalism, mixed with our observations, should be seen as indicators that distributed urbanism will inevitably be a necessary ally to combat critical challenges such as climate change and conflict-zone proliferation, as well as massive inequality and weak democracies. Learning to mimic nature more closely, and gradually embracing an increasingly circular economy, integrating life-cycle thinking into every part of human endeavour – including placemaking – should be collective ambitions for true resilience.

Smart-city dreams may not be replaced altogether, but there are definitely benefits for cities from deploying strategic micro-planning and a greater sense of organicity, rather than somehow hoping the self-regulating magic of the market and top-down macro-planning will provide a greater sense of well-being in urban and exurban environments. What is at stake here is the ecology of urbanity, and that includes the future quality of life of billions of citizens keen for methods and inspirational paths out of the vicious cycles of commercial interests that govern the outcomes of the many at the bottom of the pyramid.

The ecology of urbanity is not only about raising the quality of life of the less fortunate in urban contexts, but also one of balance. The legacy of Modernism and automotive-centric planning has deprived cities of equilibratory means, but through a participatory approach to placemaking, a win-win effect can be achieved for all community stakeholders – citizens as well as government bodies, business owners and developers, who get added value in the process. Today many city dwellers know how to be more resourceful and less wasteful. A greater number of mayors, developers, architects and policymakers, and all aspiring new-generation placemakers, need to discover the advantages of getting in on the act.

Thomas Ermacora and Lucy Bullivant
18 April 2015

The Rise

of bottom-up placemaking

Participatory placemaking has developed across various regions and in various economic and social contexts in very different ways, largely due to local legacies of policymaking, degrees of political stability, ownership structures and cultural preferences. The field evolving today is not a wholly novel one, but rather a sophisticated amalgam of a number of socio-spatial developments and initiatives, some of which have their roots in the past.

The examples that thread across this book's many chapters demonstrate the consolidation of knowledge pooled from many disciplines and skill sets as well as of the essential learning emerging from each project. But they also represent modes of thinking and acting that go back a number of centuries, now culminating in a contemporary expression of a driving force for urban change.

In order to fully understand today's bottom-up placemaking activities, with their more equitably distributed systems, we need to trace the origins of their complex relationships with different identities of top-down command and control structures across time. The story is more than simply a historical series of contestations: it is one of negotiations, mutual leverage, challenges and loopholes that have enabled the emergence of participatory placemaking as a vital cultural practice. Tracing the mutuality and its lack in the shifting relations between institutions and innovations of the day, and their respective claims to power, helps to understand at a deeper level how today's participatory placemaking – augmented through the capacity of wiki culture (see page 34) – stands tall thanks in part to a much longer cultural history than we might imagine, one that has its fascination.

The first human settlements had leaders, but no lordships as such; understandable, given that in the Neolithic period the average life expectancy was just 20 years. Hunter-gatherer tribes formed extended families, living and travelling nomadically as social networks and enforcing a strong division of labour. It was over time that they became sedentary, putting increased effort into camps and gardens that acquired an increasingly permanent status.

Grand ideals of antiquity

In the epic public-works projects of the ancient world – pyramids and the like – there was a master builder, a figure who was a high-status individual: trusted as a nobleman in the court and a close advisor to the ruler, leading teams of workers. This model of labour organisation came to include a rational division of labour among later craftsmen in Greek and Roman contexts.

When it came to empire builders generally, who needed to emphasise both their advanced view of the world and the identity of their empire as a commonwealth of civilised people, they expressed these through architecture, art, literature and public ceremonies. As the Roman poet Virgil wrote in the Aeneid, 'Others [the Greeks] shall hammer forth more delicately a breathing likeness out of bronze, coax living faces from the marble, plead causes with more skill, plot with their gauge the movements in the sky and tell the rising of the constellations. But you, Roman, must remember that you have to guide the nations by your authority, for this is to be your skill, to graft tradition onto peace, to spare those who submit, but to crush those who resist.'[1]

However, in the wake of societal fragmentation when, after 500 years, the Roman Empire eventually disintegrated, most of western Europe came to be populated by small-scale, self-sufficient economic units; these included Christian monasteries that functioned as outposts of civilisation. In the agrarian medieval society the noble class (vassals) controlled the land on which production relied, having been given these 'fiefs' by kings and lords. After the collapse of the Roman legal system, the vassals gave protection to the agricultural labourers (serfs) and defined social divisions related to labour and the largely communal way in which farm work was organised, suiting the land tenure.

The Catholic Church, the only universal institution in Europe, was also the people's government as well as a giver of spiritual guidance. With its theological and spatial precepts it licensed a new model of spatial planning that was widely adopted to bring structure to communities; monks experimented with improved farming techniques and became food entrepreneurs. In the lay fiefs, the self-sufficiency of the lords' manors at a time of unrest was vital. However dominant the lords were, there was arguably more scope for self-organisation and for spontaneous growth within this predominantly agrarian society than there was after the Industrial Revolution, for example.

In the fortified towns and cities – no more than glorified villages – that existed before populations soared in the late Middle Ages, individual merchant-craftsmen were usually masters of many trades: skilled workman; foreman supervising journeymen and apprentices, as well as being their employer; buyer of materials; and seller of products. The commercial expansion of the craft guilds led to differentiation in classes within each craft. Journeymen excluded from the profit-driven system eventually became free labourers who practised their craft outside the walls of the town and its restrictive guild regulations. From this disintegration of the craft guild system in the 18th century emerged the conditions for the development of the early industrial system.

The story is one of negotiations, mutual leverage, challenges and loopholes enabling the emergence of participatory placemaking

In Europe during the Renaissance that ended the medieval period, the city adopted its architectural language from the civilisations of ancient Egypt, Greece, Babylon and Rome, and integrated Florentine ideas about scale and organisation. The extraordinary urban ideals of Lorenzo de Medici and, later, Louis XIV emulated the way the Church developed locations on theological precepts, but these worldly leaders based their expressions of power on enlightened ideals. This reconnected with the antique legacy of Rome and Babylon, and the spatial formulation of authority gave birth to grand masterplans intended to illustrate the glory of man at the centre of the universe, the Copernican revolution applied to planning. This spawned an academic culture of top-down practice for commissioning the design of cities that still dominates today.

Renaissance plans segregated the fundamental functions of the city: power, commerce and health. In Italy, the architect Sebastiano Serlio and other planning theoreticians segregated living quarters by class and trade, whereas Parisian planners mixed the classes. The world has therefore inherited both within academia and at the level of strategic political decision-making certain cultural tenets from this period. These form the basis of ways in which the city has been made, influencing scientific progress until the Enlightenment and the Industrial Revolution, and the pioneers of city planning thereafter.

The Renaissance introduced a centralised process in urban planning and commissioning of architecture, and most of the world has copied this centralised and often bureaucratically controlled spatial development. Since the Industrial Revolution, development has been achieved with ever greater speed and an emphasis on technological mastery. This has left the artisanal city to persist in poorer or more remote areas, but also to expand informally in response to population growth and lack of top-down provision.

Locke envisages scenarios in which citizens are justified in resisting the authority of a civil government and, if necessary, establishing a better one in its place

The birth of modern cities

From the late 17th century, the Enlightenment produced a dichotomy in people's sense of construction of place. On the one hand was the law of capital, through which industry leaders would create paternalistic urbanism, with a single main employer in an area defining the rules, motives and functions in place. However, on the other hand, the rise of humanistic and social perspectives was in contrast to this top-down reinforcement of the industrial age. This dichotomy would persist in people's minds through two world wars in the twentieth century, until challenged by the civil rights movements and the emerging age of civil society organising from the 1950s, marking a critical shift from top-down to a more horizontal approach to urban governance.

In the 18th century Immanuel Kant, the practical philosopher and éminence grise of rational ethics, identified an essential obligation to contest abstract, top-down decision-making. As the social scientist and critical systems thinker Werner Ulrich lucidly put it, the 'reason why we ought to act morally is not because some external authority obliges us but simply because we recognise such action to be reasonable. The moral force resides in our will to be reasonable! It is, in the language of Kant's first Critique, "reason's own plan".'[2]

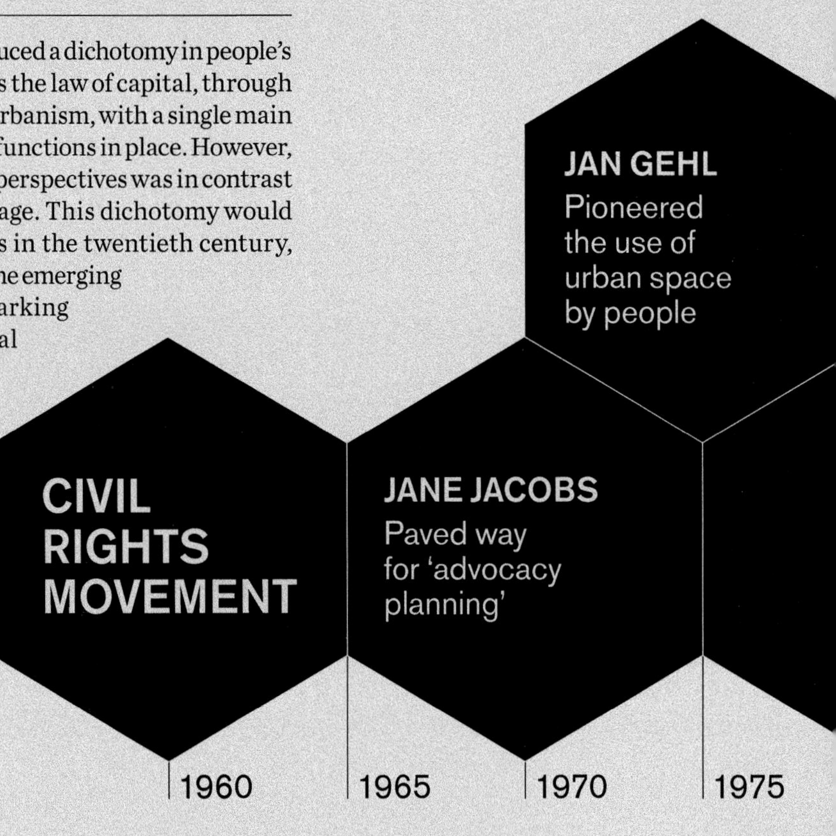

Ulrich adds that 'rational ethics need not assume that we are virtuous in the first place, but only that we want others to listen to our ideas and arguments, as they recognise that we speak reasonably. It is not because we are (or want to be) particularly virtuous but because we want to be rational that we will act morally! Virtue may then perhaps be reserved for a few (Mother Teresa comes to mind), but rationality is for all', with 'authentic thinking encompassing responsibility both to oneself and to others'.

Defining the framework for liberal democracy, the 17th-century philosopher John Locke coupled his belief in individualism as the basis for a truly free society with provision for the protection of the people's rights assumed by a government whose authority rests only on the consent of the governed. For Locke, the moral and philosophical concept of 'the state of nature' is not about individuals but about the making of a body politic realised only through explicit consent, and he also envisages

scenarios in which citizens are justified in resisting the authority of a civil government and, if necessary, establishing a better one in its place.

In these endeavours the agency of 'human capital' is indispensable; this concept was first defined by the philosopher and pioneer of political economy Adam Smith in his magnum opus of 1776, *An Inquiry into the Nature and Causes of the Wealth of Nations*, as 'the acquired and useful abilities of all the inhabitants or members of the society'.[3]

Just as the relational ideas behind the Enlightenment's 'social contract' theory have had to be expanded to rethink human nature and human relations, so too, in the 21st century, concepts of human value have needed to acknowledge and embrace wider contexts and emotional capacities. For example, the Five Capitals model defined by the environmentalist Jonathon Porritt combines human, natural, social, manufactured and financial capitals to make sustainability, quality of life, education and training key levers.[4]

Modernism's collateral damage

When it comes to the ethos of a city, planners and architects can realistically affect it only up to a certain point. The Industrial Revolution, with its rapid pace of urbanisation and steep increase in city populations, brought disease, crime, overcrowding, overheated workplaces, dirty housing and homelessness. In response to these drawbacks, in the early 20th century Modernist urban planning ushered in such radical visions as Le Corbusier's Plan Voisin for huge tower blocks in central Paris (drawn 1922–25) and his influential Cité Radieuse in Marseille (completed in 1952), in which the sheer presence of buildings edited out streets.

For Le Corbusier, the planning expert worked out plans free from partisan pressure, special interests and other opposition. This attitude could have negative consequences. Brasilia, for example, planned and developed from scratch in 1956 as the capital of Brazil, was designed by Lúcio Costa and Oscar Niemeyer around a circulation module (dubbed *ihla da fantasia* by locals); despite best intentions, this design led to an increase in segregation between rich and poor.

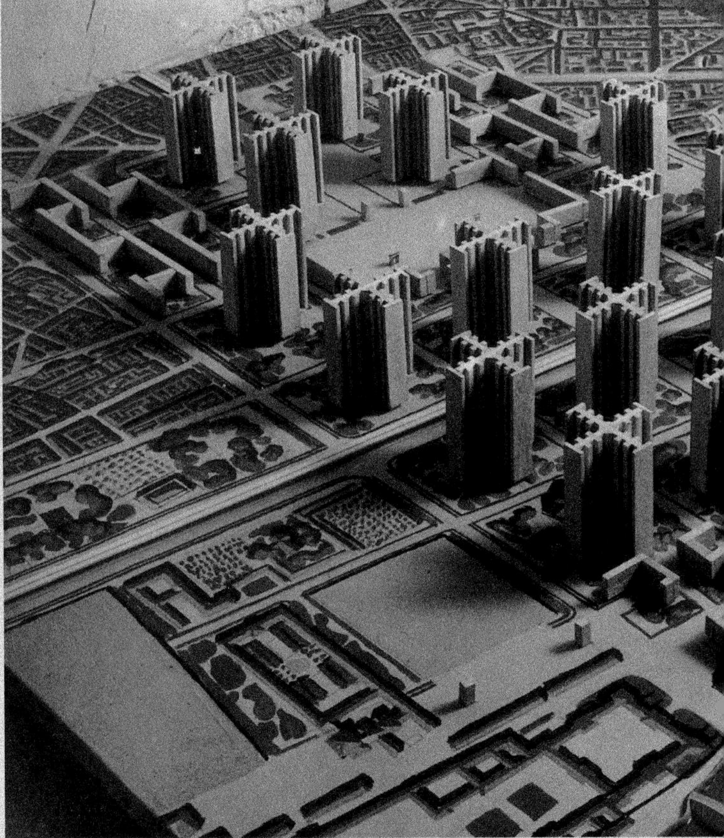

Le Corbusier's design for Plan Voisin, Paris, 1922-25, a proposed business district on the north bank of the River Seine. Its 18 skyscrapers and empty spaces replace historic buildings and characterful streets.

Such aspirations for an ideal order, and the paradoxically inefficient consequences of the early 20th-century City Efficient movement in the USA (among whose leaders was the landscape architect Frederick Law Olmsted, co-designer of New York's Central Park and many others): these were just two facets of a legacy that made urban planning a generic and apparently scientific, objective, professional citywide activity of codes, ratios and other quantitative measures.

Such a technocratic arsenal preserved a sense of distance from what was being planned, and removed placemaking as a cultural practice. As the collaborative community planning specialist and writer Leonie Sandercock has noted, 'in the post-war rush to turn town planning into an applied science much was lost – the city of memory, of desire, of spirit; the importance of place and the art of placemaking.'[5]

The end of World War II in 1945 and the long period of subsequent Cold War political and military tension saw growing polarisation and contestation concerning the production and significance of public urban space among planners, policymakers and community organisations. As society embarked on major post-war modernisation programmes, policymakers gave Modernist urban planners carte blanche to recast the city anew on supposedly self-sustaining, utopian lines.

Cities that had suffered extensive wartime bombing, such as Rotterdam, Paris and London, were reconstructed with new morphologies, as were, in America, the urban centres of Chicago and Los Angeles. New Towns proliferated around the world. Centres of science were incubated, such as Japan's Tsukuba Science City (on land designated in the 1960s, becoming operational in the 1980s); this planned city, one of the first and largest of its kind, was modelled on Brasilia and the educational and scientific cities of Akademgorodok in Russia and Palo Alto in the USA.

In Germany, war-damaged cities underwent a phoenix-like resurrection, with architects, planners, entrepreneurs and building cooperatives forming teams, although there were rumblings of ideas to abandon the ruins and rebuild nearby. With zoning rules stemming from the Athens Charter published in 1933 by Le Corbusier, by the mid 1960s the uniform results led to psychoanalyst Alexander Mitscherlich deeming them 'inhospitable cities'.[6] But after the Council of Europe's European Architectural Heritage Year (1975), citizen action groups mobilised to save and preserve old buildings and districts, leading to battles between squatters and developers in Frankfurt's West End district, for example.

The demands of growing cities led to planning orthodoxies as ways of coping. In France, peri-urbanisation or cités dortoir ('dormitory towns'), a phenomenon that appeared in the 1950s, featured hastily constructed housing developments for industrial workers and others forming part of a rural exodus which were deserted by day. This model generated centre-less cities completely dependent on the pendular migration of residents, with the consequence on people's sense of belonging likened to 'root shock' – a concept adapted from gardening by the psychiatrist Mindy Fullilove.[7]

As the architectural writer and critic Reyner Banham commented in 1962, objections to the Modernists, including condemnations of their elitism, fostered 'a kind of environmental populism, a demand for participation by the public, for the right of people to determine their own environments – all of which was not so totally unlike the ever-present concept of the modern architect as the humble servant of social need'.[8]

Banham observed that an alternative for those fearing a spectre of horizontal formlessness was the megastructure, advocated by such protagonists as the Archigram group (Banham was the first critic to write about the group following the publication of the first Archigram magazine in 1961). In the huge megastructural framework, he wrote, 'whole communities could contrive their own environments, as a means to reconcile the irreconcilable: the freedom of the individual and the mastery of architecture'.

> “
> **Concepts of human value have needed to embrace wider contexts and emotional capacities, as exemplified by Jonathon Porritt's Five Capitals model**

Cities such as Mexico City, which gained the world's first skyscraper successfully built on highly active seismic land (Torre Latinoamericana, 1956), experienced explosive growth in the 1960s, as well as serious problems of air and water pollution. The city saw ever more sprawling barrios like Neza-Chalco-Itza (one of the largest slums in the world with around four million people), which originated in the early 1900s when the railroad brought new industry and therefore new zones to accommodate it. By the 1960s, 45% of the population of Mexico City lived in slums (the same percentage as in Ankara, Turkey). Elsewhere the figures were over 33% in Rio de Janeiro, Brazil; 35% in Caracas, Venezuela; 25% in Lima, Peru, and Santiago, Chile; 65% in Algiers; and 15% in Singapore.[9]

What urban environmental historian Harold Platt calls 'the revolt of the grassroots' presented a huge narrative arc through the Cold War period (post-World War II to 1991), a time during which the Modernist planners' fortunes first rose, and then fell as cities went into crisis and struggled with ever more disasters, bureaucracy and corruption as well as 'global restructuring in the wake of the oil-energy embargo of the 1970s taking its toll'.[10]

Jane Jacobs, the American-born Canadian urban activist and author, wears a sign reading 'Conscience - the Ultimate Weapon!' at a boycott at Public School (P.S. 41), New York, 3 Feb 1964.

Many academics in the late 1960s backed a widespread change in ethos, advocating challenging structures of authority and neo-liberal democracy, and valued freedom of expression, independence of thought and responsibility taking. For Marshall McLuhan, 'the Age of Anxiety is, for the most part, the result of trying to do today's job's with yesterday's tools!', and he decried the politician's abdication of responsibility 'in favour of his image', maintaining that 'propaganda begins when dialogue ends'.[11] This is reflected in Noam Chomsky and Edward S Herman's book *Manufacturing Consent*, which analyses the advent of the 'fifth power' – the media – and the issues arising from its manipulation by established powers, damaging the democratic process for which the civil rights movement was fighting.[12]

Cities are for people

The history of community organising dates back to the American 'settlement houses' of the late 1930s, but it was during the 1960s that the civil rights movement, which had been organised from the late 1950s, shifted society towards more integrative and egalitarian forms. Participatory placemaking took its cues from the activism of Jane Jacobs in New York and others earlier in the 20th century, such as Jane Addams in Chicago and Charles Rowley in Manchester, who led campaigns to clean up their cities' slums.

Their indefatigable work on villages and neighbourhoods, along with Jacobs's seminal writings (first relayed in her book *The Death and Life of Great American Cities*), represent a direct critique of top-down planning decisions by the ruling classes, which ignored community needs and served to fragment cities.[13] They perceived a yawning gap between experts' technocratic positions and citizens' own needs, values and wishes, and made powerful objections to the Modernist legacy of unitary planning and narrow focus on physical aspects of urban areas.

Jacobs's mantras, that 'cities are for people', that urban diversity on both a social and an economic basis is vital, and that slum clearance in the name of high-rise development and main roads is deeply compromising, hit a nerve. Local people mobilised to challenge the plan for Jacobs's Greenwich Village neighbourhood that was championed by Robert Moses, the 'master builder' of New York and political scientist.

In her ideas about cities, Jacobs included the concept of 'social capital' stemming from the value of personal networks. She paved the way for advocacy planning (a term coined by Paul Davidoff in 1965), which developed from the sharing of knowledge between planners and local communities and confronting planners' narrow focus on the physical city to the detriment of civil rights.[14]

Nonetheless New York's early to mid 20th-century grand-scale public works projects and transport infrastructures, initiated by Robert Moses from 1922 onwards and designed to hasten the city's modernisation, were copied by planners all over the USA and Europe, resulting in cities for cars. Zoning of urban land, introduced to New York from Germany with the chief intention of keeping the poor out of desirable new suburbs along the tram tracks and subway lines, also had a corrosive effect on urban environments. A strict separation between home, the workplace, the marketplace and social life led to uniformity, monocultural uses of space and the dispersal of some facilities that now became accessible only by car, while streets lost their multifunctional nature.

Pervasive forms of Modernist utopia, epitomised by, for example, Brasilia – the masterplan as a catch-all for a new, perfected micro-society – have their top-down equivalents today. The more recent wave of 'smart cities' (Masdar City in Abu Dhabi, Songdu in South Korea, the discarded Dongtan eco-city project outside Shanghai in China, and the King Abdullah Economic City in Saudi Arabia) bear strong traces of similar methodologies to that of their ancestors from the 20th century and aspire to control the future. But unless the smart city has 'a bottom-up innovation eco-system', as MIT's SENSeable City Laboratory director Carlo Ratti and Matthew Claudel put it (see page 212), it is merely an urban product.[15]

In the first decade of the 21st century, however, the more pronounced (albeit more humble) emergence of adaptive planning and its more flexible

Jan Gehl, the Danish urban designer, in central Copenhagen's Strøget, the famous 1.1km-long pedestrian shopping street he designed and which was realised in 1962.

Jan Gehl took the social sciences' research methods more directly into the toolkits of architects and urbanists. His work created a new relationship between the physical environment and public life by making the everyday life of the city statistically visible

frameworks represented a huge migration away from things being 'set in stone', freeing up the city's evolution over time and people's involvement with it, through the mobilisation of new processes and systems. The veteran Danish urban designer Jan Gehl feels keenly that a new paradigm of urban development is emerging, driven by a fundamental concern for life. Gehl has probably said more than any other living architect about the value of making cities better for people. His approach is directly opposed to that of his predecessors, who saw the city as a machine, and for him 'nothing in the world is more simple and more cheap' than a people-centred approach.[16]

On his travels, Gehl drew profound inspiration from the typical Italian city, and he often refers to Siena and its great traditional place, the Piazza del Campo, in particular. What was perceived by many architects and urbanists as an impediment to that city's growth – namely the densely populated, car-free environment – Gehl evaluated as a worthy quality-of-life element to stress in urban design. It was a chief concern of his to establish it as an enlightened criteria for city-building: pedestrian, semi-private, promoting outdoor living, with cafés and shopfronts embedded within the life of the street.

Planners in Denmark had been heavily influenced by Moses's work in the USA, and one legacy of the 1950s and 1960s was the use of urban-planning analytical data that considered only highways and cars, rather than community design or public transport needs. At that early point, finding a yawning gap in suitable data, Gehl pioneered an expanded approach to understanding the use of public urban space by people, by generating new data sets about their activity patterns.

For Gehl the future lay in the past, when cities were designed around people. Noticing the disappearance of the concept of the agora or gathering place, he moved away from the influence of the car in urban planning, towards the experience of the medieval town centre, and made a grand shift, proposing a more pedestrian- and cyclist-friendly city that became his global signature.

In making the everyday life of the city statistically visible, Gehl took the social sciences' methods more directly into the toolkits of architects and urbanists. With his psychologist wife, Ingrid, he began documenting where they sat, how they walked or played, and the like. Gehl applied a 5km/h speed limit that enabled them to fully experience a sensual and interesting world of colours, smells and sounds. Their work created a new relationship between the physical environment and public life, enabling him to evaluate the qualities of the public realm and to apply them in a lifetime of work in urban design globally.

Aerial view of the Piazza del Campo, Siena, Italy, an inspirational pedestrian space meeting Jan Gehl's 12 quality criteria for urban design.

Gehl's professional contribution has been extraordinary in its improvement of cities, starting with Copenhagen which today appears in many polls as the happiest city in the world. His work there has given his practice authority to pedestrianise and design slow-mobility options for such varied cities as New York, Mexico City, Melbourne, Cape Town and Chongqing, leading to awards and accolades. By making data on how people live relevant, Gehl has created the tools for placemakers to understand the significant changes required in the design of public space.

Gehl credits Jane Jacobs with having focused attention on human scale: 'Fifty years ago she said – go out there and see what works and what doesn't work, and learn from reality. Look out of your windows, spend time in the streets and squares and see how people actually use spaces, learn from that, and use it.'[17]

Hariharpur village, Uttar Pradesh, India: Leika Aruga's design workshop with families, 2013, for WORKSHOP architecture's new school building (see page 282).

Experiments in collective dwelling

The 1960s was an age of utopias: social, material and technological utopias, all bumping up against one another. As a result of community polarisation, some people had a vision of a utopia that offered a new social order altogether. Many were disillusioned with society as it was progressing, despite the emergence of a more democratic order, as its ideologies were a muddled blend of political and commercial interests. Large numbers of people preferred to escape and create their own micro-societies, intentional communities that cut loose from the conventions of mainstream society and established self-sufficient models. The self-determination Jacobs advocated planners should take their cues from was increasingly manifested by the wider public in individualised ways.

This thinking originated in the colonisation of the New World by the Spanish and the Portuguese, and the later utopian intentional communities have their DNA in the phalanstery, a centre developed in the early 19th century by the French utopian socialist and philosopher Charles Fourier, who believed that gender roles could progress better in such centres than in the domestic home. As was noted by Sir Thomas More in *Utopia* (1516) and by Francis Bacon in *New Atlantis* (1627), what utopias have in common is that they are insular and ideal frameworks, obliging the administered citizens to abide by theocratic or social norms and codes.

The acceleration of post-war urbanisation spawned a series of initiatives that expressed strong disagreement with the commercialisation of space and production; the Situationists' cash-free dérives (unplanned journeys) through the city was one major art-driven countermove against official culture. The bipolarity of geopolitics up to the fall of the Berlin Wall in 1989, expressed in examples ranging from the Khmer agrarian villages to the Israeli kibbutzim, provided a fertile ground for further experimentation detached from either capitalistic or communist ideals, but connected to civil rights, hippyism and other trends in libertarian societies.

The writings of both Fourier and Karl Marx fuelled utopian models and associational communities (what Fourier called 'phalanxes') promoting dreams of a free society. Overcoming the weakening effects of capitalist production on civil society, the urban laboratory, led by its own rules, is epitomised by a number of projects incubated in the late 1960s and early 1970s.

Arcosanti, the experimental development in the Arizona desert established by the Italian architect and environmentalist Paolo Soleri in 1970, was dedicated to the investigation of 'arcology' (a mix of architecture and ecology first conceived in the 1950s). Arcosanti was cumulatively built by more than 7,000 volunteers; today it has about 80 residents, and the urban laboratory receives over 50,000 visitors from around the world per year. Soleri once said of his project, 'the people were very ready to obey my orders, also because I was mixing with them, and we were working together'.[18]

In southern India in 1968 Mirra Alfassa founded Auroville, an international, community-led township which she conceived as a 'universal town' that would grow from an ashram and would belong to humanity as a whole so that no nation could claim it as its own. Originally intended to house 50,000 people, the township today has some 2,300 residents from many countries and more than 5,000 staff, each of whom contributes to its budget; the building of community facilities continues.

In Denmark, the self-proclaimed autonomous neighbourhood of Christiania, in Copenhagen, was established as a direct consequence and offshoot of the student revolution of 1968; in essence, formal Danish society granted a mandate of self-governance to a Marxist fringe of society. Christiania began life in 1971 after a newspaper article questioned why young people who needed somewhere to live could not use the disused military buildings on the site. With their self-built housing and car-free streets ranged over an area of 34 hectares of land, today's 1,000 residents live in what is now one of Denmark's most popular tourist attractions.

Aerial view of Favela da Rocinha, the largest of its kind in Brazil, on the Sugarloaf mountain in Rio de Janeiro, with the skyline of the city beyond.

Challenges to welfare and growing inequalities

Whether because of suburban sprawl or owing to social inequality due to the harsh impact of market domination of governance, the top-down modern city has alienated people. In the 18th century the laissez-faire economics of Adam Smith had dictated that economies function best when markets are free of state intervention. But in the 20th century the economist John Maynard Keynes successfully promoted the concept that governments, as the ultimate protectors of public good, should play a major role in economic management in order to overcome an arbitrary and unequal distribution of wealth. Today, however, the servicing of capital has overshadowed so-called civil rights.

Global capital has created more opportunities for investment with borrowed capital, but also much disregard for the consequences of the investments. The commercialisation of contemporary urban space and the tyranny of capital have created a political mindset that is neglectful of the welfare of people, and successive events around the world have demonstrated strongly the upsurge in popular wishes for people's needs to be respected.

In today's global market, land speculators may have very little connection to a place. Compare this with the relative sense of ownership and responsibility felt by the lords of the city in feudal times. However unscrupulous lords and princes have been depicted as in literature throughout history, a great number of them had redeeming features because of their shared responsibility for making the city function.

Keynesian economic policy gave the state a responsibility to lend a hand to boost society's welfare through debt. As a consequence, that mechanism gave more fuel to centralised planning, as seen particularly in France, for example, where almost all infrastructure is state-funded. In situations of economic strife governments can be tempted to devise absolutist power structures that reinforce centralised planning. We can make parallels between, for instance, the French Sun King Louis XIV, who enjoyed a 72-year-long absolutist reign, and the socialist François Mitterrand, who after being elected President of France in 1981 renationalised much industry, in the most radical nationalisation plan adopted in any developed nation after World War II.

In Britain during the 1980s, mega-planning on a political level was heavily influenced by the policies and ideology of prime minister Margaret Thatcher (Thatcherism), which fragmented society between the haves and the have-nots and cut back on government support for the latter. These developments came after the era in which the civil rights movement was in full flow, creating a social landscape in which many different types of people were left out of the picture, marginalising them in such a way that they had to find ways to self-organise.

In addition, the contemporaneous privatisation policies of American president Ronald Reagan, intended to boost growth and defeat the USSR during the Cold War, further reinforced globally a sense of social ostracism. After

Whether because of suburban sprawl or owing to social inequality due to the harsh impact of market dominance of governance, the top-down city has alienated people

almost half a century of continents-spanning Cold War, the fall of the Berlin Wall on 9 November 1989 (incidentally the same year as China's Tiananmen Square protests and subsequent massacre) opened a Pandora's box for all the aspirations that had been suppressed for centuries for a fairer, more socially attentive approach to placemaking, appropriate for the times.

Little more than a decade after the fall of the Wall, the first World Social Forum was held in Porto Alegre, Brazil (in 2001), to formalise a relationship between an extensive group of radical, anti-globalisation movements and to speak of a need for a Global South consciousness to counter the world's North–South socio-economic divide.

The Forum was probably too controversial to be accepted by dominant groups in society, but led nonetheless to conversations in what is today a more acceptable and distinguished ensemble of voices that needed to be heard. One of these voices was that of the landless peasant movement of Latin America. These groups began a dialogue with regional political institutions that they felt had either ignored or been dismissive of their plight to secure decent living conditions, as well as of the need to start saving the Amazon rainforest from absurd exploitation.

However 'noisy' the anti-globalisation proponents have been in the media, the Forum and a string of related events have been crucibles for the growth of a number of institutions for the poor, such as the Bangladeshi microfinance organisation Grameen Bank. Importantly, these institutions have expressed the capacity to provide alternative governance models, which are establishing new norms.

Mega-planning vs micro-planning: bottom-up activism's impact

Today, 21st-century imperatives and global socio-economic shifts are challenging the traditional urban design professions to adapt; placemaking is also evolving to become more relevant in its overall dynamics. Bold, mega-solutions and bottom-up schemes with a more low-key approach can coexist. But there seems to be a problematic lag between people's aspirations for self-governance and the way in which urbanism and planning laws are developing.

In many respects planning legislation is anachronistic. Planning legislation, however well intended, is developed within the context of a political mandate and spans a number of years, facilitating growth and withstanding recession but also possibly contradicting the speed of change and the actions required to protect social equity. This means that even if a large number of the world's cities would probably benefit from more enlightened and well-anchored policies for urban planning, there is a need to not limit the forces of positive urban adaptation through rules that may soon appear obsolete or inadequate.

> **There is a need not to limit the forces of positive urban adaptation through rules that may soon appear obsolete or inadequate**

Countries with young regimes lack legislation strong enough to protect social equity at the expense of economic growth, whereas countries with 'mature' democracies struggle to react adequately due to their rigid settings that have been built through layers of legislation. So on the one hand, as a more distanced, global speculative type of development is being conducted, the city is being reconceived irrespective of social concerns; but on the other, organised civil society groups act without formal approvals to take what actions they see fit to make the most of what they have where they live.

Observers of the growth of urbanisation may note an unfortunate sequence of events in which certain developers, committed to their profit margins in a stretched and volatile market, display a deep, if involuntary disregard for

“

The new field of placemaking is creating a more reactive and resource-efficient set of choices. It can respond in situations of crisis and scarcity of means, to support communities in pursuing more holistic and characterful options for local identity and self-governance

social reality and local identity. However progressive a large development might be, the sheer scale at which the developer has to operate gives birth to some odd places.

In Abu Dhabi, Masdar City's commissioners and the architectural firm Foster + Partners have designed a state-of-the-art smart technology R&D cluster with innumerable merits. Nonetheless, looking at it as a place to live, one might wonder whether 'spatial eugenics' could be a description for this typology of 'out-of-the-blue' project. At the other end of the spectrum, rather than building a city from scratch, enlightened developers are attempting to programme and curate transitional phases of new schemes that engage with 'meanwhile uses'.

There can be disingenuous motives behind new urban schemes, but, as we see it, many schemes represent genuine claims for balanced developments, which include provisions for true affordable housing and high-quality public spaces. In London, the landmark project run by the Battersea Power Station Development Company to convert the disused power station and its grounds into a complex array of residential properties, office space and recreational amenities is led by the intention to create responsible, good placemaking. As part of this the company is steering a number of incremental and imaginative activities to include locals. But these may not buffer the extreme gentrification that is taking place in such contexts as metropolitan London, which concentrates opportunities to preserve the value of capital while much of the rest of the world experiences market volatility and banking crises.

Evaluating developments is a difficult matter. However, it is important to probe developers' creative risk-taking and their capacity to develop land in ways that have positive externalities and public benefits. The value that enlightened developers can bring to regenerate and transform cities is considerable, whether they are entirely private initiatives or public-private partnerships. The bidding process for obtaining prime real estate for development often includes demands for certain benefits for locals, such as, in England and Wales, those outlined in Section 106 of the Town and Country Planning Act (1990).

The subtlety, however, is to distinguish between developers masquerading their commercial interests – or what Alastair Parvin, initiator of the Right to Build (see WikiHouse, page 278) calls 'tacit corruptions' – and those investing in the long-term value of good placemaking, with perhaps more patient capital funders. In other words, cities growing fast in a chaotic economic climate are more prone to be deprived of investment.

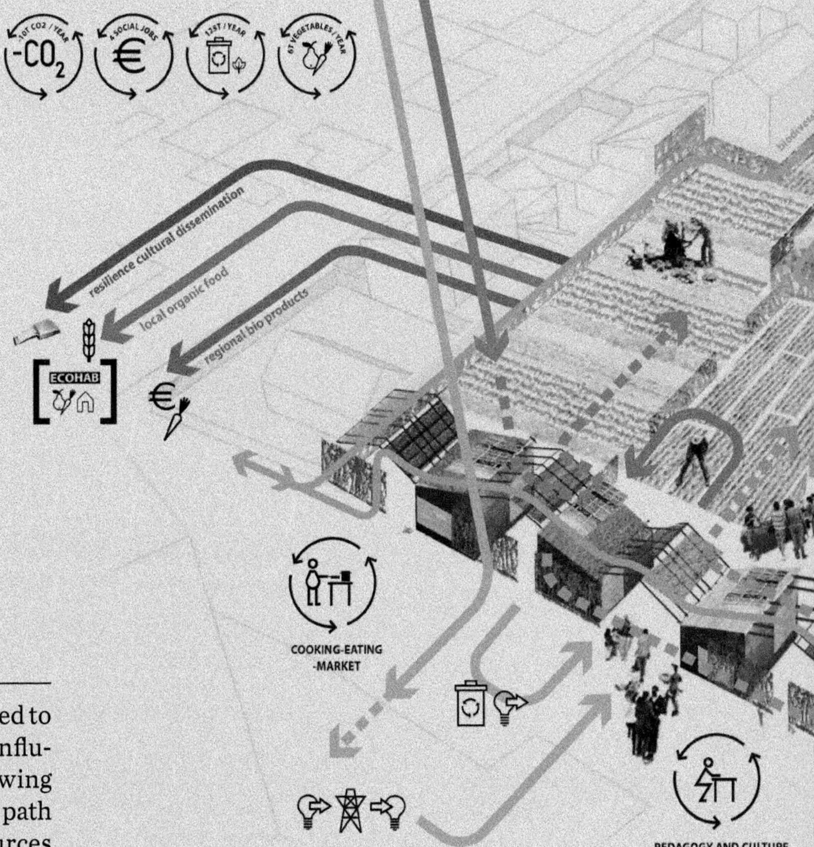

Breaking the mould and aspirations for new governance

The rise of participatory planning is not simply linked to people's natural rejection of losing their power to influence where and how they live. It also stems from growing realisation by practitioners that continuing along the path of mega-planning will further use up precious resources in unevenly distributed ways, creating 'green ghettos' for the few and further alienating the many. At the heart of the question is the cost-to-impact ratio of top-down mega-planning.

The new field of placemaking is creating a more reactive and resource-efficient set of choices. It can respond in situations of crisis and scarcity of means, to support communities in pursuing more holistic and characterful options for local identity and self-governance.

As governments have scaled down and decentralised their responsibilities, a vacuum has been created that deserves to be filled. Relationships between citizens and the state have changed, and in some cultures local community groups and organisations have become more intensely involved with managing processes of urban change. Furthermore, issues of liveability and sustainability have added stresses to the delivery of public services and adequate infrastructures.

In 2011, the majority partner in the British government coalition, the Conservative Party, in its efforts to reshape its core policies in the aftermath of the 2008 financial crisis, looked to solve certain structural public deficit issues by decentralising further and drafting the UK government's Localism Act (2011). The grand architect behind this shift was the political thinker and director of the ResPublica think tank Phillip Blond. As a driving

R-Urban Agrocité, Colombes, France, 2011-ongoing, an agro-cultural hub with a farm, community gardens, cultural spaces and a range of prototypical eco devices. Architects: atelier d'architecture autogérée (see page 114).

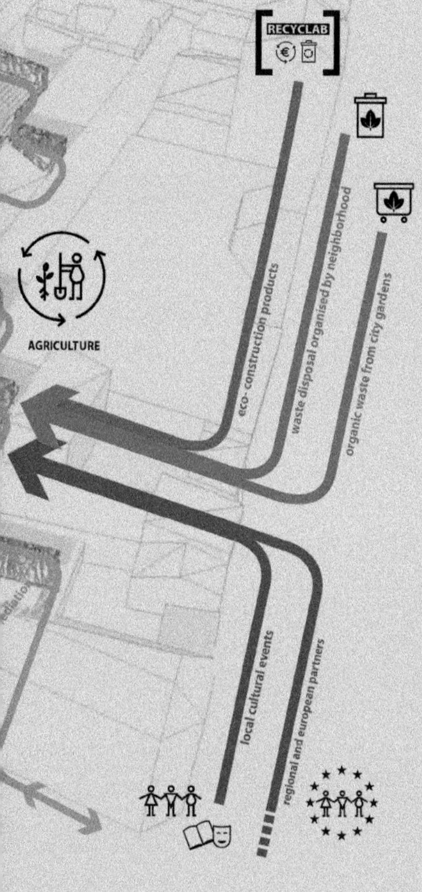

force behind the 'Big Society' concept, he devised an innovative approach to greater shared governance that would lighten public spending while also allowing active citizens the chance to have a greater role in the development of their local communities.[19]

This pioneering national policy unfortunately became caught up in political squabbles and has been rejected by many proponents of greater self-governance. Indeed, the process through which responsibility might be delegated to community groups was set in a framework that could be counterproductive at a local level, giving the louder voices a vehicle to achieve their own agendas rather than truly granting communities the capacity of local governance. This was the direct consequence of obliging communities to hold a referendum to obtain validation from local authorities. The necessary efforts from community volunteers to instigate this step have proven to be too demanding, and would succeed only if activists had their own resources or tremendous ambitions.

This makes the Localism Act an unbalanced and unresourced piece of legislation; as the architect Richard Rogers put it, 'the success of localism depends on knowing what you are doing, so if [central government] don't put money into expertise in local areas, who will make the decisions?'[20] Assessing the UK's situation ahead of its national election in 2015, there needs to be a fresh social contract between civil society, a newly enabled local government through devolution of powers from central government, and responsible businesses, allowing increased co-creation of customised services (or measures of responsible 'subsidiarity') closely relevant to everybody's lives.

We can clearly observe that, in attempting to adapt to the innumerable complications in sustaining welfare and managing growth, the UK central government's capacity has been overstretched, and in many areas it has diluted its authority. A new need has been generated by the Localism Act for active civil society members of all ages to evaluate how they might acquire legitimate authority over their administration and integration within the formal state. In other words, the Act is one of the most radical attempts to formally revisit constitutional law and the social contract derived from it. Perhaps the coming decades will see a dualistic attitude deepen the divide between a laissez-faire approach and a more interventionist 'build it and they will come' ethos.[21]

Beyond partisan politics and economics, participatory placemaking can thrive in the grey zone left in the fall out from a century of ideological clashes. The choices ahead of us are not so much about Marxism or liberalism, collectivism or individualism, but more to do with changing our approach to these historical divergences, away from an 'or' model and towards an 'and' model within an arising open society.

Beyond partisan politics and economics, participatory placemaking can thrive in the grey zone left in the fall out of a century of ideological clashes

Wiki Culture

Open society

An extraordinary wind of change has brought about the 'open society', which has created great expectations and affects the nature of placemaking at a deep level. The open society means different things to different people, but it is essentially one in which everyone is free to participate fully in civil, cultural and economic life, supported by education, an independent media, public health and legislation. This calls for governments to be accountable to their citizens, through public policies that are fair and protect fundamental human rights. In order to achieve for a society the reality of tolerant and transparent democracy, its members need to be both attentive to, and active on, questions of systemic change, at both the local and the global scale.

In the early 20th century, philosopher Henri Bergson's 'open morality' was concerned with creativity and progress; it aimed at an 'open society' based on self-determination, and that validity can never be denounced. However, the notions of democracy and freedom that sociologist Zygmunt Bauman points to in his lecture 'The Demons of an Open Society' need to be secured on a global scale, or not at all.[1] These notions have changed hugely since the days of the Greek city states, an era when advocacy and criticism were regarded as noble ways in which to communicate. The much more recent tradition is for decisions to be made by elected politicians and technical specialists, or by legally authorised bureaucrats, who have in the past hermetically retained data pertinent to governance and protocols.

There are legitimate concerns around the consequences of an open society in which decision making can be challenged, and a number of political scientists and economists question the ability of the state or the market to protect social interests and the rights of people and nature. 'Society is no longer protected by the state: it is now exposed to the rapacity of forces it does not control and no longer hopes or intends to recapture and subdue', Bauman explains. Globalisation creates new challenges, and the openness of society can also be seen negatively as a 'fate' of negative globalisation, because 'a citizenship consensus (or a "constitutional patriotism", as [sociologist and philosopher] Jürgen Habermas defines it) cannot be built on assurances of protection against the vagaries of the market that play havoc with social standings and sap the rights to social esteem and personal dignity'.

Bauman points out the reality that 'on a planet open to free circulation of capitals and commodities, whatever happens in one place has a bearing on how people of all other places live. No well-being of one place is innocent of the misery of another.' Moreover, 'the demon of fear won't be exorcised until we find (or more precisely construct) such tools' to overcome today's difficulties. However the presence today of all ten of writer Naomi Wolf's 'Ten Steps to Close Down an Open Society', including the harassment of citizens' groups, has cut deep.[2] Those in power cannot necessarily be trusted. Expectations have been placed on alternative models to theirs, ones that are not allowed or that are in gestation as ideas.

Zygmunt Bauman, the Polish-born sociologist, Professor Emeritus of Sociology, University of Leeds, photographed speaking in Prague, Czech Republic, on 10 October 2010.

As Bauman says, we do indeed need new tools with which to conquer today's fears, but we lack them. His challenge, raised a decade ago, remains an immense one. The tools appropriate to meet the complexity and velocity of today's unfolding issues – including those for placemaking – are under continual invention, testing and adaptation.

Defining wiki culture

The wiki as an online genre – a web application enabling people to modify its content – was perhaps first exemplified by WikiWikiWeb, launched on 25 March 1995 by its inventor Ward Cunningham: it enabled anyone to play, contribute, modify and collaborate with others.[3] Today's active use of the wiki, and of a range of softwares, continues to allow for incremental, shared change, and gives room to accommodate different personal preferences. Seen more widely as part of cultural behaviour, the wiki factors in other people's needs, desires and cost-effective options, rather than ruling them out.

As a means for technologically enabled sharing, the wiki is an embodiment of the sort of tool needed to address Bauman's challenge. It can be seen as part of a growing culture of new concepts, uses and legal frameworks that affect placemaking and social space more widely. Representing a whole ecosystem of activities and networks enabled via the Internet, the wiki has increasingly come to stand for an entire emerging social system. That it gives room for multiple cultures, including those with differing viewpoints, to collaborate is one of its vital defining features.

This attitude of responsible and shared contribution leverages the potential benefits of collective intelligence, provided the tenets are sound and the motivations for collaboration are successfully exposed

Open source – similarly a subject of evangelical advocacy – which has evolved with the rise of the Internet, is now a movement promoting software that can be freely used, modified and shared and distributed under specific licences including the open-source code. Today, with the advent of 'the Internet of Things', open source increasingly extends beyond software into hardware solutions, with downloadable digital fabrication files for 3D printing, computer numerical control (CNC) milling and so on.[4] The principle is the same, however, as the Internet of Things facilitates software-defined networking (SDN) with the inter-operational benefits of cloud technology. As open-source protocols continue to diffuse, open-source networking understandably will take time to mature, but there is no doubt that in time its current proliferation will lead to it replacing a number of conventional practices. One feature of the open society in alliance with the Internet of Things is an 'always on', time-shifted experience merging the physical and virtual worlds through digital networks, available in many parts of the globe but not to those socio-economically disadvantaged.

A key characteristic of wiki culture in its encompassing of open source is the hybridisation of expertise and incremental definition, in the sense that most of the work may be conducted by more active and experienced members of an information-sharing platform, yet at any moment there is the opportunity for anyone to challenge the content and its expression. This attitude of responsible and shared contribution leverages the potential benefits of collective intelligence, provided the tenets are sound and the motivations for collaboration are successfully exposed.

There lies the rub. Wikipedia, the free-access, multilingual Internet encyclopedia founded in 2001 by Jimmy Wales and Larry Sanger and hosted by the non-profit Wikipedia Foundation, is now much larger than the Encyclopedia Britannica, and claims, probably with reason, to be the Internet's largest and most popular general reference work, including recent significant scientific and technological knowledge.[5] But as an exponent of wiki culture it remains controversial: critics describe it as possessing some systemic bias, a lack of accuracy and an inconsistent quality of writing. It has therefore perhaps not yet fully replaced the authority of most paid-for encyclopedias such as Britannica and the French-language Universalis as go-to benchmarks of knowledge.

Nonetheless, as open-source activities are developing daily and demonstrate high transparency, focusing on specific aspects of this cultural territory, while invariably fascinating, offers only parts of the story. Wiki culture enables combined, differentiated behaviours by individuals; this is generating what one might optimistically term an emerging 'wiki civilisation' of advanced social development and organisation, lending the 'open society' further legitimacy.

Definitions have not yet crystallised for new societal models that merge ideologies of free capital and the commons in a global networked sharing economy. But wiki civilisation embraces the wide-ranging open-source, do-it-yourself (DIY), self-organising and bottom-up cultures across the developing world as well as the developed one.

English social reformer Octavia Hill in a 1898 portrait by John Singer Sargent. Hill left a huge legacy thanks to her work in social housing, welfare reform and conservation, connecting cultural philanthropy to social reform.

An interesting aspect of the democratisation of goods and services that wiki culture encourages as its lifeblood is that, by scaling up global production of everyday objects and products, and by developing technologies to accelerate manufacturing and miniaturisation, the cost of these products drops to a point where almost anyone with a decent standard of living can afford each of these modern comforts. While there is probably not a full correlation – and it would be a difficult one to prove – there seems to be a rather direct connection between this phenomenon and the aspiration of most people to make or customise their own products in order to define themselves in the consumerist world with its remarkable reach of standardised products.

Building operating systems for self-organisation

Just as there is a growing culture of technologically enabled sharing and new legal frameworks for collaboration, there is also an increasing tendency for individuals and groups around the world to build things themselves. The generators of toda y's self-organised activities are diverse. Self-organising – in many ways inherited from hyper-liberal, subversive or 'alternative' ways of thinking about society largely originating from the wide-ranging alternative groups of the 1960s, and markedly diverging from 'creative' participation in consumer culture – is reinforced by contemporary DIY movements. The past few years have seen regained interest in notions of co-housing and shared agricultural plots, for example, both traditions with long histories. In our view there is a very significant change in perception of phenomena that were once pejoratively labelled as hippy or communist, or as standard practices only in times of war and necessity.

Discussing the origins of the DIY movements proliferating today is complex. To generalise somewhat, DIY activities are merging from two particular places in the social spectrum. Communities in need use DIY's various associated benefits (in particular, affordability, access and adaptability) to get by and to access technology, if not the material comforts that the more wealthy enjoy today. Secondly, DIY is also used by people as a way of expressing their identities and fundamental value sets divorced from manufactured consumerist goods and their role in defining lifestyles.

While Dougald Hine, founder of Space Makers (see Recoding: the Art of Participatory Placemaking, page 70) and the sociologist Keith Kahn-Harris exult in 'the spirit of improvisation which is the life of the network', DIY culture has many facets to it.[6] DIY is just not about informal, self-managed solutions, or affordable, anti-anodyne off-the-shelf solutions or imposed answers, but also about tinkering and hacking. Hacking – the practice of cracking

the code of how things are made and governed, without permission, but also without necessarily being malign in its effects – is a key part of contemporary engagement in inventive practices in fields ranging from crafts and electronics to digital open-source platforms and participatory learning.

A 'make do and mend' attitude links people who are in survival mode, as it did in Britain and elsewhere during World War II rationing, but it is also deeply ingrained in social innovation. DIY activities are rooted in Arts and Crafts social thinking of the late 19th and early 20th centuries, and are inspired by British social reformers and philanthrophists of the time such as John Ruskin, George Peabody and Octavia Hill who, observing the social alienation brought by the Industrial Revolution, took matters into their own hands.

Machines Room fab lab in London's Limewharf, the cultural innovation hub founded and directed by *Recoded City*'s co-author Thomas Ermacora (left), with Daniel Charny of Maker Library Network.

Those excluded by restricted means, or outright poverty, from the world of consumer durables associated with modern living, such as a phone, a fridge or a car, have the need and the want to obtain that standard of living through their own means: either by creative reclamation, or by self-created advanced bricolage, or, more recently, thanks to distributed manufacturing opportunities offered by 3D printing and such devices. DIY therefore relates to modern material dignity, as well as to the needs of personalisation and customisation.

The effects of DIY culture are profound and yet to be fully measured. As curator Daniel Charny eloquently states in his book *Power of Making*, there is both a need to partake in the creation of things we use and surround ourselves with, and a joy in doing so.[7] There is ultimately a convergence in the deployment of DIY, representing both an ethos and a pathos of living.[8] From an empirical standpoint, around the world in 2014 there were almost 300 fabrication laboratories ('fab labs') and 2,000 community-operated 'makerspaces' (also known as hackerspaces or hackspaces) that operate according to their own modus operandi and are generally run as not-for-profit open innovation and research bodies without subscribing to a particular body of laws.[9] These technological and cultural incubators are among the most significant new expressions of DIY culture impacting the nature of innovation, as well as the emerging relationship between the corporate world and distributed research and development.

The Internet of Things: networks and empowerment

As evidenced by the maker community, the new paradigm of collaboration pioneered by the software community has now permeated into hardware development. This is influencing every field of work and study, including the facilitation of citywide and regional infrastructural and planning processes, as borne out by the work of SENSeable City Laboratory at the Massachusetts Institute of Technology (MIT; see page 212) – an initiative of MIT's City Design and Development Group at the School of Architecture + Planning, established in 2004 by its director, architect and engineer Carlo Ratti. Retrofitting and reorganisation is needed across all sectors to face economic, social and environmental challenges. When it is not in service to armed conflict or corruption, technology is our ally in forging change, as the expression goes, 'one light bulb at a time' – but not the determinant.

Joi Ito, director of the MIT Media Lab – first conceived in 1980 and founded in 1985 by Nicholas Negroponte, a pioneer in computer-aided design and its first director (now Chairman Emeritus) – also at MIT's School of Architecture + Planning, points out that at the time the lab was first envisioned there was only a rudimentary version of the Internet and social media did not exist. When Ito took up the post in 2011, he said that the innovations made possible by open-source software around the time of the new millennium, which among other things minimised business start-up costs, were likely to be followed by an equal wave of new creativity thanks to freely available hardware. People could source the parts and the designs online for free, and adapt the product as they assembled it, carrying out rapid prototyping with ease.

'What's changed is that we've made a lot of progress in empowering the individual', Ito asserts, 'so now we have a network, and suddenly when you have a network, you have to look at things as systems, instead of objects. Now it's less about empowering the individual and more about empowering the community.'[10] With distribution, collaboration and communication costs reduced to virtually nothing, innovative activity of all kinds transformed to become more of a vast, decentralised and agile grassroots operation – one which requires no permission from anyone, and can make changes where they are most needed without boundaries or borders. As with the participative growth of the Linux computer development community, this innovation can be applied to everything we can think of or build, and as a result, having an impact on urban environments is more possible now thanks to these movements.

> **DIY relates to modern material dignity, as well as to the needs of personalisation and customisation**

Adhocracy exhibition at Limewharf, London, 2013, with Raul of Blablablab operating Be Your Own Souvenir.

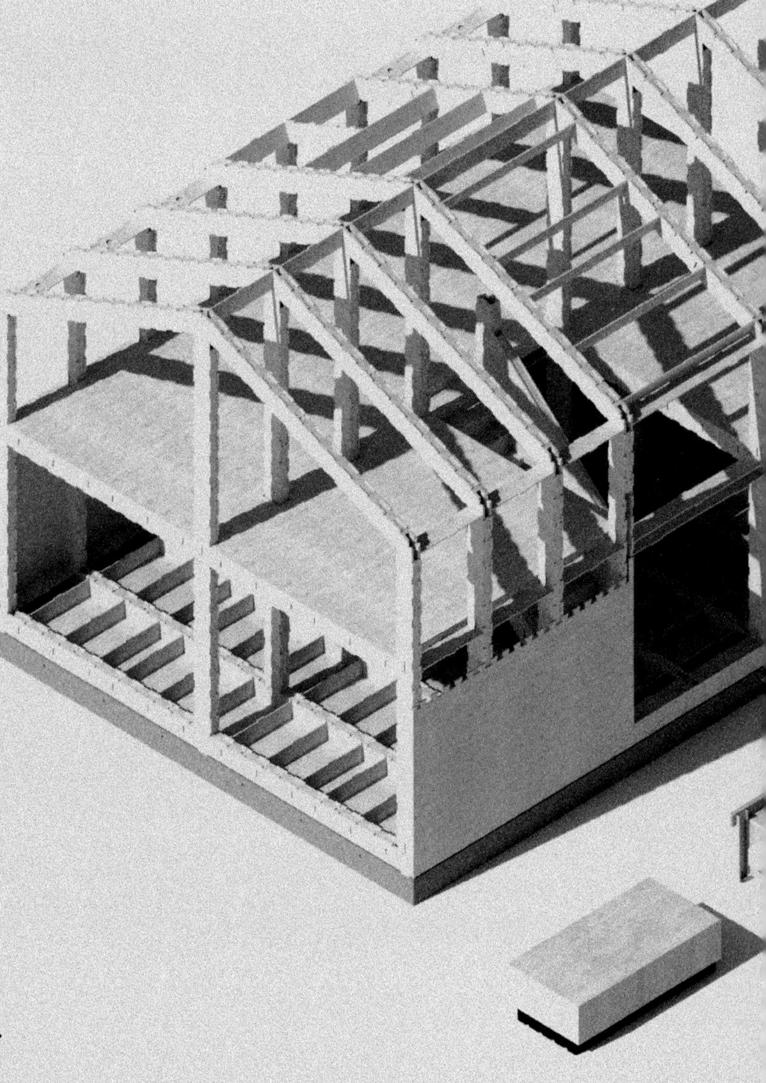

When it comes to skills, Ito's advice to students is to 'deploy or die' (in other words, use skills and tools at hand), and he strongly encourages them to build fresh 'combinations' of things that may 'grow' and be useful within the complex ecosystem of the world. This overall sensibility, he believes, more closely relates with the spirit of the age than to the old world of 'Newtonian, Euclidian laws before Internet when you could predict things'.

In *The Rise of the Network Society*, the sociologist Manuel Castells writes that today's global networks reflect deep changes in relational patterns of all kinds, some of them explosive in their implications – two prime examples being outsourcing of work and dating.[11] These networks represent new, intentionally less hierarchical dynamics that radically alter human capacities to create, maintain and develop identities of institutions, firms and individuals.

Whatever the motives, contemporary networks have emotional impacts, in that they create new bonds between social processes and the values they represent, and in that emerging social structures are facilitated by the Internet. Information control, and coercive behaviour as a means of persuasion, are now being countered by a different kind of challenging power: one wielded through an intense public sphere of communication, that frequently goes viral – and is both global and local in its effects.[12]

Ito too is a strong believer in the agility of networks. He cites the value of the Japanese online employment agency Otetsudai Networks. In a society where many young people value their freedom, this location-based, peer-to-peer service offers flexibility. The job seeker signs up, takes a

WikiHouse, designed in 2011 by Alastair Parvin and Nick Ierodiaconou, is an open-platform project for open-source construction, creating affordable blueprints for people to build their own homes.

GPS reading on his or her smartphone, and waits for a job opportunity; both parties – seekers and offerers of jobs – are rated for their reputation. Ito defines a decentralised 'pull' paradigm, with firms, agencies and individuals pulling resources from networks – whether local, national or global – when needed, rather than keeping them permanently in one single centralised location.

A decentralised pull paradigm is also operating in the field of placemaking. The early wiki project WikiHouse, consisting of an open-source construction system designed by Alastair Parvin and Nick Ierodiaconou (see page 278), empowers amateurs. Anyone, anywhere, can design, share, download, adapt and digitally print house parts from a standard sheet material like plywood through CNC milling. The method – which combines open-source materials and locally sourced ones – is a radically 'disruptive' one, as Parvin puts it (especially so if it is scaled up to impact on conventional housebuilding practices), reducing the threshold time, costs and skills needed, and enabling the user to augment his or her capabilities.

Essentially an experiment in open hardware built on a larger scale than before, WikiHouse also opens up a new economy for design. The project's design standards are not proposed as a fixed set of rules, and people are able not only to use them, but also to develop and alter them as they themselves improve on the elements available from WikiHouse. The concept shifts the 'factory' into any context, democratising the otherwise hierarchical production of architecture through a new system driven by common purpose. The new local factory will undoubtedly influence urban development, as more projects open up opportunities for the development of other WikiHouses or variants. For example, the Cradle to Cradle Products Innovation Institute for architectural-scale digital fabrication, started by architect and sustainable development specialist William McDonough and chemist Michael Braungart in 2010, is focused on 'upcycling' of waste materials.[13]

Anyone, anywhere, can design, share, download, adapt and digitally print house parts from a standard sheet material like plywood through CNC milling. The method, combining open-source materials and locally sourced ones, is a radically 'disruptive' one enabling the user to augment his or her capacities

The sharing economy

The economics and social theorist Jeremy Rifkin describes the process of reorientation of economy and society towards a collaborative commons, a concept endorsed by the P2P Foundation, created in 2005 to analyse and advance this transition.[14] The reduction of overhead costs transforms the dynamics and possibilities of social organisation, and a vision of the state and the market in harmonious alignment with the commons is evoked. While institutions we are familiar with are finding obstacles to maintaining their status, the collaborative commons is a major means for establishing 'new-generation', democratic, alternative institutions, or at least for upgrading the relevance and competence of existing ones.

Atmos Totnes consultation hub designed by Encounters Arts for Totnes Community Development Society to consider the Dairy Crest site and the UK's first community 'right to build'.

The concept of the sharing, or peer-to-peer (P2P) economy – promoted by the P2P Foundation (founded by Michel Bauwens) and others, and made a reality via distributed networks – brings the prospect of real-time, on-demand skill trading, with a vast pool of digitally connected 'talent' that competes freely to provide the best service when and where necessary. P2P encompasses the creation, production, distribution, trading and consumption of goods and services by different people and organisations.

If asked to explain what the sharing economy means, some people may – off the tops of their heads – think of cars (Zipcar, car2go, Liftshare, Nextgreencar), homes (Airbnb), dogs (Borrowmydoggy, DogVacay), bicycles (globally there exists more than 600 urban bike-sharing schemes), clothes (for example, 'shwapping' schemes such as Rentez-vous, or friendrobes), money, Wi-Fi, or headline-grabbing taxi-sharing schemes (Uber, Wheels). But Bauwens's P2P philosophy has far wider applications than simply being an inventory of modern conveniences, as he explains: '"Peer to peer theory" addresses itself not just to those who are network-enabled and to knowledge workers generally, but to the whole of civil society (the "multitudes"), and to whoever agrees that the core of decision-making should be located in civil society, and not in the market or in the state, and that the latter should be the servants of civil society.'[15]

The sharing economy has a strong allure, as well as some controversial aspects. It contradicts certain norms in current labour markets of seniority and proximity, and there are probably a number of values attached to those norms that are worth retaining in the shared economy as ethical standards to protect employees and hired help. If given full momentum, the sharing economy can dramatically improve performance and optimise costs. It is likely to trump the owning economy with its narrow adherance to classical hierarchical structures, as entrepreneur Lisa Gansky notes in her book *The Mesh*.[16]

Creative Commons and shared property rights

As technology platforms and tools abound, society is moving towards more open and transparent information. E-governance and mobile commerce are now practices people have adopted, following the changing habits of institutions and firms, while information-gathering via Wikipedia and open-source self-publishing have been deeply influenced by MySpace, Facebook, Linkedin and Foursquare.

This shift is transforming ideas about remodelling community governance, and in fact now there is a plethora of examples, and literature, on how the adoption of new standards has accelerated decision-making, financial transactions and more. Examples include Microsoft-led testing grounds, such as the towns of Parthenay or Chooz in France, that launched 'early day' e-governance platforms for all citizens via 'fibre-to-the-home' way back in 2000. When it comes to placemaking, there are urban districts such as Kilen in Ronneby, Sweden, or the Park 20/20 business park in Haarlemmermeer, the Netherlands, aiming to adopt 'Cradle-to-Cradle' (C2C, the sustainability concept introduced by McDonough and Braungart) in their design, through C2C-licencing, allied to a total digitisation of their systems and governance.

A key consequence of the coming of an open society is the need for 'tribes' – groups of people and cultural niches – with defined identities and a sense of direction about sharing their resources and capacities, as suggested by author and marketeer Seth Godin, in his book *Tribes: We Need You to Lead Us*.[17] Patterns of 'tribal' sharing are manifesting themselves globally, producing friction with current practices of sharing and value definition, and this calls for the establishment of adapted and acceptable codes.

Not only is it now easier to work with others in any context involving intellectual property rights (IPR), but also the development of legal frameworks for collective creativity is establishing new norms of acceptance of authorship. The most advanced set of rules and principles is set out in the licence terms of the Creative Commons, a non-profit organisation founded by Joi Ito that proposes a range of licences for groups and individuals developing intellectual property (IP) of some form. Ito captured the multiple types of collaboration, both commercial and non-profit, in such a way that individuals

“

While institutions we are familiar with are finding obstacles to maintaining their status, the collaborative commons is a major means for establishing 'new-generation', democratic, alternative institutions

and organisations can choose how to adequately place trust in, or safeguard, their intellectual property globally, in ways that are often more cost-effective, and therefore more competitive-to-market, than allowed for by conventional intellectual property l aw.

The philosophy behind Creative Commons, whether related to product or content – and even legislation – is about protection and freedom. Authors, artists, designers and educators share IP openly in such a fashion: intuitive, innovative, spontaneous and reversing the usual norms.

The intention of Creative Commons is not merely to license transactions, but rather to augment the capacity for shared invention and creativity by enabling a system of mutual reputation and crediting of each other's contributions in a way that honours the intentions of the originators of source material. This radically dynamic, mutual-attribution ecosystem of production is fundamental to areas and domains of work that traditionally have been locked into orders and 'charters' that were certainly not decided upon through contextual conventions, but rather through conventional, top-down decision-making. It is a great achievement in the face of the 'siloing' of knowledge and solutions of any sort which offers the party who owns IP disproportional authority on matters related to the general good, and which protects creators through what one could call omni-directional validation.

Setting up new value and transaction systems

Economic forces and tools, including Bitcoin and other parallel or complementary online currencies, are offering game-changing options to new entrants facing incumbents in markets, from telecoms to media and infrastructure. Who is to say what wikinomic option will be the most viable in a few years, when collaborative consumption becomes the norm?

Wiki culture fundamentally challenges the ways in which we define value, and that helps creative communities to self-organise their priorities of change beyond governmental or local authority definition processes. For example, in the UK a number of the Transition Towns groups, a movement for low-impact living started by Rob Hopkins, have set up their own currencies and attribute preference to exchange of local goods and services that have less carbon impact. This in turn produces a propensity for collaboration on other issues pertaining to placemaking, because the systems for such collaboration are already in place, as well as the value systems guiding choices. Setting up new value systems in this way makes it easier to kick-start participatory placemaking projects.

The tendency in placemaking has been to have proportionally low levels of sharing decision making, as a way of influencing the stakes at hand. In order to introduce valuable input from users that balances more top-down placemaking schemes, it is vital to make a strong case for placemaking platforms, so that case studies can be appropriately and dynamically documented, and to understand the relative responsibilities to be shouldered by each stakeholder, and their optimum relationships.

Vinay Gupta, the mastermind behind the Hexayurt, the most replicated open-source shelter to date, has faced the challenge of how to increase quality in design through the instruments of mass collaboration. He has observed that in fact very few members of the public are capable of personally furthering the designs. In other words, involving various design specialists throughout realisation processes will invariably lead to improvements. Concerns about whether networked knowledge alone ends up delivering better solutions are valid.

A backlash is being produced by the constant stories in the media about major computer hacking activities and other attempts to destabilise servers

Hexayurt at Burning Man Festival, August 2007, in Nevada's Black Rock Desert, where thousands gather to create Black Rock City, a temporary participatory metropolis.

> Wiki culture fundamentally challenges the ways in which we define value, and that helps creative communities to self-organise their priorities of change beyond governmental or local authority definition processes

handling our energy grids, financial services or traffic-control devices managed through reactive algorithmic automation. Whether this backlash is on the same scale as the scare produced in its time by the discovery of nuclear energy and its significance for warfare and weapons of mass destruction, for example, is debatable. There are also risks facing the proponents of more, rather than less, openness. What is undeniable is that it is not an easy task to gain public support for the clearly redeeming qualities of wiki culture (or wiki civilisation): its massive, real-time, relevant and creative contribution to almost any organisational challenge, or to the research and development of products and services.

Fast Forward Now

Individuals' roles as actors in history are shifting. Slowly but surely, as more of those who were formerly merely observers become participants, a new era of collective human intelligence is manifesting itself. Everyone is a voluntary or an involuntary maker of history through his or her presence in today's ecosystem, and in decision chains. One does not need to be an activist to contribute and to become a maker of change.

Places everywhere around the world are under stress from trying to adapt to human aspirations for quality of life, and for less fortunate people these stresses restrict their opportunities to define themselves. The digitisation of the world and the ubiquity of technology introduce a new factor of complexity in self-definition. The speed at which we are moving through history – not simply fast, but faster and faster still – is rendering a number of once trustworthy institutions and bodies of thought vulnerable to increasing pressure of scrutiny. Within this destabilising context, the professions collectively responsible for making cities both liveable and workable are expected to rise to the challenge; but currently commercial considerations often block, rather than allow for, adequate responses to these challenges in a timely manner.

Entering an age of acceleration

We live in an age of exponential growth in almost every aspect of knowledge creation, science and technology. Change that was once perceived across a century can now be perceived in a decade.

In computing, Moore's law, originating from around 1970 and now often referred to as a measure of change, states that the overall processing power of computers will double every two years.[1] This era of rapidly accelerated change has spawned phenomena such as the Singularity University, a non-profit teaching organisation dedicated to encouraging, through the application of growing technologies such as biotechnology, artificial intelligence and neuroscience, sustainable solutions to some of the most difficult challenges facing humanity.[2] The intellectual framework of the hypothesis of technological singularity, which has its roots in the writings of the early 20th-century mathematician John von Neumann, hinges on the concept of a moment beyond which 'technological progress will become incomprehensively rapid and complicated'.[3] This takes the simple concept of Moore's law into another paradigm.

In his book *The Singularity Is Near: When Humans Transcend Biology*, the inventor, writer and Singularity University co-founder Ray Kurzweil anticipates a time rapidly approaching when the pace of technological change will alter every aspect of human life.[4] With super computers rivalling human intelligence in nearly all its aspects, and with measurable information technology everywhere, there will also be exponential growth in bio-tech machines based on artificial intelligence (AI). Human intelligence captured in a machine already supports many endeavours, and while singularity has existed in the realms of science fiction, now, with such a profound transformation, it can extend who we are, amplifying human existence.

Ray Kurzweil, the inventor, computer scientist and futurist, CEO of Kurzweil Technologies and a director at Google, heading a team developing machine intelligence and natural language understanding. Pictured onstage at Expanding Our Intelligence Without Limit, 2012 SXSW Music, Film + Interactive Festival.

Although Kurzweil sees this singularity era as 'neither utopian nor dystopian', the spectre persists of the technological determinism first envisaged in the 19th century by Karl Marx and by the sociologist Thorstein Veblen.[5] To alleviate and confront negative social and environmental outcomes needs more than commercial production values, and tech firms pushing out multiple new technological enablements need to adopt more socially responsive mindsets that go beyond legally and politically correct corporate social responsibility policies. These by any measure reflect a time lag between action and reaction, rather than responsible and visionary anticipation. The work ahead of us is to engineer and manage processes and platforms so that they engage with both the practical and ethical consequences of an open society.

The democratisation of technology

The democratisation of technology and its ever-increasing influence on our day-to-day life have dramatically increased the ways in which people – unless they are materially marginalised – can access information on the fly and make decisions of all kinds, including beyond those of a transactional nature. The epitome of the penetration of the digital sphere into human life is the 'smart phone'. The term appeared in the mid 1990s to describe a mobile phone containing an operating system – a revolution in its time. Today the smartphone is the number-one important global device. It is possible that by 2020 there will be one smartphone per person in the world. In the past decade smartphone market penetration has increased to the extent that there are more handsets in the world today than any other consumer electronic device, and this is at last bringing the Internet to the most remote parts of the world. This in itself is an open door to e-learning, e-medicine, e-governance, e-commerce and

6 IN 10

Global 4G-LTE connect

Global 4G-LTE connections will come from the developing region in 2020, up from 5% in 2013, largely driven by growth in China

e-banking through local entrepreneurship. It means that all but rare indigenous tribes or voluntary technophobes are unaware of the possibilities presented through the web.

Even before today's immense cloud computing capabilities, the nature of the game for decision making concerning the urban realm had been transformed by the simple fact that the Internet and mobile telephony have made information real-time and remotely accessible. The sheer ubiquity and speed of connection, the transparency, the ability to be continually iterative 24/7, have nurtured certain relational and interactive capabilities, replacing top-down, hierarchical decision making and its claims to greater efficiency.

Furthermore, technology itself, in its multiplication and commoditisation, has led to the challenging of the notion of closed source and associated 'silo' thinking – systems

500 M

Tweets per day (2012)

According to Twitter CEO Dick Costolo, the number of tweets posted in 2012 was estimated at 500 million per day

200 BN

Tweets per year (2012)

According to internetlivstats.com the tweets per year was estimated at 200 billion

2.5 BN

Global 4G-LTE connect

4G-LTE (FDD/TDD) connections expected worldwide in 2020

> **Technology itself, in its multiplication and commoditisation, has led to the challenging of the notion of closed source and associated 'silo thinking'**

and procedures of intellectual property development of any kind that assume the need for separated disciplines in order to achieve greater performance and results. The traditional reaction to complexity in scientific research and development has been to fragment knowledge areas into distinct specialist fields, operating a justifiable but unfortunate over-simplication. It is worth noting that the most advanced current collaboration efforts, such as the Large Hadron Collider built by the European Organisation for Nuclear Research (CERN) near Geneva, Switzerland, are being pioneered by the scientific community itself.

The smart city

The emergence of 'smart city' practices has been one manifestation of new technologies. Narrow kit-based and crowdsourced, data-focused 'smart city' concepts are still in their infancy, and while the infinitely larger capacities of wiki culture (see page 34) have begun to influence opinion formers, they have yet to filter through widely to transformations in urban design and planning.

There is a big difference between 'smart city' defined as a growing market of 'kit' products with which cities can manage and control energy use, traffic congestion, flood alerts and public-services coordination in an integrated way, and genuine, technologically enabled citizen power. Another point to consider is how to maximise the beneficial aspects of the smart city – in monitoring resource consumption, traffic flows and other related matters – without hindering individuals' capacities to act outside the parameters fixed by the network and server owners and administrators.

In any case, citizens have become deeply sceptical of formal politics, and any person who feels the freedom to act in a community's interests must become a good cultural broker in order to

64%

Global 4G-LTE connect

of the world's populaton will be covered by 4G-LTE networks by the end of 2020

4.4BN

The world wide web

The Indexed Web contains at least 4.4 billion pages (Sunday, 25 January, 2015)

avoid further dangerous democratic deficits accruing in different societies. With the emerging tools of the wiki culture, citizens themselves can build new relations and networks, share their knowledge across sectors and boundaries of professional and non-professional, and explore actions and proposals to deal with challenges on every front.

With the atomisation of data intelligence comes a range of problematics vital to assess. As regards how this affects the building of cities, while new and necessary relational decisions involving a much wider array of participants are enabled, traditional control mechanisms are threatened. A race to acquire data sets that are perhaps of public interest is being waged between corporate bodies for commercial benefits at the expense of privacy, urban quality management and e-governance.

It is with tremendous care that the burgeoning realm of urban data needs to be analysed, in order on the one hand to empower legitimately organised civil society, and on the other, to facilitate access and well-intended moderation by pre-digital institutions we may want to retain. Participatory placemaking certainly opens a can of worms, and debunks the goals of the smart city. At this point arbitration is definitely needed between accepted institutions, progressive civil society and important corporate bodies' data greed.

At Liverpool's Flyover Festival, 13 July 2014, Talkaoke ran a live chatshow to ask local people what they wanted to see done with the Churchill flyover, which was threatened with demolition; now Friends of the Flyover plan a new elevated park here instead.

Crowdfunding

Truly worth putting effort into, in order to maximise the potential of the technologies and software solutions coming to maturity, is civic crowdsourcing, and its low-cost collaboration infrastructures and computer-assisted archiving and decision-making. A tool increasingly used for public-space projects, crowdfunding democratises the design of towns and cities by enabling anyone and everyone to create and fund civic projects online. In placemaking, crowdfunding has often functioned as a top-up to other, larger sources of funding, including donations, and this continues to be the case. Nevertheless, it is catching on because, in the age of austerity, cities and towns need additional and more effective means of sourcing finance for enhancing both people's quality of life and the local economy. Having crowdsourced funding also helps to democratise ownership of a project (or a product) and its potential benefits.

More than 1 million successful crowdfunding campaigns were undertaken in 2011, mostly in Europe (where they generated some $654,000) and North America ($532,000); most of these campaigns were donation-based rather than reward-based. In April 2012 there were 452 CFPs – crowdfunding platforms – in the world. The estimated level of funding raised worldwide that year was $1.5 billion, and a report by the professional services firm Deloitte estimates an expansion, with £1.9 billion in funds raised for this sector in 2013 and a forecast of £14 billion by 2016.[6] One representative of the trend is Spacehive, the world's first funding platform for neighbourhood improvement projects (created in 2011) and the first successful placemaking and crowdfunding firm in the UK; the donation-based platform was set up by planning journalist Chris Gourlay to focus on reviving British towns and high streets.

At the time of writing Spacehive had helped to fund 57 projects across the UK worth £1.8 million. In 2014 it raised £1.3 million in funding from the Belgian SI2 Fund, an 'alternative' investment fund targeting social returns as well as financial ones, and Big Society Capital, a body set up to boost investment in British social ventures. While Spacehive is often described as a 'Kickstarter for places', Gourlay points out that there is a substantial difference between its donation-based structure and the reward-based systems of such crowdfunding platforms as Kickstarter.

Pledges of funding for Spacehive projects come from ordinary people as well as businesses and local municipalities, and, as with Kickstarter, they are charged only if the fundraising campaign is successful and the project goes ahead. Gourlay regards crowdfunding as 'a turnkey solution for councils and corporates wishing to help communities shape their local civic environment'. He wanted to affect 'that very bureaucratic, opaque world of urban planning', and 'translate it into something more user-friendly, that would allow people to engage with it'.[7]

Gourlay cites the case of a former mining town in a deprived area of South Wales, with 50% unemployment. 'People really got it, because the model was one where they had the vast majority of the money they needed for a civic centre, [with] a mixture of locals chipping in, corporates doing their bit, and the government picking up the lion's share of the burden. They had some giant pledges which they couldn't collect, so the fundraising they did online unlocked those grants. It was something the

“

Participatory placemaking opens a can of worms, and debunks the goals of the smart city…arbitration is definitely needed between accepted institutions, progressive civil society and important corporate bodies' data greed

Scrap Tall Bikes were part of Friends of the Flyover's Flyover Festival, promoting the conversion of roads into pedestrian- and cycling-friendly routes.

community desperately needed – literally the figures were there two weeks later, so [it brought] a sense of unblocking people's aspirations for their area. And it wasn't just about the money: it made people think it was also possible to do stuff again.'[8]

Despite crowdfunding's undeniably alluring promise, enabling the marketing goals of community-focused projects through its social media features, it is still difficult to empower local communities and activists through this means alone. Campaigns may bring a number of networking benefits, but the reality of crowdfunding's gap-filling identity is that it needs to be part of a larger strategy for fundraising for placemaking.

Crowdfunding has a gap-filling identity – it needs to be part of a larger strategy for fundraising for placemaking

New alliances and platforms engaging bits and atoms

With the advent of social media and the spread of ubiquitous technology, the reduction in the cost of creating the infrastructure for collaboration has been such that virtually any organised group can now easily develop participatory projects with excellent communication and archiving. This accessibility, forging a new mutuality across boundaries, is one of the consequences of the emerging DIY culture. Social media enable people to believe that they can achieve what they did not previously think possible. Adherents of DIY culture are becoming 'prosumers' by individually elevating their own skills incrementally through e-learning. As a figure in society, infused with DIY cultural value, the prosumer is also going to have a cumulative economic impact.

The economic and social theorist Jeremy Rifkin has described how the prosumer is now 'producing and sharing music, videos, news, and knowledge at near-zero marginal cost and nearly for free, shrinking revenues in the music, newspaper and book-publishing industries', and this 'zero-marginal cost revolution is beginning to affect other commercial sectors'.[9] Rifkin regards the 'precipitating agent' as being an 'emerging general purpose technology platform – the Internet of Things'. He also sees fragmented distributive ownership structures as 'a collaborative challenger ... entirely bypassing the conventional capitalist market', in the sense that these structures can clearly become so large that local policy does not have the capacity to legislate or regulate their activities, and that is problematic.[10] However, while the new possibilities clearly bring new issues of concern, that does not mean that the changes should not be embraced. The challenge is to marshal initiatives and guide processes in such ways that they bring about positive effects.

In June 2014 American President Barack Obama welcomed the inaugural Maker Faire on the White House lawn, in the hope of fostering a renaissance in US manufacturing. A few weeks later the largest maker gathering to date took place in Barcelona, Spain: the FAB10 event on world-changing open and accessible technologies (slogan: From Fab Labs to Fab Cities). Present were the innovation directors of Google, Airbus and Nike, who stated to the counterculture underground constituency attending the event that they might need help from the group. The science-fiction author and social critic Bruce Sterling discussed the emerging public protests against new digital ownership behemoths including

Airbnb and Uber. This is a scenario of unlegislated distributed structures that Rifkin warned about, and Sterling pointed out the irony of a future in which the keys to local transportation and hosted homes are handed over to an international corporation uncontrollable by local legislation.

Time will tell whether Neil Gershenfeld, director of the Massachusetts Institute of Technology's Center for Bits and Atoms, founder of the Fab Foundation (formed in 2009 to support the growth of the international fab lab network) and director of the Fab Academy, manages to broker a truce between the maker community present at the event and the corporate world following their surreal deal-making contest. Observing this association of 'Robin Hoods' and 'Sheriffs', it seems that there is a natural reluctance on the part of the DIY maker community to contribute their skills to help what they reject. Both sides need each other, however: the talents developing in the DIY sphere have the capacity and the inclination to scale up, while the corporate players require help to innovate with appropriate technologies, to be more relevant and, in many cases, more competitive.

Alliances between once largely opposing sides are being formed, in which it is beyond party politics and financial systems to define appropriate technologies and scaleable solutions. This is an extraordinary turn of events, and it is good news. It is not new that radical innovators have been hired to challenge product development or business models, but this has now culminated in a fresh formula: open-source hardware and the advent of the 'Internet of Things' are imposing an awareness on radical innovators and corporates alike that collaboration is necessary in the interests of mutual self-preservation. But such developments need to be carefully monitored so as to avoid some parties taking advantage, which would risk disrupting the new balance of powers wrought from those mutual ambitions.

When numerous stakeholders all want to have their say, the collaborative spirit is often brittle; so when things are becoming evidenced naturally, the lesser voice can participate through an intrinsically fairer process. There is a common misunderstanding that it is the software or the specific kind of technology that are making things different. In fact, what has really changed is the ease of access to new developments and the available options, so that in the pursuit of fairness and the exercise of collaboration, the opportunity cost through the benefits of an alternative option has been reduced.

Technology is an ally of the less fortunate and their quest for empowerment. Many examples demonstrate how a sense of enterprise and ambition can be augmented by the simple facility to connect online. Ushahidi (Swahili for 'testimony'), for example, was started in 2008 by Erik Hirshman, Juliana Rotich, Ory Okolloh and David Kobia as an SMS platform to help people in riots in Kenya locate each other and provide real-time information that could be critical for their survival, as well as for relaying opinions about information that needs to be shared, that government cannot stop.

US President Barack Obama talks to Neil Gershenfeld, the director of MIT's Center for Bits and Atoms, at the first Maker Faire in June 2014, hosted by Obama on the White House lawn to highlight new tools and techniques.

The system acts as a parallel information channel and creates a precedent for online participation in the most remote places in the world. It has been widely used in Africa, in the field of disaster relief and situations of political unrest, as well as in other contexts requiring unmediated real-time information. Even if it has not as yet been used in the space of participatory placemaking, it is a key tool for unlocking potential, which has helped people to understand what can be done without the approval of official bodies.

The growing impact of participatory culture on education through new media has made it possible not only to appropriate and retransmit online material, but also create new, hybrid social platforms

Participatory learning and self-learning

The pervasiveness of network culture partially accounts for the growing impact of participatory culture on education through new media, which is putting the focus on learning as a process. This has made it possible not only to appropriate and retransmit online material, but also to create new social platforms that link education, creative activities, community focal points and goals with ideals of democratic citizenship. The media scholar Henry Jenkins defines this arena as having 'relatively low barriers to artistic expression and civic engagement ... with strong support for creating and sharing one's creations with others', involving informal mentorship and social connections.[11]

Academies of renown are adapting to this novel academic landscape in which the institutions coach and vet knowledge acquisition of all forms, rather than simply teach in the traditional ways. Open college educational practices – such as Stanford and Harvard universities putting all their courses online for free, iTunesU and amateur videos on YouTube – contribute to a seemingly more democratic access to knowledge. This of course means that there are new rules in establishing reputation, and, having built academic capital over decades or even centuries, old players are not easily trumped. But the ambitious student without means has more options to make meritocracy actually work for him or her.

One of these options is the online University of the People, launched in 2009 to provide tuition-free education in business administration and computer science for underserved areas of the world, empowering networks as a new meta-authority of learning. Instead of competing with traditional institutions, it is bridging their expertise with the needs of the many to rapidly augment their capacity. This can radically impact the opportunities for certain countries, and for currently limited, high-potential demographics, such as teenage girls in Africa, India and the Middle East.

This impact is illustrated by the Khan Academy, created in 2006 and now the largest, fastest-growing online education platform. It has radically transformed the way in which millions of children in their teens, before they decide on directions in their later education, help themselves to learn topics they have struggled with. It has largely eliminated learning problems with professors who may not be sensitive to different learning abilities.

The Khan Academy has established a new benchmark for how to provide educational support to students where teachers and educational resources have failed. Other platforms include TED.com, and particularly ed.TED.com, which pairs a great teacher with a talented visual communication person or studio to make short YouTube-style videos to help students of all ages to learn key curriculum topics; these too also accelerate the learning of complex subjects and eliminate language barriers through translation, and, more importantly, age barriers.

Taken together, these platforms for self-learning – professional and amateur, institutional and academic – represent an emerging global trend. As a consequence, almost every person capable of reading, and with the time to do so, can gain vital professional knowledge and eliminate some forms of academic exclusion.

Open data and achieving transparency

Beyond the realm of education, open data platforms are being created daily based on private and governmental data sets – including military-level information – coming into the public domain. This changes the notion of accountability on major decisions related to placemaking at a regional and occasionally national and international level. One example is the Satellite Sentinel Project (SSP), conceived by the actor George Clooney and the human rights activist John Prendergast during a visit to South Sudan in 2010. By employing satellite imagery, SSP acts a rapid alert system concerning mass atrocities globally.

Many companies, in working closely with local government, have reduced the size of their bureaucracy and have made cost savings in a recession. An unexpected consequence of this is a transparency in newer data sets, which represents a radical opportunity for enlightened placemaking. A good example is the Ecological Sequestration Trust founded by Peter Head in 2011. The Trust performs open mapping through its online Knowledge Exchange of bio-regional land use potential, making use of software that pulls in publicly available satellite data. The Trust's work promotes transparency, curating real-time data intelligence that is visually rich, and through a software platform empowers citizens to make more informed decisions.

The case for technology as a tool of empowerment is an easy one to make. That the impacts of an open-source wiki culture need monitoring if platforms, processes and mechanisms are to be genuinely socially beneficial, is also not difficult to advocate. New relational processes and networks, built by citizens and asserting their own authority, may not need arbitration with corporate players when it comes to social ideals. However, in order to be economically viable, and in turn to trigger local benefits, new hyper-local platforms, whether in the developed or the developing world, must have patronage and the moral support of those backers if they are to be allied further with participatory placemaking goals.

Behind the emerging model of crowdfunding for placemaking lies an immense opportunity – and imperative – for new discussions and alliances. Wiki culture is not just to be made; it needs to be negotiated, every step of the way. One major step necessitates the building of a new relationship between owners of previously exclusive information and communities in need of it, for the sake of people's sense of ownership and empowerment.

The impacts of an open-source wikiculture need monitoring if platforms, processes and mechanisms are to be genuinely socially beneficial

Reframing Placemak

The professions that form placemaking alliances today include urban design, urban planning, landscape architecture, engineering, geology, agricultural engineering, social science, ethnology and activism – as well as liveability research, as tough as it is to pin down the full meaning of 'liveability' in the context of cities. Working for clients in the public sector and, increasingly, the private sector too, these multidisciplinary battalions' common modes of operation today include zoning of land uses; masterplanning is deployed in various guises, sometimes more as a conceptual framework, and public space regeneration and landscape schemes are applied to a mix of goals, commercial motives being predominant.

Responses are made, as well, to overall governmental growth strategies, to the requirement to accommodate and decentralise populations in order to meet environmental agendas. Considerations need to be given to economic and carbon costs, and performance criteria, as well as to the creation of benchmarks against international exemplars. But set against this noble picture of holistic procedures, it remains a fact that the traditionally reforming dynamic of urban design is today tempered by too much compromise in favour of expedient solutions, rather than socially beneficial ones. Yet urban design possesses so much potential of social value that it is no surprise that alternative means of advancing urban placemaking for people – as opposed to statistics – are a justified central focus of this book.

Contemporary urban design genres vary: the widely influential New Urbanists favour pedestrianised neighbourhood design subsisting on a restricted diet of design codes, for example; and the hermetic gated community model has not waned in popularity among developers globally. Joined-up development plans are not a given, and relationships with transport infrastructure

range on a spectrum from wholly integrated live-travel-work solutions to plans alarmingly disconnected from transport hubs and other services and heavily car-dependent.

Whatever identity a public urban design scheme takes, the norm is huge dossiers of project design development diagrams and assessments, rarely shown to the public. Urban design jobs are invariably clinched at the outset by private-sector or local-government clients tempted by a smorgasbord of alluring computer-generated imagery, area makeover and branding concepts and local job opportunities, with only a desultory minimum of public consultation about intentions.

Then, although there are many notable exceptions, in too many cases project stakeholders, given augmented powers by the public sector, neglect their responsibilities to build a percentage of affordable housing, adhere in any case to a land bank policy that retains the best land, and lack the incentive to incorporate sustainable land-use policies into their schemes. A narrow cycle of dysfunction perpetuates itself in the name of development, leaving aside urban design's powerful regenerative potential – unless, that is, newer marshalling forces enter the process.

In 2010 the UK government stated its intention to solve a housing crisis by supporting major development schemes billed as 'eco-towns', converting largely disused brownfield land. This gave developers an incentive to build more ecologically in line with pioneering European schemes, such as Vauban in Freiburg, Germany, and BedZED (Beddington Zero Energy Development), in Hackbridge, in the London borough of Sutton, designed by Bill Dunster Architects (now BDa ZEDfactory) in 2002, and realised with BioRegional and Arup and funding from the Peabody Trust. BedZED has 100 homes, community facilities and workspaces sufficient for 100 people; the project was shortlisted for the Stirling Prize in 2003, and the UK eco-village became the poster child for sustainable affordable housing in the UK.

However benign the intentions of the government of the time, many of the 11 subsequent eco-town projects selected met with civic resistance and rejection of presumptions made and the arbitrary nature of decisions taken. Even if the locations were good, the schemes potentially created parallel urban developments threatening existing services, and there were concerns that they would siphon public funds towards private developers. The economic crisis has expanded debate about options for solving the UK housing crisis but reduced the capacities of local authorities to plan.

The proposal by the town planner David Rudlin, winner of the Wolfson Economics Prize in 2014, to double the size of up to 40 existing towns, each one accommodating a further 150,000 people, has been resisted by politicians and councillors at the localities concerned. Ahead of a national election in 2015, central government announced its commitment to development (one first planned in the early years of the 21st century) for 15,000 homes at Ebbsfleet in Kent, in a disused quarry by the Thames Estuary near the station for High Speed 1/Channel Tunnel rail links. This would take place through the means of an urban development corporation (UDC), using public funds for infrastructure alongside the investment of the private sector. A top-down, unelected quango of this kind would take the project out of local government control, and the scheme is promoted by central government as a quick-fix solution and magnet of businesses, rather than as a test

In-situ housing prototype built by Urban-Think Tank and NGO Ikhayalami as part of U-TT's Empower Shack R&D project, Khayelitsha township, Cape Town, 2012- (page 266). Ikhayalami/ Empower Shack.

If the term 'liveability' is to have real significance beyond the media vogue for annual city rankings, it needs to stand for building social capital, inclusive planning and holistic systemic thinking, design and organisation

bed for enhancing the planning process to include public interest objectives, innovative sustainable design and green infrastructure.

Advocating alternative practices in the face of adversity and rapid change is complex, but not exactly rocket science; especially when, today, as architect and academic Irena Bauman observes, 'there is uncertainty about impacts on society of unstable economies, unregulated banking practices, rising wealth discrepancies, global warming, diminishing resources and unresponsive political bodies'.[1] If the term 'liveability' is to have real significance beyond the media vogue for annual city rankings, it needs to stand for building social capital, and for applying inclusive planning, holistic systemic thinking, design and organisation geared towards adaptation of urban environments in the face of all these perils.

Private sector developers do not all sing from the same hymn sheet on sustainability, and many do not sing much at all about matters of sustainability except to collect their sustainable badges of honour. But the harsh reality is that the majority of world cities, including ports and water filtration plant locations, are hugely exposed to climatological catastrophe and geological transformations, and many also suffer from drought and inundation, affecting their liveability. It has taken almost half a century to rally most of the world behind the idea of mankind's impact on the environment. The 2009 United Nations IPCC climate summit in Copenhagen sharply emphasised the increasing number of climate-related catastrophes striking humanity.[2]

Unfortunately the diplomatic negotiations between developed and developing nations at the summit failed to forge the global unity needed to formally reduce carbon emissions and pollution in general. This goal was politically perceived as a 'white man's burden' when compared to other concerns that developing nations face, such as building competitive infrastructures, reducing poverty and promoting health and education. Yet in late 2014 the World Meteorological Organisation stated that the year was on course to be the hottest on record for Europe (and in the UK the hottest for 350 years), with not only higher heat levels across vast areas of the world's surface, but also torrential rainfall and flooding.[3]

The discussions in Paris, where the next milestone UN Climate Change Conference will be held in 2015, may change things a little. American politician Al Gore and his Climate Reality Project organisation are working towards finally achieving a more promising, binding agreement between nations, following the announcement in 2014 by the USA and China of a joint climate change agreement to reduce their greenhouse gas output. Just mitigating the effects of climate change is not enough. The task now is to adapt to a different climatic reality, and to develop new strategies and action plans that come to terms with the impact climate change is having on hydrological resources, energy consumption, flooding and natural catastrophes. This calls for a great deal of public-private ingenuity to achieve for citizens, the natural environment and for business, win-win outcomes that are not dominated by short-termism or party political games. It is a time when enlightened developers, large and small, have to step up and bridge the divide between the interests of the few and those of the many.

When it comes to civil society playing a more active role in placemaking, in many contexts it is now strong enough to conduct solid campaigning against schemes not deemed appropriate, exerting pressure on developers. Fewer projects of any scale can now get off the ground without public support. Nonetheless, democratic uplift is still hugely lacking in many societies, and autocratic visions are alive and well. This is illustrated by Turkish president Recep Erdoğan's new palace, costing over $615 million and extending over 50 acres of forest land; the

The Three Gorges Dam, Sandouping, Yichang, China, was approved by the country's National People's Congress in 1992 and completed in 2012.

palace has been widely objected to as the land was bequeathed to the nation by modern Turkey's founding father, Mustafa Kemal Atatürk, and was supposed to be protected. Another instance is the Three Gorges Dam in central China, the world's largest hydroelectric project, approved by the National People's Congress in 1992 and completed in 2012, which has been strongly objected to from the beginning by human rights activists, environmentalists and scientists.

Participatory institutions

Despite – and also because of – many impediments, since the late 1990s participatory institutions have spread globally, delegating decision-making authority directly to citizens, in order to help to generate more accountable governments, strengthen social networks, develop new programmes and encourage citizens to get involved, and open up the processes of policymaking to public scrutiny. According to the Participatory Budgeting Project, there are now more than 1,500 participatory budgets around the world, with Brazil leading the way in letting citizens make decisions about city budgets.[4]

In Paris in October 2014, the mayor of Paris, Anne Hidalgo, after just six months in office allocated 5% of the overall city hall investment budget – €426 million – for the next five years to participatory budgeting. For implementation in 2014-15, Parisians were given a week to decide which of the fifteen proposed public space projects they wanted to vote for. Some €20 million was assigned to the nine winners, which included projects for co-working spaces, green walls, 'learning gardens' in primary schools, mobile refuse collection points

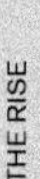

and other socially beneficial schemes reusing disused land around the city's ring road for concerts, exhibitions and film screenings. For those who have been against public spending policies, the advantage of the scheme is that they now have the chance to get involved with backing new initiatives. And while the funding allocation has also been contested in the face of the city's overall budget deficit, Hidalgo has set up a website for citizens wanting to propose their own schemes.[5]

Hybrid forums

It is becoming clear that many new types of forum are opening up in the field of participatory placemaking and in fields of science, technology and politics. One hugely welcome effect is the blurring of the boundary between professional specialists and laypeople. Michel Callon, Pierre Lascoumes and Yannick Barthe, discussing this theme in their book *Acting in an Uncertain World: An Essay on Technical Democracy,* advocate the benefits of public hybrid forums to which 'experts, politicians, technicians, and laypersons who consider themselves involved' contribute. 'It is the entry of new actors on the scene that causes the border [between professional and lay spheres of activity] to be called into question', they state.[6]

Those transcending this 'border' today are myriad in identity. They range from the Dreaming New Mexico initiative by the Bioneers (see page 152), the RE.WORK Future Cities Summit and the Urban Age programme staged by the LSE Cities and the Alfred Herrhausen Society (see 'Voices' – Ute Weiland, page 304); to the European Union-funded Transitioning Towards Urban Resilience and Sustainability (TURAS) initiative and Kenya's iHub (see 'Voices', page 298), as well as the Spanish political party Podemos's scheme dealing with such issues as the need for affordable public housing.

Brad Pitt, founder of Make It Right (2007-), tours the devastated Lower 9th Ward after Hurricane Katrina, August 2005. Make It Right builds sustainable housing that is LEED Platinuum-certified and Cradle to Cradle inspired.

The Open City

Although every city has its own character, cultural history, demographics and challenges, in developed cities the public meeting spaces over which members of the public actually have some measure of control, have been subject to change. With 'business improvement districts' (BIDs) dotted about the place, confusion is rife about what is actually public space, and what is private. The architect Richard Rogers, a strong proponent of building on urban brownfield sites allied to changes in planning in order to respond to the current housing crisis, speaks for many in his field when he says that 'it's better to have semi-public space than no public space at all'.[7]

Hotlinks duplex house, combining two shotgun homes to provide living space residents can customise, New Orleans' Lower 9th Ward. Designed by architect Hitoshi Abe for Make It Right, 2010-11.

The sociologist Richard Sennett is a stalwart for human solidarity and the bottom-up open, egalitarian city.[8] In the final lines of his book *Corrosion of Character: the Consequences of Work in the New Capitalism*, he predicts that any regime 'which provides human beings no deep reasons to care about one another cannot long preserve its legitimacy'.[9] Sennett makes ongoing investigations of detrimental practices perpetrated, above all, in the area of labour conditions, and has identified in his books and talks many different tangents of the consequences of an open society.

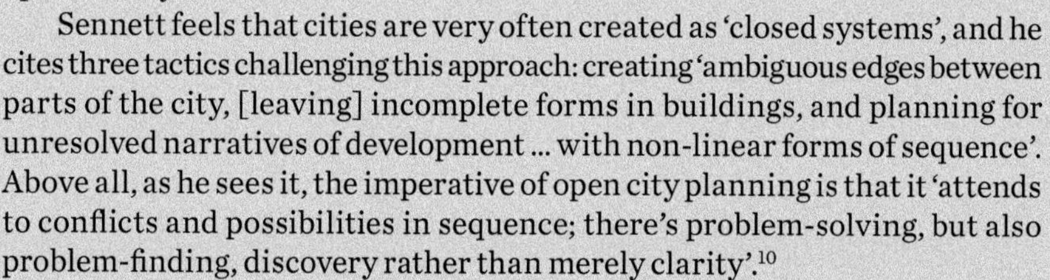

Sennett feels that cities are very often created as 'closed systems', and he cites three tactics challenging this approach: creating 'ambiguous edges between parts of the city, [leaving] incomplete forms in buildings, and planning for unresolved narratives of development ... with non-linear forms of sequence'. Above all, as he sees it, the imperative of open city planning is that it 'attends to conflicts and possibilities in sequence; there's problem-solving, but also problem-finding, discovery rather than merely clarity'.[10]

Discovery through first-hand research, debates of issues arising and design activism as part of urban design and placemaking: this trend is a powerful force challenging 'business as usual' mentalities. It needs to be, not only in light of climate change, but also because of the increasing number of communities that are now uprooted and living in refugee camps.[11] According to the UN Office for Disaster Risk Reduction (UNISDR), in the first 12 years of this century 2.9 billion people, 80% of these in Asia, were directly affected by natural disasters such as tsunamis, flooding, fire, earthquakes, hurricanes and typhoons, many losing their homes. In 2011 alone, 42 million were forced to leave their houses, more than the total of those displaced by war and armed conflict.[12]

Accordingly there has been a proliferation of disaster relief projects in the world. A number of organisations are professionally dedicated to these issues, such as the long-standing Architecture for Humanity (which closed in 2015, but the work of its 'chapters' around the world continues; see page 108), UK charity Article 25, EarthKaya in South Africa, the international Habitat for Humanity, Architects without Frontiers (Australia), Community Architects for Shelter and Environment (Thailand). Initiatives include the American Rebuild by Design competition (launched by the Hurricane Sandy Rebuilding Task Force), and the Rethink Relief workshops.[13] Today's multitude of precarious habitats globally creates an urgent new requirement from placemakers to support social cohesion through the building of long-term resilient infrastructure, by a process of understanding community aspirations at a deep level. What were once considered tragedies with little that could necessarily be done, with the advent of human rights are now scenarios calling for appropriate intervention.

Awareness of this possibility has induced many architects and urban designers to be more actively concerned global citizens. Some practitioners in this field, like Lizzie Babbister, Eric Cesal, Brett Moore and Maggie Stephenson work for NGOs and international aid bodies. Others, such as Anna Heringer, MASS Design Group, Kéré Architecture, Elemental, Urban-Think Tank and TYIN (see Stories, starting on page 107), Hsieh Ying-chun and Patama Roonrakwit, operate as private practices. Architectural students have founded non-profits Operation Resilient Long Island and WORKSHOP (see pages 196 and 282), among others, or been greatly influenced by the pioneering work of figures such as Nathaniel Corum of Architecture for Humanity. Some architectural practices have established their own charitable foundations – Kéré's Bricks for Gando, PITCHAfrica (page 228) and Home for All (page 184), founded by Toyo Ito, Klein Dytham architecture and others, being three examples; and Voluntary Architects' Network (VAN), founded by architect Shigeru Ban and active since the 1990s, creating prototypes for post-disaster housing and community amenities, being a long-standing example.

The growing attempts by practitioners such as these, united by common belief in a consultative process of placemaking, to synergise multidisciplinary placemaking skills in such contexts, in a low-cost, low-impact manner, are based on extensive research into a mix of building skills. The complementary strategies of each are profiled by Esther Charlesworth, founder of Architects without Frontiers, in her book *Humanitarian Architecture*.[14] Architects, designers, engineers, philanthropists, corporations and individual citizens also now share knowledge through online platforms (for example Design4Disaster) to develop better sustainable infrastructure and methodologies to guard against crisis in the future.[15]

With adaptive design thinking applied to transitional situations of all kinds, from emergencies to situations in which local people can build post-disaster self-sufficiency, the tactics are to ensure resilience rather than perpetuate a status quo that is destroyed or inadequate, limiting and degrading. 'Building back better' is a commonly used slogan describing such efforts. It encompasses the building of social capital, including local skills, in the face of precariousness as well as its attendant precarity, to use the French neologism referring to the crisis of the society of work, which dates back to the 1970s and '80s.

Khayelitsha Township, south of Cape Town's city centre, is home to an estimated 400,000 people and the focus of Urban-Think Tank's Empower Shack R&D project (see page 266).

Liveability

Urbanisation continues to accelerate, making the territory of engagement a much expanded one for alternative placemakers. Developing countries are undergoing slum upgrades, and while innovative mixed-use schemes are galvanising city and town districts, liveability is becoming a luxury in many city centres, with surging property values pushing out the vast majority of residents in favour of the top 10%, who may have little vested interest in the well-being of their community context. Placemaking strategies are urgently needed to boost liveability across the board. Certain councils and municipalities have even gone back to building their own affordable housing, after the combined effects of market dominance and the economic crisis minimised the possibilities available, and diminished the role of the public sector to that of a weak standby.

A sensitivity to liveability also entails registering demographic shifts. In Japan, for example, a country with an ageing and shrinking population, settlements have to attract migrants to survive. There, in the creation of places that are desirable environments in which to live and work, the emphasis has shifted

away from the sole historic concern of attracting industry and jobs. The move now is towards the provision of qualities that make contexts highly liveable, with a positive atmosphere and amenities of a high standard.

This imperative has affected local governments' strategies and encouraged everyone – from architects to developers and community organisations – to knuckle down and create liveable places with more of a community spirit. The Japanese concept of *machizukuri* – community placemaking through community building groups and processes – spread during the 1990s, resulting in new parks and community centres, influencing historical preservation, creating new housing types, revitalising declining shopping areas and prompting environmental remediation projects.

'Machizukuri' has also generated greater participatory environmental management, as residents increasingly volunteer; significantly, local government supports this process.[16] The severe impact of the recent environmental disasters in Japan (including catastrophic earthquakes, tsunamis and radioactive pollution) has triggered further commitments to participatory processes by architects aghast at the destruction wreaked on their country's environment, as the work of Home for All (see page 184), Ban and Atelier BowWow exemplifies.

Similarly, in approaching informal settlements and their capacity for self-organisation and upgrading – for example as carried out in South Africa by 1to1 Agency of Engagement and Urban-Think Tank, helping to overcome the scars of social segregation (see pages 192 and 266) – an acute sensitivity to social psychology and cultural diversity is inherently required, as well as innovative techniques such as collaborative building and cross-generational educational activities. However unfortunate the situation may be, there is nonetheless great hope that a transdisciplinary approach can improve the living standards in these fragile settlements.

With adaptive design thinking applied to transitional situations of all kinds, from emergencies to situations in which people can build post-disaster self-sufficiency, the tactics are to ensure resilience rather than to perpetuate a status quo that is limiting, inadequate and degrading

Relatively new types of urban design programme abound: mixed use; landscape urbanism; retrofitting of neighbourhoods and buildings with various legacies. While improvisatory, cheap fixes have been undertaken in communities for centuries, 'tactical urbanism', a term coined by Mike Lydon, co-founder in 2010 of the Street Plans Collaborative, was based on the idea of creating models as alternatives to top-down planning, that could be emulated. Mostly only short-term, the varied work of the Vancouver Public Space Network (see page 274), proves the exception to the rule.

The boundary lines between soft and hard, short-term and long-term planning are perhaps now becoming more blurred. But the social and economic wounds of a location must be directly addressed through related initiatives, or projects remain of superficial value. Sustainable design practices have been proposed since the 1960s but only recently have truly integrated activities been set in motion. However, professional codes of conduct are constrained by long-established legislation, which in some cases is anachronistic and lacking in the capacity to open up new possibilities for a more equitably organised urban design scene.

Alongside the emergence of new, broad and socially inclusive constituencies, the demonstrations in the public spaces of cities around the world since 2010 have brought to civil society a sense of its new ground, opening urgent discussions on what is necessary and incubating new dreams for the future. They also ushered in the use of the word 'we' as 'the 99%' (referring to the concentration of wealth in the USA among the top earning 1%), as the historian and activist Rebecca Solnit underlines.[17] Along with this passion to militate has been increasing use of the phrase 'design for the 99%' or for the '90%'. Many in the fields of architecture and design, especially students and young practitioners, are demonstrating a strong interest in aligning their professional skills with the needs of the majority rather than a privileged minority.

The strength of presence of design for the 90% is borne out by the processes generated by architectural practitioners in this book's Stories (page 107 onwards). Social needs, broadly perceived through a perspective of sustainable social capital, are the brief to which architects respond, breaking with the traditional hierarchy of top-down commissions that are still the basis for the majority of architectural work. It is vital to concentrate further on a placemaking approach that goes beyond the overly simplistic area-ratio approach and cost-effectiveness.

Design standards must be allied with a strong embrace through direct engagement with the complex realities of the context, as exemplified by the Rural Urban Framework projects for various villages around China (page 238) or the city-wide Calama PLUS scheme in Chile by Elemental (page 164). The Stories included in this book offer a number of narratives about the ways in which open-city urban design and planning philosophies and strategies are being put into action on the ground around the world. While they have yet to be anchored widely in institutional protocols, the range of ideas emerging about placemaking are increasingly being tested out through hyper-local processes of various kinds, under the banner of sustainable design, resilience and liveability.

The traditional assumption is that urban change is conceived in a relatively linear fashion involving commissioners, then designers, followed by public consultation,

Syrian boy receiving food in a Turkish refugee camp on the Turkish-Syrian border, June 2014.

before entering legal, financial and formal execution; and this presumption has by no means been thrown out. By contrast, participatory placemaking enriches the options and the ideation stages, creating better briefs for professionals and experts and ensuring a long-term tacit agreement between owners and users. It augments traditional planning and is more cyclical in nature, and participants can join its cycles in different steps or at different moments to help maximise the outcome for communities. This is helped by a transparency in procedures as well as the less opportunistic nature of the endeavours.

Class in progress at Bethel Secondary School, Gourcy, Burkino Faso. The school was built by the UK charity Article 25, which designs, builds and manages buildings for vulnerable communities around the world.

Architects now forge participatory platforms of various kinds – such as the open-source WikiHouse (page 278), the Home for All community centres (page 184), the wide-ranging network of partners created by 1to1 Agency of Engagement (page 192), and Collectif Etc's Détour de France involving the stakeholders of 22 cities (page 136). Each, in its own way, is addressing Zygmunt Bauman's challenge of creating and deploying new tools, appropriate for the era (see Wiki Culture, page 34).

It is fair to say that participatory placemaking is still being shaped as a discipline. It is by no means a magic wand to wave at problem areas of rapidly urbanising places; it does, however, augment the chances that what is happening on so many levels of society with the spread of wiki culture can be more widely implemented. Tools to manifest intentions, devised amidst an array of useful and not-so-useful political instruments and institutions, are today either slowly undergoing reform to survive the test of distributed decision making, or coming apart at the seams.

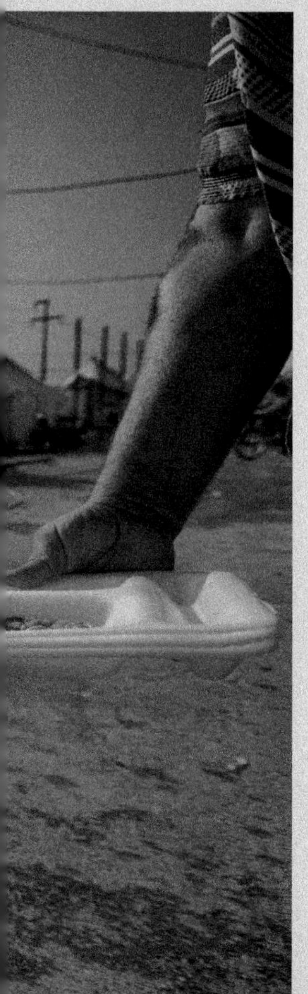

Every new tool and protocol constructed comes with a motive. While participatory placemaking offers legitimate and valid responses to pressing matters through creative and equitable processes, enabling a transition through complex and fast-moving societal change, it needs to be practised with a full critical awareness of the Janus-faced identity of the open city.

Digital tools of placemaking

In the hands of professionals genuinely concerned to facilitate open city concepts, since the mid to late 1990s the contemporary tools for participatory placemaking have increasingly integrated the analogue and digital in an open-source way. Hyper-local – or 'relational urbanism', to use the term coined by engineer Eduardo Rico and architect Enriqueta Llabres – enables the modelling and interplay of any number of complex socio-economic and cultural data through platforms that collaborators and stakeholders can access and influence.[18]

Placemaking tools now include geo-location technologies such as GPS-enabled mobile devices; GIS (geographic information systems), a tool traditionally used by geographers; digital visualisation through augmented reality; and drone cameras (which can now be bought online at little cost). These enable a deep exploration of evolving

Accelerators of change

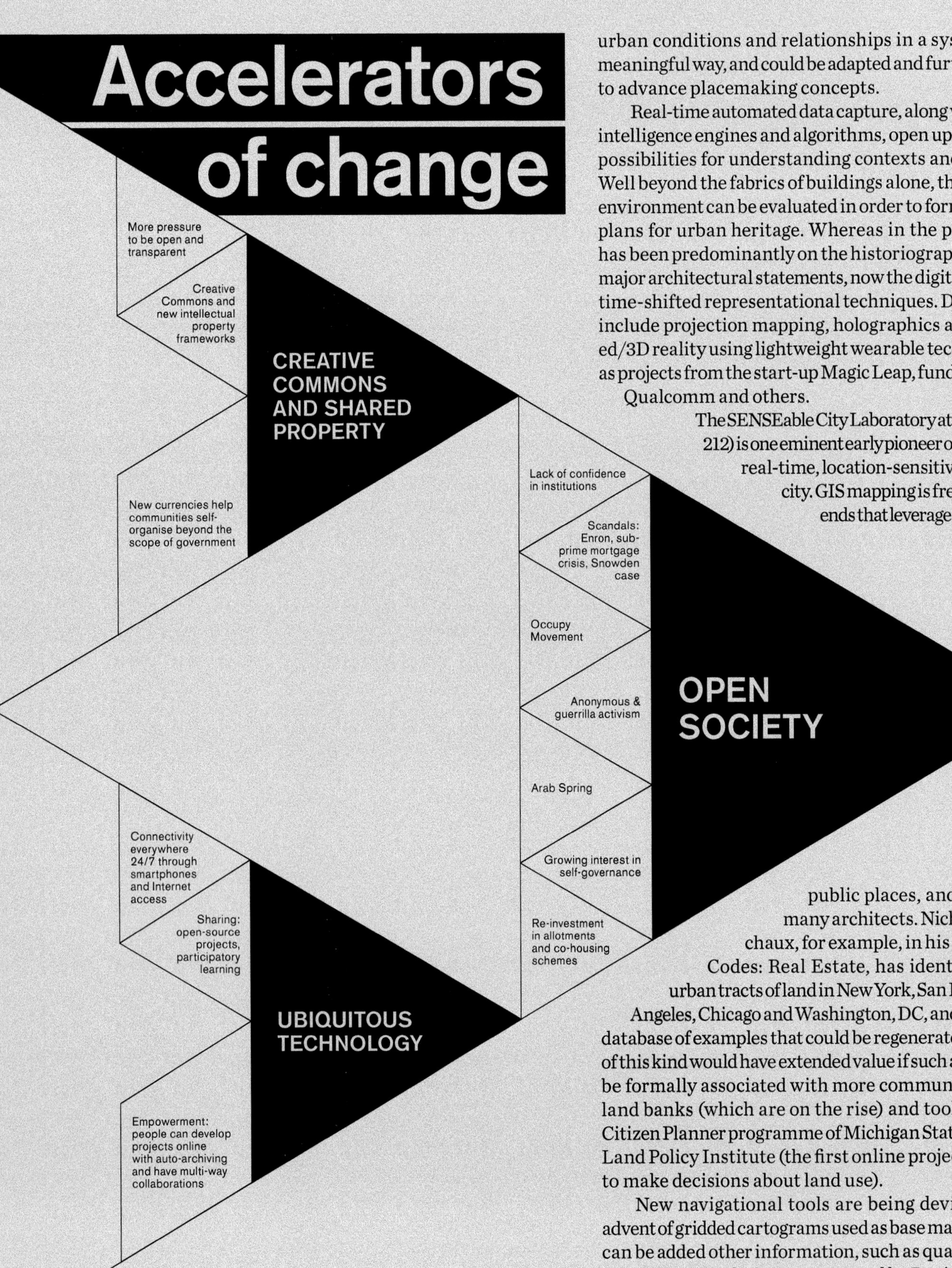

urban conditions and relationships in a systematic and meaningful way, and could be adapted and further deployed to advance placemaking concepts.

Real-time automated data capture, along with artificial intelligence engines and algorithms, open up very exciting possibilities for understanding contexts and their value. Well beyond the fabrics of buildings alone, the entire built environment can be evaluated in order to formulate legacy plans for urban heritage. Whereas in the past the focus has been predominantly on the historiographic quality of major architectural statements, now the digital age enables time-shifted representational techniques. Developments include projection mapping, holographics and augmented/3D reality using lightweight wearable technology such as projects from the start-up Magic Leap, funded by Google, Qualcomm and others.

The SENSEable City Laboratory at MIT (see page 212) is one eminent early pioneer of open-source, real-time, location-sensitive tools for the city. GIS mapping is frequently put to ends that leverage social value in public places, and it is used by many architects. Nicholas de Monchaux, for example, in his project Local Codes: Real Estate, has identified disused urban tracts of land in New York, San Francisco, Los Angeles, Chicago and Washington, DC, and has created a database of examples that could be regenerated. A resource of this kind would have extended value if such a project could be formally associated with more community-equitable land banks (which are on the rise) and tools such as the Citizen Planner programme of Michigan State University's Land Policy Institute (the first online project for citizens to make decisions about land use).

New navigational tools are being devised with the advent of gridded cartograms used as base maps on to which can be added other information, such as quantitative data relating to population, as proposed by Benjamin Hennig, author of *Rediscovering the World: Map Transformations of*

“

Placemakers need to focus on urban design that synthesises collective intentions and drives local development dynamics through the nurturance of meaning, values and liveability

Human and Physical Space.[19] And the trajectory of community mapping resources – such as Worldmappers, introduced in 2006-7 – continues to introduce scope for new layers of information that can be manipulated, through techniques akin to gaming and other shared activities.

As many of the 43 Stories in this book demonstrate, what we term 'wiki culture' is manifesting itself in placemaking through many new technologically mediated platforms prioritising sharing of skills, knowledge and activities. But wiki culture is equally meaningful as one dedicated to sharing its knowledge, skills and then collectively modifying the results. It involves much more than online activities alone. The Center for Urban Pedagogy (CUP; see page 122) is perhaps unique in its focus on pairing of information designers and artists with advocacy organisations so as to decipher and convey complex public-policy issues in the form of accessible graphic materials. Use of print media, as well as online availability, makes CUP's materials, distributed across the low-income, multilingual communities directly affected by these issues, more directly effective.

A community's facility with online and social media can be considered high, and its existing social networks relatively strong. But such assets and the scope for new ideas can still be transformed through the agency of a particular participatory project. As part of Ecosistema Urbano's Dreamhamar process, in Hamar, Norway (see page 160), weekly broadcasts were followed by a digital lab participatory web platform linked to social networks, and online workshops were staged. Snark space making's regeneration project in Auletta, Sicily (see page 248), demonstrates a way of overcoming the common polarity of 'hyper-local vs. hyper-global'.[20]

The holy grail in all these endeavours is a community's authentic sense of ownership engendered through their participation. To achieve this, placemakers need to focus on urban design that synthesises collective intentions and drives local development dynamics through the nurturance of meaning, values and liveability. Urban planners, designers and managers are facing demands from communities and individuals for more inclusivity in planning adaptive strategies, and to avoid the perpetual marginalisation of groups. More authentic and lateral consultation processes are therefore needed, along with qualitative cost-benefit analysis, so that parties are commissioned to incorporate genuine social measures appropriate to the specific context.

Art as actor

Art-driven activities are tremendously important as mediatory practices within participatory placemaking, because art is increasingly being accepted as a way of communicating within society and transforming it. In the context of participatory placemaking, it can also be an engaging, low-barrier means to trigger civic engagement, highlight neglected issues and engender a fresh sense of collective creativity – as demonstrated for example by the work of Gap Filler (see page 174), Partizaning (see page 224) and the artist Candy Chang (see Neighborland, page 220).

Participatory art – focusing on the active participation of the viewer in the conceptual and physical realisation and reception of the artwork – came strongly to the fore in the 20th century. The swapping of the role of the professional artist as sole creator, or author of the artwork, for something shared gives placemaking a source of inspiration about methods of collaborations and building social bonds. Today within the visual arts, music and drama, a range of arts practices are deployed in an interdisciplinary fashion, and the agencies collaborating include local authorities, community development groups and other bodies devoted to social inclusion.

Informed by early 20th-century avant-garde movements – Dada, Constructivism and Surrealism, all of which questioned ideas of originality, authorship and the passive identity of the viewer – relational or participatory art was deeply influenced by the profound social, political and cultural upheavals of the 1960s. Conceptual art, movements like Situationism and such networks as Fluxus critiqued notions of elitism, as well as the commodification of socially disengaged art, promoting in their stead collective engagement and other co-creation activities that did not necessitate the presence of the artist.

Art became time-based, open to chance and interpretation. Allied to the dissolution of disciplinary boundaries, and given impetus by the evolution of new technologies that enhanced and widened methods of communication and distribution, the emerging forms of artistic practice were open and inclusive. In the wider world too, many free-thinking people, not satisfied with the status quo, favoured small-scale agricultural communities based on shared ideals and committed to socialism, local democracy, worker self-management, feminism, psychoanalysis and post-colonial, critical and literary theory.

The dream was an agenda for a liberated and democratised society, but what allied all these permutations of art was nonetheless the relationship between the work of art and its audience. Conceptual artists emphasised a concept rather than a concrete art object, but the activities of Fluxus adherents included performances and events such as workshop-style activities and publications, which drew in the spectator and in which the artist played the role of facilitator. Meaning evolved from everyone's collective involvement, and boundaries between art and life blurred. Yet these ideals were appropriated by the market with its crude logics and sold back to people, and scepticism reigns about a marketplace that supplanted the arena for individual agency in a corrosive way.

Nonetheless, today's participatory arts practices are informed by formidable artistic roots, as a key part of building solidarity and consensus as well as strengthening political positions on controversial developments. Practitioners and curators working in the UK in the 1980s, when the first postgraduate university course in the social history of art was offered by Leeds University's Department of Fine Art, perceived the arts as a potent vehicle or set of mechanisms with which to take up issues of social inclusion. It was a decade when many community arts bodies were set up and projects began, and funding bodies more strongly stressed the importance of the participation of the public in the arts. The arts in turn were used as media arenas in which to discuss social and political issues.

This dimension of participatory culture was further expanded by the concept of 'relational aesthetics' – a term coined by the French author, curator and director of the École Nationale Supérieure des Beaux-Arts art school Nicolas Bourriaud to denote an open-endedness in art practices that enhance human networks and their social contexts, not through visual or textual metaphors but thanks to strengthened social connections. Art projects could take the

An open-endedness in art practices enhances human networks and their social contexts, not through visual or textual metaphors but thanks to strengthened social connections made at different types of events staged

form of meetings, discussion platforms or dinner parties – any event in which art was perceived by those present as information to be exchanged, related to and used further as a creative spur.

The former arts professor Edi Rama, currently prime minister of Albania, as culture minister in the late 1990s transformed the Eastern Bloc dereliction of Tirana, the country's capital, thanks to a colourful upgrade with public green spaces. To citizens who had been depressed by the failures of democracy, this spectacular and affordable facelift to safeguard their city alleviated some of the maelstrom of issues that had burst into public disgrace. It demonstrated a new role for art elevated to an urban scale without questions of ownership and attribution, and helped to build paths to trust in relatively new government institutions.

Yet another proof that cultural and arts figures are being appreciated as new brokers and arbitors involving civil society is the example of the famed musician Gilberto Gil, chosen in 2003 as the Brazilian minister of culture by the incoming president, Luiz Lula da Silva. Gil made significant creative inroads into reformulating procedures and relationships between mass digital culture, the market, technology and intellectual property regulation. Among his initiatives are *'pontas de cultura'*, or cultural hotspots, to promote and protect cultural diversity, and he negotiated tensions between the traditional and the modern.

Mayors, too, have risen to become cultural impresarios and icons. The strategies of Antanas Mockus and Enrique Peñalosa in Bogota, Sergio Fajardo in Medellín (both in Colombia) and Jaime Lerner in Curitiba, Brazil, have been four exceptional Latin American examples demonstrating the impact of the alliance between cultural expression and social mandates, which can be further empowered by participatory actions. There is disputable, but growing evidence that cultural icons can improve the relationship between civil society and organised government, and can broker advances which would not be possible to achieve without an accepted 'translator'.

Participatory art-based practice has become feasible through newer concepts about communities, facilitated by the rise of social media and wide-ranging responses to globalisation, urbanisation and a myriad of emerging questions about place, identity, nature and human agency. It is in this context that has occurred the rise in notions and practices that are ad hoc, DIY, guerrilla, pop-up, crowdsourced, small-scale aggregations, based on sharing and networking – notions and practices that are new but also part of an older tradition. 'Altermodern', Bourriaud's other concept – and the title of the Tate Triennial exhibition he curated in 2009 at Tate Britain, London – referred to alternative modes of interpretation that are facilitated by a migratory cultural framework not confined by political and geographical boundaries, and to alternative modes of art practice in which digital technologies are deployed in a hyper-local way.

Alternative strategies for urban placemaking cannot be both socially driven and beneficial through a distanced approach and minimal public consultation. The newer participatory marshalling processes create test beds for enhancing the practices of planning and placemaking by making public interests, innovative sustainable design and green infrastructure the objectives. Taking responsibility for genuine liveability gives social capital a high priority. The work hinges on citizen activism and an interdependent relationship between the expert placemaker and the amateur user of places, and entails the continual discovery of human beings' adaptive sensibilities and capacities as well as of the potential of places themselves.

Participatory-based art practice has become feasible through newer concepts about communities, facilitated by the rise of social media and wide-ranging questions about place, identity, nature and human agency

Recodin

the art of participatory placemaking

The concept of 'recoding' alluded to in the title of this book, denoting the art of participatory placemaking, is a central one that Thomas Ermacora, in his capacity as the founder of the urban regeneration non-profit outfit Clear Village (see page 128), has developed over many years through a variety of on-the-ground projects and via conversations with peers. The word 'recoding' is a metaphor drawn from the worlds of biological systems and computational intelligence, both of which rely on simple formulae or programmes that replicate and iterate to generate functional systems. The notion of recoding brings together three distinct elements.

First, recoding aims to convert neglected spaces and places into community assets that maximise place capital. 'Meanwhile uses' are one means to achieve this. Canning Town Caravanserai, in east London, is a key example of a 'meanwhile' – or interim – use project in the context of a long-term, developer-led masterplan, won in a competition specifically for projects of this kind (see page 118). Secondly, recoding focuses on a deep understanding of the specific context – the people, the infrastructure and the environment – before any placemaking 'programme', strategy or proposals are developed further. Three excellent examples of this approach are the deep research staged by high-school students as part of the Center for Urban Pedagogy's Urban Investigations (page 122), the CivicEcology framework by SERA Architects (page 242), and the collaborative 'action research' work of La 27e Région with French regional government civil servants over many years, carried out with François Jégou, founder of Strategic Design Scenarios (page 256). With both CivicEcology and La 27e Région, a strong focus is placed on the generative aspect of 'programme' to both enable the community stakeholders to sustain the projects locally, and to create inspirational templates for projects that may be used in other neighbourhoods or regions.

Recoding's third critical focal point is the space between buildings. In his seminal book *Cities for People*, Danish urban designer Jan Gehl, whose work is discussed earlier (see page 26), talks about these spaces being the core of the city.[1] It is largely in the space between buildings that replicable and iterative placemaking solutions can be built, largely because the public realm is where place capital (see 'Futures', page 94) can be developed for the benefit of all users and community members.

'Place capital' is an expression used by Ermacora and his Clear Village non-profit body, as well as others such as Ethan Kent, director of Project for Public Spaces (see page 232), and the Centre for Local Economic Strategies in Manchester, to denote the shared wealth of the built and natural environment. These assets are the foundation of a more holistic approach to sustainable growth, resilience and innovation. They contribute to what makes a particular place successful for those living in it, and also, importantly, to what makes a place attractive to others – which is key in a world that sets store by reputation and in which places are 'branded' as part of the process of enabling them to thrive. Cities are made up of a myriad of different communities anchored in physical space, and their contexts, which, when successful, radiate and attract all forms of capital.

The ethos of recoding is premised on the idea that placemaking is not static: it is a continuous adaptation of a context. It is difficult to create a successful participatory placemaking project if one is simply an external 'clockmaker' or technical engineer. The placemaker needs to be actively involved, accompanying every step of the process, or working in alliance with a body or group rooted in a particular place, one that is able to carry on an intervention, giving priority for resilience and long-term benefits. From the outside this may make recoding seem like a messy or imperfect process, but the skill of a recoder lies precisely in navigating through this surface appearance of messiness and imperfection. Every practice has different art forms attached to its successful execution and purpose; and in part, the art of recoding has some affinity with the Japanese concept of *wabi-sabi* in its embrace of transience and imperfection.

A concept and a method

Recoding is both a concept and a viable method that comes with a defined set of processes. It encourages stakeholders and citizen actors to work together on the basis of four core value principles:

- Dialogue is key; the recoding cycle starts with listening to all the stakeholders involved in a local context, as part of 'action research', in order to better understand that context at a deep level.
- Trust must be built on a variety of levels to ensure that effective ideas can be put forward, collectively developed, agreed upon and implemented.
- Recoding is not a one-off process, but an ongoing cycle that moves from ideation, to engagement, to co-design, and then back to ideation in a manner based on the new situation and the challenges and opportunities it brings.
- Good solutions and designs need to be evaluated on their self-replicating or generative component.

Recoding is a significantly more responsive and sensitive approach to the built environment than traditional placemaking. It replaces the narrow focus on building procurement alone by fully valuing the rich array of relationships, as well as the potential for new social networks, in the places concerned. If the importance of these actual and potential relationships and ideas about the guardianship of places in the future, are underestimated or neglected, the results tend to be not urban spaces for people, but isolated buildings lacking

> **Recoding aims to convert neglected spaces and places into community assets that maximise place capital**

meaning, or grands projets that are rather less grand in their social, cultural, ecological and economic impact. Recoding avoids this risk by putting relationships at the heart of the process. Moreover, thanks to the intimate relationship it builds with history, context and local people, recoding can evolve with fewer resources and less effort than traditional placemaking.

The methodology of recoding as an open framework, discussed in this book, is neither a linear nor a universal one. It is defined by its ethos and cyclical nature, involving a collection of processes and strategies that make up a multiplicity of activities and entry points. It is a well-judged mix of predetermined and spontaneous activities. In order to maximise the outcomes for all stakeholders, people join the cycle at different points or moments, encouraged by the transparency and positive ethos of the recoding process. Involvement in one part of the recoding cycle is not a prerequisite for taking part in others.

Recoding is powerful for a number of reasons, not least because it offers a strategic tool to increase 'soft power' – a term coined in the late 1980s by Joseph Nye, the political scientist and former dean of the John F Kennedy School of Government at Harvard University.[2]

6. HAND-OVER

5. CO-CONSTRUCT

PHASES OF RECODING

Placemakers enter at different stages and are often involved with every step of recoding. Identification is about proactively finding a problem that can be solved; Enquiry is associated with action research of the place; Development is more concerned with building a project; Co-design focuses on the actual ideation and designing of preferred scenarios; Co-construction is about implementation; Hand-over is about helping local communities manage and take ownership.

POSITIVE: **BUILDING MOMENTUM**

Each recoding cycle, however complete, if conducted with the same inclusive approach, generates more place capital and anchors local identity (as shown with thick arrows).

NEGATIVE: **GOING OFF COURSE**

Breaking the participatory spirit potentially disrupts a complex set of intangible values that are key to lasting urban quality. It is wasteful as it takes a lot of energy to (re)create the conditions for constructive collaboration.

Recoding cycle

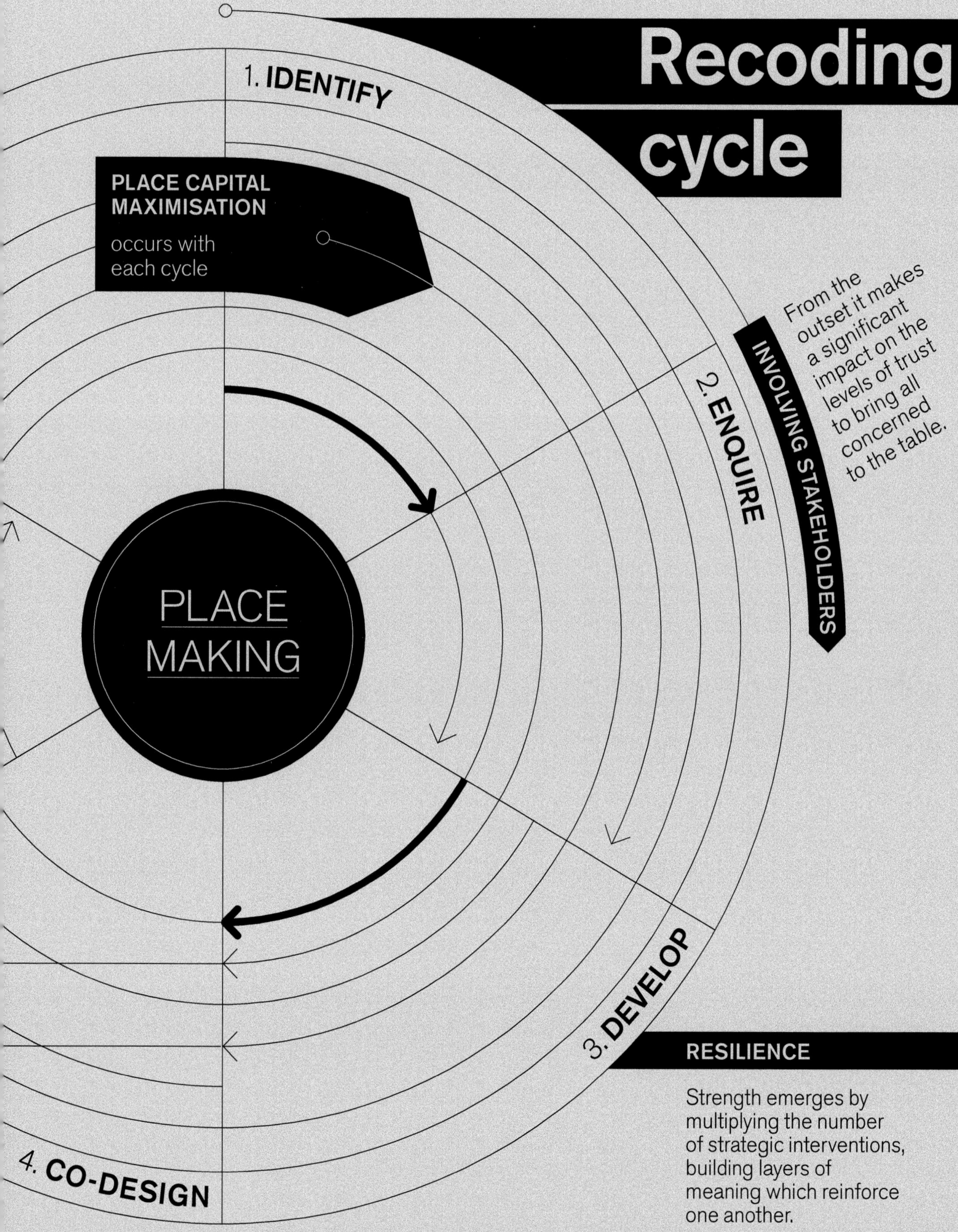

1. IDENTIFY

PLACE CAPITAL MAXIMISATION

occurs with each cycle

2. ENQUIRE

INVOLVING STAKEHOLDERS

From the outset it makes a significant impact on the levels of trust to bring all concerned to the table.

PLACE MAKING

3. DEVELOP

RESILIENCE

Strength emerges by multiplying the number of strategic interventions, building layers of meaning which reinforce one another.

4. CO-DESIGN

Even if professionals are proven right in their assumptions, the beauty of involving crowd intelligence is that the contextual wisdom and emotional empathy will build a more long-term, consensual dimension into any solution

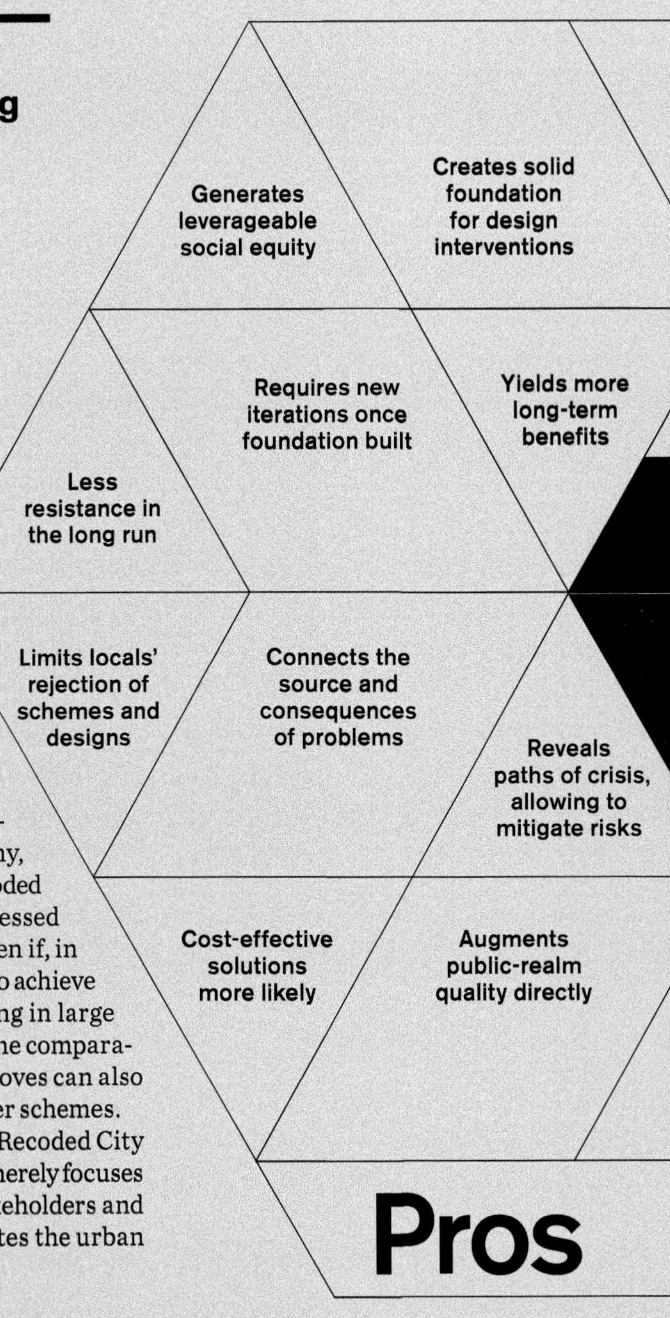

'Soft power' describes the ability to attract and co-opt people, rather than coercing them, using force or giving money, in order to achieve a result at the urban scale. Nye's concept points to the intangibles in creating wealth, health and political authority. Cities in the 21st century are engaged in ever greater competition for intellectual and creative capital, and those that thrive do so partly thanks to their attractiveness in terms of well-being and other soft power factors.

Rather than calling up the old slogan 'less is more', the notion of recoding embraces a philosophy of reform one could call 'small is smart'. Efficient placemaking codes have a powerfully viral nature, which contributes further to building a healthy, self-sufficient and connected city: the post-analogue city or the Recoded City. The urgency with which urban questions need to be addressed calls for a reframing of the notion of socio-political reform. Even if, in the light of environmental and social challenges, societies need to achieve many improvements extremely rapidly, the notion of reforming in large increments needs to be re-assessed taking into consideration the comparative advantages of multiple small steps. Smaller incremental moves can also involve the actors on the ground more profoundly than do larger schemes.

Finally, it is important to recognise that the concept of the Recoded City does not exclude the notion of exurban interventions. This book merely focuses on the fact that placemaking contexts exist when multiple stakeholders and functions are concentrated in one place, which naturally denotes the urban context more than it does the rural.

Pros and cons: key considerations of recoding

Recoding comes with massive benefits in many cases, particularly in the medium and long term. But it also comes with a set of risks that need to be mitigated and analysed. The following points are derived from our research into how to maximise success, based on evaluating over one hundred examples and the work of practitioners from Palestine to Hong Kong, via the back streets of second-tier cities in the UK, all the way to the favelas of São Paulo.

Our goal is to highlight instances of excellence in the field – the art of participatory practice – in order that readers can consider how best to implement and adopt processes that fit the particular context in which they are working; we also need to point out some of the hazards to bear in mind. The following points discuss: involving the professional and the non-professional;

strategies for developing relevance and credibility; using time wisely; funding and funding solutions; evaluating the process; and building a legacy and sustaining the results.

1. Involving the professional and the non-professional

A significant issue with participatory placemaking lies in determining the degree of involvement of professionals and non-professionals. The Canadian journalist and author Malcolm Gladwell came up with a 10,000-hour rule for how much practice time people need to develop an expertise need before it becomes truly phenomenal: an 'outlier', as he put it.[3] An expert is not at this level, but has a profound comparative and analytical understanding of problems. Nevertheless, both types can confuse this relative authority on a matter with knowing what is best for others.

Even if professionals are proven right in their assumptions, the beauty of involving crowd intelligence is that the contextual wisdom and emotional empathy will build a more long-term, consensual dimension into any solution. Certainly there are exceptional instances when a so-called 'grand architect' performs an act of placemaking that transcends the context. Mediocrity in results, stemming from striving to find a common denominator – especially when there are major disagreements and different interests between parties and stakeholders – inevitably pushes the bar lower. This is not a matter of diminishing the notion of expertise, but of foregrounding the value of proceeding from a brief based on everyone's input through crowd intelligence, and of giving greater emphasis to this as a means to increase the number and impact of lasting and successful acts of placemaking.

While there is no direct correlation between the collective intelligence of human groups and that of colony organisms, it is worth referencing the visionary mycologist and biomimicry expert Paul Stamets, who highlights slime mould intelligence as an example of the power and logic of complex problem-solving, a faculty usually attributed only to mammals, of so-called unintelligent life forms around us.

Stamets told the story in his 2011 Bioneers lecture[4] of a team of biologists in Japan in 2009 led by Atsushi Tero, of Hokkaido University, that on a piece of wet bark created a map with nodes representing the centres of activity of Tokyo.[5] They let a slime mould species resembling funghi populate the map, placing oak flakes in further-away in positions denoting surrounding urban centres. It turned out after 26 hours that the moulds had self-organised, 'optimised mathematically', and created an efficient network from a process in which they progressively selected a myriad of pathways and communication networks. Quite possibly, Stamets surmised, they solved their problem more effectively than subway system designers struggling to find the quickest destinations between separate routes in a transportation system.

This wonderful and amusing scientific discovery injects a dose of humility to the notion of *Homo erectus*'s engineering genius and computational superiority. This underlines the importance of also involving non-professionals in the recoding process, an approach that does not lead to the mediocrity anticipated by cultural elitists who believe that this is the inevitable result of letting too many people take part in solving problems of a certain magnitude and complexity.

2. Strategies for developing relevance and credibility

The goal of a placemaker is to bring value to a community of interest. In order to achieve this in ways that circumvent the traditional top-down commission-based placemaking models, a series of tried and tested techniques can build the necessary trust and understanding before any interventions are carried out. This is a complicated process and should in most cases be costed as part of the project budget. As in the field of remedial psychology, or any other type of therapy with intangible benefits in the beginning and during the entire process, there is an added cost due to the sheer amount of time required. Obviously in many instances participatory placemaking can be started by a local resident or activist, who has the advantage of being from the place itself. However, practice shows that this is not always the best solution, as it can be perceived as confrontational and self-interested by other locals.

Conventional placemaking tends to tackle this part of the process through consultation. This is essentially a single organised event (or, depending on the scale and sensitivity of a project, a series of events) at which questions can be asked by locals and answered by commissioners and placemakers such as architects and urbanists. Unfortunately, there is a tendency to commission consultation that will be carried out only after most of the critical decisions have already been made, which can lead to locals viewing the process as limited and disingenuous, and to a legacy of distrust ensuing.

Moreover, in many cases a disproportionate amount of blame is shouldered by placemakers because they effectively operate within a framework that favours the landlord versus the tenant. The point is not to criticise the landlord, but to advocate the value of developing an honest and mutually empowering relationship with locals and users of the place in question, so that an ongoing dialogue can augment the relevance of interventions. One could compare this shift to outsourcing product testing and open-sourcing parts of code in software development. It is standard practice nowadays for major firms in the software industry to create focus groups from the product concept stage and to maintain a relationship with the groups all the way through to product release. This process, which is often referred to as 'beta

Clear Village's Barcelona Launch Lab, November 2009.

testing', is something that is rarely done in the field of placemaking, which is ironic considering that the longest-lasting 'products' we create are the places in which we live. The consequences of failure can last for generations and cannot be replaced or upgraded easily.

All sorts of resources are at stake, including time, natural resources, financial resources, and less well recognised factors such as emotional resources. The cost of failed placemaking is so high that we are only slowly beginning to be capable of evaluating it. The hospitality industry is very astute at understanding the need to establish good client relations; yet cities and decision-makers, despite their sensitivity to appearances, rarely appreciate the tremendous boost that can be yielded from the soft power that comes with satisfaction with placemaking.

Looking into concrete methodologies that have proven effective and that need to be modulated and customised to the act of placemaking, three main categories or types of activity are recommended:

- action research, which combines research in the studio and on the ground;
- a design residency carried out by the placemaker(s), which should take place prior to collaborative workshops;
- collaborative workshops with exercises that are engineered to take into account different stakeholder perspectives and to ensure that the underdogs' interests are represented, too.

The value of the participatory design process is directly correlated to the spread of inputs. If only the loudest voice speaks (which is an inevitable risk), the outcomes are either skewed or even wholly unrepresentative of group interests. On the other hand, if the process is successfully carried out, it has the potential not only to address the topics at hand, but also to create collateral benefits in terms of building capacity and strengthening local relationships, which can spawn other initiatives or develop an effective feedback loop to the project. The advantages of setting up a robust ethos of group dynamics can be widespread, enormously valuable and potentially long term. Participatory placemaking may not only provide great design solutions to places in need, but also 'code' a number of positive externalities into an area.

In creating a setting for participation, if the relevance of the project is not made clear there can be resistance from participants to engaging more than once or for a certain period of time. A series of strategies can help to soften this defensiveness:

- On the one hand, the rhythm and typology of involvement need to accommodate immediate responses and intuitive reactions that are profoundly connected to people's concerns. On the other, they need to open up the conversation and allow for more fluid and imagination-driven aspirations and questions that support the group's baseline set of values.

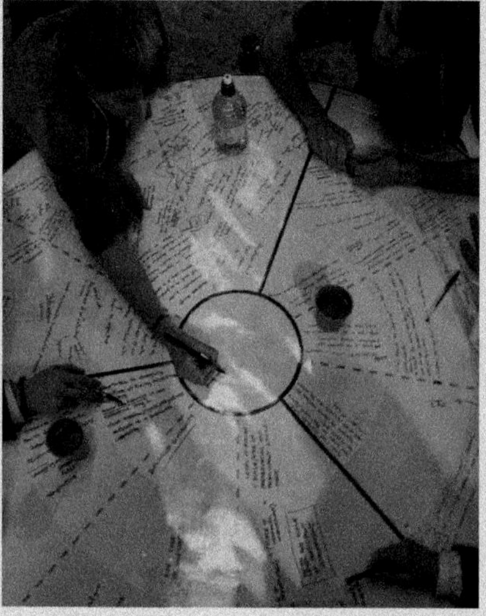

Clear Village's Barcelona Launch Lab, November 2009.

Beta testing is rarely done in the field of placemaking, which is ironic considering that the longest-lasting 'products' we create are the places in which we live. The consequences of failure can last for generations

'What Residents Want' consultation at the Marlborough Square Project, outside Small Works in Hackney, east London, September 2013.

- The exercises people are exposed to should play on the variety of intelligences of the group. On top of more intellectual shared experiences, there could for example be opportunities for participants to engage physically through outdoor activities, or for stimulating emotional intelligence through meals and other social gatherings.
- Given that participant interest is key, people should be free to choose preferred activities within the parameters set. Process orthodoxy is less effective than having an adaptive framework. In other words, the core competency of a 'recoder' is to be a good facilitator for the specific group assembled at any given time. This is analogous to the quality of a teacher or mentor, who ideally responds to the particular psychologies of the group members, rather than treating them generically. This is a radical paradigm shift similar to the ways in which societies have developed from a focus on acquiring knowledge, to learning how to learn and use knowledge in the more progressive educational systems emerging today.

3. Using time wisely

There is a perception that participatory activities slow down the development process. The participatory process is a

> With democratic systems and the complexity of resolving questions around the use of place, it is only natural that the process should be relatively slow

time-consuming one, entailing diagnosis, proposals, consultation, adaptation, further proposals, voting in some cases, and so on. Furthermore, there is the challenge of managing expectations as projects develop slowly, often more slowly than was planned. With democratic systems and the complexity of resolving questions around the use of place, it is only natural that the process should be relatively slow. This is indeed an argument against participatory placemaking, though it should be challenged over the entire span of a project, as solid foundations will allow the process to gain speed over time and require fewer iterations.

In many instances slow is better, especially if there is an incrementally evolving understanding of place and a learning curve in the process. A project may start slowly, and then begin to accelerate. In the process, a substantial amount of shared value will have been created in terms of relations between stakeholders, social capital in the community, and capacity building in terms of competences.

4. Funding and funding solutions

While contemporary commercial architecture relies on the patronage of the market and, to a lesser extent currently than used to be the case, on the direct support of local government, the economic model of participatory placemaking is driven largely by a high degree of self-sufficiency. Few, if any, local governments formally allocate funds to this field. Innovative participatory placemaking projects have often had to create their own funding mechanisms, through crowdfunding and other means, to transcend the customary 'silo' structures around which municipalities centre the funding of their community design efforts. In addition, the strong social ethos of the field has meant that groups have needed to explore different sources and processes of funding that are consistent with their values.

The result of these factors is that 'recoders' often find it extremely challenging to secure funding for their projects. Until there is more official acknowledgement of the value of participatory placemaking and economic support is increased accordingly, there is a risk that participatory placemaking will remain marginalised as a cultural activity. It is to be hoped that governments will eventually see the need to scale up this field, especially when budgetary restrictions call for alternative solutions. It could also be argued that such legislation as the British Conservative Party's Localism Act of 2011 (see 'The Rise of Bottom-up Placemaking', page 18) should have included a greater emphasis on different means of funding new or existing participatory placemaking projects.

Until there is a change in the official position, 'recoders' will continue to struggle with the funding challenge. This is made particularly acute by the fact that participatory placemaking, by its very nature, cannot guarantee a predetermined final result. Predetermined results, however, are precisely what institutions providing grants, whether private or public, expect from organisations seeking financial support. Addressing this catch-22 situation can require considerable ingenuity.

An interesting case of achieving financial support by adding functions into a locality for both community and city is the East River Blueway Plan, New York, by WXY Studio (see page 286). The plan developed a clear solution to the problem of the need for flood protection after 2012's Hurricane Sandy, and built in a participatory placemaking project on top, with the base funding being associated with the first issue being solved. In other words, funding strictly for the placemaking aspect would not have been possible without the

Recoding Spectrum: Mapping practices & Strategies

There are different types of recoding strategies. Each has its own level of design focus (left side of graph), level of participation (right side of graph), scale of operation (size of circle) and scope for impact and replicability (size of the outer circles). The groups shown at the top right of this graph (featured in the Stories section from page 107) apply the most design focus while involving more actors in the creation of place capital – which needs to be both a cost-efficient and a long-term process.

VISUAL KEY

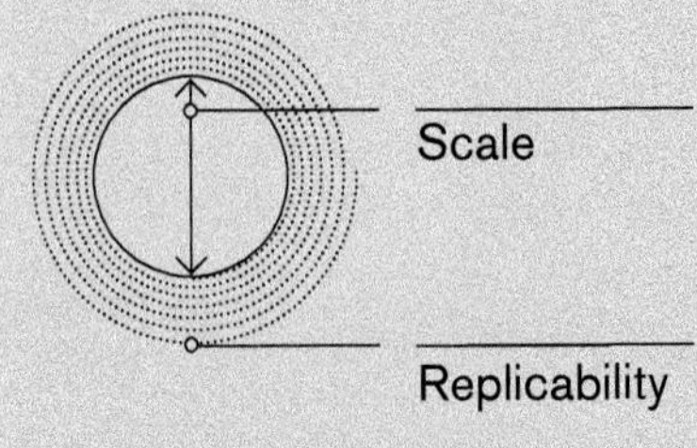

HIGH

Operation Resilient Long Island

Friends of the High Line

Cost-efficiency + long-term place capital thinking=

DESIGN DRIVEN

LOW

ENGAGEMENT

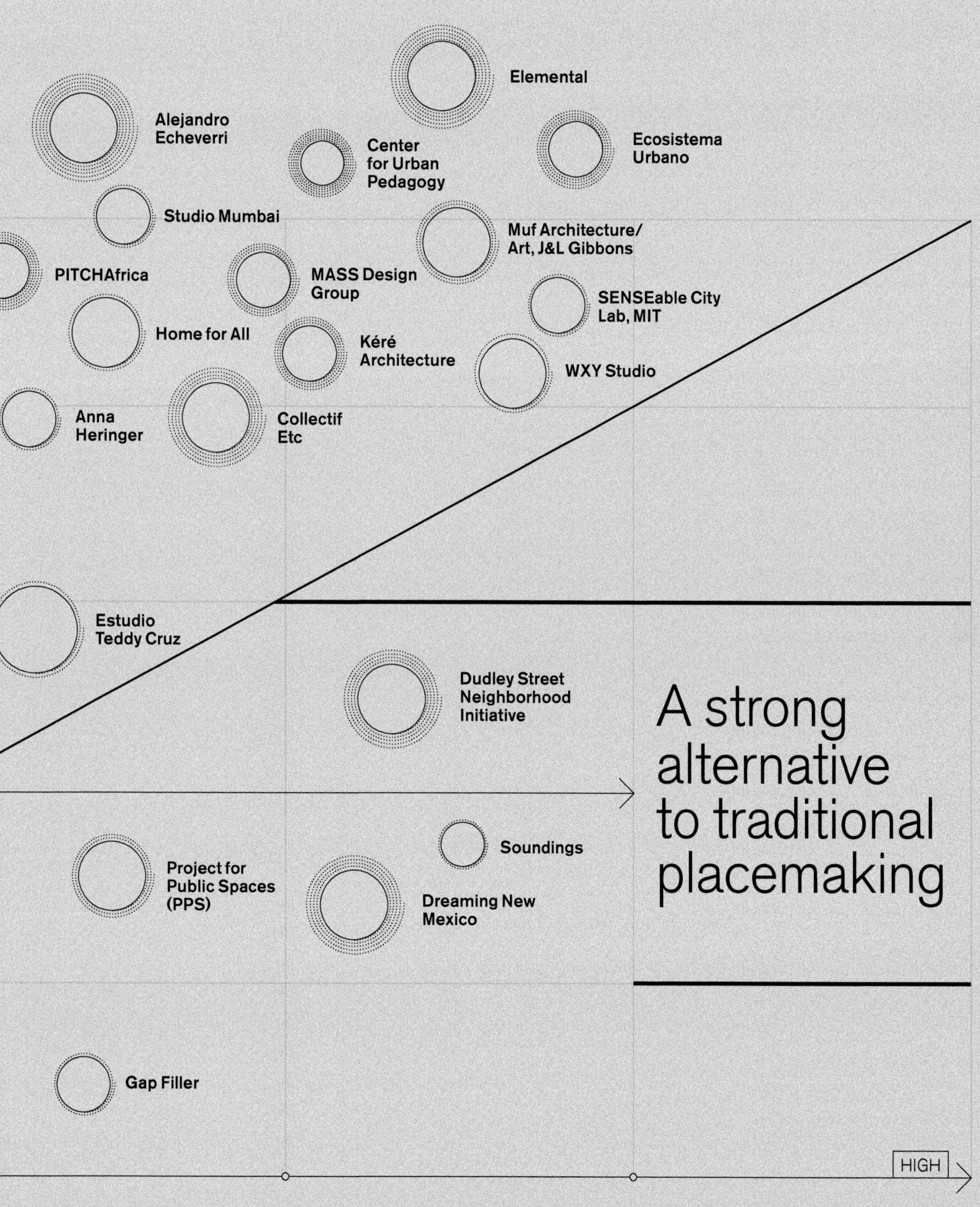

A strong alternative to traditional placemaking

element of creating a storm surge barrier on the East River of Manhattan, as well as aligning with the local policy against privatisation of space along that attractive stretch for developers.

Another obstacle is that in order to attract funding it is often necessary to cater for a specific community or interest group. Participatory placemaking, with its relatively holistic perspective that aims to bring value to more than one party and to balance the interests of different stakeholders, is limited by the orthodoxy of fundraising. In view of the hurdles, it is not surprising that many placemakers lose their motivation. Carrying out a participatory placemaking project, in the current funding landscape, requires an exceptional degree of determination and commitment. Yet there are some very clear things that can be done to increase the chances of fundraising success.

Firstly, it is essential to brand the project and position it at the right level to gain public support and political backing, which can be used as valuable supporting arguments when reaching out to funding bodies. It is also important never to stop searching for funding. Marketing and public relations are vital strategic activities and should be carried out well to ensure that a simple compelling version of the bigger (and inevitably more confusing) picture is communicated. And finally, one needs to be aware of the 'stacking' options for funding. Combining traditional approaches such as grant applications with more exploratory routes such as crowdfunding can make for an effective overall strategy.

5. Evaluating the process

When it comes to evaluation, participatory placemaking can be viewed as a 'soft' science that is trying to get 'harder' every day. Evaluation of the benefits of participatory placemaking needs to be conducted on a number of integrated fronts. Does it lead to better design results? Is it something that can conceivably touch a large part of the 90% not currently affected by professional design? Does it lead to greater well-being and health? Does it lead to more resilient neighbourhoods and cities? Even an imperfect participatory placemaking project can be considered a step forward, in terms of developing incremental awareness and learning about how places can be changed. For this reason one should perhaps take a philosophical approach to failure and success. For example, although the Brixton Market project developed by the non-profit Space Makers in London (see '6. Building a Legacy and Sustaining the Results', below) could be perceived as an unfortunate accelerator of local gentrification,

Does participatory placemaking lead to better design results? Is it something that can conceivably touch a large part of the 90% not currently affected by professional design? Does it lead to greater well-being and health? Does it lead to more resilient neighbourhoods and cities?

it remains an outstanding example of how to activate a community. Rather than criticising the project, therefore, one should acknowledge its failed mitigation of gentrification while applauding its success in activating the community.

As a new field of urban intervention, participatory placemaking often lacks the benefit of a track record to support funding applications. It is becoming critical to develop solid Key Performance Indicators (KPIs) and monitoring and evaluation techniques that reflect measurable impact. This way, backers or endorsers will feel that they can put their name to projects. Even if it is worth bearing in mind that not all the outcomes of participatory placemaking projects can be predefined or rationalised, there should be an effort to predefine and rationalise at least a few to the greatest degree possible, and to integrate hard performance indicators into the project design.

This is where we can perhaps differentiate between amateur and professional 'recoders' in the future. Amateur 'recoders' may want to adhere to the romantic ideals that exist in the field: namely that serendipity and spontaneity of interaction will generate results that may not be measurable or quantifiable. Professional 'recoders', on the other hand, will establish benchmarkable criteria for social innovation and an implicit certification of their activities.

Amateur 'recoders' merely adhere to romantic ideals. Professional 'recoders', on the other hand, establish benchmarkable criterial for social innovation and an implicit certification of their activities

6. Building a legacy and sustaining the results

All placemaking projects can be debated in two lights. One is of financial viability and economic solidity of a project, which in itself justifies actions by decision-makers managing cities at large. The other is how users benefit from the place and manifest their enjoyment of it. Obviously the latter is also a question of time, for observation and analysis, as evaluating the legacy of an implemented urban masterplan requires more than five to ten years for it to make sense. Last but not least, if in order to create a place the natural systems are destroyed, however green the city itself may be, it is an abstraction that can perhaps not be counted as a favourable legacy.

All participatory projects potentially have an ambivalent legacy if one considers the question of gentrification. Many of the projects chosen to exemplify the state of participatory placemaking in this book are in the peripheries of cities or in areas in regeneration or recovery, and if they are not they may be in developing areas or disaster relief contexts. As such, there are more cases of 'recoding' associated with places in need of stimulation than with places considered to be 'working fine' from the standpoint of high net worth individuals choosing to live in them. Instead of judging how fair a view this is, it is critical to understand the inherently ambivalent result one might obtain from a participatory placemaking project that is considered successful when most view it as an accelerator of gentrification.

The main problem is not gentrification, but the nature of the gentrification. Making places gradually more attractive will always have the perverse effect of pushing socially marginalised groups further to the peripheries of cities. If people take part and understand the changes they can help to engineer, it is hoped that a great number of individuals will be able to participate in and benefit from the gentrification itself. In other words, gradual and inclusive gentrification is a relatively positive legacy whereby no extreme capitalisation of the benefits of a recoding intervention will polarise a community.

Valuable insights into these issues emerged from one of the 'recode conversations' Ermacora has conducted over the course of many years of his participatory placemaking work, with Dougald Hine about the Brixton Market project in Lon-

Shoppers at Brixton Village, south London, 2013.

don by Space Makers, the non-profit regeneration agency Hine founded in 2009. The conversations covered ways in which the underlying narratives of place could be recrafted, and analysed the legacies of projects with which both Ermacora's Clear Village and Space Makers were involved. The Brixton Market case was unusual in that it had attracted coverage from the national press and New York Times, and after the project was completed in 2010 it was perceived by many as a poster child for accelerated gentrification. This image was far from the original intention, and an important operator of high street markets took over the Market, quickly evicting the artists and activists that had taken part in its makeover and rendered it so attractive. For anyone trying to build a positive legacy from a participatory placemaking project, a number of the arguments arising from this conversation are of value:

A key way to turn a project into a sustainable achievement is to successfully play the role of a catalyst.

Dougald Hine (DH): 'At Space Makers we have always said our role is to be catalysts. We have succeeded [when] we can go back on the road heading off to the next thing we do and leave behind something which is sustained by the people we've been working with, because we weren't making magic happen through some extraordinary injection of resources or whatever. All we were doing was having fun with people whilst drawing their attention to possibilities that were already there within the situation.'

Being a catalyst means empowering local people to be the experts of change in their neighbourhoods.

DH: 'A lot of it is giving people the confidence to do what they're already capable of. Perhaps that's another route into how we can play with the word "expert" and the idea that even though expertise can be a bit problematic, it's a way of exercising power and authority because you're an expert, rather than because you know what to do next. But if you go into a situation and you name the people who are conventionally described as the people with least power in the situation as the experts, there's a playfulness, a subversiveness of taking that marker of privilege and authority and saying: "we're not the experts here, you guys are the experts."'

The catalyst needs humility to help enable a community to achieve lasting results.

DH: 'It's really important to me that when I come into a place I'm not coming in with great expertise or authority. I'm there to have fun and hopefully it'll be fun for the people we're working with. We might notice some things and learn some things from each other along the way, but it's absolutely not about coming in with any kind of bounty or magic. We have to quickly hand that role over to whoever we're working with, because it's only going to work when it's them who are really providing the energy. That's part of being a catalyst. You don't bring the energy to the equation; what you bring is something that makes it possible for the energy that was already present in the situation to come out.'

A 'recoder' is like a journeyman who travels from place to place, helping people to solve problems. In the process, he or she adds to his or her own stock of knowledge by learning from others.

DH: 'Did you ever read Walter Benjamin's essay "The Storyteller"?[6] He talks about the two kinds of storyteller: the person who stays in a place and holds the stories of the place and is responsible for them, and the person who travels from place to place and brings the stories and the news from the other side of the hills. Benjamin also talks about the guilds and craft workshops of the Middle Ages as this social form that had room for both of these things. On the one hand you had a master who was holding that place and was responsible for the workshop and that particular craft and trade in that particular place. And you also had the journeymen who were travelling from place to place, adding to their skills by spending time learning from different masters. I don't know enough about the history of this to know how far that is romantic, but even just as an idea what it offers is a kind of paradigm.'

It is important to be ready to pass the project on to local people sooner rather than later.

DH: 'My happiest moment in a project is the point where local people who've got involved in it push us out of the way and say: "you guys are going to make a mess of this, this is where we live, we're going to be here when you're gone, we're going to take over this bit of it."'

A great deal can be achieved, even on a shoestring budget, by activating local enthusiasm and capacity.

DH: 'My hunch is that in most scenarios I could imagine, it will become more, rather than less, useful to be able to bring people together on a shoestring budget by working with the desires, and the passions, and the enthusiasm, and the skills that are already present within a place, rather than being as dependent as maybe we're used to being on bringing in resources and professional skills from outside. And equally, being able to bring underused spaces to life and arrest a spiral of decline feels like something that it's worth being able to do in a world where we can't take for granted some of the things we used to.'

Focus on what is good and meaningful to the people who are there.

DH: 'The thing I know is good is that when people come together to do something they care about and they do it on a shoestring, amazing stuff happens, compared to what happens when either the public or private sector throws huge amounts of money at things. Because it's real. We know this – we know that so many of the things that matter most in life cannot be bought. And I think that what both of us believe in is doing projects that mobilise the stuff that money can't buy. And that's not to do with being cool, because cool has a hell of a lot to do with money.'

The 'recoder' is always faced with the challenge of gentrification.

DH: 'The kind of placemaking work that we both care about is vulnerable to people saying: "this is all you're doing, you're coming in, you're gentrifying an area, you're attracting new visitors to it, you're bringing more money into it." And the cost of that is that the people who were there already feel marginalised or the businesses that have been there a long time are driven out. Gentrification is the bogeyman that's haunted me with what we've been doing with Space Makers. If someone says to me: "you came into Brixton and you gentrified it", I can see the elements within what we did when we took on those 20 shops in the market, and brought them back to life, and it suddenly generated all this momentum. I can see the elements in that which are why they're unhappy about it, because it feels that what you're doing is coming into an area and making it the new cool place to live. But cool is scarce. Everywhere can't be the new cool place to live, but everywhere could have a community-owned and -run street market.'

The way to mitigate the risk of gentrification is to always focus on what is good and meaningful.

DH: 'One of the people who taught me most in life is Charlie Davies, the last features editor at *The Face* magazine [before it closed in 2004]. And one of the things that he taught me was: don't be satisfied with creating something cool and counter-cultural. Make stuff that everyone likes; make stuff that's real; make stuff your mum likes; make stuff that the people you see standing at the bus stop, who you'd never normally meet, like. And to me that's much more important. I don't get a kick out of making something cool. The thing that excites me is creating stuff that's just good.

'There are lots of different forms that [good stuff] might take, but there is a certain kind of intrinsically good stuff that is not about being able to show off. It's just about the fact that it makes it a nicer place to live and it's part of the social fabric, and a lot of what I'm trying to do is to show that there are talents, ideas, energies, resources and possibilities just about anywhere you can go. With a little bit of help with mobilising, and with the pressures of the systemic level of stuff off their back, people can make good stuff happen in a way that isn't inherently scarce. So, to me, [it's important to make] that distinction between gentrification as the process of making something extrinsically desirable, and the kind that gets good things happening in a place which is intrinsically desirable and then sharing what you've done, de-professionalising it, making it clear that there are some commonsense rules that people can take and adapt to do their version of the thing you've been doing.'

Find the positivity in the legacy of the project.

DH: '[The food critic] Jay Rayner wrote a piece for *The Observer* newspaper about Brixton Village in which he said that every week he received press releases from people who are opening new restaurants where they've spent up to a million pounds. They've got a concept; they've got a PR agency working for them. That's his life, that's what being a restaurant critic in London, with the amount of stupid money that there is flowing through the city, brings with it.

'And then he stumbles across Brixton Village on his own doorstep and he says: these restaurants don't have concepts. They've been fitted out for about the cost of a trip to Ikea. But they're full of people who care about what they're doing, and some of [the restaurants] are really outstanding in terms of the food, and it feels like a good place to be. What I loved about that was, that was a year after we had left. We'd handed over Brixton Village back to the owners and said: we've done the stuff we're good at, we don't want to build ourselves into the fabric of the place. Rayner didn't know the story of what we'd done, but what he's describing there is the thing that matters about what we'd done.

'In Brixton, what I see now that makes me feel happiest about the legacy of Brixton Village is not so much walking through the place itself. It's the way in which the street traders on the outdoor market there have taken the initiative and have got these new community markets several times a month; the way that projects like Makerhood [the showcase for local makers in Lambeth] have got off the ground – there's a website that's encouraging people to buy and sell locally made stuff and to meet each other through it.[7]

'There's a DIY culture, which was already part of the genetic code of Brixton anyway, that was part of why Brixton Village worked in the way that it did. It wasn't primarily about bringing in outsiders; it was to some extent about bringing out of the woodwork people who lived in Brixton, but didn't necessarily spend their money or their time on their own doorstep so much. But these threads of continuity that you see: some of that to be honest is having been fairly open about the fact that we were making it up as we went along, that we were not experts or specialists. That seems to have had a legacy of other people looking at what we do and thinking: well, if they can do it, we can.'

The bigger picture

The perceived role of Gross National Product within society was questioned by Robert F. Kennedy, in an address at the University of Kansas, Lawrence, Kansas, in March 1968.[8] A US Senator at the time, he had run for the presidency, and tragically was assassinated less than three months after this stirring address, using words that clearly conveyed his strength of feeling: 'The Gross National Product does not allow for the health of our children, the quality of their education, or the joy of their play... It measures neither our wit nor our courage, neither our wisdom nor our learning, neither our compassion nor our devotion to our country; it measures everything, in short, except that which makes life worthwhile.'

Since this voiced challenge to the way progress and well-being were measured, Gross National Happiness initiatives have been spreading. The term 'gross national product' was coined in 1972 by Bhutan's fourth Dragon King, Jigme Singye Wangchuck, and the concept was the pillar of his young constitutional monarchy of Buddhist Bhutan. This is nothing new however, as the Chinese philosopher Confucius, over two and half millennia ago, was quoted as saying 'Good government obtains when those who are near are made happy, and those who are far off are attracted.'[9] Attempting to understand dynamics of well-being and effectively measuring them and correlating them to the success of societies, as the New Economics Foundation in London has done, is proof that a profound reassessment is taking place of how to value things that matter more than pure economics. That re-evaluation is also shifting the perspectives of the 1% all the way into the World Economic Forum, which gathers 1,000 of the top global leaders every year in Davos, Switzerland.

Recoding is in some respects a form of design and local development alchemy. Because of its intrinsic focus on well-being and participation, it constitutes a worthy approach to help anchor in place these progressive ideals.

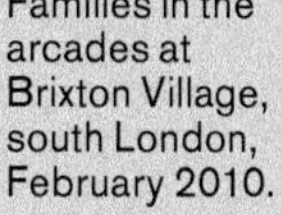

Families in the arcades at Brixton Village, south London, February 2010.

Open Society,

inequality and the post-individualist spirit

Crumbling institutions and global turmoil

While the concept of an open society is evidenced today by disparate, atomised, individual activities almost everywhere across national boundaries and on the web, its impact is being limited. This is evidenced, by the swift retaliation of national defence interests against Julian Assange's Wikileaks monitoring their reach and judging what is worthy of being open to civic participation and what closed. When it comes to certain sovereignty and national defence matters that have so far functioned on the basis of secrecy, effectively opening up fully is uncomfortable for those guarding them.

The brilliant US hacktivist Aaron Swartz, who died in 2013, campaigned for a free and open internet in the face of censorship bills, and Demand Progress, the group he co-founded, promotes online campaigns on social justice issues. As cyberwarfare and hacking are increasingly in the news spotlight, there is a more encouraging aspect to free and open data, which governments and private institutions share and sometimes operate on an open-source basis. Indeed open data is making for a blurred boundary between professional specialists and lay people. As a field it has potential to be given support as a whole, across national boundaries.

Wikileaks, the non-profit online journalism organisation initiated in 2006, underlined the fact that public lies are a bad business model. It generated incrementally a new ideal of a truthful social contract between the established authorities and the administered citizens – to the point where more radical, neo-Marxist/anarchist sections of society, such as the hacktivist network Anonymous, concluded that governance is not best conducted by government.

From the beginning of the 21st century we have witnessed a string of catastrophic, sometimes epic, collapses in public management. The Enron case, 'redlining'[1] and pension scandals, the 2008 financial crisis, toxic assets, illegal credit financing and the Edward Snowden affair – to mention but a few cases – remain in the collective memory due to their continuing effects. They are perhaps the final blows to the belief that we can trust government officials and their ambition or capacity to rein in serial virulent threats such as fundamentalist terrorism and financial cybercrime.

There was a time when it would have been unthinkable that government stability could be threatened through social media. But while official media downplay or exclude coverage of many issues, social media has proved to be a connecting thread in many contexts, conveying and underlining the realities of situations and issues brought to the fore. Today individuals like Snowden have the temerity and self-appointed legitimacy to hack central governments, exposing truths and voicing preferences in a viral manner – something earlier radical activists such as Marshall McLuhan and Noam Chomsky would have been thrilled to see in their generation.

It is a laudable and ethical outcome when the negative effects of an open society in which power is used to control citizens, are counteracted through increasing distribution of authority and improving accountability and transparency. However, along with the advantages come challenges, as is being experienced by NGOs such as Transparency International, the global civil-society charity fighting corruption worldwide. But there are also examples of philanthropists and activists who are risking their reputations and finances to support a wise transition towards more open forms of governance. The business magnate and investor George Soros may for some people be marked by a dubious past, but through his Open Society Foundations is a generous sponsor of more vibrant and tolerant democracies.

The late US hacktivist and founder/ director of Demand Progress Aaron Swartz (1986-2013), who campaigned for a free and open internet.

At the other end of the spectrum, there exist irrational and extremist attitudes and an information totalitarianism that aim to crush any shred of freedom of thought and expression: for example, fundamentalist groups such as the Taliban and ISIS, organised crime syndicates, human trafficking networks, and their complicit circles of influence. In their hatred of openness, these entities represent frightening provocations to well-intentioned and progressive societal values.

The advent of social media has been a huge pivotal point in opening doors that were previously shut. Social media connects people in ways that allow them to understand what is happening on the ground in real time, and how to use public space collectively in mutually empowering ways. A turning point was the global insurgence, facilitated by the new digital media

People are being proactive in response to the fact that not since the end of World War II have human rights been more severely under attack

culture, against public lies in two waves of Arab Spring protests in North Africa in 2010.

The impact of the revolutions of the Arab Spring against economic inequality, corporate greed and financial injustice was one of the triggers in the coalescing of the Occupy movement. The Occupy protests heightened people's awareness of the power of their unofficial membership of the 99% and of their common cause on tense issues of inequality regarding housing, jobs and the economy.[2] Occupy's amorphous group of adherents around the globe discovered that combining voices and physical energies created an authority. The recent protests – which include Hong Kong's 'umbrella revolution' of Occupy Central with Love and Peace, echoing the 1989 Tiananmen Square occupation in Beijing – have been symbolically defining moments for democracy in the 21st century.

Increasing sections of society seem capable of militating against what they perceive as arbitrary political motivations and decisions. There is a renewed determination to fight against disenfranchisement and inequality. For some, the battle is against abuses of power; people are joining forces to wage 'class warfare' in the face of decreasing wages, rising unemployment and government-enforced austerity policies. All are staking a claim for democratic ideals.

A post-individualist spirit is on the rise, spurred by the realisation that people can have a collective influence on the established powers and their policies. People are being proactive in response to the fact that, as the UN Secretary General, Ban Ki-Moon, has said, not since the end of World War II have human rights been more severely under attack.[3] Certain issues are no longer being kept hidden under the

Hong Kong's Occupy Central with Love and Peace of October 2014, campaigning for genuine universal suffrage.

carpet, and social media are playing a key part in this new transparency and awareness of the drawbacks of neo-liberalism's meritocracy. Social media support the emergence of new ways of considering alternative activities to build resilience, across every field of public life.

While Occupy may have to date led only to certain minor concessionary financial reforms within a depressing economic climate, it hugely changed the conversation about income inequality, as historian and activist Rebecca Solnit discussed two years after New York's Occupy Wall Street in 2011 (the first such protest to receive widespread attention).[4] Occupy's General Assembly model, which proliferated globally at Occupy encampments in the months following the New York protests, emphasised 'egalitarian participation and consensus decision-making'. It strongly influenced many individuals taking part, and precipitated new alliances in different cities on such matters as housing rights – a development that has strong implications for placemaking as a civic practice.

In Turkey, for example, the popularity of the protests started by environmentalists at Istanbul's Gezi Park in 2013, where the architectural group Herkes için Mimarlik staged workshops (see page 178), were direct contestations of the government's plans to build over the park as part of an urban development plan. There were strong feelings about yet another retrogressive instance of public planning in a city already scarred by developers who had ignored its natural topography.

Street protestor in a stylised Guy Fawkes mask worn by Anonymous supporters and an Uncle Sam hat, Occupy Wall Street, 26 October 2011, New York City.

The protests in Istanbul had been preceded by many others in the fields of environmental and human rights, and they ignited a spread of protests in other Turkish cities – including in parks in Izmir and Ankara – and in other countries. The broad range of participants from many sections of society has been widely acknowledged in print and on television. Such was the potency of social media as part of the protests that the Turkish government claimed that non-national conspiratorial forces were behind the demonstrations. It was far more credible that locals simply cared about the public amenity of their own civic spaces, and decided to take action.

Inequality, its discontents and new paradigms

Growing urbanisation and the power of social media have made inequality increasingly transparent. In the face of this, mobilisation on the streets is backed by massive conviction. Referring to the Turkish situation, Daron Acemoglu, professor of economics at MIT, writes that 'if the ballot box doesn't offer the right choices, democracy advances by direct action'.[5] Acemoglu acknowledges that there is no established correlation between countries' levels of economic growth and their democratic tendencies.

As notable exceptions he cites South Korea and Taiwan, where a close connection between growth and democracy has come about through 'a combative political process – and a far more violent set of confrontations between the military and protesters, trade unionists and students'. The events taking place here need to be seen in the light of the new political paradigms arising from industrialisation and urbanisation locally. With their new participatory democracies, each country has severed itself from historic identities and 'nomenklatura', or extended dynasties. Global affairs and the lack of dominant ideologies have triggered the formation of many strong, sceptically minded

A member of the Turkish architectural group Herkes için Mimarlik (see page 178) at one of the Gezi Park festivals the group organised at Taksim Square, Istanbul, in April 2012.

youth movements. This has particularly been the case since the early 1990s with the end of the Cold War, which had created two ideological camps that mostly fought for a similar self-determination.

For more than 40 years we had the 'good' and the 'evil', the liberal society versus the communist ones. The lack of contrast between the leading ideologies today is notable. Gone is the perception of a bipolar world, with liberal capitalism clearly triumphant over more repressive communist societies. Yet predictions of 'the end of history' have proven to be a false dawn. In the context of a lack of the old oppositional and aspirational models, what are the dreams of youth now? Where people place their energy today is no longer in old ideologies, nor in an abstract fight for freedom, but in a quest for the power to influence their own well-being through democracy.

There are strong implications for the future of placemaking in the fact that an ideological vacuum has fomented fierce fights revolving around universal suffrage, human rights, local identity, housing issues and architectural heritage, notions of sovereignty, environmental and endangered species protection, and sustainability. Alliances across issues are being forged at a wider level, too. In New York, for example, the People's Climate March of 2014, the largest climate change demonstration to date with over 300,000 participants, had been coordinated by more than 1,000 environmental justice, faith and labour groups.

With the free market conquering most of the globe, its failure to distribute wealth and capacity is distressing and radicalising a significant percentage of the developing world's youth. This is nuanced by the fact that in certain instances, privatisation and connection to free markets are unleashing the creativity of whole developing nations or cities. When countries have access to important telecommunication nodes, they can have exceptional results, as in the case of Ghana and Mauritius, two examples of the occasionally remarkable effects of liberal policies in expressing a mature and educated youth's choices.

Today the technologically augmented ability to search for information is accompanied by an unbridled thirst for openness. Information can be hacked, or engaged with in a myriad of different ways. The sheer range of specialist domains encompassed in the probing of questions fully opens up a 'socio-technical controversy', which 'unfolds in time and space', as described by Michel Callon, Pierre Lascoumes and Yannick Barthe in *Acting in an Uncertain World.* Such a scenario, with exploratory philosophy 'in the wild', taking 'time to explore conceivable options before deciding', enables democracies to absorb scientific and technological debates and controversies. This process of bringing about 'technical democracy' involving 'new actors' is especially relevant in an era when citizens are most likely to mistrust official information sources.[6]

In the UK, the social alienation brought by Thatcherist revision of the role of the state has seen the rise of non-governmental organisations focusing on various forms of structural inequality through qualitative research and ethnography, such as the non-profit Young Foundation (originally the Institute for Community Studies founded by social innovator and visionary Michael Young in 1954). Such a broad-based strategy is justified when no single discipline is adequate in understanding and dealing with the causes of fragmentation and breakdown of trust.

Also in the UK, the Kids' Company charity, founded by psychotherapist Camila Batmanghelidjh in six London railway arches to provide support to vulnerable children, at the time of writing operates in three cities. That this first-rate organisation is under threat of closure as government may not in 2015 renew its support alongside that from celebrity philanthropists, shows the fragility of new, emerging systems of meta-welfare and of local organising capacity through social enterprise. All the more reason to continue to forge local placemaking, local powers and hyper-local tools.

New, emerging systems of meta-welfare and the local organising capacity of social enterprise are fragile and need local placemaking capacities and tools

Tent for a children's workshop organised by Herkes için Mimarlik in Gezi Park, Istanbul, in June 2013. Hundreds of people stayed in the Park at night so as to avoid police intervention.

Future

There is an acute need to reinvent urban design and placemaking practices in the 21st century. To successfully do so would radically improve human development and well-being, and assist economic growth and political stability. It would reduce the inequality of entire nations, help to provide wider education and health care, significantly lower the world's ecological footprint and heighten our multiple civilisations' commitment to more sustainable living.

The next generation of innovative decision-makers will need to find ways to counter the acquiescence of Brad Pitt's heroic character Wardaddy in the World War II war movie Fury, when he says 'ideals are peaceful but history is violent'. A lot is at stake. As the Stories in this book (from page 107) demonstrate, the responsibility is not to be taken lightly. The rising generation can, through their small and steady steps, increase the impact of their distributed micro-strategies, but also try to find the means to scale these up. Such endeavours should be far more commonly an integral part of top-down placemaking, not as a sop to communities as is too often the case with public consultation processes, but to genuinely spread the benefits of plans and frameworks through the use of more experimental urbanist strategies that help to build local assets.

By such means incremental innovation will be spurred, embracing a new approach to and a practical philosophy

Architect and co-founder of Elemental Alejandro Aravena meets residents of Calama, Chile, to discuss the masterplan proposed by Elemental and Tironi, 2012- (page 164).

of urbanism: a practice that encompasses 'ad-hocism' and DIY, one in which everyone has a say and a stake, that relies less on accreditation, status, or intellectualism for the sake of it, and far more on direct involvement. Taking such an active stance towards placemaking calls for a thorough evaluation of the pros and cons of different participatory strategies, and of the tools and methods available to be shared.

It is essential to understand that there are consequences to letting inefficiencies cripple the pressing development imperatives for more balanced cities, and that we must take a pragmatic stance towards the range of opportunities at all scales that technology and an open society afford. Short-termism, partisan policymaking and insensitive mega-planning need to be seen for the inadequate sticking-plaster solutions they are. In order to forcefully drive further attention and resources towards the support of social and natural capital, it needs to be noted how divisive land use strategies can be, leading to the drastic neglect of the importance of the public realm.

In this book we investigate localist tactics that boost dormant or damaged community cycles which, by empowering networks and by activating material and intangible resources and assets, support social capital. To make cities more resilient and to future-proof neighbourhoods, new ways are needed for city dwellers and professionals alike to become more engaged in the challenges, tasks and responsibilities of placemaking. With time and patience, these will establish common ground between all stakeholders in different places.

Placemaking management roles have traditionally been exercised by local authorities and other administrative agencies and their contracted architects and urbanists. The reinvention of not just architecture, urban design and planning but also local government in response to what one might see as an age of austerity in the aftermath of the global financial crisis, is also a fascinating story of emerging innovation, more informal in methods than ever before. Those local governments which work with pioneering groups in communities, making the most of fewer resources, helping to facilitate active involvement by their constituents, promoting social inclusion, well-being and future-proofing, deserve a book in their own right. These priorities are at the heart of the Bloomberg Philanthropies' Mayors Challenge, for example, and the ongoing work with local government, through such initiatives as La 27e Région (see page 256), is propelling new knowledge whose significance we continue to explore.[1]

The crisis of place, in which the land of the public realm is sold as a commodity in the interests of untrammeled 'growth', is not a new phenomenon, but as urbanisation increases pace, the pressures to adopt new methods become stronger. Concepts for the adaptation of the commons as a sustainable human habitat are also not new kids on the block, as this book explains, but have been tested out with varying degrees of success over decades. However the compromising, polarising changes emerging through the narrow goals of growth mean that adaptive planning is required more than ever before.

Today the urban population accounts for 54% of the total global population.[2] Cities account for some 70% of the global GDP – a wealth concentrated in a voracious minority of city-dwellers. It is estimated that between 2010 and 2013, 200,000 people per day became new urban

One of the biggest challenges ahead is to bridge the polarising divide between the mega-wealthy and the extremely poor in both horizontally and vertically sprawling megacities

residents – 91% of them in developing countries.[3] Many of these new arrivals end up in informal conditions on degraded or marginal land, ill-served by infrastructure and in areas of flood zones, or with vertiginous hills or swamps. In 2013 the UN World Economic and Social Survey estimated that the 1 billion people living in slums would soon increase to 3 billion if rapid urbanisation was not addressed.[4] One of the biggest challenges ahead is to bridge the polarising divide between the mega-wealthy and the extremely poor in both horizontally and vertically sprawling megacities.

In the face of these challenges, clear-headed, resilient, socially equitable and collaborative placemaking contributes impetus. The work of courageous practitioners and activists deserves to be prioritised, put under the spotlight, legislated and campaigned for more heavily. The volatility in global economics and the focus on the shortest-term return on investment, geopolitical instability and the prevalence of insulated tax havens for the wealthy have meant that participatory placemaking is adopting two main profiles, each of which must be incubated further.

First, those working in participatory placemaking have sought to influence local conditions, practices, networks and platforms in order to help local people feel empowered in taking an active, creative role in the transformation of their living environments, despite residual scepticism and the prevalence of older legislative and behavioural barriers to change. That means speaking out, and having the confidence to do so, knowing that there is a kinship and an open society that will be responsive.

Secondly, as with any innovation, the task is also to consider tactics for scaling up such hands-on practices so that participatory placemaking becomes a more widely accepted and adopted part of urban design and planning – both of which have traditionally been characterised by top-down modes of operation.

After extensive consultation in 2012, the residents of Calama, Chile, were given the opportunity to vote for the plan proposed by Elemental and Tironi (see page 164).

Evidence that this is possible is underlined by the reality that, in other fields, millions of people can be positively impacted by the incremental effects of thoughtful micro-scale projects.

One example is the VerBien (See Better to Learn Better) scheme by the designers fuseproject: the free eyeglasses programme, operated in partnership with the Mexican government and Augen Optics, offers a collection of customisable and iconic corrective eyewear that is specifically designed for children and teenagers. The power of that potential calls for greater attention to new methods, narratives, tools and ways of reorganising relationships between the public and private sectors. It is the challenges of funding participatory placemaking that present the greatest obstacle to its expansion as a practice. Backing calls for great understanding and support by decision-makers.

We consider participatory placemaking to be an emerging science, in that it is based on theories. Not fly-by-night ideas or hunches, not fanciful marketing strategies, but socially driven theories that have been tested out – and in a number of cases formally adopted in pilot schemes – in challenging conditions, and that demonstrate community innovation and cohesiveness.

Pilot schemes are likely to be shifting towards an 'Internet of Things' model (see Wiki Culture, page 34), using open data, gamification or voting to encourage engagement by members of the community; they may also hopefully bring 'prototyping' into the new lexicon of local government in a way that has lasting effects, drawing on local resources. They may have a more loose-fit character to them, but they are focused on building place capital (see page 105), irrespective of the institutional, financial and psychological barriers to change perceivable in a particular location. This holistic quality, including the sense of ownership by those involved, results from the iterative effects of a limited number of problem-solving strategies for placemaking that have been defined and applied to a wide range of circumstances – and can be again in the future.

The 43 Stories at the heart of this book, along with further examples more briefly referred to throughout, represent some of the evidence we built up during the course of our research. This evidence has helped us to organise knowledge about participatory placemaking in its various forms, as it has been applied in different contexts over the past few years. These narratives about activities in the UK and Europe, the USA, South America, Africa, India and elsewhere in the Far East, across both formal and informal contexts, as extensive and varied as they seem, are together just the first chapter in the unfolding story of participatory placemaking in the 21st century.

As more information is gathered, any of the practices and theories outlined in this book is open to improvement or modification. This process, if critically

66

Participatory placemaking is based on socially driven theories that have been tested out in projects demonstrating community innovation and cohesiveness

Cover of Camilo Calderon's PhD thesis *Politicising Participation: Towards a New Theoretical Approach to Participation in the Planning and Design of Public Spaces* (2013).

documented as it needs to be, will continue to strengthen the foundation for furthering the scientific knowledge about participatory placemaking and for putting the information gathered to practical use, that will help to bring about further positive change.

The systematic study of the structure and behaviour of participatory placemaking through observation and experiment is still at an early stage, and rigour needs to accompany passionate enquiry at every step of the way. The architect and urban and regional planner Camilo Calderon, in his PhD thesis, *Politicising Participation*, for example, valuably examined the gap between the theory and the practice of participation in placemaking.[5]

Calderon's research findings showed that 'although participatory processes can have highly beneficial results', this is dependent on the 'social, political and economic processes and dynamics of the context' in question. The challenges arise in the yawning gulf between the status quo – a locality's resources and the means of access to them, regulations and other procedures in place, and specific cultural identities of civil organisations – and citizens and groups wishing to engage in participatory placemaking. These make creative decision-making a particularly uphill task.

The 'wiki culture' at the heart of good placemaking, with its ethos of shared responsibility and collective envisioning and implementation (see page 34), does not mean that quality management is no longer necessary or can be taken for granted. On the contrary, this role falls to a moderator, whether self-appointed or commissioned, to ensure that high-quality participatory strategies and results are upheld in a transparent fashion. This person can of course be contested and challenged while also being helped and supported by the process.

One sterling quality of participatory placemaking that is of incalculable depth, giving many dimensions to its value, is its great embrace of the non-professional. No longer subject to the traditional polarity between experts and those without their formal specialist training, placemaking's collaborators – professionals working alongside community members, who may include people with specialist knowledge and skills of many different kinds across the arts, sciences and management – enjoy a symbiotic relationship. This new equilibrium of knowledge transfer is further enabled through new technologies, platforms and networks.

The 'local person' is therefore certainly not reducible to a single type or an abstract group, as urban planning's agendas of the past were based on, but exists as part of a multitude of different individuals. Each has his or her own specialisms, priorities and needs. Community groups also encompass a myriad of ages, backgrounds and circumstances. These diverse individuals must also not be confused with 'the amateur'. When members of communities take part in conversations, and in the planning and making of a place, a project becomes a process of sharing of existing wisdom of a place that enables knowledge to be culled from very many diverse sources.

Such a practice may well have been enacted more widely by pre-industrial societies, and contemporary forces exist that unfairly negate or push aside the potential of such elements of place capital. Today, when there is scope to do so, and the imperatives are growing, such a rich, narrative-based approach makes great sense because there are many values and goals at stake. Participatory placemaking enables a multi-modal geography of meaning through a cross-pollination, one that fertilises the processes, rather than limiting the creation of places to standardised procedures.

To centre on the concerns and needs of the 90%, who are increasingly located in cities and peri-urban areas, but also, in the case of endangered minorities, increasingly displaced from their native lands (as Paul Virilio critically chronicles in his book with Raymond Depardon, *Native Land*), means that the tasks of participatory placemaking have to be about finding, preserving and deploying the appropriate resources in all their diversity.[6] Very many of these resources already exist locally, even if they are in a latent or disregarded form. That is especially the case when most of the more traditional urban design models do not prioritise serving the world in such a way.

In Dewsbury, Yorkshire, the participatory arts group Encounters took over a disused shop for its 2010 Ambition and Aspiration project for developing the town centre (for Kirklees Borough Council). The project attracted 4,000 people who brought memories of the past and ideas for the future of Dewsbury.

Some agencies are working along the right lines in evolving localised, neighbourhood planning tools for capacity building, favouring open-sourcing, peer-to-peer, DIY, transparency and ease of relational modelling. They may place focus on traditional building techniques, a field upheld by the creativity of many architects featured in the Stories section of this book, including Anna Heringer (page 180), Kéré Architecture (page 188), Studio Mumbai (page 260), MASS Design Group (page 208), TYIN (page 262) and WORKSHOP (page 282). Not many agencies do both. One that does is the Sustasis Foundation, founded in 2007 by Michael Mehaffy, author and sustainable urban development practitioner, and which has as board member Ward Cunningham, who programmed the software for the first wiki, WikiWikiWeb (in 1994) and was a pioneer in software design patterns. The foundation has recently devised Federated Wiki, new open-source scenario-modelling tools.

Sustasis hosts the American chapter of the International Network for Traditional Building, Architecture and Urbanism (INTBAU), a UK charity dedicated to the study, protection and regeneration of resilient local neighbourhoods and buildings around the world. INTBAU's 18 international chapters unite some

4,000 members, active as practitioners around the world. They work in such contexts as Haiti, for the rebuilding of areas devastated by the 2010 earthquake, Cuba, Romania and other developing countries, where they advocate for locally abundant materials to be used rather than reinforced concrete, for example. As Mehaffy's co-author on *Design for a Living Planet*, the mathematician, design theorist and consultant Nikos Salingaros says, 'traditions are incorrectly dismissed as something "old-fashioned" and unnecessary, but in fact they are sophisticated forms of collective intelligence. They give us important solutions for today's critical problems, like finding more ecological and sustainable ways of settlement.' [7]

Moreover, there is considerable interest in the future commitments and legacies of design practitioners who have been veterans of disaster relief, having battled a proliferation of crises around the world in recent years. Their swelling numbers include student groups such as Operation Resilient Long Island (page 196), a group of NYIT architects in the Institute's innovation programme led by Frank Mruk, associate dean at the School of Architecture and Design. They take fast, preventative action to mitigate the effects of disaster, but also to adapt environments, through the building of resilience in inhabited areas everywhere with various degrees of precariousness.

To create credible and feasible liveable cities, personal memories and cultural histories and visions are needed as part of placemaking, so that those taking part in processes feel that they belong

Patrick Mwaura, headmaster of Uaso Nyiro Primary/ Waterbank School, Laikipia, Kenya, demonstrates PITCHAfrica's Rainchute rain harvesters made from decommissioned military parachutes (2012).

Both the scale of these activities and the need for them have led to a shift in preferred terminology, away from the woolly, tired word 'sustainable', which is used as a smokescreen for all manner of aspirational commercial development, and towards the terms 'resilient city' and 'resilient landscape'. To achieve resiliency through urban design and planning calls for what David Orr, professor of environmental studies and politics at Oberlin College, Ohio, describes as 'whole systems thinking' and 'full-spectrum sustainability', encompassing social and economic activities including food production and jobs creation as well as the active, incremental application and germination of environmental wisdom.[8]

Furthermore, in order to create credible and feasible liveable cities, what is needed is an approach to placemaking that engages personal memories, cultural histories and visions in such a way that those taking part feel they belong. If participatory placemaking is to be effective, it must foster a politics of belonging, and from this support of local democracy, a foundation of spaces of belonging can grow. Such a stance matches the newer approach to placemaking that leads away from normative, context-less, standardised procedures and methods. As Calderon advocates, it allows for 'discussions of difference, conflicts and power at [placemaking's] very centre', and for 'context-based theorisation' and 'the transferability of knowledge and experiences among different contexts'. Among the work that exemplifies this approach is that of 1to1 Agency of Engagement (page 192), PITCHAfrica (page 228) and Kéré Architecture (page 188) and the bringing about of the Proyecto Urbano Integral for Medellín, Colombia (see Alejandro Echeverri, page 142).

This vision of placemaking complements the pattern language approach promoted by the architect Christopher Alexander and his colleagues in the 1970s as part of multiscalar urban design and planning; in a nutshell, they argued that all elements of the man-made landscape were fundamentally orders of relationships. The apparent separation of elements was – and is – an illusion. The failure to perceive that web of relationships was part of the problem behind developments leading to a denuded public realm. Pattern language, with patterns based on psychological needs, can be used in unique individual ways that are pertinent to the specific context and aspire to an 'aliveness';[9] its use supports, rather than disrupts, a set of multi-sensory and symbolic connections.

Activism and vigilance are needed to ensure that such valuable, relational visions are not buried as urban development marches forward. The definition of 'activism' that interests us most, as the driver of participatory placemaking's future, is activity that creates new social behaviours through new sustainable design frameworks intentionally developed as examples, in the hope that others will follow. In his book *Blessed Unrest*, the environmentalist and entrepreneur Paul Hawken estimated the number of non-profit, non-governmental groups working towards ecological restitution and social justice across the globe, organising from the ground up, at 1 million or more, 'involving tens of millions of people dedicated to change'.[10] His book, written in the first decade of the 21st century, included a taxonomic guide to the widespread projects being developed by these people. 'The very word movement is too small to describe it', but '[the movement] has deep and ancient roots', he said, speaking at the Bioneers conference in 2006. It 'has no name'.[11]

How have those numbers swelled since Hawken wrote his book? It is impossible to say, as no one seems to be keeping consistent tabs on the question across the globe, but certainly the scope for expansion is huge. As regards today's breed of resilience activists, Hawken's more recent personal assessment of the chief climate actors today is that they are mostly 'technology-driven' and 'almost all top-down'. This is one motivation for his next book, *Project Drawdown* (at the time of writing, to be published in 2015), that 'will encompass a broader set of solutions and include those that can be carried out by individuals, communities, building owners, companies and local governments'.[12]

Echoing Hawken's environmentalism, Pope Francis, as widely reported by the media, has recently argued for an ethical economic system that supports human equality and ecology, warning of the dangers of the Anthropocene era.[13] 'Socio-environmental processes are not self-correcting', said the Vatican's Sustainable Humanity Academy group. 'Market forces alone, bereft of ethics and collective action, cannot solve the intertwined crises of poverty, exclusion, and the environment. However, the failure of the market has been accompanied by the failure of institutions, which have not always aimed at the common good.' In strengthening communities, 'we have the innovative and technological capability to be good stewards of creation.'[14]

The identity of participatory placemaking in the coming years will be closely allied to the forms democracy takes in the future. In the UK, for example, this relates to the way localism, regionalism and devolution develop. The economist Mauro Bonaiuti is among the many people who believe that exponential change will bring new patterns. In his book *The Great Transition*, he maintains that 'when the framework changes, as the sciences of complexity teach us, there will be other forms of economic and social organisation more suited to the new situation'. Bonaiuti's argument is that these new forms of organisation are particularly likely to come into being amidst 'global crisis, or even stagnant growth', and that 'cooperation among decentralised, smaller scale economic organisations, will offer greater chances of success. These organisations can lead the system towards conditions of ecological sustainability, more social equity and, by involving citizens and territories, even increase the level of democracy.'[15]

Pope Francis greets the pilgrims during his weekly general audience at St Peter's Square at the Vatican, Rome, 22 October 2014.

Where does that leave the figures proudly holding aloft their badges of 'smart city' top-down proficiency: the property developers? As brokers between big and smaller interests, their identity is called into question. Pioneering non-profit bodies such as the US-based Make It Right, which operated in New Orleans' 9th Ward after Hurricane Katrina in 2005, prototypes alternative models of housing development in tandem with community support in ways that can be applied in other cities. However socially impactful its work is, using truly ambitious design, there remains the question of how community cohesion is supported through greater focus on public realm strategies. But, as Oliver Wainwright, architectural correspondent to *The Guardian* newspaper, has written, flouting the affordable quotas laid down by local authorities has become the new norm by property developers.[16] This has to change, through new models of land use, new land trusts, and a bridging of the gap in trust and amenity to match growing expectations by city dwellers.

Participatory processes are a long-term sustainable means to upgrade deprived neighbourhoods. They focus on improving the allocation of resources and making plans, and bringing about better, more socially equitable cycles of programmes and policies, with occupants seen as 'genuine development partners and agents'.[17] They still need further financial backing, as crowdfunding and philanthropism are not yet sufficient sources in their own right.

One of the participatory workshops staged by Ecosistema Urbano (page 160), 2015, in the Chacarita informal neighbourhood, Asunción, Paraguay, part of its revitalisation masterplan for the historical centre.

> **The identity of participatory placemaking in the coming years will be closely allied to the forms democracy takes in the future. In the UK, for example, this relates to the way localism, regionalism and devolution develop**

The unexpected bankruptcy announced in early 2015 of Architecture for Humanity (AfH; page 108), widely acknowledged as the leading global humanitarian design organisation, might be attributable to naivety or recent miscalculation in tactics by management. But AfH's demise is more likely to have been brought about by a scissor effect between growing operational costs and diminishing financial support and interest from funding bodies.

Inevitably, over the past decade a variety of competing organisations have popped up to intervene in the landscape once dominated by AfH and other pioneers. They often have alternative financial and operational models to the grant- and sponsor-based AfH model; some, such as IDEO.org, are divisions of successful studios and design groups, acting on a pro bono basis.

While participatory placemaking is fully endorsed by many international donor agencies including the World Bank, the United Nations and UN-Habitat, it needs more bodies and generous philanthropists to enter the fray. To heighten awareness of the processes and issues that need support, it would be useful to fashion a repository of knowledge in the manner of appropedia, an online platform for sharing knowledge about collaborative solutions in sustainability, appropriate technology and poverty reduction.[18]

While participatory placemaking does not need a union of any kind, it could do with breaking free from the burdens of its identity as a charitable practice in order to evolve further as a professional practice, one in which self-reliant social enterprise replaces the traditional donor models. That, however, is dependent on the acceptance of participatory placemaking by clients and communities – and, as Rory Sutherland, vice chairman of the advertising agency Ogilvy Group, explained in his popular 2009 TED talk, perhaps also on an association of participatory placemakers that tracks and assesses the intangible values of work carried out, as was done in the fields of marketing and reputation assessments.[19]

As a number of the Stories in the following pages demonstrate, helping with problems in local 'backyards', rather than more widely, makes it easier to argue for funding for projects either started with, or servicing a local group. On the other hand, the capacity to work across cultural boundaries is demonstrated by the work of MASS Design Group (page 208), PITCHAfrica (page 228), Urban-Think Tank (page 226), TYIN (page 262), WORKSHOP (page 282), Ecosistema Urbano (page 160), SENSEable City Laboratory (page 212), Anna Heringer (page 180) and SERA Architects (page 242). There are a few exceptions transcending this dual profile orientation of participatory placemaking, and the particular genesis of each project is unique. However, extraordinary tenacity is called for if placemakers are to implement sustainable systemic thinking with greater value, extending beyond institutional norms.

As societies move towards more open models of collaboration, participatory placemaking will become more common. But in order to reach its full potential, practitioners will need to be able to demonstrate the value that they provide, and find a deeper capacity to fund their activities. The two go hand-in-hand, and there needs to be a step change in more decision- and policy-makers innovating and opening up to giving a mandate to newer sustainable practices to enrich the practice of placemaking.

One big difference between the arsenal of tools available to the pioneers of sustainable placemaking in the 1970s and today's is the internet, which has become a general purpose technology on which societies are now hugely dependent. The academic and journalist John Naughton has written, 'the network has become the nervous system of the planet', and he acknowledges that 'we're also stuck with its downsides'.[20] However, as Jeffrey Sachs, economist and director of the Earth Institute at New York's Columbia University, recently said, 'all great social movements look impossible until they are inevitable'.[21]

Time will tell how far participatory placemaking – or what Ermacora calls 'recoding' – will become accepted, and over what timescale. Time will also reveal how precisely these practices will scale up, becoming a truly vital force behind the regeneration and recovery of places where high-quality design and governance is presently lacking, or cannot penetrate. The obstacles as they are currently perceived include lack of resources. They may also include potential resistance by repressive authorities worried that such an approach will open a Pandora's box and liberate the energies contradicting the status quo of power structures and financial privileges.

Place capital equation

To what extent participatory placemaking may actually become a fundamental a part of societies in the short-term future is not yet known. The continuous research and development – representing a substantial body of work and success stories – this book contributes towards, helps to galvanise the necessary continuity in prototyping meaningful ways to contribute positively to the evolving open society. Whether in conflict zones, disaster relief contexts, sprawling suburbia or central business districts with their high building densities and land values, the ideals outlined in *Recoded City* can sow new seeds for a generation of citizens who face having to live their lives adapting to the rising constraints enforced by an increase in global competition for resources.

The planet's abundance should inspire us to nurture systemic well-being rather than to – consciously or unconsciously – perpetuate the exploitative models that characterise too many urban plans. In *Recoded City* we have attempted to shed light on processes and approaches that express the richness and potential of micro-planning in order that cities may form and thrive in a more humane fashion. We hope that, in time, these will relieve some of the tensions mankind has accumulated through policies and designs that have lacked common sense and the wisdom to care.

Extraordinary tenacity is called for if placemakers are to implement sustainable systemic thinking with greater value, extending beyond institutional norms

Afterword

A number of the participatory placemaking and design projects featured in *Recoded City* are experimental in mode. Their strategies to nurture and augment place capital illuminate how best the open society's goals, allied to this field, could constitute an advance for civilisation.

Place capital could perhaps also be formulated on the printed page as an equation that both captures and expands capacities for human development and happiness, including a vital specificity in location and the notion of replicability, which in itself has analogous behaviour to DNA. To do so helps to consider the potential leap forward that building place capital will bring, alongside the power of the natural sciences. Referring to their actual and future kinship, the cover of this book is conceptually, a cross between an X chromosome – found in both males and females of all mammals – and a night photograph of the world taken from space.

The optimum behaviour of societies is surely forthcoming by being as aligned as possible with the nano dimension of genetics. This connection limits temptations to conceive of cities as fabric dominated by bricks and mortar, encouraging more attention to be paid to the relations and soft features that truly define their habitability.

The potential to maximise place capital is reflected by the following equation, in which the amount of participation is multiplied by well-being strategies, by open society policies and by sensitive design, divided by social and natural capital*, by the Gini coefficient* and by localised GDP. Our ambition is to continue to refine our understanding of how to grow the value of places for people.

*For notes on natural capital and the Gini coefficient, see Introduction note 1 and Open Society note 2, in Endnotes starting page 307.

(Participation quotient X Well-being strategies X Open society policies X Sensitive design)

DIVIDED BY

(Social capital X Natural capital X Gini coefficient X Localised GDP)

Stories

These Stories about participatory placemaking projects and those behind them, as listed on the right, discuss a wide range of recoding activities responding to needs across all continents around the world, in formal and informal contexts. Our 43 essays, based on fresh research, explore ways in which to regenerate, develop or repair places cost-effectively and sensitively, applying more dynamic and user-centred urban design approaches.

Architecture for Humanity

atelier d'architecture autogérée

Canning Town Caravanserai

Center for Urban Pedagogy

Clear Village

Collectif Etc

Alejandro Echeverri, Sergio Fajardo, Municipio de Medellín

Estudio Teddy Cruz

Dreaming New Mexico

Dudley Street Neighbourhood Initiative

Ecosistema Urbano

Elemental

Friends of the High Line

Gap Filler

Herkes için Mimarlik

Anna Heringer

Home for All

Kéré Architecture

1to1 Agency of Engagement

Operation Resilient Long Island

Marcos L. Rosa

Marko and Placemakers

MASS Design Group

SENSEable City Laboratory, MIT

Muf Architecture/Art, J&L Gibbons

Neighborland

Partizaning

PITCHAfrica

Project for Public Spaces

Project H Design

Rural Urban Framework

SERA Architects

snark space making

Soundings

Strategic Design Scenarios and La 27e Région

Studio Mumbai

TYIN tegnestue Architects

Urban-Think Tank

URBZ

Vancouver Public Space Network

WikiHouse

WORKSHOP architecture

WXY Studio

Architecture for Humanity

'My focus isn't the heart of the city, I'm interested in where the city meets nature', says the architect Nathaniel Corum, who until 2015 was the long-standing head of Educational Outreach at Architecture for Humanity (AfH), the American non-profit organisation established by London-born architect Cameron Sinclair and writer/producer Kate Stohr in 1999.[1] For Corum, asset-based design, conducted through a locally specific approach to the use of land, brings resilience to communities' dwelling places.

Sinclair and Stohr were also co-founders of the Open Architecture Network for open source humanitarian design (2006). Honoured by multiple awards for AfH, notably its work in disaster relief housing after Hurricane Katrina in August 2005, they stepped down from their executive positions in 2013, with Sinclair becoming the executive director of the Jolie-Pitt Foundation and Stohr founding 99 Antennas, a digital design and curating firm.

In spite of AfH's immense track record in pro bono design and construction in 48 countries – particularly in the US, Haiti, the Philippines, South Africa and Japan – involving 90,000 design professionals at its height and with 70 independent, city-based chapters, in January 2015 the organisation announced it was filing for bankruptcy. By way of explanation it cited a spate of serious funding challenges from both budget overruns and decreasing donations, challenges faced by many charitable bodies.

However, as part of what is seen as a foremost asset of AfH's legacy, many of the international chapters sharing the AfH name have continued their work as separate legal entities. The contemporary era is marked by extensive practical knowledge of high-level humanitarian design – not the case in the late 1990s when the organisation was set up – and a wider informed awareness of AfH's activities and strategies globally.

From very early on in its operations, AfH's reach was larger than any other comparable entity's. 'Where we had the ability to do so, we not only moved there, but set up shop', says Corum. Besides its base in San Francisco, it also had five offices including in Biloxi, Mississippi, and in Haiti (led by a team of 10 full-time workers). The overall staff of 30

↑ **Above:** Tsunami-impacted coastal conditions near Shizugawa, Japan, showing storm-damaged boats and other jetsam. A group of fishermen who lost everything asked AfH for help in 2011.

↗ **Top right:** Site plan by students at Kyoto University of Art and Design of Shizugawa, where they designed and constructed a new workplace and warehouse for local fishermen as part of an AfH post-tsunami workshop.

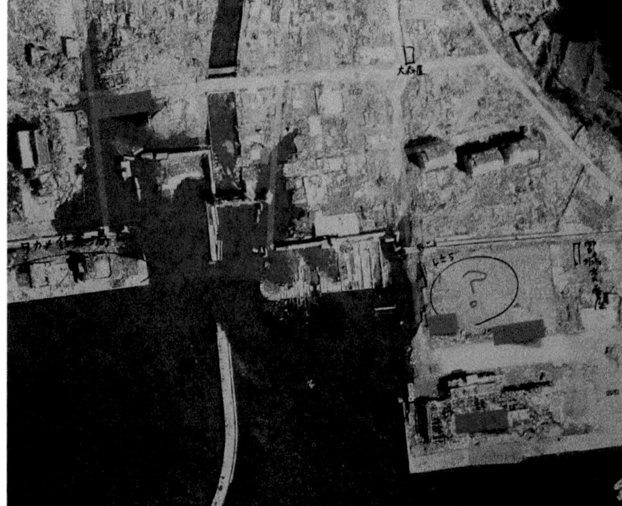

> **We use the word ‘acupuncture’ a lot. Building community facilities shows a way to a more resilient future, not an ephemeral one.**

was complemented by design fellows and consultants, as well as international students on internships, some of whom went on to become staff.

Corum led AfH’s Native American community initiatives, which did not get as much exposure in the media as its work in New Orleans and Haiti. He worked alongside tribal members to research and develop culturally and climatically appropriate building prototypes and materials. However he was also an instrumental part of AfH’s wide ‘exchange across cultures’, and remains engaged in humanitarian design projects in Japan, Haiti, and the Galápagos Islands, where AfH was invited by various partners to be part of long-established networks, for example, a nation’s indigenous groups. For each endeavour he has connected university design programmes to humanitarian design projects, involving research, design and hands-on assistance, and creating design teams. Students frequently join projects, contributing their goodwill and skills, and Corum has worked hard over the years to get more architectural schools involved.

Rather than bringing a generic methodology or system to projects, Corum comes with questions, first listening to the replies and then working with what is there, to make an asset-based response: what can be built on with local place forms and the community’s skills and latent ideas – including tribal intelligence and indigenous technologies. The process relies on ‘inperts’ – local people who are ‘experts about things that we’ll never know’, who will understand a Navajo elder living in an off-grid location, for example, or someone whose family members have just died in a natural disaster – to express what they might need. ‘We get them to draw, show us a place they like.’

‘We’re not doing charity’, Corum asserts, ‘we’re going for a mutually supportive and productive exchange across cultures – mutual understanding that builds things beyond the facilities themselves, and actually helps people to better sustain themselves in the world. We use the word “acupuncture” a lot.[2] We’ve gravitated away from housing to community facilities, which affect more people. A building that is very useable by many people shows a way to a more resilient future, not an ephemeral one.’

AfH’s first really big project was one of rehabilitation after the deadly Hurricane Katrina hit the US coast of the Gulf of

Above left:
Shizugawa, Miyagi, Japan, 2011. Students from Kyoto University of Art and Design working with local fishermen, attaching kelp fronds (seaweed) to ropes to be floated in the sea.

Mexico in 2005. Here in Biloxi, Mississippi, AfH collaboratively designed over 300 new-build and renovated homes, and partnered with long-standing local groups to create a public-access design centre in a disused building, where people could talk extensively about problems in their devastated community. With all the road signs destroyed in the storm, the group also mapped the area to redesign an orientation system.

After the 2011 Tohoku earthquake and tsunami AfH also assisted in Japan's reconstruction efforts. Japan, Corum says, is 'essentially a megalopolis, so densely settled, and every inch of land is spoken for by someone's family. Tsunami stones exist on the hills, etched with the year of the tsunamis in the 17th and 18th centuries, saying, "don't build beyond this point"', but people have done. Fishermen worked competitively before the tsunami, but after the disaster boats were scarce so the men formed a collective, which was more fun. 'It was the only way for them to survive, but it resulted in a lot more community.' In assembling the team for Japan AfH gathered as many Asian architects as it could, especially suitable personnel able to provide technical rehabilitation support. Beyond the problems of nuclear contamination and ongoing threats of earthquake and tsunami, the team had a lot to learn, 'because the Japanese have been at the forefront of "base isolation" and of a different kind of seismic approach in their codes' to that taken in the USA.

'I'm really learning a lot from these folks working [in Japan] about seismically resilient design. In America we tend to build things strong so they'll break, but in Japan it's much more about flexibility, being able to roll with it. Like taekwondo versus aikido. Both approaches are right, but I feel theirs is the more elegant.' AfH's project in the devastated coastal town of Shizugawa saw students working alongside community members in workshops held to clarify needs and refine designs. Together they built tables, chairs, platforms and furnishings for work, cooking, eating and resting, all made from local wood.

To achieve consensus, a wishlist was compiled. In this ravaged environment, temporary buildings were needed – places to store fishermen's nets, prepare lunch, and potentially to sell some things from. The project was therefore more of an acupuncture scheme for 'a shelter in a place inside the red line where they will never build again'. A demountable prefabricated building was made of shipping containers, kitted it out with

> Showing up with ample time, actually getting to know people and walking in their shoes, is a really amazing ice-breaker

Left:
A community meeting to discuss the Banya building for the local fishermen, attended by ocean farmers, local stakeholders, AfH representatives and students from Kyoto University of Art and Design.

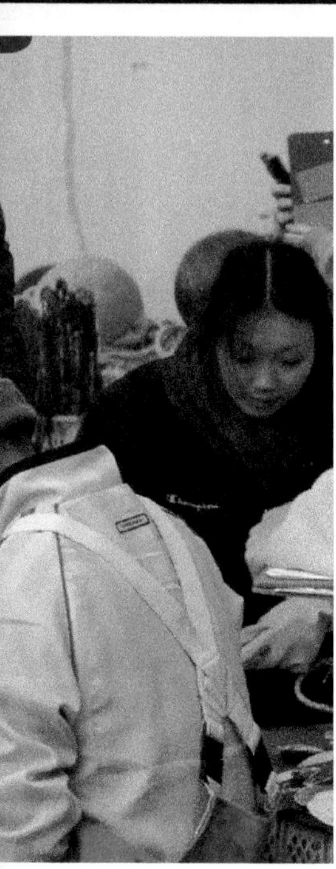

Above Left:
The completed Banya building, Shizugawa, a new workplace for the fishermen, to help develop a collective acquafarming business. Its furnishings were designed and built through the AfH workshop with Kyoto University of Art and Design.

Left:
Fishermen in Shizugawa and students from Kyoto University of Art and Design working together as part of the AfH workshop in 2011.

shelving, bookcases, tables, chairs for relaxation and meetings. The team went out on the boats and worked with the fishermen, while asking them questions about their life and their needs. For Corum this is 'a really important process. Actually getting to know people, and walking in their shoes a bit, is a really amazing icebreaker. Some of the best ideas come out of that.'

In the USA, AfH collaborated with the organisation Make It Right (through the Ford Peck Foundation) on a community project in Montana for highly insulated tribal housing, involving the staging of design charrettes. Held over several days with AfH team members and local citizens, these intense meetings served to jointly formulate solutions and options responding to declared needs. 'We need to make beyond-LEED village expansions with the full collaboration of the community and respecting the ecology at large,' said Corum, 'helping them expand through improved systems for agriculture, permaculture and habitat, and new, regenerative community buildings, rather than through solely LEED criteria.'[3]

AfH design team members frequently become embedded in the physical contexts of projects. When he started, Corum lived for nine months in the Navajo Nation, which extends into the states of Arizona, Utah and New Mexico. 'I'm not a tribal member but I got immersed in it. I learned some words, how people spend their days. Developing trust allows you to understand what people need and to apply design knowledge to that challenge.' Native communities 'have only recently regained control over their finances, through a Native American self-determination act. There were always government handouts before. You got certain things but couldn't decide what the money was spent on. Now tribal governments have a budget, and are able to hire technical assistance, or decide to build a community centre.'

Corum is excited by the fact that many tribal members who grew in the Crow Tribe of Montana up went on to Cornell University's architecture school, and are now returning to their homes with professional expertise. Working on a study of 20 exemplary tribal architecture projects sponsored by the US Department of Housing and Urban Development (HUD), he has found not historical artefacts or reconstructions, but LEED platinum buildings with culturally appropriate features.

Architecture is ideally a profession of apprenticeship, says Corum. 'A lot of the tribal members I've met are looking for ways to include indigenous designers in their staff and project teams.' A happy trend has been the increase in Native American students involved with projects, and this is reflected at professional level: a Crow architect won awards for his work on a large housing initiative; another was the

first native tribal member to win a three-year Enterprise Rose Architectural Fellowship. This has helped to develop a network of knowledgeable practitioners who support their work with different tribes at a high level.

'We allow for traditional practice and lifestyles, especially with elders' housing.' Indigenous clients often ask for non-toxic materials. One tribe in California, the Pinoleville Pomo Nation, was attracted to straw bale (Corum is an expert on designing and constructing with this material, and co-author of *Building a Straw Bale House*).[4] With the involvement of the University of California, Berkeley's engineering and architecture departments, and funds from the Department of Energy, a few prototype homes made of natural materials were constructed; 'but they also have these souped-up technical features like ground source heat pumps that you don't see in houses'.

Corum sees how people want to relate to their direct environment, and how very different tribespeople are – the Najavo Nation are sparsely settled, do cattle ranching, and 'don't want to be able to see another house from their house', while the Hopi tribe prefer adjacent, traditionally built prehistoric apartment buildings. In the Najavo project details were crucial: 'where the fire's placed, the stick that you mind the fire with, all in terms of relationships to the four directions, so the entry doorway and the way you enter and move around the house, there's a hierarchy of privacy and specific utility'.

AfH teams catered to these needs with the use of non-toxic, passive solar building, space plans with an aesthetic sensibility and a novel use of materials. 'It's a lot of things to puzzle together, but it's a process that's very rewarding, and gets to true homes, not housing. The client teaches you something about the building, despite their ignorance of our funny profession.'

In 2013 the team presented an exhibition, Self-published Sustainable Native Communities, at the National

Museum of the American Indian, and published an initial 17 community case studies. This showed HUD – keen to develop better solutions in this sector – and other policymakers that it is possible for tribes to make first-rate housing that reflects green building values, whether built of straw bale or using more traditional protocols. While earlier housing designs appeared uniform in style and materiality and were often technically substandard, 'not tuned to landscape, now we are starting to see collaborations that are really linked to unique cultures and places, off-grid, some of the oldest continually inhabited contexts, as well as some forgotten environments.' New projects are also financed by innovative funding sources.

In 2013 Corum responded to a request for technical assistance on several sites in the remote Galápagos Islands (approximately 15,000 people live on Baltra, Santa Cruz and San Cristobal islands). It raises 'the big issue of the oceans doing most of the work of keeping

Left:
View from the coast showing the impact of Hurricane Katrina in August 2005 on the extension to Biloxi, Mississippi's O'Keefe Museum of Art, designed by Frank Gehry.

Bottom left:
The Parker House designed by Brett Zamore Design (2007), part of AfH's Biloxi Model Homes initiative to help families repair and rebuild their homes in the aftermath of Hurricane Katrina.

Bottom right:
A renovation of the John Henry Beck Red House into a police substation and community meeting room. Biloxi, Mississippi, led by the Gulf Coast Community Design Studio, AfH, 2007.

The collaborative work has hugely strengthened communities, human relations and connections with land, sharing ideas about long-term resilience

the planet clean. People think of forests for dealing with carbon and oxygen, but it's actually the oceans by a factor of about four... So it's exciting to do projects that bring some awareness of that.'

On several sites in these island communities, his team created indoor/outdoor classrooms to boost existing facilities, to collaborate on building a permanent school on San Cristobal, and set up exchange programmes and training, with support from a local architectural school and a local architect. As in Haiti, little in the Galápagos is built directly on the ground, and it is forbidden to chop down trees on the archipelago, therefore many things are brought in from outside. Lava rock is quarried here, and locals are interested in structural bamboo. The climate makes it appropriate to construct pavilions, offering shade and the right kind of platform, rather than closed-in facilities and utility cores.

The islands and their waters are a biological marine reserve, but as Corum points out, motor traffic, housing demands and commercial fishing have all led to increased conflicts between residents and those seeking to conserve the islands' natural resources. And despite the fact that human settlement is restricted to only 3% of the archipelago, immigration continues. 'Galápagos residents ultimately will be the best stewards of their natural heritage. Their lives and livelihoods are uniquely intertwined with the successful protection and preservation of the islands.'

AfH's Pac Rim studios of this kind over the years considered holistic solutions to several major Pacific Ocean crises, focusing on issues of sea-level rises and oceanic and coastal resilience. Architectural student team members come through various partner university design programmes in locations as far apart as California and Asia, and they get involved a real-world design challenges, assisting the design teams.

The collaborative work carried out by AfH under Corum's direction has hugely strengthened communities, human relations and connections with land around the globe by sharing ideas about long-term resilience. Creating game-changing places and facilities through various forms of acupuncture, it has offered compelling resistance in the face of the deracinating impacts of urban development and natural disasters worldwide.

atelier d'architecture autogérée

Above:
The plots at the Agrocité agricultural hub, Colombes, Paris (2011-ongoing), on a suburban social housing estate are cultivated by inhabitants, June 2013.

'A city can only become resilient with the active involvement of its diverse inhabitants. To stimulate the democratic engagement of the largest number of citizens, we need tools, knowledge and places for testing new collective practices and initiatives, and for showcasing the results and benefits of a resilient transformation of the city.'[1] Such was the motivation of architects Constantin Petcou and Doina Petrescu, who founded atelier d'architecture autogérée (aaa) in Paris in 2001. Their goal was to bring about a much needed and truly resilient urban regeneration involving residents in the transformation of their neighbourhoods, through a process of radically new collective dynamics.

Traditionally the 'commons' referred to the natural resources of an environmental space managed and used by the whole community, but today the meaning of the term has expanded to signify all resources collectively shared by the population. Aaa – a team of architects, artists, urban planners, sociologists, activists, students and residents working as part of a fluid

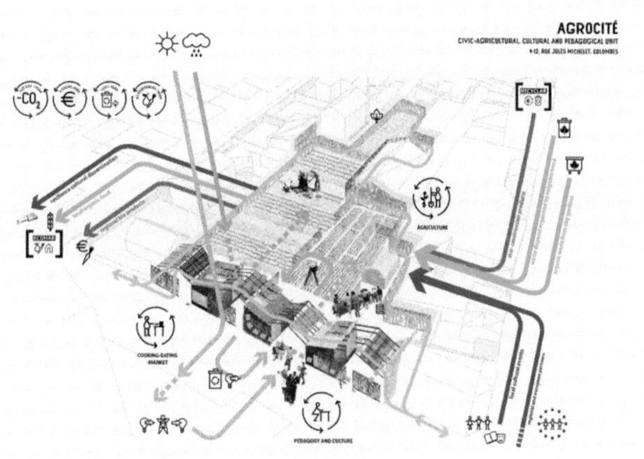

Left:
Agrocité, Colombes, includes a farm, gardens, composting, rainwater collection/use in garden irrigation, solar energy generation and grey water phytoremediation.

Below:
R-Urban collective hubs, Colombes, 2011-ongoing. Agrocité agricultural unit; Recyclab recycling/eco-construction; Ecohab, housing cooperative.

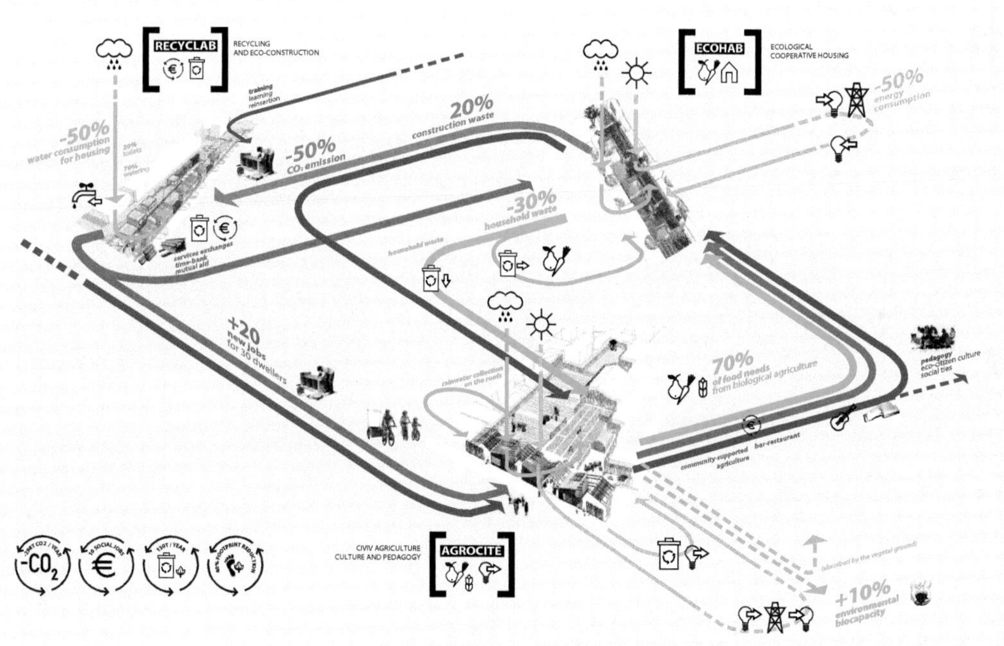

> **Through a network of hubs with complementary, collective facilities, a new sense of spatial and ecological agency enhances urban resilience**

network – is small in scale. However, it is one of many such initiatives to have emerged as a reaction to the sluggardly pace of governmental processes in Europe affecting urban regeneration, and also to the lack of agreement about meeting challenges of an environmental and economic nature and their consequences on people's lives.

R-Urban, aaa's bottom-up framework created in 2008, was intended to 'trigger short circuits' between complementary urban hubs and developing practices across local, regional and international scales, in order to promote new collective dynamics and forms of urban 'commons'. Aaa began implementing R-Urban in 2011 in Colombes, a small town in the suburbs of Paris, in partnership with the local municipality, a number of organisations and local residents. Through the team's gradual generation of a network of hubs with collective facilities that complement one another, a new sense of spatial and ecological agency enhances the capacities of urban resilience.

The first two R-Urban hubs, Recyclab and Agrocité, have been built and are fully functioning, and further additions will be added to the R-Urban network over the next few years, managed by a cooperative land trust that will buy space, facilitate development and handle its democratic governance. Recyclab is a recycling and eco-construction unit set up as a social enterprise with facilities for storing and reusing locally salvaged materials that →

atelier d'architecture autogérée

Thinking of new systems of governance by restructuring resource cycles

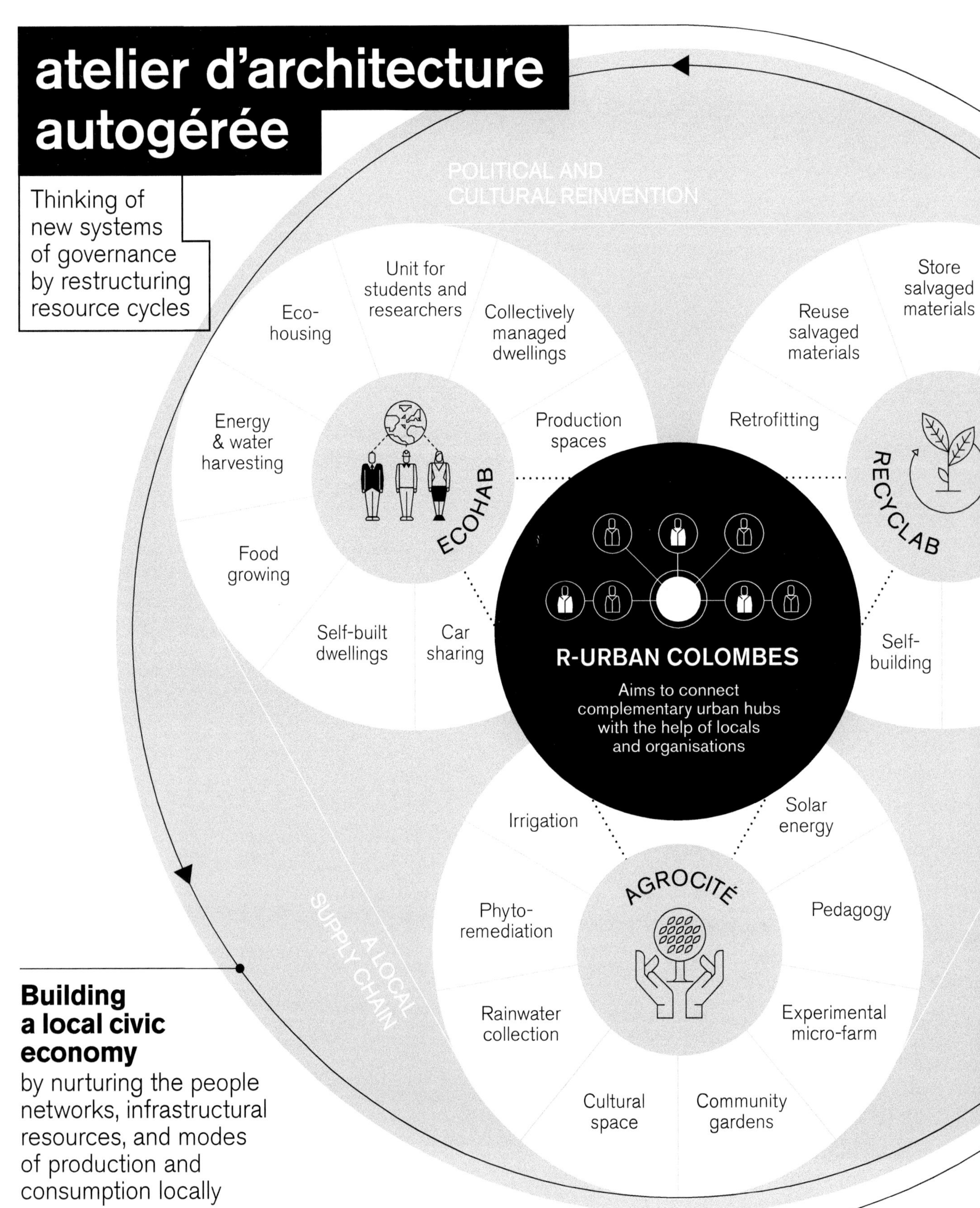

Building a local civic economy

by nurturing the people networks, infrastructural resources, and modes of production and consumption locally

Ecological construction

Fab lab for residents

SUSTAINABLE AND RESILIENT

are intended for ecological construction projects of self-building and retrofitting. Recyclab includes an associated 'fab lab' (fabrication laboratory) for residents' use.

Agrocité is described by aaa as an 'agro-cultural unit'. It has an experimental micro-farm, community gardens, pedagogical and cultural spaces, and a series of systems for compost heating, rainwater collection and garden irrigation, solar energy production and grey-water phytoremediation. Some elements are run as social enterprises – for example, the micro-farm, the market, the worm compost farm and the café; while others, such as the community garden, the cultural space and the pedagogical space, are run by local organisations. Ecohab, by contrast, is a cooperative eco-housing project with a number of partially self-built and collectively managed ecological dwellings. It has shared facilities and schemes including car sharing, food growing, production spaces, and energy and water harvesting, as well as two public housing units and a temporary residential unit for students and researchers.

Aaa sees its role as '[teaching] the necessary skills and [creating] opportunities for people to invent their own jobs as part of an alternative economy, which is not only financial, but also social, cognitive and affective'. R-Urban nurtures networks and cycles of production and consumption between the collective facilities and the neighbourhood in a way that 'closes chains of needs and supply as locally as possible'. The benefits accrue to citizens but also to the municipality as a partner, which will help with land, funding and logistical support. 'This is the passage from the welfare state to a civic economy in which new forms of public-civic partnerships should be key components.'

What makes R-Urban unique is its broad interpretation of this production-consumption chain, extending beyond material aspects to those that are cultural, cognitive and affective. It also reconsiders at a deep level the relationship between the urban and the rural as part of the retrofitting of these metropolitan suburbs.

'R-Urban is not only about "sustainability" but also about societal change and political and cultural reinvention, addressing issues of social inequality, power and cultural difference.' Instead of acting solely as building designers, aaa calls for architects to be initiators, negotiators, co-managers and enablers of processes and agencies that strengthen existing civic resilience. 'It is by micro-political acting that we want to participate in making the city more ecological and more democratic, to make the space of proximity less dependent on top-down processes and more accessible to its users. The (new) "self-managed architecture" is an architecture of relationships, processes and agencies of persons, desires, skills and know-hows.'

The benefits accrue to citizens but also to the municipality as a partner, helping with land, funding and logistical support

Right:
Agrocité, Colombes, 2011-ongoing. An urban agricultural hub in the middle of a suburban social housing estate, on a temporarily available plot of land.

ENGAGEMENT REPLICABILITY DESIGN DRIVEN SCALE IMPACT

IDENTIFY → ENQUIRE → DEVELOP → CO-DESIGN → CO-CONSTRUCT → HAND-OVER

Canning Town Caravanserai

'Drab', 'unfriendly', 'McDonald's is more exciting'... In 2011 the public spaces in the east London district of Canning Town South elicited nothing but negative comments. One of the UK's most deprived wards, and also one of its most ethnically diverse, it remained on the edge of the city and out of the spotlight placed on the nearby Canary Wharf business district, and until recently was untargeted for comprehensive regeneration.

But the successful staging in east London of the Olympics in 2012, and moving into gear of the legacy plans, have been factors in changing expectations for this part of the Royal Docks area, and a new town centre for Canning Town was planned by the local Borough of Newham; the borough's Sustainable Community Strategy for 2010-30 states intentions to establish the district as 'a place where people choose to live, work and play'.

Two years before the Games, a prominent 0.5-hectare brownfield site was cleared directly opposite Canning Town station, a key east London transport interchange, and a competition was held for its 'meanwhile' use. A new chapter in the area's history was started with the opening, a few months before the Games in 2012, of Canning Town Caravanserai – a community garden with 18 allotments, an open-air theatre, a children's play area, sheltered tables

with seating for 60 people, a 'micro-manufacture' workshop, market kiosks for local entrepreneurs, and the Oasis café/bar. Showcasing local talent, it also develops economic opportunities with and for the local community.

Canning Town Caravanserai began life as a winning entry by the architecture firm Ash Sakula to the 2010-11 'Meanwhile London' competition for the regeneration of Canning Town and the Royal Docks. Together with two other sites to be regenerated, the scheme covered an arc of land running from Stratford, the main site of the Games, down the River Lea to the Thames and east to Woolwich Reach. The sites' potential as part of an area of significant development opportunity was identified. The £3.7 billion mixed-use Canning Town project to transform the area's physical, social and economic horizons (due for completion in 2024) was launched by the London Borough of Newham, with developers Bouygues behind a £600 million regeneration of

Above:
Architect and academic Sarah Wigglesworth at Canning Town Caravanserai's Self Made City event discusses the potentials of self-building, 2014.

Right:
Canning Town Caravanserai's north gate is kept open to local residents and other visiting members of the public, 2013.

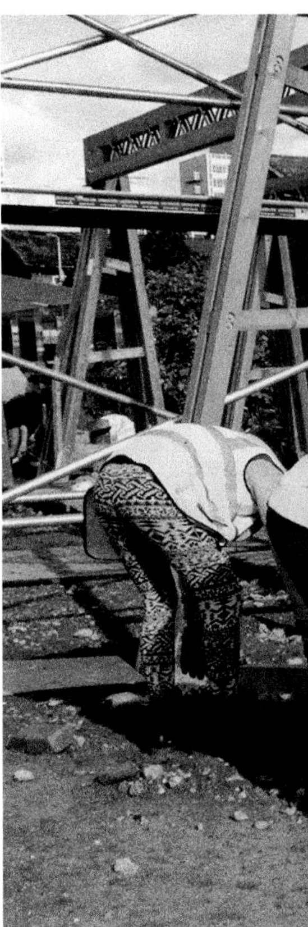

the town centre, along with One Housing Group, Countryside Properties, the London Thames Gateway Development Corporation and the Homes and Communities Agency. The main part of the Meanwhile competition site was to be available for at least three years, and the southern part – which was used for Canning Town Caravanserai – potentially for five.

The competition brief asked how people could be enticed to the area, and how the site could be animated by a 'destination' of 'meanwhile' uses signalling the potential of the Royal Docks area to locals, visitors and the market. Ideas needed to be visually attractive, while also promoting entrepreneurial activities and encouraging business start-up and/or incubator activities, thereby creating new jobs for local people.

'The Canning Town Caravanserai is a kind of small village', explains Ash Sakula's co-director Cany Ash, an inveterate lover of storytelling, 'inspired by the medieval network of safe, hosted spaces along the Silk Route, which allowed travellers and traders to rest, and so ensured the flow of goods, knowledge and culture between Europe and Asia.'[1]

Local resident Iman Ogoo says that Canning Town Caravanserai is 'a hub essential to community cohesion ... a place where my family and I can explore new concepts, socialise, and even use as a trading space alongside other local business owners.'[2] The firm she founded, Imanmade Natural Skin Care, trades from one of eight micro-enterprise units supporting local business start-ups, rent free.

Valerie Segree is another such business owner, running Anais Crafts using upcycling techniques. Her young daughter has been involved since the beginning, looking after the plants. '[Caravanserai has] made the area a bit brighter', she says. At first local people 'didn't want to be involved' in a more active way, probably due to shyness, but many have got progressively involved.[3] Ash likes to ensure that the streetside windows and the →

Left:
Erecting the pillars of the Flying Carpet Theatre, an open-plan performing space at the heart of Canning Town Caravanserai, 2013.

A hub essential to community cohesion... a place where my family and I can explore new concepts, socialise, and use as a trading space alongside other local business owners

gates at either end of the site are kept open during opening hours, so that locals and visitors feel free to enter and experience a connection with the project.

The on-site facilities were built incrementally over two years, with more than 50 volunteer trainees working alongside experienced tradespeople. Everything was constructed without prefabricated systems, using remediated and salvaged materials, including for the kitchens and toilets. The timber used incorporated sleepers taken from the construction of the Velodrome on the Olympic site; wood was also obtained from ISG, the contractor of the nearby Crystal sustainable-development exhibition centre run by Siemens; scaffolding was donated. The waterproofed sari-fabric roof on the theatre, and the brick construction by Iliona Outram Khalili, are two examples of experimental building techniques used at the centre.

The multi-use 'Flitched' workshop on the site was designed by architect Tina Patel and engineer Roberto Mirabella (winners of the Upcycler's Design Competition for collaborations between career-starters and established professionals), and constructed by 53 architectural and structural engineering enthusiasts. The many activities that have been held under its rafters include drumming and steel-pan lessons, timber workshops and social art studios.

All this has taken place in tandem with collaborations with local individuals and community groups to organise pilot events, in turn feeding back into directions taken for the site's user-friendly design and further plans for activities. In 2013, more than 1,500 people attended events, ranging from secondary and further education days and corporate volunteering days, to arts events (the biggest being Light Night Canning Town with many other local community organisations), performing arts shows and community events. The project is a hive of creativity: live events have taken in puppet shows and a bank holiday weekend at which 25 bands performed. Festivals and community feasts have been hosted, language classes

It qualifies as a 'third space', or a place of informal public gathering beyond home or work, helping to nurture social interactivity and equality

offered. The workshop houses a disabled gardening group, and will be the site of experiments with gravity watering systems – anticipating the project's move in 2015 to a new site off the nearby A12 road that has some water pollution.

Ash believes that the project demonstrates the potential of 'creating modern oases' in the context of the city's 'harsh realities' as a place 'where huge differences divide populations who in fact have much to offer each other'. It is 'a meeting place where alternative interests can be discovered, and new connections can be forged'. The visitor to Caravanserai is 'a stranger until he or she meets us', she adds. 'Thereafter the conversation might be short or rambling but the warmth of the greeting is paramount, and this concept of hosting has shaped everything we do in the project.' It easily qualifies as a 'third space', or place of informal public gathering beyond home or work in which there is a sense of civic engagement, helping to nurture social interactivity and equality.[4]

Canning Town Caravanserai is run as a not-for-profit limited company, of which Ash is chair and executive director; funding has come from the London & Quadrant Foundation, the Development Trusts Association, the London Borough of Newham, Comic Relief and the European Union's Youth in Action programme. More than 100 trainees have developed their construction and design skills through the project, representing a unique form of career mentoring, and new ideas competitions – such as Parks on Wheels in 2014 – continue to generate possibilities with existing and new collaborators.

Ash sees the project encouraging 'a grassroots form of personal, economic and community development, building local resilience, through a model that is scaleable'. She also believes that the network it has established 'enables us to connect with people who often feel excluded from community activities, through engaging with project leaders whom they already trust'. The four guilds established there – growing, making, trading and performing – are also highly facilitative social structures, enabling new bonds and networks to develop.

Canning Town Caravanserai is an entirely unique – and vital – social-space resource, an all-too-rare type of space in London, let alone in east London as developments slowly bring the area away from the margins, and some areas benefit more directly than others. Canning Town lacks safe, public events spaces that have the capacity to bring people of all ages together, and Ash points out that 'with the Newham population growing at more than twice the London average, this need will only intensify'. Canning Town Caravanserai is intentionally a cumulative process with participatory opportunities emerging, enabling the local communities to become active in their public realm. The new connections benefiting local people – who could not otherwise afford Canning Town Caravanserai's activities and facilities – encourage 'a sense of ownership and community, which counters the upheaval of local developments'.

Left:
Self Made City event talk at the Flitched workshop space at Canning Town Caravanserai, 2014.

Below:
Summertime performance at the Flying Carpet Theatre, Canning Town Caravanserai, 2013.

ENGAGEMENT
REPLICABILITY
DESIGN DRIVEN
SCALE
IMPACT

IDENTIFY → ENQUIRE → DEVELOP → CO-DESIGN → CO-CONSTRUCT → HAND-OVER

Much of the most important information urban residents need about their city is unspoken and downright elusive. When details about a topical question – such as zoning rules, regulations on street vending, or the workings of the youth justice system – are finally tracked down, they are often presented in a visually and textually arcane form. While in most larger cities there are plenty of mentors, counsellors and teachers, it is often difficult to engage with them one-to-one. An individual's particular questions may not be answered by watching an online lecture. Even in the digital age, for city dwellers, it can be hugely frustrating trying to find out what they need in order to enlarge their knowledge, to become more 'street smart' about the city and its policies. Yet, in the process, the autodidact is not only rewarded by an armoury of knowledge, but also empowered to engage with decision-makers and to question limited and limiting processes and policies.

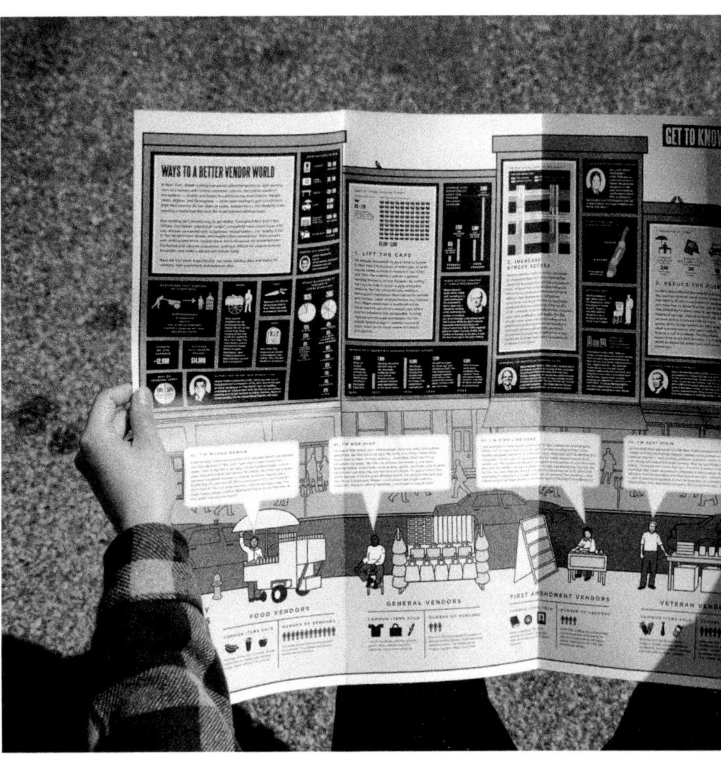

Center for Urban Pedagogy

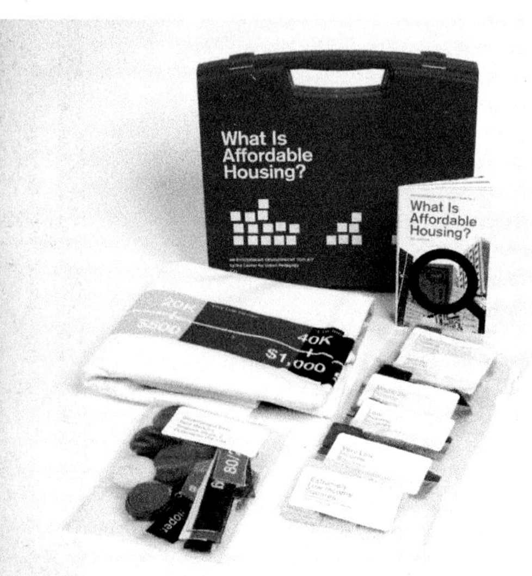

Learning more about how the city works usually cannot be achieved by looking in one single location. To help raise awareness about a specific subject, material needs to be closely geared to the specific needs of particular city dwellers, but this is not always the case. Visual tools, too, have to be seen from these particular citizens' point of view, allowing for cultural and ethnic difference. Furthermore, they should function as an open door for further engagement, so that the individual is not alone but encouraged to take up a DIY attitude through collective activities geared to his or her local contexts. In addition, they should enable people to advocate more effectively within the systems they are involved with, using the same terms as specialists and elected officials.

Left:
CUP's What Is Affordable Housing? toolkit includes a guidebook, wall chart and an interactive online map, 2010.

In New York City, the non-profit Center for Urban Pedagogy (CUP) adheres to a successful mission of using 'art, design and visual culture to increase meaningful civic engagement, particularly among historically under-represented communities', says Christine Gaspar, Executive Director since 2009.[1] CUP was founded in 2001 by Damon Rich with co-founders Oscar Tuazon, Stella Bugbee, Josh Breitbart, Jason Anderson, AJ Blandford, Sarah Dadush, Althea Wasow, and Rosten Woo. Many of them had gone to college together, and they had a range of backgrounds in art, architecture, film, policy and government.

While CUP had no preset trajectory in those early days, invariably its work led to visual products. This activity by the voluntary collective fostered a couple of zines and an exhibition at Storefront for Art and Architecture in Soho, NYC, in 2001. This included video of multiple stakeholder interviews, primary research displayed in posters, models, and drawings, and was created in collaboration with a range of partners, including high-school students. Many of CUP's current methods emerged from this early exhibition. Over time, the organisation shifted away from creating exhibitions, and instead began to create visual explanations of complicated policy issues with and for community

Left: Vendor Power! is an issue of CUP's Making Policy Public. The poster helps street vendors to know their rights, 2009.

Below: Over 90 community organisations use the What is Affordable Housing? toolkit to run community workshops, 2010.

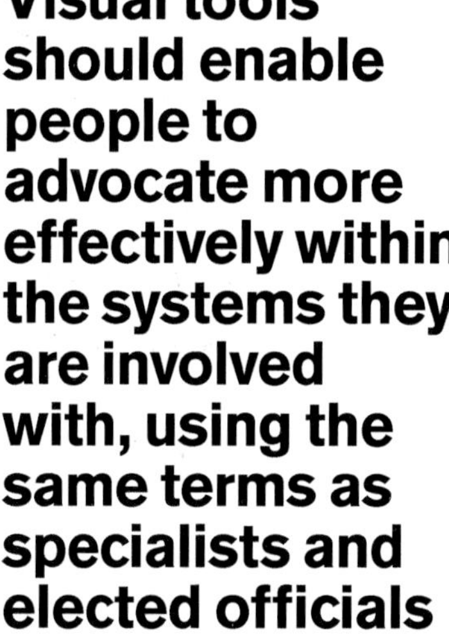

Visual tools should enable people to advocate more effectively within the systems they are involved with, using the same terms as specialists and elected officials

organisations who wanted to use this work to educate and organise their community members.

This focus on using visuals to make issues accessible, and the principle of making and sustaining impact, prevalent throughout all CUP's work, has benefited tens of thousands of community members to date. CUP subscribes to a process of creation of appropriate and accessible visual education tools for community organisers and city dwellers. Its aim is to help people to overcome the inherent difficulty of comprehending complex urban policies and decision-making processes that shape neighbourhoods, and to empower individuals to take further action.

Gaspar, a long-standing community design leader whose background is in architecture and planning, was formerly assistant director of the Gulf Coast Community Design Studio (GCCDS) in Biloxi, Mississippi, which provided architecture and planning services to low-income communities recovering from the devastating effects of 2005's Hurricane Katrina. 'At GCCDS I realised that design is a tool of power', she says, 'and, as designers we make decisions about whose hands we put that power in. Both at CUP and at GCCDS, the work is about putting that power in the hands of communities who are often left out of decision-making.'

CUP partners with bodies keen to advance their active knowledge of some aspect of public policy, and through this means reaches a wide range of individuals. Partners range from →

We are interested that students should see that the physical, the social and the economic in the places where they live, aren't givens

↑
Above:
CUP students interview Congresswoman Nydia Velazquez about her bodega bill for their research on the project Bodega Down Bronx, 2009.

community organisations and advocacy groups to high-school teachers and students. At the outset of each project, CUP issues an open call for project partners, encouraging groups to come to them with issues that are impacting their communities. The partnerships brokered are a key first step.

CUP has eight full-time in-house staff, who manage collaborations with teams of commissioned artists, graphic and user interface designers, educators, activists and researchers. At the next stage CUP identifies suitable artists, graphic and industrial designers needed for the project. The multidisciplinary collaborators work together to ensure that everyone has a say in the project's goals and understands the process agreed to, and the group proceeds to create an appropriate visual tool designed to achieve the specific aim of the project. This is then distributed by the community partner to help enable the partner's constituency of individuals to achieve a deeper knowledge of the issues involved, 'so that more people can understand how those processes and systems work, and more people can be engaged in shaping them'.

It is vital that CUP's visual products create an impact, speaking to their respective recipients and their particular needs. CUP often creates print items such as posters and booklets because they are easily accessible by low-income communities, but also produces some multimedia and video projects. Everything is available for sale (at a subsidised rate for community organisations), and for free download from CUP's website, including the videos for streaming. It is no surprise, given the care taken by CUP in commissioning art and design, that many of its products have been exhibited by museums including the Cooper-Hewitt and NYC's New Museum of Contemporary Art, and at such events as the Venice Biennale, and has won awards from bodies including the Curry Stone Design Prize and the Rockefeller Foundation NYC Cultural Innovation Fund.

In the realm of youth education CUP works with high-school students, exploring key questions about how the city works. The principal after-school programme is Urban Investigations, in which project-based learning is used to take students out of the classroom to engage in in-depth field research, visiting sites and interviewing decision-makers and stakeholders – often quite prominent people, such as the police commissioner and congressmen and women. 'The ultimate goal is that they [students] understand that places that they live in are not naturally occurring, but the products of decision-making', says Gaspar, and 'see that it is knowable,

and that they can be agents and hold those decision-makers accountable.'

Each Urban Investigation takes 80-120 contact hours, including a preliminary week of face-to-face coaching with student groups, engaging art and design to create effective educational tools based on their focused research around a question about how the city works. Through these means, students come to see 'the city as the product of a decision-making landscape and are empowered to participate in it'. A typical scenario, says Gaspar, is when 'you think you know the answer to an urban question', but in trying to explain it to someone, realise that 'you don't really know how it works'.[2] The resulting understanding of related social, political and economic issues also enables CUP collaborators to grasp the processes, problematics and nuances of decision-making that form part of shaping policy.

The ethos of Urban Investigations is one of everyone – students and teachers alike – figuring things out together. The Big Squeeze project, for example, brought CUP together with teaching artist Chat Travieso and a group of high-school students from Bushwick's Academy of Urban Planning in Brooklyn to investigate small modular living spaces. The students asked urban planners about

Bottom: A street vendor shows off his Vendor Power! publication, which helps vendors to know their rights and avoid fines by making the rules easier to understand, 2009.

Below: Shelter Skelter project: CUP students review final design changes for a poster they created on the way in which homeless shelters are sited in New York, 2014.

regulatory hurdles, architects about prefabricated units, developers about funding and community advocates about their concerns about this housing type and whether it meets community needs, and created a 'Big Squeeze' poster based on their research. 'We're really interested in collaborating with the students for their visual sensibilities', says Gaspar, and 'for them to see that the physical, the social and the economic in the places where they live, aren't givens.'

As Gaspar also stresses, 'we train students to be really good interviewers', to ask the 'different stakeholders tough questions', to document interviews through video, photos and notes, to look closely and deconstruct the scenario, and to critically evaluate the wide-ranging answers.[3] CUP is now making a guide about interviewing strategies. It encourages students to switch roles, and after their interviews to explore ideas through making things – for example, visual media such as animations, or even puppets representing different policies – and to reenact some of the interviews and hypothesise about alternative outcomes. The next step is for the students to present their findings in public, as an opportunity to show where they have reached in the process and their awareness of the issue. The work they create is always shown publicly. For example, Bodega Down Bronx, a video about food deserts and food access issues, has been shown more than 50 times at venues around the world ranging from the New Museum and New York's MoMA PS1 to the Rotterdam Architecture Biennale. The community organisation interviewed as part of these projects will often distribute the final product, helping to raise awareness, both as regards social justice and in an art context.

Another CUP Urban Investigations project, Shelter Skelter, explored homeless shelters in New York, where there are more than 55,000 homeless people. The key issues examined were who decides where they go and why some boroughs have taken on more than others. Teaching artist Patrick Rowe with CUP worked with students at CUNY College Now, a programme designed to prepare NYC's high-school →

The toolkits don't have an agenda. It's more about breaking down policy and seeing what the neighbourhood looks like

students for success at college, at Hostos Community College in the Bronx. The students interviewed the Department of Homeless Services, an advocacy group, a Community Board Member, a shelter provider and a City Council Member. While many may associate youth with cynical thinking, Gaspar says that at CUP they think that cynicism is 'the root of critical thinking. We try to find where it comes from, find out what's behind it, and try to help the students develop it as a criticality which is about participating in the decisions' being made around them.

When it comes to CUP's community education programmes, 'it's really critical to have the groups being impacted by the issues work with us. We're not interested in civic engagement as an abstract idea', but rather in 'specific scenarios where it can have an impact, if people are already concerned about an issue they want to do something about.'[4] From very early on, CUP set up programmes to enable the groups to respond: 'Making Policy Public', centring on complex social policy issues that would benefit from visual explanation; 'Envisioning Development', hands-on workshop tools on development issues, such as zoning; 'Public Access Design', a multi-media programme launched in 2013; and 'Technical Assistance', for groups wanting to collaborate on issues that may not fit into the first three headings. The proposals resulting from the open calls are selected by juries of leading design world figures and leaders in community organising.

The range of issues to which CUP's unique form of advocacy responds extends to vital, but often neglected areas of public communication. Its visual tools addressing each area are designed to match the specific context, and serve as catalysts for group discussions and activities, such as workshops and campaigning. A very popular pamphlet in the Making Policy Public programme is 'Vendor Power', outlining street vendors' rights. It was created in collaboration with the Street Vendor Project organisation and designer Candy Chang (see Neighborland, page 220). Because vendors speak many different languages, the pamphlet is visually focused, with illustrations, rather than text heavy. It is also intended to educate those who are not vendors and who may be unaware of policies affecting this informal sector. New York police officers apparently find it hard to understand the regulations for street vending, and issue many fines erroneously. Street vendors across the city's five boroughs now use the pamphlet to demonstrate that they are following the rules.

From street vending (2009) to fracking (2013), and from 'redistricting'[5] (2010) to federalism (2011), the range of social justice issues impacting urban communities seems endless. For young people who have been arrested and need to learn about their rights, with graphic novelist Danica Novgorodoff and the Center for Court Innovation, CUP created 'I got arrested! Now what?', a comic-book guide to the juvenile justice system; this is now distributed widely by the New York City Department of Probation to young people who are arrested.

In its Envisioning Development programme, CUP launched 'What is Affordable Housing?' in 2010, now used regularly by more than 90 organising groups in New York, and 'What is Zoning?' in 2013. These are toolkits with hands-on activities using different visual elements to make issues that confuse even the most rigorous researcher, crystal clear for a wide audience, empowering them to take positive action. 'It helps people understand the

Right:
Parents of New York schoolchildren review 'Schools Are Us', another issue of 'Making Policy Public', at the poster's launch event, 2014.

Left:
City residents learn about how to advocate for park improvements at the launch of How Can I Improve My Park?, another issue of Making Policy Public, 2014.

issues better, but also to remember them better, as it gives them a mental map', Gaspar explains.

CUP's 'What is Affordable Housing?' includes info-graphic elements that allow communities to see neighbourhood incomes and how they relate to rent costs, as well as what affordability programmes are available and who qualifies for them. The toolkit can be used by groups to advance in-depth discussions about the specific workings of housing policy and issues of eligibility in relation to income levels, and what members wish to see happening in the development of their neighbourhood. Understanding the system, because it has been visualised so clearly, is a fast door opener for workshop participants, who also have access to an interactive map they can use after the workshop.

'Organisers all over the country need tools like this. The toolkits are meant to increase the capacity of organisers to do the work they already do – they fit into their work', says Gaspar. 'The toolkits don't have an agenda. It's more about breaking down policy and seeing what the neighbourhood looks like. Then it's down to the organising group to layer in their own agenda, or to start working with their constituency group to create their own agenda.' It can happen that two opposing groups use the same CUP tool kits to contest each other.

What makes CUP work in New York is that there is 'such a robust community organising culture', born from its history of social justice groups and labour organising, along with 'an equally robust design culture to collaborate with'. CUP's advocacy work strongly influences other bodies in the public sector in New York but also further afield. CUP is adapting 'What Is Affordable Housing?' for Chicago, which also has a robust organising culture. In Pennsylvania, Pittsburgh's Urban Redevelopment Authority hired CUP to train some community leaders and educators to set up their own version of CUP's Urban Investigations. In 2014, Pittsburgh launched Urban Matters, and worked with local students to create their first project, a short video about land banking.

CUP is looking to continue to expand the impact of its existing programmes and projects. As the range of tools and the networks expands, there is increasing scope to discuss with partners possible evolutions of existing tools. As a small non-profit, CUP measures impact by counting numbers of 'anything we can' on the distribution side, says Gaspar. 'We also get the community organisations to quantify their proposed impact in advance', so that there is a road map. CUP carries out post-project evaluations with the project partners, immediately after the project and then again once a year, to get an overview with anecdotes and other feedback. 'We try to stay in people's orbit a little', she adds.

As a strategic network-based 'extra-actor' in the field, devoted to issues-based citizen engagement and learning in New York through information design, and to participatory planning tied to decision-making, CUP's methodologies stem from the very genesis of the body. One of the most discerning community design and urban ecologies to date, it is an intelligent role model for others based elsewhere in the world, who need only to adapt it to their own contexts.

Clear Village

City branding and starchitecture-led planning alone cannot hope to create a transformative legacy for any urban context; indeed, any kind of 'copy-paste thinking by developers is a limited approach to placemaking', maintains Thomas Ermacora, the founder of design-driven, non-profit creative regeneration agency Clear Village – and co-author of this book.[1] He regards this 'tendency for urban spaces to be designed abstractly and in a distanced way from the people living in them' as a recipe for disaster.

Fuelled by his mission to build local capacity and resilience from the ground up, Ermacora also observes the paradox that, as funds for urban regeneration grow harder to find, instances of 'the city as product with a peacock attitude' are proliferating. Creating workable places for people calls for a full-blown alternative to current practices, investigating the DNA of a context. 'We need enquiries to attempt to understand the dynamics that govern places, or in other words, their operating system – one that conceives of them as intimate and interconnected social spaces, where the buildings and infrastructures are manifestations of life and not just the containers of it.'

Ermacora, who has a master's degree in geography specialising in sustainable and digital urbanism, and an undergraduate degree in international affairs and philosophy, is a self-taught architect and designer, who founded a boutique practice consultancy, Etikstudio, in 2003, doing eco-housing and low carbon footprint masterplanning, as well as curating exhibitions about 'slow living' cultures and their branding. He has collaborated and worked on projects with many prominent practices including Gehry Partners and Gehl Architects.

Finding limitations with commissioning models, and having diversified his time as a new media and technology investor-entrepreneur, Ermacora felt there was a need to shift his role in the field of urbanism and architecture towards social issues. These, he felt, were more pressing than the strict environmental focus he had been dedicated to, and if not resolved, would become a worse problem. Firstly he switched format to become a micro-scale developer with a conscience. Then the financial crunch in 2009 led him to

↑
Above:
Dynamic Dialogues, co-creative workshops created and staged by Clear Village at the City Theatre, Helsingborg, Sweden, November 2012.

Right:
Sketches made during the consultation Labs at MyPlace Cultural Centre, Harold Hill, as part of the Bedfords Park Walled Garden, a Clear Village project in Essex, March 2013.

Right:
Clear Village's Barcelona Launch Lab, November 2009.

adapt again, setting up Clear Village, specialising in integrated, participatory, process-driven interventions to help places reinvent themselves and build social cohesion, through high-level strategic consulting for social landlords, community groups and local authorities.

'Through our design processes and collaboration tools we initiate and curate strategic transitions, empowering communities to self-organise and turning neglected spaces into valuable assets that help mend broken neighbourhoods', says Ermacora, who chose the name Clear Village because 'the village scale is optimal for achieving sustainability through clear systems thinking, building on existing assets through a process that happens on the community's terms.' Clear Village's seasoned catalytical activities in participatory and tactical urbanism (such as urban acupuncture, see Architecture for Humanity, page 108), in various urban settings of segregation and decline, are driven by his fervent belief in the power of the open society, and particularly its contemporary capacity to enable ground-up activities and empowerment through the shared physical-digital platforms and tools of wiki culture. This expression of DIY in the face of changing political, economic, climatic and social shifts, interprets needs for sustainable lifestyles and activities geared towards particular communities which offer greater resiliency for all members.

Ermacora's concern has always been about how to design for the other 90%, and therefore how to scale appropriate designs in that context. From early in his career, he was convinced that 'a hands-on, ground up approach through co-creation of projects was a stronger way to embed lasting change because I have witnessed the devastating effects of eagle-eye decision-making removed from realities'. He has always been moved by a sense that community members' lack of scope – rather than any lack of ability to act – prevented them from playing determining roles affecting their own public realm, as well as appalled by absurd bureaucratic burdens and constraints, empire building and corruption.

Over the years Ermacora has registered the evolution in placemaking tactics. Widespread regeneration of post-industrial spaces now takes place, with varying degrees →

Ermacora's concern has always been how to design for the other 90%, and how to scale appropriate designs in that context

of long-term success; emergency/disaster relief architecture has forged advanced approaches pretty much globally; and slum upgrading is a much more widespread endeavor than it was. However, he has also observed a widening gap between the few who can afford the talents of great architects and urbanists, and the rest, who lack that luxury of skill and vision. There are 'perennial resource conflict zones', between, for example, 'idyllic villages' supported in their revival, and 'lost villages needing a reboot. There is no sense in claiming a monopoly on happiness in gated places.'

Taking action, Ermacora began to instigate micro-scale design interventions in abandoned urban spaces, seeing them as potential local game changers. The participatory and co-creation design tools, processes and frameworks he began to formulate, and continues to develop, were and are inspired by insights gained from empirical research, appreciative enquiry and a detailed pattern language-driven analysis of a locality and its inhabitants.

Below:
The Garden Angels Lab held in October 2011 at Bedfords Park Walled Garden, Essex, a Clear Village project.

In the past few years alone, Clear Village has tested out a range of methods in over ten different countries – ranging from Italy, the Galapagos, Finland and Sweden to the UK's east London. Its assignments are always strongly culturally driven in the sense that they aim to respect and augment local knowledge, deepening and broadening social potential: giving a theatre a new identity as a community hub; bridging social divide through new curatorial angles and programming; 'designing out' street crime after riots in Tottenham, north London, in 2011 (for the Design Council); creating a new task force to undertake urban prototyping for the World Design Capital Helsinki; nurturing the dreams of small-town residents; and curating a programme of interventions to bring more attention to the Grand Canal in Hangzhou, China, with aspiring spatial reformers and students from CAA (Central Arts Academy).

Clear Village is currently steering three major projects with multi-year funding: Bedfords Park Walled Garden, Essex, with Havering Council, funded mainly by the Big Lottery Fund and Veolia; Small Works, beta-testing social enterprise hubs to deliver alternative welfare solutions in the derelict spaces in low-income communities, with the Peabody Trust and supported by a range of grant-giving organisations; and Human Cities, a four-year programme focused on the revitalisation of the public realm in Europe, supported by the Creative Cities programme of the European Union in collaboration with a consortium of academic and research institutions including Cité du Design Saint-Etienne.

Clear Village's USP stems from its a series of interrelated modes of operation. 'We research and produce custom-designed tools for participatory design projects, and curate and realise a variety of kinds of spatial interventions, programmes and social enterprise activities for community-led organisations', says Ermacora. These tools, partly developed in-house, partly borrowed from other contexts, include well-being analyses, a kind of place-scan Ermacora invented and intends to turn

into digital format soon, and World Café or IDEO-style co-visioning. 'We sow seeds for positive urban futures in a variety of ways. We can also formulate and carry out appropriate coaching activities based on our evidence-based interpretation of what is needed in a particular place, to help enable community groups to become capable, in time, of managing and advancing the outcomes themselves.'

Highly significantly at this pivotal time when localism needs to come into its own, Clear Village is also 'a campaigner, building fund-raising and branding strategies with community members. All our projects serve as catalysts for local visions that each local community we work with can embrace, and funders can take on until the time that a social enterprise we spawn can build a sustainable foundation for self operation in which we also assist with the handover.' What Ermacora knows is that 'it is hard to rely strictly on grassroots tactics, which often lack method and tend to disregard the value of tried and tested ideas from elsewhere. Creative regeneration is a hybrid, bridging between the formal and the informal to create healthier ground', he adds, 'allowing people at times to become guerrilla activists if necessary.'

Creative regeneration is a hybrid, bridging between the formal and the informal to create healthier ground – with people as guerrilla activists if necessary

Clear Village is deliberately versatile and hands-on, and also attempts to deliver the 'full recode, instead of partial recodes' (see page 70) commonly undertaken by other participatory agencies, which often do not take responsibility for such a wide spectrum of activities. Many also do not physically locate themselves on sites over an extended period, nor take on long-term leases, but come and go. Ermacora views Clear Village's style of community presence as what he terms 'participatory entrepreneurship'. This is a vital element of his concern to develop novel ways and means to stimulate the build-up of place capital. His organisation designs and deploys a range of competencies, from design and anthropology to social enterprise and coaching, all of which aim to engage communities and stakeholders in open dialogues about their future.

'Our participatory placemaking journeys usually start by structured and recorded listening, in order to better understand the context, then advance on action research and what we are calling a well-being analysis, composed of qualitative and quantitative data; these are followed by co-design workshops and scenario planning. All of this together forms a body of work geared to reconfigure the local narratives and play a part in →

↖ **Top:**
Clear Village team members Frank Van Hasselt, Robin Houterman and Paul King discuss plans for new greenhouses at Bedfords Park Walled Garden.

↑ **Above:**
At Clear Village's consultation Labs for its Bedfords Park Walled Garden project, MyPlace Cultural Centre, Harold Hill, Essex.

Left:
Workshop staged as part of Clear Village's Make Your Space event, Small Works Hackney, 27 October 2012.

strategic regeneration', Ermacora says. These actions and steps are each marked by strong design and media inputs to support the fund-raising efforts and awareness as well as continued involvement by the local community, which are the bedrocks of Clear Village's sustainability and resilience thinking. It is the journey from piloting a project to finding ways for self-sufficient social enterprises embedded within the community that truly distinguishes Clear Village.

Ermacora came into the field of participatory placemaking with experience in sustainable architecture and urban design at multiple scales, and could have continued as a specialist in creating 'green' neighbourhoods, but was frustrated with a vision of sustainability revolving around clunky 'smart city' kits, that in his opinion were aggravating social segregation. As he says, 'what is the point of green neighbourhoods if only the few can live in them? How is that going to improve our overall carbon emissions?' Instead, he is convinced that participatory placemaking and social enterprise as vectors, using the vocabulary and techniques of architecture, represent the road forward, not just for him but many of his peers, too.

Realising participatory placemaking full cycle, from the earliest stages of inception and conceptual thinking, fund-raising and piloting, to developing management and appropriate staffing, including volunteers, designing, branding and marketing, requires a recognition that every situation has its own differences and potentials. New stakeholder dynamics need to be orchestrated ahead of the point when 'we progressively step out of the picture and hand over to a competent local community group, which Clear Village assists in pursuing self-sustaining operating models relying on reciprocity and civic volunteerism'.

Many scenarios today represent reduction or neglect of facilities and spaces, and Clear Village's antennae track contexts in which the agency can perform a genuine turnaround in fortunes, creating new centres, hubs and networks. The Small Works Programme is an example of such. In the UK, among the decimating effects of the financial crisis of 2009 was the closure of many community centres on housing estates and others funded by local authorities. In Haringey, north London, for example, about two-thirds of the community centres in Haringey were closed down in one season alone. After the riots in

What is the point of green neighbourhoods if only the few can live in them, asks Ermacora

Left:
Bedfords Park Walled Garden, Essex, before any work done, winter 2010.

English cities in August 2011, a number of activist groups engaged as social enterprise charities and philanthropic bodies emerged across the UK and debated the crisis. They proposed that many of the disused spaces in housing estates should host a new kind of community centre favourable to social enterprise, replacing some of the services that these bodies would have provided through a principle of reciprocity that would give low-rent opportunities in exchange for space management and activation.

Michael Norton, founder of UnLtd (providing support to social entrepreneurs) and the Centre for Innovation and Voluntary Action (CIVA), decided to champion this cause, obtaining funding from the Esmée Fairbairn Foundation and the Tudor Trust to support a pilot project through the Art In Empty Spaces programme developed by Hackney Council. An initial organisation called Rollmop Art was set up with the support of CIVA representative Chris Vaughan, to activate space on the Regent Estate in Hackney.

Clear Village, based close by the project, got involved in 2011, providing process and design intelligence. 'We conducted a well-being analysis that studied mapped tenants' levels of satisfaction, aspirations and preferences. We used our tool both to visually comprehend and communicate some of the gaps and to define appropriate types of interventions to deal with them in the public realm and within the spaces allocated. The extra benefit of this approach was to further a relationship with the local community as well as with Hackney Homes and Hackney Council', says Ermacora.

The work enabled Ermacora to develop branding for the project, and to extend the conceptual framework into a programme geared to transform the estate's abandoned places into a new-generation empowerment and enterprise hub. A number of social enterprises were invited to sign up to hot-desk in the space, and Clear Village organised a number of events such as baking, dancing and bicycle repair workshops with different organisations in the area. These helped to kick-start a new round of fund-raising and business development, to enable the project to scale up from this single location to others. In 2013 a second hub was opened in Victoria, for another demographic housed by the Peabody Trust (part of g15, the body representing London's largest not-for-profit housing associations, which together build one in four of all new homes in London). Today a third centre is open and busy near King's Cross, and Small Works has been shortlisted for awards such as European Social Business Innovation Award as well as the Big Venture Challenge to scale the programme, and make a significant outlet for tailored social services and enterprise incubation across the UK, while improving the public realms of tired housing estates.

Another current regeneration project Clear Village is leading is a unique take at converting an abandoned heritage site. Concentrated currently due to funding avenues on developing a new local food and gardening culture in a context of great historic interest, the project revolves around both restoring a walled garden and providing an experiential and professionalising learning ground for the groups in its catchment area. Bedfords Park Walled Garden, on the edge of London in Essex, is a community food growing and gardening space set within a small nature reserve. A walled kitchen garden was first built on the site in the 1770s, and fruit and flowers were grown there for the owners of the Bedfords country estate (where there was once an ancient manor dating back to the early 13th century, now only visible in the form of its front steps). →

Left:
Clear Village's Small Works Hackney consultation, September 2013.

I see Clear Village as a meta-design organisation experimenting with how to re-engineer welfare in the interstices and edges of cities, where it has failed or never reached

Right:
Clear Village's Small Works Hackney consultation, September 2013.

Once royal hunting grounds and now part of a piece of suburbia that has reduced the old village of Havering-atte-Bower to a minimal footprint, the park is on a hill that separates London from its green belt. 'The park is a gate between urban areas and rural areas of Essex, as well as a bridge between an affluent and a disadvantaged community, symptomatic of the effects of uncontrolled sprawl', says Ermacora. The wealthy estate, replete with greenhouses and hothouses, exemplified 18th-century horticultural innovation, with its pineapple house ingeniously heated by manure, one of very few such examples in the UK of that period. In the 100x62m garden the owners grew delicate peach trees through the winter, thanks to steam engines heating its north wall; the engines also pumped water from ponds, still visible today outside the garden walls, to the main house.

In 1933, the Bedfords estate was bought by Romford Urban District council, now the London Borough of Havering, and the house and its gardens were opened to the public. The walled garden operated as a nursery, growing the bedding plants needed for all the borough's urban parks, but was also used to grow food for disadvantaged local communities. Although the whole site was covered in greenhouses, nothing was growing in the ground itself and the valuable topsoil had been removed many years before. Because of safety concerns about the deteriorating walls, the nursery was forced to close in 1999. After many years of neglect and the further dilapidation of the walls the site became a jungle.

In 2008, the Friends of Bedfords Park, seeing the garden's potential as a community asset, attempted with the council to reopen the site by searching for grants to restore the garden into a usable plot. Ermacora was shown the space by Simon Parkinson, the Council's head of culture and leisure at, as he was planning a festival in the park with his creative partner, artist and local resident Imogen Heap. He offered to help activate the space and campaign for it through a collaborative lab, to which Imogen drew attention through her social media and fan base. Clear Village brought local stakeholders together, in particular the Essex Wildlife Trust and the Havering-atte-Bower Conservation Society.

Having reached that point, steps could then be taken towards incremental change: building the new vision for the garden, gathering a team of 'Garden Angel' volunteers from all over the globe, and successfully securing a substantial Big Lottery Food Grant in 2012 – the first of nine sums in grant-aid Clear Village secured overall from public, charity and private donors, including Veolia, making it one of the largest open-air charitable schemes within the greater London area. All these enabled the garden to be brought back to life, this time as an active and engaging community space, enhancing local well-being. 'Growing food and learning to cook bonds people and is a channel for awareness of health

and rekindling a relationship with the natural world, all while breaking the barriers between generations and welcoming individuals from all walks of life, even the most challenged ones. Gardens can be our mini Edens that make the "big society" idea – not the political one [see The Rise of Bottom-up Placemaking, page 18] but the conceptual one – actually happen.'[2]

From the beginning the local community has been deeply engaged in the project, day by day, seeing evidence that change is possible through collective dreams and actions. Workshops in schools from 2012 involved some 300 children. Big Digs in 2013 and 2014 saw around 80 people. The team's effort has been to connect with organisations such as Seetec, which focuses on reintroducing young offenders to society, with the long-term unemployed, people with physical and mental disabilities, children in low-income situations, and with groups like Age Concern, to deliver high social impact. These form the main bulk of volunteers working in the walled garden today.

The 'Grow, Cook, Eat' programme Clear Village started in the summer 2014 is now heralded as an example by the local council and may be taken into other sites as an extra-curricular activity to help avoid the early onset of obesity and diabetes, and diminish the effects of degenerative mental diseases. But more importantly, locals are proud of it: 'This is the most exciting thing that has happened in the community in the last 30 years', said one local volunteer.[3]

In the space of three years the Walled Garden has been almost fully restored. While the design does not respect the original configuration, the 3.4m-high perimeter brick walls are partly rebuilt to heritage standards, and a 60m section of lean-to greenhouses has been built. The various growing techniques and climate options (from oceanic to Mediterranean and tropical biomes) within the greenhouses make them extraordinary demonstrators of horticultural techniques, including traditional, permacultural and biodynamic. Some 6,000sq metres of land was transformed; half of this is now productive growing space, which registered 3,850 meals from the 2013 harvest with the Capital Growth Harvest-ometer. 'We may be the first to show how pineapples where grown prior to the industrial revolution' says Kirsty McArdle, project manager.[4]

Bottom:
Bedfords Park Walled Garden, Essex, autumn 2014, after three years of care by Clear Village.

Ermacora also curates events and happenings to expand the mandate of the place beyond growing food. In 2013, Midsummer Night was marked by festivities and a public exhibition, and the London Contemporary Orchestra played at a Harvest Moon festival attended by 150 visitors, 600 schoolchildren and 40 disabled young people. 'Culture serves as a lubricant in the complex equation of regeneration here', he maintains.

'I see Clear Village as a meta-design organisation experimenting with how to re-engineer welfare in the interstices and edges of cities, where it has failed or never reached', says Ermacora. 'It is in those contexts that our efforts are the most valuable and add most to people's livelihoods.' To achieve this he is attempting to create a new type of contract for places informed by what people want, because in fact 'it has not been the norm to establish a social contract in urbanism, and our work is really about preventing chronic disaster patterns in a cost-effective way, healing rather than treating the pains of uninspired placemaking'.

Collectif Etc

'Our projects try to get the people involved in the making of the city', says Victor Mahé, co-founder of Collectif Etc, a young architecture and urban design studio based in Strasbourg, eastern France.[1] 'Civil society lacks autonomy. That's a reason why urban planning is disconnected from its interests. We are less acting for urban consultations organised by public authorities, than working for social empowerment and community organising.'

Collectif Etc began life in 2009 when a group of architectural students began making art in the streets of Strasbourg, leading to some commissions for small-scale urban projects. 'We wanted to experiment with real interventions outside the university boundaries', says Mahé. Gradually the group learned how to work with locals on the streets. Collectif Etc has architectural, graphic design and urban planning skills, and now, after more than 35 projects in different urban locations, the group's fortunes have reached a turning point. Its work has contributed to an emerging movement in France adopting transversally effective approaches cutting through the traditional, top-down system through which French cities have been made, to create new, open-source and trans-disciplinary networks.

Collectif Etc's experience is that 'politically, it's always great – no municipality can say "no" to somebody who comes and says, "Ok, I'm trying to legitimise any action on the public space: do you accept that or not?" They can't say "no", or they will lose votes at the next election.'[2] Mahé explains that 'some citizens, urban professionals and public authorities are willing to introduce this transversal approach'. But it is tough to 'make the different entities currently involved in the decision-making process of urban planning work together in a fair and equal manner. Our projects attempt to create democratic means by which people coming from different backgrounds can find solutions together.'

For at least the last two decades, urban and town planning in France and Western Europe has followed a complex and very hierarchical logic, and users are often excluded from the decision-making process. As Mahé says, 'the work of professionals remains distanced from [users'] reality'. Citizens can participate in city making in one of three ways. First, they can act passively, in which case they have only weak margins for manoeuvre in future plans; secondly, they can take part in framed deliberations and final outcomes through public meetings and polls. In both these scenarios, they are not always the originators of the process,

Above left:
The Détour de France team cycling through Provence in their tour of of 21 French cities to meet residents, local government officials and private firms, 2011-12.

Above:
The Détour de France team looking at a former charcoal factory in Montceau-les-Mines.

and professionals and elected officials take decisions on the basis of a synthesis of individual judgements. The public is disengaged from the responsibility of creating the project.

But a third scenario presents itself: when people interact, drawn out through various methods such as practical workshops, debates and meetings, they can start to propose solutions and experiment with them. Furthermore, they are involved as being among those responsible during the various stages of conception, becoming motors of the project with a say in the 'fabrique citoyenne de la ville' ('the urban factory of citizenship').

Collectif Etc's activities straddle many disciplines and fields of intervention, reaching a highly varied public across France. An atmosphere of apprenticeship pervades its projects. Local people are engaged in construction, conversion, gardening, painting and furniture-making. Collectif Etc also involves those who are rarely given responsibility in traditional urban planning – for →

> **An emerging movement adopting transversal approaches cutting through the traditional, top-down system to create open-source, transdisciplinary networks**

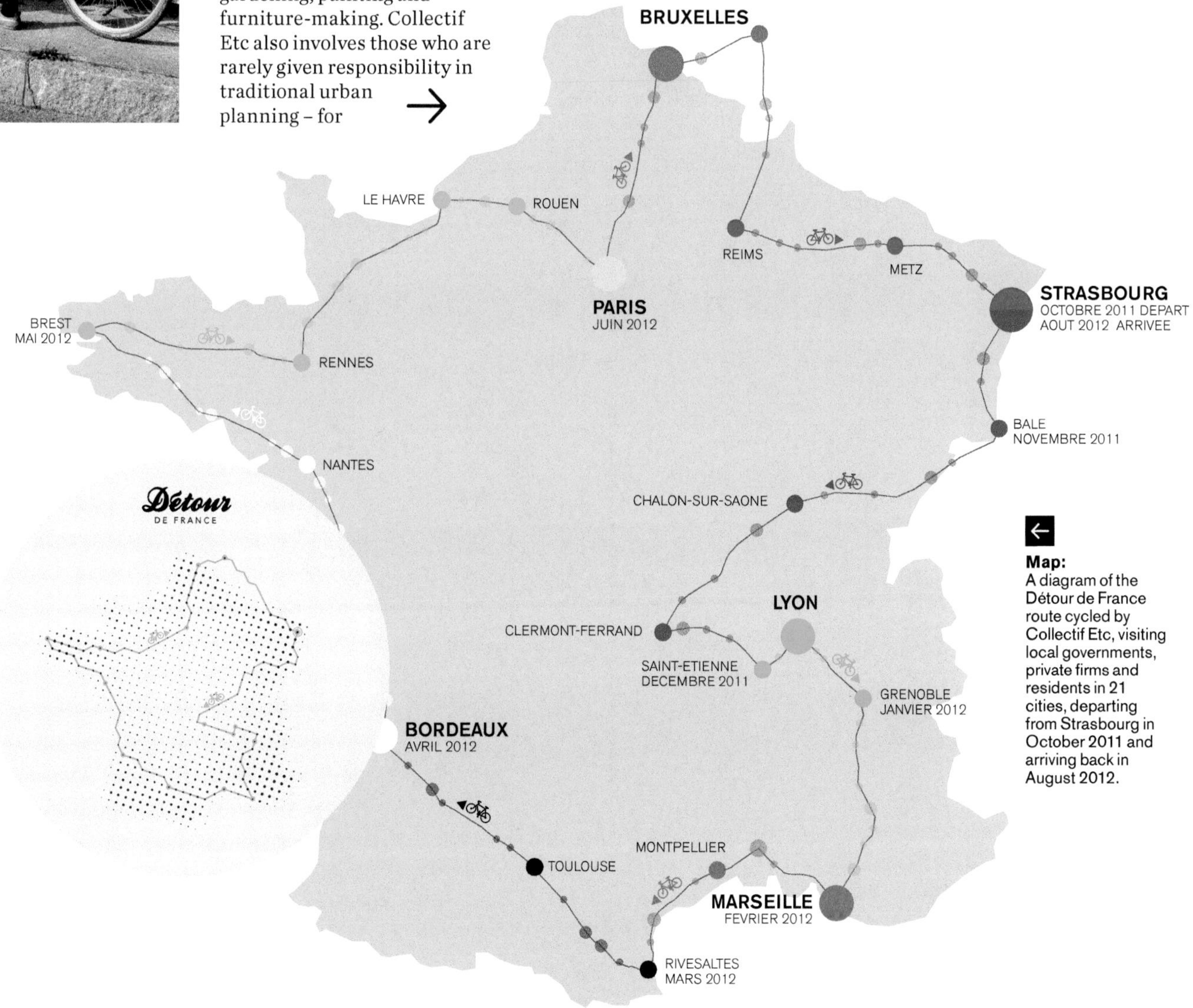

Map: A diagram of the Détour de France route cycled by Collectif Etc, visiting local governments, private firms and residents in 21 cities, departing from Strasbourg in October 2011 and arriving back in August 2012.

example children, pensioners and the unemployed.

The group is closely identified with its Détour de France project, which was backed by EU funding. In 2011 12 members of Collectif Etc – 11 architects and a graphic designer – cycled to 21 cities including Saint-Etienne, Lyon, Grenoble, Marseille, Montpellier, Toulouse, Bordeaux, Nantes, Brest, Rennes, Paris, Lille and Brussels, and made two tours of their home city of Strasbourg. At each urban centre they met stakeholders to probe issues and make connections, but also central and local government departments and private firms.

Collectif Etc is keen to emphasise that the Détour de France initiative was based on pre-existing underlying networks. Many of the protagonists had been working in a socially participatory way for 10-15 years. The group's initiatives are best thought of 'as the outcome of some European and US urban struggles in the 1970s. What is new is the multiplication of these actions, their increasing positive reception by public authorities and in the wider media coverage (which tend to omit these broad and political roots).'

Below:
On the Moon, Hénin-Beaumont, July 2012, Collectif Etc and Les Saprophytes. Making a film in a private garden with some of the neighbours in acting roles.

Right:
On the Moon, Hénin-Beaumont, July 2012, Collectif Etc and Les Saprophytes. Village party with a space-age feel, on top of the abandoned slag heap left behind by the local mining industry.

On the moon

Turning a 'lost' coal-mining ground into a memorable play area for local community

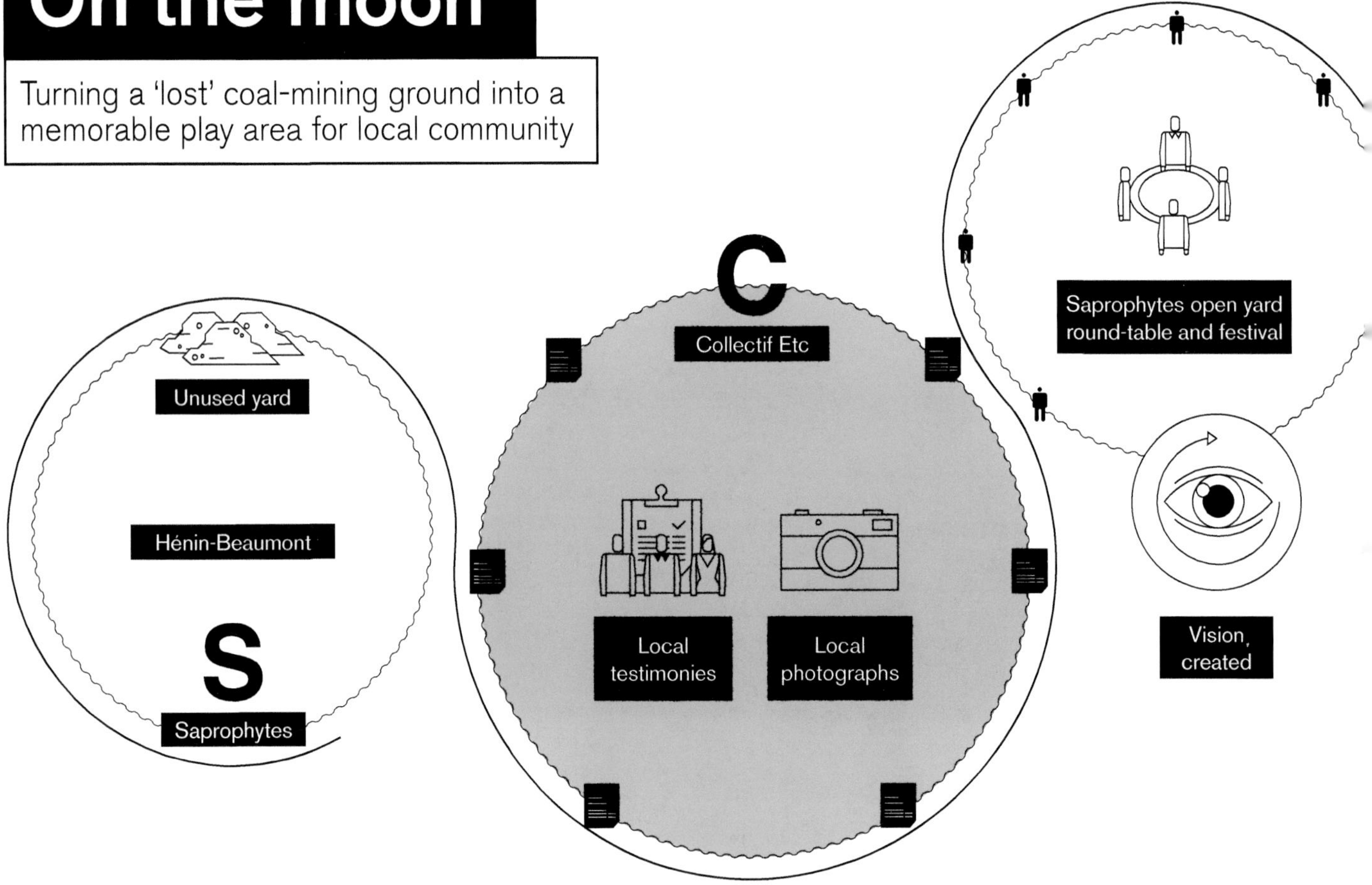

Unused yard

Hénin-Beaumont

S

Saprophytes

C

Collectif Etc

Local testimonies

Local photographs

Saprophytes open yard round-table and festival

Vision, created

The urban contexts of Détour de France vary immensely, from inner-city areas to suburbs and villages, but much of the terrain is 'left-behind' places. Among them are wasteland in Strasbourg, a derelict town-centre square in Bordeaux, unclassified public space in Rennes, a psychiatric hospital in Montpellier, and the impoverished northern districts of Marseille. There are also forgotten tracts of urban heritage in Hénin-Beaumont, a former coal-mining town in northern France where the French National Front party has made advances in recent years. Sometimes Collectif Etc's work has parallelled emerging political and urban opportunities, such as →

ENGAGEMENT
REPLICABILITY
DESIGN DRIVEN
SCALE
IMPACT

> **During project conception, local people are its motors: they have a major say in the 'urban factory' of citizenship**

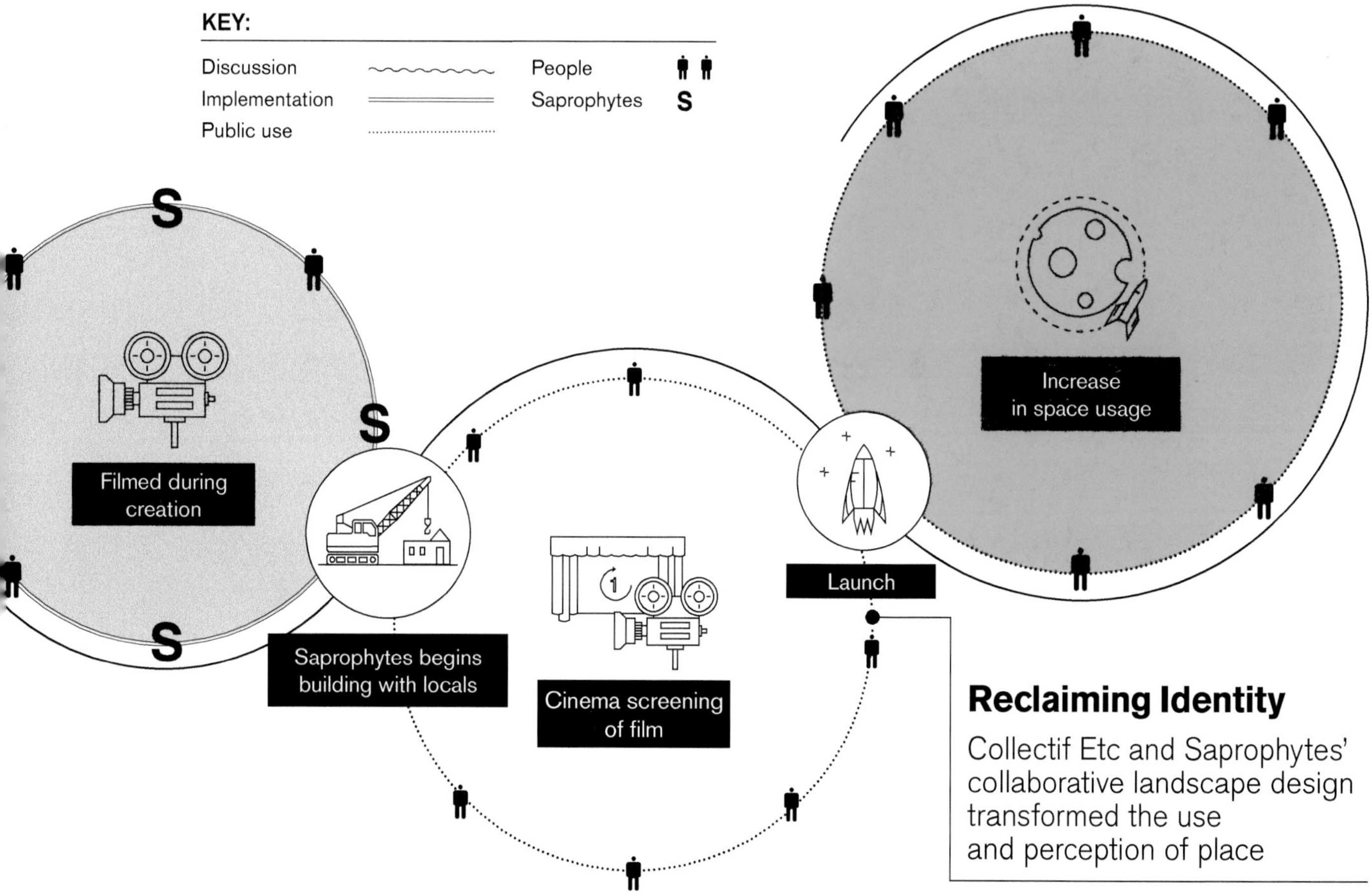

KEY:

Discussion
Implementation
Public use
People
Saprophytes S

S
Filmed during creation
S
S
Saprophytes begins building with locals
Cinema screening of film
Launch
Increase in space usage

Reclaiming Identity

Collectif Etc and Saprophytes' collaborative landscape design transformed the use and perception of place

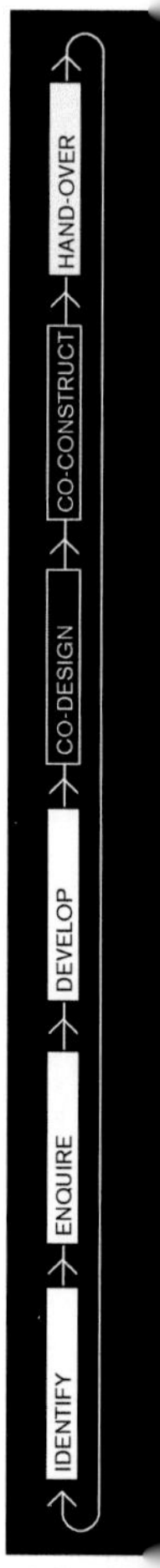

IDENTIFY → ENQUIRE → DEVELOP → CO-DESIGN → CO-CONSTRUCT → HAND-OVER

large-scale urban planning projects in Bordeaux and Rennes; on other occasions it has taken place during times of political turmoil, as in the case of Hénin-Beaumont.

A full analysis of the sites led to findings that have been published online and in print, and to small projects with locals defined at each location – for buildings, street furniture or public spaces. Collectif Etc met professionals, citizens and public-authority planning staff for discussions, leading to a second stage: the creation of a network of French urban plans and participants in each case. 'Some people in the different urban locations knew about each other; others didn't. We wanted them to interact and create a network of "collectifs". All the invitees were particularly interested in the fact that this network was timely, one among many others, constantly moving, not institutionalised.' The network existed simply because people had knowledge and wanted to communicate or work with one another.

In 2013 the group staged a reunion of the various 'collectifs', to which most of the people met during the Détour de France were able to gather to share their thoughts. The three-day meeting centred on several debates. Most of the cities represented 'have a strong need for new tools to rethink their urban policies', says Mahé, and he calls for public authorities and urban professionals to trust in civil society. 'We should especially rely on citizens' associations and workers' communities, but also on a new network of public departments and institutions at a communal or regional scale.'

As catalysts for a new urban order, Collectif Etc advocates a participative urbanism that is diversified by formal and less formal frameworks structured via a combined focus on aim, output and context in each case. Through a programme staged with Aix-Marseille University, the team is inventing new modes of citizens' responsibilities in local decision-making on urban planning, combining its research with that of academic researchers in sociology.

Transversal civic politics – challenging the traditional, top-down system operating in French cities with new open-source, holistic networks directly tackling social needs – is on the rise. So as to further mobilise such a process, Collectif Etc collaborates and shares skills with different civic entities in order to understand the different interests involved. The group enjoys working with rural villages, leading carpentry workshops for locals on building sites. 'We use our skills as architects to create moments, pedagogic activities, workshops, debates, where people can meet.' It becomes part of civic dialogues so that it can 'convince urban planners that people should have a say'.

In Bordeaux, Collectif Etc's Café sur Place project helped a local association to open a café. In Rennes's place de Prague in Rennes, with the graphic designers Le Fabricatoire the group conceived an 'enchanted forest' consisting of a wooden

Below:
On the Moon, Hénin-Beaumont, July 2012, Collectif Etc and Les Saprophytes. Neighbours acting in the film made for the project, at the foot of the staircase from the street to the peak of the hill.

Right:
On the Moon, Hénin-Beaumont, July 2012, Collectif Etc and Les Saprophytes. Staircase and toboggan run shaped like a spaceship launch ramp, and installed from the street to the very top of the hill.

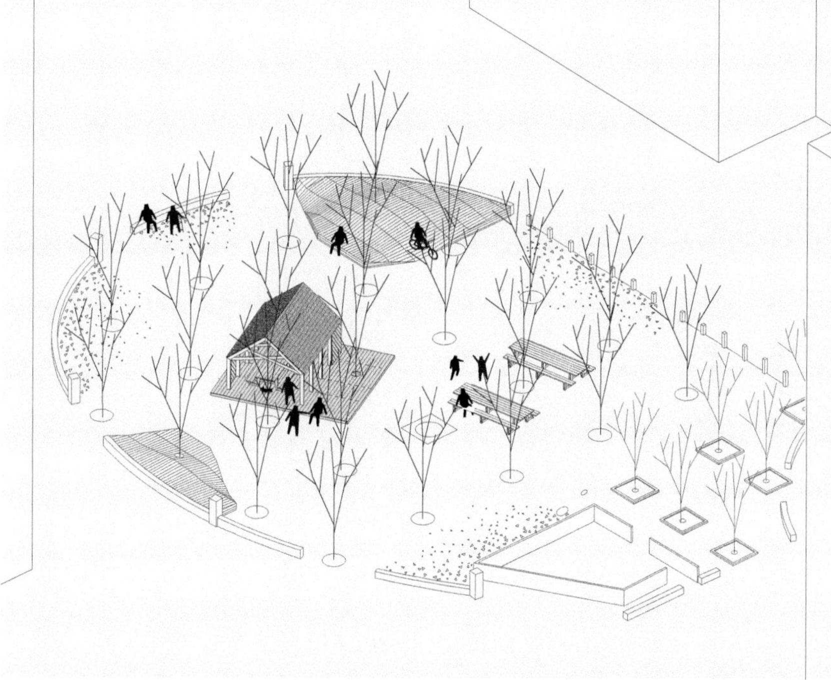

> The aim was to show the public authorities, as well as inhabitants and local associations, an alternative way to occupy a huge charcoal mound left by the mining industry

cabin, some picnic furniture and a raised fringe area where people could meet. The process also built up the local group's prominence in the eyes of the authorities.

For the On the Moon project at Hénin-Beaumont, Collectif Etc collaborated with the architects and landscape designers Les Saprophytes, who had originated the project. The aim was to show the public authorities, as well as inhabitants and associations, an alternative way to occupy a huge charcoal mound wasteland left by the local mining industry, redefining history and topography, memory and culture. Collectif Etc designed wooden geodesic domes on the site, plus stairs and a giant slide, a new means of climbing the difficult, inaccessible hill and returning to ground in a more playful way.

For Mahé, 'what matters is living together in a place'. Collectif Etc has staged social events such as concerts, dinners, games of pétanque, open-air cinema and round tables. Publicity was generated through its website and blog, posters, flyers and even postcards, and the local, national and international press covered the activities. The group emphasises being optimistic, open and oriented towards a spontaneous audience. With names like Dérives, Bon Plans pour le Refuge, Cuisine Mobile, A Nous le Parking, Conversations Lumineuses, Légende Urbaine, La Façade Habitée and Médaillon Funk, many of Collectif Etc's projects denote playful, pop-culture suggestiveness directly expressing deep-rooted community aspirations for their localities.

Across the board, through dialogue and encounters Collectif Etc's projects open up new networks of social allegiances and skills to create wider processes. A building project's commissioning, design and construction process often takes place in a defended, territorial space, but under Collectif Etc's direction it becomes 'an opportunity for people to gather and exchange ideas', says Mahé, adding that the ritual of 'building time is a time for gathering, like a feast'. Through each event the cold, closed logic of hierarchical planning can be reversed into something profoundly generative and socially empowering.

Above left:
Place de Prague, in the district of Blosne, Rennes, June 2012. Transforming the derelict square into a small multifunctional 'enchanted forest' with a wooden cabin, picnic furniture and a raised fringe area for meetings.

Below:
Place de Prague, Rennes, June 2012. The wooden cabin at the centre of the transformed public square.

Alejandro Echeverri, Sergio Fajardo, Municipio de Medellín

At the end of the 1980s Medellín, the second most populous city in Colombia and capital of the province of Antioquia, was in the ranks of the world's most violent cities, with drugs cartels-related murders and crime spiralling in and around the *comunas* (slums) such as Comuna 13, La Candelaria and La Sierra. The city was the centre of operations and the final the hideout of the drug lord Pablo Escobar, killed in a shootout here in 1993. Since those days the painstaking building of a new narrative and programme of public works has led to a widely reported turnaround in the fortunes of the city. Through its strategic, holistic commitment to social urbanism and education, bringing the poorest areas into the heart of the city, Medellín has become a global reference point for those concerned with putting urban design in service to realising a new, equitable reality.

Today, while Medellín, which experienced a population explosion in the 1970s, has become a famous tourist destination, it still has a number of no-go areas for the vast majority of its population of 3.5 million inhabiting the metropolitan area. But the mix of new, transformative facilities includes new parks and plazas, including one along the rechannelled banks of the Medellín river, high-quality schools, the new Explora Park children's museum and the innovative renovation of the city's Botanic Gardens in the centre, at the intersection of districts, as well as an entirely new Metrocable gondola transportation system inserted into the vertiginous Andean river valley, giving the poorest communities better access to the rest of the city.

The new resources complement ongoing community programmes such as the Talleres del Sueño ('workshops of dreams'), promoting identity and a sense of place. Such concepts as transparency, participation, non-violence, innovation and resilience are not mere buzzwords; in alliance with social urbanism, these concepts have been the fundamental building blocks of its governmental policy and citizenship. This new era of hope bears witness to the success of the social consensus that, in the face of many

Top right: PUI Integral Urban Project, for the informal settlements on the slopes of north-east Medellín connected by cable-car lines, Alejandro Echeverri and team, Urbam, 2005-7.

Right: Fernando Botero Library and Park, San Cristóbal, one of five new library-parks positioned in areas of most need in the city, G Ateliers Architecture, 2008-11.

segregating tensions, drove the promotion of social urbanism – a term articulated by Sergio Fajardo, former mayor of Medellín and now the governor of the province of Antioquia. During his 2003-7 period of office in the city, Fajardo put all his energies behind the regeneration.

Academics, journalists and businessmen were part of a group of around 50 people who took on Fajardo's goal before his election as mayor, first thrashing out the axioms on which the plan was built, and then campaigning for him by walking the streets, handing out leaflets and establishing relationships with people. 'The way you get into power determines the way you govern', says Fajardo. 'We followed what we had been dreaming [of] all our lives. The ends justify the means... Every step that we take never contradicts the steps already taken. We have been consistent, building trust, and that you can never buy.'[1]

'Medellín, the most educated' and 'An engine of social transformation' were

slogans used to promote the group's plans for the city. Instead of a more limited approach, the programme of social urbanism in the poorest, informally occupied neighbourhoods of city turned the usual model of gentrification – as well as of traditional politics – upside down. 'Our most beautiful buildings must be in our most humble areas', Fajardo has said, so that people there feel recognised.[2] The urban team prioritised 'planning to not improvise', but to achieve defined long-term goals. 'We had to come up with an opportunities door. We decided to create a political city movement, in the city.'[3]

The social urbanism design and implementation programme was carried out by architect and urban designer Alejandro Echeverri, director of the Centre for Urban and Environmental Studies (Urbam, a new civic movement supported by other academics and NGOs) at Medellín's EAFIT University. As the municipality's director of urban projects, Echeverri's priority was to change the dynamics of the city, which is positioned in a cup-shaped valley full of creeks and with the informal settlements extending up the hills. His multifaceted and comprehensive plans included all the city's 16 districts, aiming to connect its divided territories. 'The plans really helped to build a →

new form of civility', which was necessary because 'Medellín is a very segregated city, physically and socially', says Echeverri. 'Our reality is very fragile, and very complex'.[4]

The plans encompassed projects for the city centre and for the Poblado (Medellín's wealthiest area, in the south-east), but also for districts high up on the hills that were especially impoverished. The city's new infrastructures, including a range of new amenities, was created in record time. The streets of the informal parts of the city have always been a focus of social life, and the improvements to streets such as Paseo Andalucia in the north-east of the city have also enabled a number of new businesses to be started. As part of the plans, Integral Urban Projects (PUIs) on the valley sides developed specific participatory strategies, involving many meetings with members of the *comunas*, and affecting physical, social and institutional aspects of these areas of the city that were at risk and had problems of inequality. While it is still quite early to assess the major changes brought by the PUIs, it is hoped that their impact has genuinely deepened local democracy.

The way Fajardo chose to solve the city's problems, opening new 'opportunities doors' for the future, was to improve through inclusive growth the urban context and quality of life for previously neglected community members. Education, science, entrepreneurship and culture have been treated as long-term means to reduce social inequality. People came to believe strongly in what Fajardo, his community director David Escobar, Echeverri and their respective teams were doing collaboratively, because they could both see and feel that 'architecture meant social transformation', as Fajardo puts it, and felt a strong sense of ownership.[5]

Medellín is widely appreciated globally as a role model, especially as its intervention process has drawn together public policy, inter-agency management, physical adaptations and community participation. It has nurtured and extended the existing assets of the city's cultural life, and opened up areas of the city people would never have dreamed to enter before. The ways in which the social and infrastructure programme, which included participatory budgeting,

Right:
The Media Ladera Viaduct, one of the PUI Integral Urban Projects, eastern centre, Medellín. César Augusto Hernández and team/City Hall, Secretariat of Public Works, 2010-11.

Left: The cable-car line above the Santo Domingo *comuna* in the north-east of Medellín, once one of the most dangerous districts, Alejandro Echeverri and team, Urbam, 2005-7.

has been financed has been scrutinised by academics as closely as have the physical improvements. To incubate a new economic climate for the city, the programme has involved the major utilities firms, through the Empresas Públicas de Medellín, a main pillar in the development of the city, diversifying their operations to help boost employment; this measure has reduced unemployment to single figures for the first time in 20 years.

The new public transport system combines urban train lines, cable-car lines, dedicated bus lanes, bike lanes and escalators for the city's challenging topography, while an urban mobility strategy includes a plan for a new tram system. Stations were deliberately located at the heart of troubled hillside comunas, turning the streets into public places where locals can see what is going on. This reduced tensions, as well as enabling movement from place to place and the generation of new activities.

The integrated nature of the urban planning introduced new bridges and housing schemes around some of the transport stops, relocating some people from the most precarious areas. People residing in the same valley, but previously divided by disconnected territories, were for the first time able not only to feel connected to the rest of the city but also to inhabit their own neighbourhoods differently – painting façades, for example, and using new buildings as programmatic hubs.

Similarly, the schools rehabilitation programme – which saw the upgrade of 132 existing schools were upgraded, plus the building of ten new schools in troubled neighbourhoods and five new 'parques educativos', or library-parks – brought a new sense of dignity. Striking, well-landscaped new-build public libraries were positioned in areas of most need. Among the most widely discussed globally is the Parque Biblioteca España, with its rough stone forms designed by architect Giancarlo Mazzanti; it is sited on the top of the mountain in Santa Domingo in the north-east, once one of the city's most dangerous districts. Each of these 'punctual interventions', including street improvements in each district, creates a new, distinct focal point and centre of social benefit.

New promenades and emblematic streets helped to transform city centre areas such as Carabobo-Cundinamarca. The formerly squalid and dangerous Parque de las Luces and its Edificio Carré was rehabilitated, the latter turned into the Centre for Education. One of the main roads through Medellín is now closed to traffic on Sundays, giving full rein to the city's joggers, cyclists, skateboarders, dog walkers and strollers. In the past, many districts that are today very active, were scarcely discussed: now they are perceived as part of the whole urban environment. →

Stations were deliberately located at the heart of the troubled hillside *comunas*, turning the streets into public places

↓ The entire exercise of connecting space through intentionally high-quality architecture and infrastructure has helped to create a new, highly significant symbolic mental map of the city, taking in the relationships between the hills and the valleys, for both residents and visitors. Such planning tactics have another beneficial dimension, as 'the geography of Medellín is very special', says Echeverri, referring to the many river creeks which had gradually disappeared due to uncontrolled urban development, and to the city, which is close to both the Pacific Ocean and the Caribbean Sea, and has important biodiversity.[6]

More recently Echeverri has been building a new transdisciplinary school at Urbam combining urban design, environmental, social and political programmes, and has played a role with a number of local and international student workshops about the city. 'Our work is for the people', he explains. 'In the past, in the university, we did a lot of abstractions, but we have to put them on the real skin of the territory. The level of success depends on what happens to the people. We are continually learning in the process. It's very important to involve institutions and communities, and receive feedback. One of the most important things an architect can do is to understand the power of the mediation spaces you can build in the process [of realising the programme of social urbanism].'[7]

Apart from improving Medellín's relationship with nature and boosting social equity, the plans drawn up by Fajardo, Echeverri and their teams, which were realised in less than four years (by 2007), also legalised the *comunas*. In order to ensure a wide mix of housing types and tenures, encouragement has been given to housing cooperatives, other social housing operators and private building contractors. A series of projects are in process for the redevelopment of post-industrial sites, with derelict buildings converted and used for new purposes: neighbourhood business development incubators (CEDEZOS), a new convention centre to host major events and support tourism, and new headquarters for both regional and international firms, generating new jobs.

In 2014 Medellín hosted over 15,000 local, national and international attendees at the 7th World Urban Forum, which took the theme 'Urban Equity in Development – Cities for Life'. The reasoning behind this theme was that, while a 'search for equity has been on the fringes of the development policy agenda for a long time', in recent years there has been a clear urban policy and strategy to tackle it'.[8] More than any other recent urban example, Medellín, engaged with a programmatic approach to equity dating back more than 15 years, epitomised the notion that equitable development could actually be achieved.

At the Forum the city adopted the concept 'Cities for Life' to promote the transition of its social and political landscape from the violence of the past, with what has been a whole new social pact to enhance citizenship. 'Cities for Life' are for all, 'but they focus on those more in need – the poor and marginalized, who are excluded from all opportunities and deprived of the tools needed to transform their lives for individual and collective wellbeing.'[9]

The ethos linking all Médellin's urban projects is one of pedagogical urbanism. The next phase is full of plans: the Medellín River Botanical Park Project aims to transform the river into a public

Above:
Neighbourhood connections: the Independence Path and escalators, eastern centre of Medellín, one of the PUI Integral Urban Projects, Cesar Hernández and team, City Hall, Secretariat of Public Works, 2011-12.

Left:
Explora Park, north-east Medellín, Alejandro Echeverri and team, Urbam, 2005-8.

environmental hub for the city and the region, while the Garden Walkway, part of the Medellín greenbelt, is a strategy of a equally long-term nature for the areas where urban and rural zones meet, to avoid disorganised growth at the peripheries of the city. The Mother Laura Bridge will be the largest urban bridge in Colombia, linking two of the city's most populated districts. Further examples of the city's overall revolutionary approach to social equity acted on in the last few years include neighbourhood facilities for sports, recreation and culture; a new Innovation District; the House of Music; and the House of Memory Museum – treating the city's violent past as a series of lessons of human coexistence, through the theme 'remembering is not repeating'.

'Dignity is the space where you learn, the space where you live', says Fajardo.[10] As governor of the province of Antioquia since 2012, he has been busy advancing his plans for duplicating the success model of Medellín (pop. 2.5 million) more widely in Antioquia, which has a population of around 6.5 million people. Some 80 of its 125 municipalities are now creating their own, unique library parks, each designed by a different architect, as part of their integrated plans – an extraordinary means for mobilising change. Local mayors were asked to enter a competition with their plans for boosting education, entrepreneurship, culture and tourism. Fajardo signed a Quality Education Pact with every single mayor involved, and implemented a Knowledge Olympic Games to help to develop the programme.

One of the most important things an architect can do is to understand the power of the mediation spaces you can build

There were also competitions promoting entrepreneurship. The local talent is strong. Ideas included prototype devices to capture water vapour using renewable energy; others to find and eliminate the many land mines blighting rural areas; and biodegradable, biopolymer kitchen utensils. 'I have to be a teacher... A good teacher always listens to the students. You have to find a vocabulary, the explanations, to make sure why we are in a public position', says Fajardo. 'We have spent a lot of time with violence.' Today, as a result of the myriad physical improvements that connect top-down and bottom-up, Antioquia has the best quality of life of all the 32 provinces of Colombia. 'We say we are going to turn the page on violence with intelligence, decency, capabilities, opportunities. You have do to that with education, every single day.'[11]

Estudio Teddy Cruz

The contested threshold between the cities of San Diego and Tijuana, on either side of the US–Mexican border, is described by Guatemala-born architect Teddy Cruz as 'the most trafficked checkpoint in the world'.[1] He regards the metropolitan explosion of the last few years, which has resulted in an unprecedented growth of slums around major urban centres, as having led to an 'urban asymmetry'. Through the many facets of his work, he assesses the processes via which 'political economies of division have caused polarising enclaves of wealth and sectors of poverty'.

In response to the forces of control on either side of the border, the small immigrant border neighbourhoods have created their own adaptive urbanism, impacting in both directions. On the American side, migrant workers' informal land-use patterns and economies have diluted the homogeneity of San Diego's neighbourhoods. On the Mexican side, Tijuana is recycling for domestic use the infrastructural waste (including rubber tyres, garage doors and small bungalows) of southern California.

Cruz sees in these processes a 'radicalisation of the local' through a recontextualisation of globalisation. The conditions of social emergency affecting marginalised, under-represented communities in the area have given rise to interventions that engage with the 'spatial, territorial and environmental collisions across critical thresholds' – in this case, taking in contexts affected by discriminatory zoning and uneven economic development as well as by an international border. These interventions have taken the forms of 'other' spaces, arrangements and institutional protocols and models of citizenship in immigrant neighbourhoods. Undertaken in collaboration with community-based, non-profit organisations, they have advanced new models of civic participation, affordable housing and infrastructure.

Such a mix of topical themes make this a potent field of enquiry and stimulates collaboration between academia, communities and local government bodies. At the University of California, San Diego (UCSD), where Cruz is associate professor in public culture and urbanism, he is co-director with the political theorist, associate professor

The Political Equator promotes the reimagining of the border between San Diego and Tijuana through the logic of natural and social systems

Below:
Political Equator 3 event, US–Mexico border at Tijuana, with temporary but 'official' public port of entry for 24 hours, 3-4 June 2011, Estudio Teddy Cruz.

Right:
Stamping passports at the temporary port of entry at the Political Equator 3 event, US–Mexico border at Tijuana, 3-4 June 2011, Estudio Teddy Cruz.

Above:
Participants at the Political Equator 3 event, US/Mexico border at Tijuana, 3-4 June 2011.

Fonna Forman of the multidisciplinary Blum Cross-Border Initiative focused on local zones of conflict such as that of the San Diego-Tijuana border territory. In 2010 Cruz founded the Center for Urban Ecologies at UCSD, in order to research urban conflict, informal urbanisation and citizenship culture, and to develop new forms of cross-sector collaboration and urban intervention. The impetus of this academic collaborative work has led to further initiatives.

The City of San Diego set up a 'Civic Innovation Lab', a collaboration led by Cruz and Forman between the university, community-based organisations and the municipality, to rethink public space and civic engagement and improve the relationship between urban policy and public imagination. Now defunct, the Lab's one-time leaders remain special advisers to the City on urban and public initiatives.

In collaboration with former Bogotá mayor Antanas Mockus and the NGO he founded, Corpovisionarios, Cruz and Forman are conducting a Ford-funded study of citizenship culture in the San Diego-Tijuana border region. The studies will lead to a protocol document on cross-border models of planning that has evolved from surveys on both sides of the border and addresses cross-border civic infrastructure, public trust and social norms.

Amidst these emerging initiatives, Cruz's incisive curatorial project The Political Equator, a series of mobile conferences spanning the border between San Diego and Tijuana, first set up in 2006, promotes the re-imagining of that threshold through the logic of natural and social systems. Cruz's main focus has been to link two activist neighbourhoods divided by the border near the checkpoint. He has staged a number of itinerant dialogues involving institutions and communities at diverse sites between Tijuana and San Diego, such as Los Laureles Canyon (the last slum in Latin America before the border into the US, populated by 85,000 people) and San Ysidro (the first immigrant neighbourhood on the US side). Each meeting has involved different public works, performances and walks across the conflicted territories and has helped to build up evidence. The collaborators have made clear their view that the multidisciplinary debates needed to take place outside institutions and inside the sites in conflict, not in some supposedly neutral place.

The knowledge-exchanging meetings have been co-produced with two community-based NGOs representing the neighbourhoods, Casa Familiar in San Ysidro and Alter Terra in Los Laureles Canyon. 'Social justice today cannot be only about the redistribution of resources but must also engage with the redistribution of knowledge', says Cruz. Accordingly, the Political Equator project links the specialised knowledge of institutions and the activist socio-economic and political intelligence within communities. Instead of following a generic conference format, it takes the form of an experimental platform researching new forms of knowledge and public participation.

The point of departure for all the meetings has been the visualisation of environmental and political

↑

Above:
Creative workshops held with local primary school children for the Exuma garden of dreams - a sustainable future for Exuma, the Bahamas, empowering public participation. Ecosistema Urbano and Exuma Lab - Harvard University's Graduate School of Design, 2014.

↓ conflict. In 2011 the focus of conversations was the Tijuana River Estuary, which is next to the American checkpoint and border wall. Here new infrastructures of control have been built by the USA; drains in the canyons accelerate the flow of water into the estuary, impacting on the watershed systems that are key to its bioregional sustainability. Following a long process of negotiation with the US Department of Homeland Security and Mexican immigration services, the Border-Drain-Crossing (Political Equator 3) staged on 3-4 June 2011 made a 24-hour public border crossing through one of the drains. Taking part were local, national and international activists, scholars and researchers, artists, architects and urbanists, politicians, border patrol agents and other community stakeholders. It was vital for them all to directly experience what Cruz calls a 'liminal space' – a zone of environmental degradation, precarious informal settlement and expanding surveillance infrastructure.

Through the project participants could reflect on whether this nexus of contradictions could be a genuine laboratory to re-imagine citizenship beyond the nation state, mobilised around the shared interests between the two cities. For Cruz, the San Ysidro–Los Laureles Canyon threshold is also representative of many other marginal communities in other continents. 'Some of the most relevant projects advancing socio-economic inclusion and artistic experimentation will not emerge from sites of economic abundance but from sites of scarcity in the midst of conflicts between geopolitical borders, natural resources and marginal communities', he says. Central to the Political Equator project was a diagram he created that linked Tijuana and San Diego to the rest of the world: starting from this border spot, he extended an imaginary line across a world atlas, taking in the Strait of Gibraltar, where migration flows from North Africa into Europe, the Israeli-Palestinian border dividing the Middle East and many other critical thresholds.

'A community is always in dialogue with its immediate social and ecological environment; this is what defines its political nature', says Cruz. 'But when this relationship is disrupted and its productive capacity splintered by the very way in which jurisdictional power is instituted, it is necessary to find a means of recuperating its agency.' He believes that can happen only 'if architecture is reinvented as a cognitive system enabling the public to access complexity, ... building collective capacity for political agency and action at local scales', and by generating new experimental urban spaces and social programmes.

Political Equator at San Diego–Tijuana border

ITINERANT DISCUSSIONS

Solutions for shared interests were developed through the exchange of knowledge between neighbourhood NGOs, activists, scholars, researchers, architects, urbanists, politicians, border patrol officers and so on

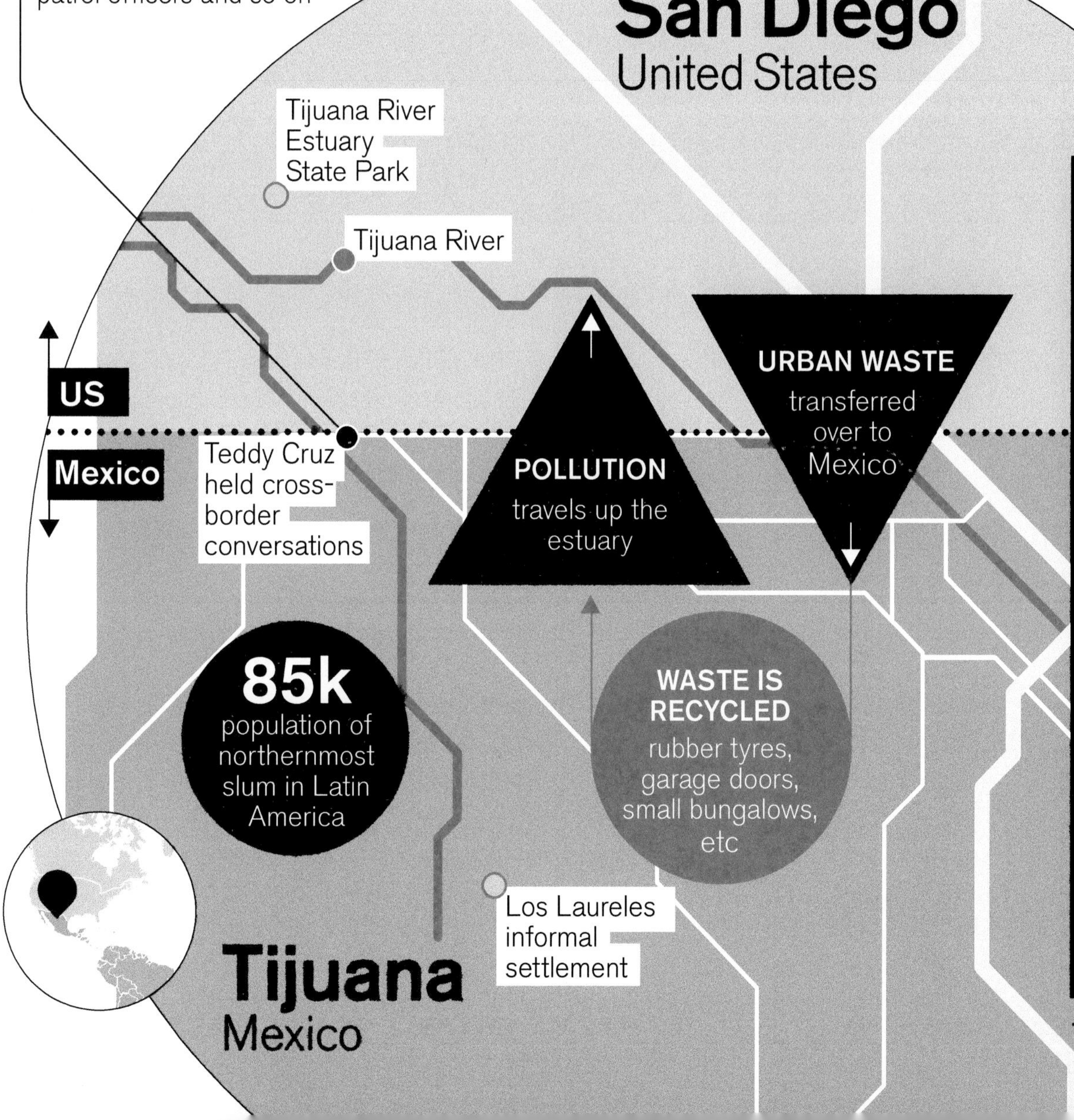

San Diego
United States

Tijuana River Estuary State Park

Tijuana River

US

Mexico

Teddy Cruz held cross-border conversations

POLLUTION
travels up the estuary

URBAN WASTE
transferred over to Mexico

85k
population of northernmost slum in Latin America

WASTE IS RECYCLED
rubber tyres, garage doors, small bungalows, etc

Los Laureles informal settlement

Tijuana
Mexico

Above:
Teddy Cruz (right) explains the intersection of the US–Mexico border at Tijuana, Political Equator 3, 3-4 June 2011.

ENGAGEMENT
REPLICABILITY
DESIGN DRIVEN
SCALE
IMPACT

IDENTIFY → ENQUIRE → DEVELOP → CO-DESIGN → CO-CONSTRUCT → HAND-OVER

Dreaming New Mexico

Participatory, restorative bioregional planning in the American Southwest has been a dream of those witnessing the blight of commercial expediency. The founding of Dreaming New Mexico food and farming initiative (DNM), by the Santa Fe-based Bioneers organisation and national conference, has been a key advance in counteracting the effects of this blinkered approach in that American state. New Mexico has 22 sovereign nations within its borders, each drawing on the legacies of indigenous and Hispanic peoples representing the majority of New Mexico's populations. Adding to the difficulties is the fact that, while small-scale initiatives have value, 'what's missing in the USA is the infrastructure for us to scale up', as the ecologist and DNM co-founder Peter Warshall has pointed out.[1]

Rising to that challenge, DNM has promoted a myriad of inspirational ways in which the problem could be tackled, and its significant breakthroughs of many unexpected kinds provide models that other regions could pay closer attention to. In founding DNM, Warshall aimed to step back from an 'amoral economic extremism' in the US, and stimulate a sense of possibility as regards 'how we want to be nourished in the next 25 years'.[2]

In the late 1950s, before he took his doctorate in biological anthropology, Warshall was an attendee at Camp Rising Sun, an American summer programme promoting cross-cultural interaction and responsible leadership. He was inspired by the Brooklyn Botanic Garden's Children's Gardens (established in 1914), where young people of all ages have been encouraged to learn about community horticulture, conservation and urban ecology.

Bioneers was founded in New Mexico in 1989 as a non-profit organisation by the social entrepreneur, writer and film-

Below:
An Age of Local Foodsheds and a Fair Trade State, poster-map, Cynthia Miller for Dreaming New Mexico, 2010.

Right:
New Mexico in the Age of Renewables, poster-map, Glen Strock for Dreaming New Mexico, 2008.

maker Kenny Ausubel and his partner Nina Simons, founder of the women's leadership programme UnReasonable Women for the Earth (both residents of Santa Fe, the state capital), in order to advance holistic education about social, cultural and environmental issues. They initially worked with indigenous farmers in New Mexico to help them to conserve their traditional cultural practices and seed stocks. Numbers attending their conferences – first held annually in Santa Fe; now in San Rafael, California – have swelled from 250 in the early years to 3,000 today. The meetings' initial themes, biological and cultural diversity, biomimicry and natural medicine, have been expanded to include restorative food and farming, biodiversity conservation, bioremediation, women's leadership development, green medicine and progressive politics and neighbourhood resilience.

Today Bioneers attests to a 'vastly greater receptivity' to the kinds of ideas and practices it has been highlighting for more than 20 years. In particular, regional and national government and the business community are now showing a new openness. It seems that change is finally coming – and now needs to be built on further.

Dreaming New Mexico has sought to reconcile nature and cultures at the state level through systemic, collaborative approaches towards a common vision of restoration. DNM's promotion of renewable energy solutions – solar, wind, biofuels and geothermal – has involved lobbying against restrictions that prevent New Mexico from adopting sustainable practices, instead offering solutions based on the collective wisdom of many people and organisations.

'What do we want?' quickly led to 'what do we know'?

Rather than fall into the trap of focusing on hair-shirt mentality and the tunnel vision of preventative legislation, DNM began by talking to over 2,000 people, from Hispanic government workers, farmers, energy consultants and non-government activists, to philanthropists and entrepreneurs. Interviewees were asked to speculate about how their work and desires could fit into a bigger picture of the state's future in 2025, emerging from today's nascent age of low-carbon energy – taking in solar, wind and geothermal energy, biofuels, micropower, distributed energy, green grids, energy efficiency, and activism for more socially geared governance and environmental justice. 'What do we want?' quickly led to 'what do we know?'

DNM combined the numerous ideas, tools, processes and strategies, dreams, insights and research of these informed grassroots organisations into a single analytical framework. This close scrutiny of the food and farming sectors of New Mexico's 'agro-eco regions' examined food and value chains for existing and new crops; the potential for new foodsheds (geographically defined concentrations of food and agricultural production) to play a role in the local economy; and the region's cultural legacy in terms of its cuisines and foods, its food insecurity and its poor nutritional health.

DNM's accumulated knowledge opened doors. Through its research it was found, for example, that New Mexico's farmers' markets represented a nascent network that could be developed, but needed support to scale up. Local people expressed dreams for new hubs in the networks with amenities with large coolers and freezers, for organic waste recycling schemes and for farms at closer proximity to urban centres.

The investigative research produced some shocks: government data covered only New Mexico's →

Dreaming New Mexico

JOURNEY TO CHANGE GOVERNANCE

Cooperative research model to generate new governance approach to food and energy resources on a state-wide level

VISION

Reconcile nature and cultures through a collaborative vision of restoration

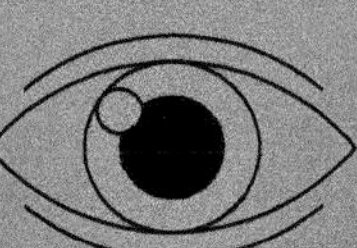

COLLABORATION

Created a 'big picture' of New Mexico which opened doors

DISCOVERY

95%

of food consumed in New Mexico was imported, research revealed. This shocking fact is one of many that prompted 'locavore' policies, community discussions and mutually beneficial systems

From inhabitants' narratives a common intellectual foundation was formed

SOLUTIONS

Important to align distant NGOs and support the work of indigenous and Hispano people

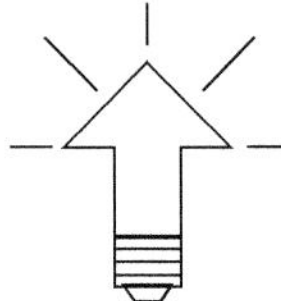

CONSULTING

2,000

state residents including hispanic government workers, farmers, energy consultants, activists, philanthropists and entrepreneurs. Each explained how his or her work could fit into the state's future in 2025

Ideas, tools, processes and strategies were accumulated

COLLABORATION

AFFECTING POLICY

developed by DNM and partners to support the work of indigenous and Hispano people

food exports, and DNM discovered to its horror that 95% of the food consumed in New Mexico was imported from outside the state. This galvanised the team into looking at changing the ratio of local to imported food, undertaking new research into, for example, whether the state had the ranches or farms, and how many greenhouses could be run on geo-thermal energy. New possibilities were seeded – including hot springs and other tourism ideas.

The new research helped DNM to identify weak points in the value chain and opened up a multitude of notions: of farmers as ecosystem managers; that a deeper collaboration between foodsheds would assist in 'figuring out how to get the food from the farm to the dining table'. It also prompted community discussions on such topics as 'locavore'-friendly trade policies, alternatives to the World Trade Organisation's rules of trade between nations, and mutually beneficial economic systems, forging further alternative dreams, including for places suffering from a paucity of grocery shops and decent food to buy. The systemic thinking facilitated through the research extended to local business schools, which considered new strategies for the portfolio management of ecosystem services by the farmers to help incentivise them.

DNM produced new maps that permitted everyone involved to navigate a future course and acted as an easily understandable communications tool that 'helped people understand that actually there is a movement', said Warshall in an interview with Ausubel at the Bioneers conference in 2010.[3] Today many schools, pueblos and reservations in New Mexico display a poster map designed by Cindy Miller of the agro-eco regions' working landscapes – some of which have been in use for over 10,000 years – revealing the differences in habits and rules across the state's regions. Ausubel hoped that these efforts would prevent 'some kind of cookie-cutter political policy that will only work in one part of the state'.[4]

Other new materials produced by DNM included an atlas of technical maps, designed by Diane Rigoli, which examined restorative processes, and booklets such as *The Age of Renewables* and *An Age of Local Foodsheds and a Fair Trade State*; a website followed. These materials supported conferences, briefing meetings, educational activities and a range of collaborative projects, with the maps helping to inform cross-sector networks about shared possibilities in restorative ecological and social transformation.

Three messages ran through it all: that cultural legacy in farming and food production is deeply significant; that it is vital to combine new and old methods; and that a piecemeal approach to policy in this field is counter-productive. DNM's new conceptual framework creates a common intellectual foundation formed from all the inhabitants' legacies and narratives. It includes research findings about current patterns of behaviour and resources that could be synthesised for benefit at all levels across New Mexico. The big-scale, emerging picture of communities forming around new energy sources also served to bring some alignment with previously distant NGOs, and multiple stakeholder collaborations have since developed. DNM presented the findings to New Mexico's state governor, its mayors and its Green Jobs Cabinet, so that, for the first time, food and farming jobs were included on the political agenda.

Transforming attitudes on governance is the hardest part of achieving appropriate support for the food and farming sectors in New Mexico, Warshall reflected. 'Ultimately, we [the people] have to govern ourselves', he told Ausubel. Talking about food production, but equally applicable to sustainable participatory placemaking more broadly, he advocated that people remember what they eat – 'that this is what we are'.

From the 1950s the Dudley Triangle in the close-knit Roxbury and North Dorchester neighbourhoods of Boston, Massachusetts, was devastated by a constellation of illegal dumping, 'arson-for-profit' and 'white flight' from the city. Discriminatory 'redlining' commercial practices either denied locals home and business loans, insurance, health care and other essentials, or offered them only at exorbitant rates.

Dudley Street Neighborhood Initiative

In the 2006 documentary Holding Ground: The Rebirth of Dudley Street, the African-American civil rights activist Martin Luther King, Jr is shown giving a speech in 1965: 'Boston must become a leader among cities. A vision of a new Boston must extend into the heart of Roxbury, and into the mind of every child. Boston must conduct the creative experiments, and the abolition of ghettos, which will point the way to other communities.'[1] The city has done exactly that in Roxbury, thanks to the work of the Dudley Street Neighborhood Initiative.

During the course of Dudley's meltdown, though, many in the area lost their homes through foreclosure. It became a no-man's land. By the early 1980s nearly a third of Dudley's land was vacant, scarred by arson and extensive illegal dumping by firms. Many people who had moved there in the early 1980s were angry and frightened for their futures. They were also determined to protect the area from speculators looking for profits from upmarket 'urban renewal', and who would ignore affordable housing and local businesses. The people of Dudley became pioneering activists against their oppressive circumstances. When the mayor at the time failed to take action against locally dumped cars, they duly put his campaign bumper stickers on them and marched against the offence on their doorsteps.

A group of women started a 'Don't Dump on Us' campaign to clean up the lots – 'Educate don't contaminate' read one of their placards. This coming together of local residents to revive their neighbourhood spurred the founding in 1984 of the Dudley Street Neighborhood Initiative (DSNI), a community organising agency partnering with residents to demand the best, helping to empower them to drive plans to improve the neighbourhood. DSNI has grown to encompass over 3,000 residents, non-profit organisations, community development corporations, businesses and religious groups.

Through its commitment to 'development without displacement', DSNI pushed doggedly for stability and affordable housing, helping residents to do things for themselves and to become confident in raising their voices about issues of concern. Its overall remit was to ensure that local residents be the primary beneficiaries of economic growth in the local communities, and that human development and environment issues be addressed; this remains at the heart of its activities. DSNI devised a comprehensive bottom-up plan centred on the concept of a lively, sustainable urban village. This successfully got the attention of the public and the mayor, and in 1987 the revitalisation of the area was kickstarted with the formal help of the city.

In 1988 DSNI became the first community group in the USA to win the power of 'eminent domain' to acquire 12 hectares of vacant land on the 26-hectare 'Dudley Triangle' for resident-friendly development activities. While half of the land there had been owned by the city, it also included 181 private vacant lots, many with absentee owners. Through eminent domain DSNI could command the territory, creating one overall plan instead of having to buy lots piecemeal over time. 'Dudley's approach turned the long-abused power of eminent domain into a tool for development without displacement', explains Holly Sklar, author with Peter Medoff of *Streets of Hope: The Fall and Rise of an Urban Neighborhood*, about the work of DSNI. 'Eminent domain only applied to vacant land. No one lost their home or business in the process.'[2] DSNI also worked with resident owners of vacant lots to help them develop these for housing or gardens.

DSNI set up Dudley Neighbors Inc, a community land trust (CLT) that would help to steer the housing development within the plan, ensuring high-quality construction, affordable housing, responsible economic development, open spaces and other amenities. At the time a land trust was more commonly associated with rural land conservation, rather than urban land. The trust leases land to developers during construction, and then to individual homeowners, cooperative housing associations and other forms of limited partnerships under 99-year leases. It protects the affordability of the housing and land over the long term, restricting future sales to buyers with low or moderate incomes; homes are deed-restricted so the sale price cannot inflate along with the market. Dudley Neighbors' admirable housing →

Left: The Dudley Greenhouse at the Winthrop School, Roxbury, Boston, MA, owned by DSNI and run by The Food Project, 2013.

Below: The Fred Woodard Collective, led by a local jazz musician and DSNI board member, plays at the annual DSNI Multicultural Festival, August 2013.

“

‘We care about the place, and the people working in the place’

↓ model also restricts loans to those from approved lenders who offer reasonable terms, and the trust helps out in cases of personal crisis. It is now helping Boston Chinatown’s land trust in its fight against gentrification.

Following an urban envisioning process in 1996, updating DSNI’s original comprehensive plan from 1987, over 180 residents drafted the masterplan guiding the revitalisation of the neighbourhood. Supported by the land trust’s mechanisms helping to root people in their neighbourhood rather than forcing them to move out, a dramatic rebuilding of human, social and physical infrastructure continued to signal the neighbourhood’s regeneration. ‘We were Boston’s dumping ground and forgotten neighbourhood. Today, we are on the rise! We are reclaiming our dignity’, residents wrote in their Declaration of Community Rights, produced by DSNI’s Human Development Committee. ‘Tomorrow, we realise our vision of a vibrant, culturally diverse neighborhood, where everyone is valued for their talents and contribution to the larger community.’[3]

The economic downturn in the late 1990s, and the accompanying threat that the foreclosure crisis would put residents back a few decades, put real pressure on DSNI. When the economic crisis of 2008 hit, forewarned was forearmed: while in Boston generally there were many housing foreclosures that year, the land trust had none. ‘Foreclosure destroys communities’, said DSNI’s former executive director John Barros, who, as a teenager, helped to found its youth committee and who designed its memorable 1993 ‘Unity through Diversity’ mural.[4] Today he is Boston’s chief of economic development.

In spite the difficulties triggered in 2008, the Dudley plan has worked over the long term. More than half of the 1,300 abandoned parcels of land have been transformed into over 400 new, high-quality affordable homes, community centres, schools and businesses. There are parks and gardens such as Dudley Town Common, playgrounds, a community greenhouse, an orchard and other public spaces. Today the 24,000-strong Dudley Urban Village, as it is called, has vibrancy, not vacancy, marked by regular farmers’ markets, performances and festivals, and further development.

DSNI takes its responsibilities seriously. It focuses on three interrelated strategic areas: community economic development; leadership development and collaboration; and youth opportunities and development. These are led by an elected board of directors, which includes 16 residents, reelected every two years, from each of the four major local ethnic groups – African-American, Latino, Cape Verdean and white. Everything they do is carried out in three languages, English, Spanish and Cape Verde Creole. DSNI’s collaborative initiatives encompass a combined programme of continuous learning and social support, which is proving highly effective.

Now, in a further elaboration of the Village vision, there is the new Dudley Village Campus. Here is the fruit of a

Above:
DSNI and The Food Project creating raised-bed gardens at the land trust led by DSNI, July 2013.

Left:
A man watering crops in the Dudley Greenhouse owned by DSNI at its land trust, and operated by The Food Project, Roxbury, Boston, MA, June 2011.

collaboration with the Boston Promise Initiative (BPI, part of the national federally funded Promise Neighborhoods Initiative), which has grown out of the work of DSNI, relating its socially supportive initiatives to the field of education. The scheme encompasses ten Boston schools and engages with parents, encouraging them to play an active role, and creates a new, integrated environment for continuous learning, health and social life for toddlers to young people up to the age of 24.

'One of the key components of this [initiative] is how do you support learning outside the classroom', explains Sheena Collier, initiative director at DSNI, 'as a lot of our students are not getting enrichment opportunities, either in school, or in the neighbourhood.'[5] DSNI is also collaborating with the long-established Project HOPE, which works with homeless families to find affordable housing for them. Schools especially appreciate the integrated approach of this alliance, as these families often approach local schools about their plight, including eviction.

The long-term visions that DSNI has implemented include its Resident Development Institute, a repository for community history, learning and innovation offering community guidance in the form of standards and data, information, tools and processes for community decision-making. Among the tools offered is a set of core leadership competency training modules based on experiential learning methods. DSNI has also joined forces with the Boston Youth Service Network to engage 'peer leaders' – a role specifically created for 'energetic young adults between the ages of 18-24 years old' to help 'strengthen Boston's youth voice in driving citywide strategies that support young people to be successful', says DSNI.[6]

In *Gaining Ground: Building Community on Dudley Street*, a follow-up to the *Holding Ground* film celebrating DSNI's 30th anniversary in 2014, Chris Jones, DSNI's executive director, asserts that 'everyone in the neighbourhood is an organiser and an agent for change.'[7] Between them, the two films capture a unique piece of social history, and show how powerfully DSNI has held hands with residents of Dudley of all ages, right across three decades. At the *Gaining Ground* launch discussion, people discussed the benefits of home-grown leadership – including seminal figures such as Barros – to the community and its visions. They were particularly happy to see that large numbers of talented young adults return to the community to play their role in the creative experiment of sustaining change.

Martin Luther King's manifesto for much-needed change in Roxbury, so many years ago, has come into being. How has this been possible? The question is not easily answered, but at the heart of the explanation is the fact that, from the very first, DSNI has not been solely place-based in its strategic goals, nor has it been focused on social issues in their own right. 'We care about the place, and the people working in the place', said Jones during DSNI's anniversary celebrations.[8]

Ecosistema Urbano

Every project affecting the city has to deal with both opposition and support, consensus and contradiction

Liberal politicians like the notion of 'trickle-down' benefits, but when it comes to creating better, enlivening facilities, furthering social interaction and empowering greater community self-organisation through urban design, these benefits simply cannot be achieved through elite processes alone. The process is also far more than just a vital relational measure to be taken in large-scale urban development, appealing for marketing reasons. When the reality is that 'urban development is what happens in the city while others try to plan it' – as Belinda Tato and José Luis Vallejo, co-founders in 2000 of the Madrid-based group of architects and urban designers Ecosistema Urbano, put it[1] – why cannot a creative, relational process be set in motion across a community to collectively reconceive a space?

It can, say Tato and Vallejo, and among the factors they cite are that '[architects'] roles as professionals are evolving, disciplinary bonds are loosening, urban projects are complex, and circumstances are continuously changing'. They try to be as open-minded as possible, 'flexible enough to adapt our roles and skills and to use unusual tools'. By 'unusual' they mean custom-designed and hybrid: with 'social software' promoting new possibilities through the use of technology to help to empower people and improve their social connectivity and interaction. By these means, alongside its urban projects Ecosistema Urbano operates digital platforms that develop social networks and manages online channels on the open-ended topic of creative urban sustainability.

Ecosistema Urbano is a pioneer in this emerging field. Tato and Vallejo define the practice's approach as

ENGAGEMENT
REPLICABILITY
DESIGN DRIVEN
SCALE
IMPACT

Left: Aerial view of Stortorget Square, the central public space in Hamar, Norway, and site of the Dreamhamar project, 2011-13.

'urban social design'. By this they have in mind the design of environments, spaces and dynamics that enhance the capacities of citizens to self-organise, while also improving scope for social interaction within communities and their relationship with their environment. The pair have applied this adaptive philosophy to design projects in such diverse countries as Norway, Denmark, Spain, Italy, France, China and the Bahamas. In these very different contexts, certain methods work best. 'Participation, like conversation, means letting all the points of view be raised and listened to. Public debate only makes sense if all the stakeholders get properly involved. Every project affecting the city has to deal with both opposition and support, consensus and contradiction.'

For the Dreamhamar project (2011-13) in the Norwegian town of Hamar, 130km from Oslo, Ecosistema Urbano developed a participation and network design process that it has dubbed Dream Your City. To encourage greater proactivity in the redevelopment of Stortorget Square, Hamar's main public square, the team employed collective brainstorming across a multitude of sectors as well as physical and digital platforms. The process included workshops, lectures and other activities, and made use of various communication and participation tools. It made Dreamhamar one of the most innovative participatory projects yet experienced in Scandinavia.

Citizen stakeholders of the Dreamhamar project could take part in numerous separate but interrelated spheres of work. They were able to intervene in urban design by contributing to the technical research and the design possibilities for the public space. They could directly experience the space and speculate on future uses thanks to a multitude of gatherings and happenings, installations, stalls and 1:1 mock-ups on the square. A 'physical lab' with an-open door policy, which also functioned as the practice's pop-up office, was the site of workshops, lectures and exhibitions attended by local and international creative guests. Such events enabled the formation of a large database of citizens' ideas.

A 'digital lab' participatory web platform linked to social networks followed weekly broadcasts and online workshops, and made use of the Dreamhamar app. Ecosistema Urbano made the participative brainstorming part of coursework from institutions ranging from the Bergen School of Architecture and the Norwegian School for Gardeners, to the Polytechnic University of Milan and the Istituto Europeo di Design. Through a 'cultural rucksack', more than 1,500 students from local schools could let rip with their ideas for the public space and become part of the design process by sharing these ideas. Once Dreamhamar kicked off, people would never perceive the Square in the same light again.

Collaborators Ethel Baraona (writer and co-founder of dpr-barcelona) and architect Paco González (founder of radarq), directors of the Tactical Urbanism workshop held as part of the project, focused on the development of urban practices that employ new technologies to improve liveability. Participants found this to be a highly satisfying work-in-progress urban project. The duo drew on the French sociologist Henri Lefebvre's definition of the urban as a place of encounter, assembly and simultaneity. They also adhered to the main concept of open-source peer-to-peer (P2P) processes: that design technology, tools and information-sharing are not sufficient in themselves to create the preconditions for successful open organisations. To achieve genuine co-design of new, open organisations and foundations for urban places, tools and technologies need to be forged and applied with the active participation of communities.

Above: Dreamhamar was a network design process including many public events, for collectively reimagining Stortorget Square, 2011-13.

Right: Creative workshops held with local people for a 'garden of dreams', a sustainable future for Exuma, the Bahamas, empowering public participation. Ecosistema Urbano and Exuma Lab - Harvard University's Graduate School of Design, 2014.

IDENTIFY → ENQUIRE → DEVELOP → CO-DESIGN → CO-CONSTRUCT → HAND-OVER

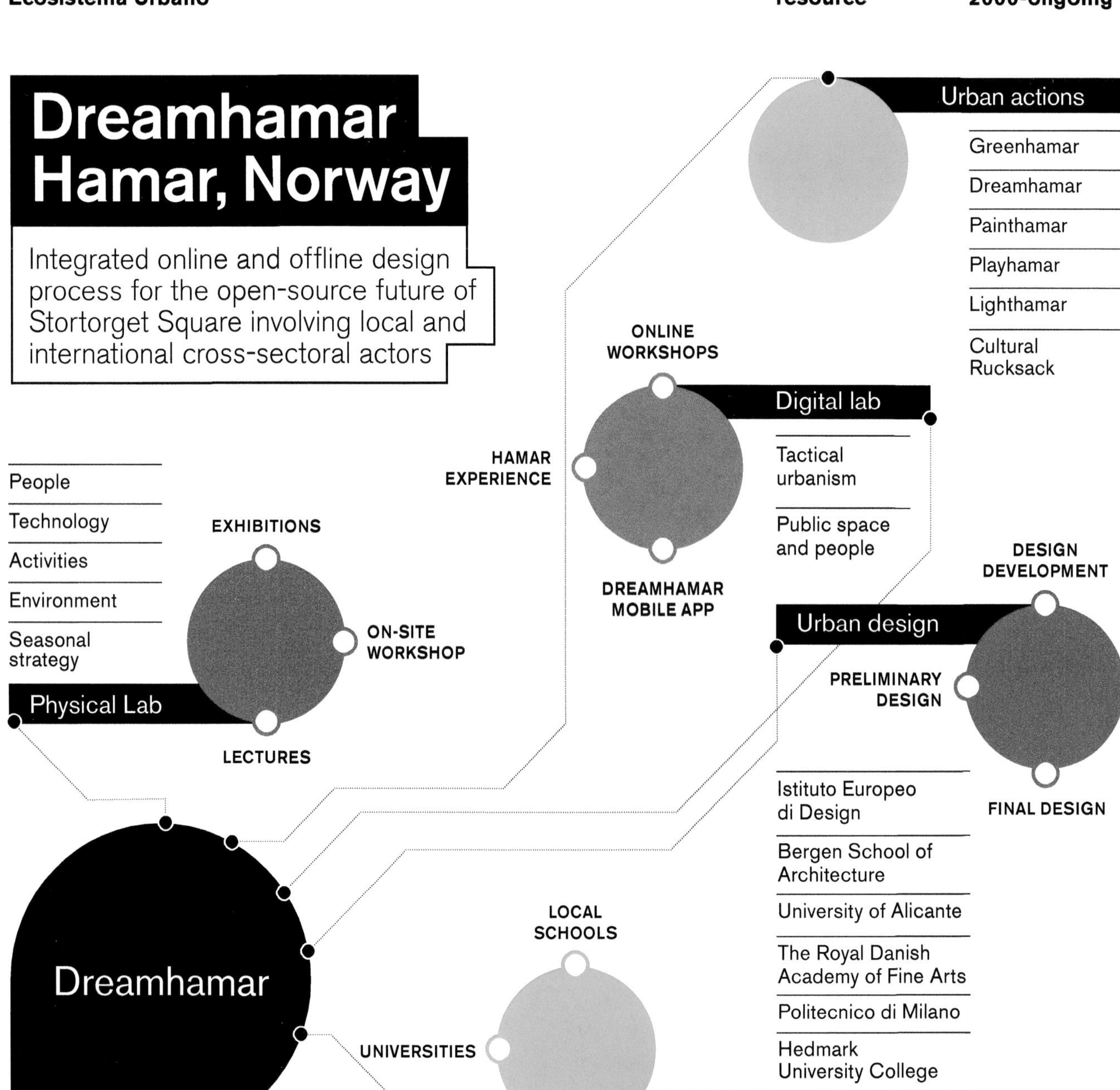

While there are a number of ways to trigger a workshop process, Baraona and González began by sharing some case studies on ‘tactical urbanism’ and other bottom-up strategies. They differentiated between guerrilla urbanism, do-it-yourself approaches and other spatial practices so as to draw out deeper reflection on the ways in which, when short-term actions have been mobilised, cities can go on to evolve and respond catalytically in the long term. They integrated four separate participatory actions: narratives/storytelling; the formation of community groups; the collection of documentation and archives; and open P2P design/network design. Participants presented their projects and discussed their ideas through the Dreamhamar blog and the Google+ Hangout, amending them as the process developed. This created a good starting point for future discussions on urban liveability.

The Dreamhamar project started life as OneThousandSquare, a competition entry submitted by Ecosistema Urbano and architect Lluís Sabadell Artiga. Their vision was that both local participants and others worldwide could take part in the collaborative process of designing an open-source space at Stortorget Square. Their design strategy booklet suggested three principles of organisation for the future square that would promote social interaction: a lively streetscape connected to the surrounding streets and buildings; a social and nature ‘ring’ with an area of trees and other fixed facilities including lighting; and a multi-use arena with many possible configurations.

At this early point the design strategy did not include proposals concerning the square’s future management (an aspect of development that ‘meanwhile use’ project leaders, in their drive to cultivate value in the here and now, often do not focus on). However Tato and Vallejo feel sure that – especially in today's climate of uprisings – it is 'far more difficult for closed solutions to be imposed by a power minority than for specific temporary actions to be applied based on grassroots talks, because sensitivity is high, and social groups are highly resistant to accepting any changes which have not come from within their ranks'.

Ecosistema Urbano bases its urban social-design processes on semi-scientific theory, assembling an engaged stakeholder constituency as the first step of every project. The parties include local and external people, groups and agencies, 'expert or not yet', affected by a common problem, so that they can all participate in the decision-making process. The team also brings in 'a politician who guarantees the administrative process', and a technician to coordinate it. This method of action requires that Ecosistema Urbano marshall the uncertain process of integrating different points of view and endorse differing positions. Bringing in people 'who don't usually meet' is a vital step 'when there are strong conflicts, actual or potential' and skills and expert knowledge are needed. As a result, the early stages of each Ecosistema Urbano project includes five operative steps: conducting social analysis; gathering place knowledge; gaining local confidence; devising and planning actions; and starting interaction.

Ecosistema Urbano sees many future possibilities in participatory processes that have already been widely 'disseminated all over the world, especially in the US and northern Europe where citizens have a strong sense of community and cooperation'. One ongoing project, Exuma Dreams, has seen the practice collaborate with the government of the Bahamas, the Bahamas National Trust and Harvard University Graduate School of Design on a wider framework for a sustainable future for the Exuma archipelago. In designing activities to promote dialogue with the local community, the design team is reflecting on the future of Exuma and the Bahamas more generally. A toolkit and workshops have probed the wishes and aspirations of the local community. The team introduced a previously developed tool, Whatif, to digitally collect ideas from participants, resulting in the Exumadreams web platform.[2] Work on this platform took place alongside development of the project's physical aspect, the visually arresting Origami Garden of Exuma Dreams that exhibited all the ideas collected – ephemeral, symbolic and embedded with desires.

Ecosistema Urbano has been keen to engage in Spain, a country hard-hit by economic crisis, and its research there has shown that in this field, 'a lack of organisation meets high-quality creativity, typical of the Latin culture'. In that country, the design team has focused on low-cost actions capable of generating responses from residents, such as the temporary Beach on the Moon Square (2006) to improve a run-down square in a deprived area of Madrid. Here the designers have tested new notions of neighbourhood connectivity by curating such events as La Noche de los Niños ('the night of the children'; 2010) at a nearby cultural centre, at which children could exchange toys, becoming both spontaneous actors and spectators.

'Cities are created and maintained by people for people, and urban development only makes sense when the community cares about it', Tato and Vallejo emphasise. 'We work to empower the communities to drive the projects that affect them, to guarantee social relevance.'

Urban development only makes sense when the community cares about it

→ **Right:** José Lluis Vallejo, co-founder of Ecosistema Urbano, leads a creative workshop with local primary school children as part of Exuma's Garden of Dreams project for its sustainable future, The Bahamas, with Exuma Lab, Harvard University GSD, 2014.

Below:
Site of the Calama PLUS masterplan, Elemental and Tironi, 2012-2025. The mining centre of Calama, in Chile's Atacama desert, has one of the planet's most adverse climates, a very high altitude, 10% air humidity, and a widening equity gap.

Below, centre:
The Calama PLUS masterplan will promote reforestation, expansion of farming activities and new public space.

Elemental

In the evolution of an urban plan today, the involvement of the whole community is vital. Conventionally, however, this is a protracted process, the convention being to start in a near independent way with in-depth analysis, then to evolve proposals and only later deign to show them to the public. But to gutsily open up the process from the beginning, conveying a greater number or rough early ideas for citizens' responses and giving real teeth to their proposals through intensive dialogue, better enables the local realities of each situation to be grasped and reflected in the plan. Above all, it rouses the community to have a sense of confidence about the plans' content, modus operandi and motives.

The Chilean city of Calama in the Atacama Desert is a mining centre with a population of some 150,000, where 22% of the country's copper is extracted, accounting for a considerable amount of GDP.[1] Despite this value, it possesses one of the planet's most adverse climates, with frequent windstorms, high ultraviolet (UV) radiation, a yearly rainfall of a mere 1mm (if that), and a variation in temperatures of 40°C between day and night. The region is located over high altitudes – above 2,500 metres above sea level – and has only about 10% air humidity. To make matters worse, an equity gap between wealth produced and poor living conditions has rapidly been getting wider, with a marked difference between the city's new eastern districts and the rest which has long been in a delapidated condition.

Codelco, the state-owned mining company and the world's foremost copper producer, asked Elemental, the leading Chilean architectural and urban design firm, founded in 2000, to produce a participatory urban plan. It was to be based on the lines of Elemental's much-admired plan of this kind for the coastal town of Constitucíon, which had been ravaged by a tsunami in 2010. Once again, the firm partnered with Rodrigo Araya, co-founder of Tironi Asociados, a strategic communication company, to conduct the participatory design process 'with neighbours as actors', a process typifying an emerging way of operating that democratises a plan, galvanising all concerned with urban standards.[2]

> **The equity gap between wealth produced and poor living conditions has rapidly been getting wider**

Bottom:
The Calama PLUS masterplan project included a strong public participatory process with the city's inhabitants and all the local institutions keen for its renewal, centred on the Open House in the main square.

Right:
The Calama PLUS masterplan proposes an expansion of the oasis, the creation of a green belt and the multiplication of greenery within Calama.

In June 2011 the team presented its first proposals, not knowing that the local community, including miners – as much as a quarter of the population, according to the media, and acting with the support of the mayor – had begun protesting on the streets and were being met by riot police. Blocking the mines and threatening the copper production, the protestors demanded better living conditions and an improved quality of urban space in Calama. As with the Constitucíon plan, Elemental and Tironi offered to come up with a set of proposals in 100 days to help to alleviate the social pressure.

The locals wanted 'beauty, friendliness and dignity', says Alejandro Aravena, founder of Elemental. The team immediately created a consortium with all the stakeholders and built an 'Open House' in the main square in which the planners could conduct their deliberations in the most public way. The team also rigorously analysed all the existing plans. But in late August 2011 a major strike immobilised the city for the second time. The mayor was even arrested for leading it.

Amidst these winds of political conflict it took many weeks to restabilise the consortium but in November the 'Open House' was inaugurated. However, the first meetings were marked by scepticism, resentment and rage from participants. The team became aware, too, that the pronounced inequalities represented a mix of polarities: left wing (municipality) and right wing (regional government), urban and rural modes of productions, natives and westerners as well as rich and poor.

The first proposals of Calama PLUS ('Urban Sustainable Plan' in Spanish) by Elemental and Tironi in December 2011 were to make Calama the best-connected city in the country with a new light rail system. But the plans were rejected, so in workshops and forums the team shifted emphasis to systems that would protect the city from the wind and dust, based on the green filter irrigation methods used in high plateaux of the Andes, and opened discussions about water and its role in the future.

These themes hit a chord with the participants of the town meeting, and at a second gathering the team addressed the 'historical debt' in Calama, evidenced by the broken promises of previous plans drawn up but not implemented in 1998, 2001, 2004 and 2008. At last, there was a sense of standing on common ground, which led to the team's masterplan synthesising its vision for the city. Encompassing geographical and environmental issues, the plan expanded the oasis from the river to the

→

Calama PLUS

Elemental helps to reform the city

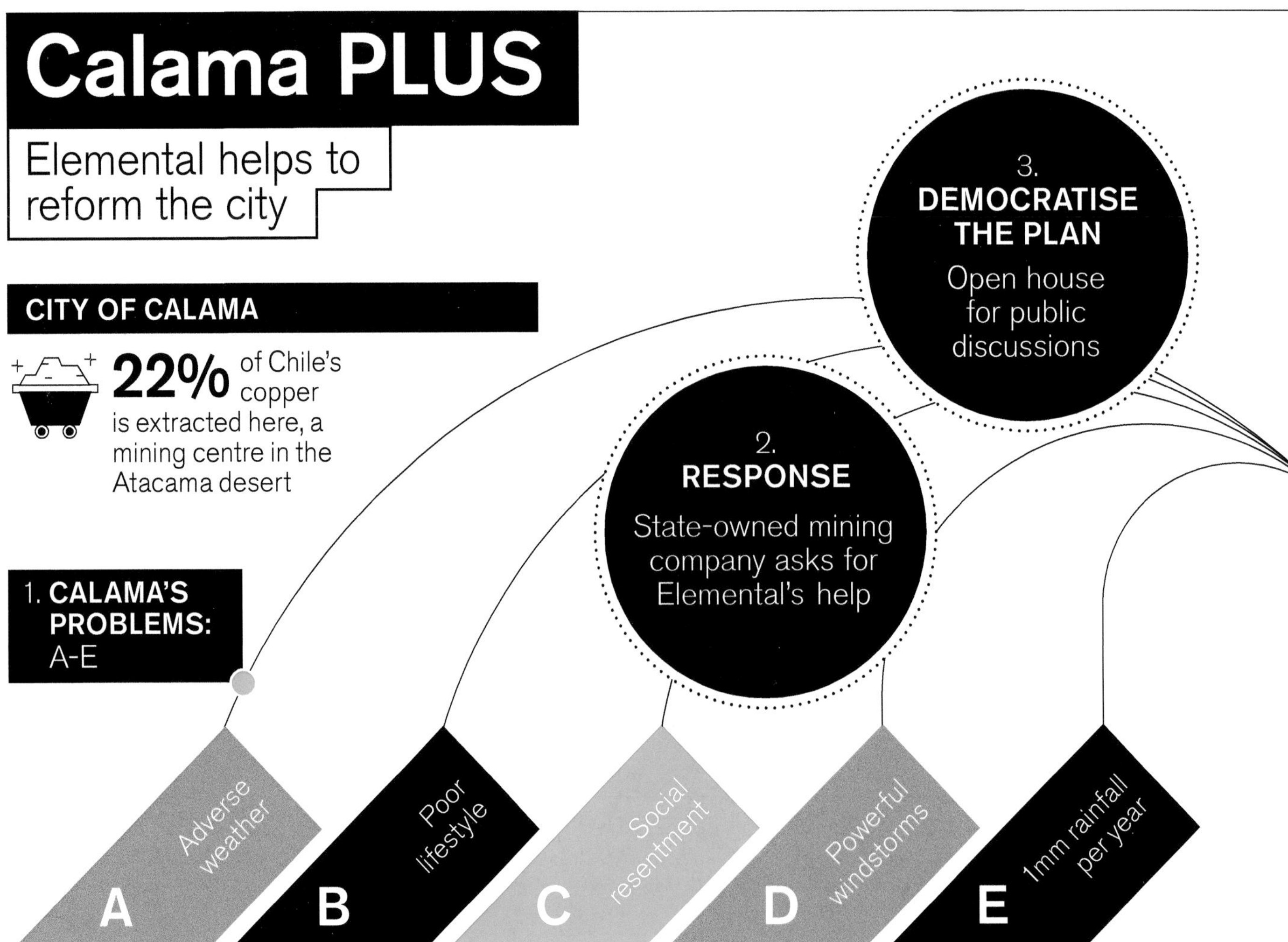

> The marketing of new urban plans can easily raise suspicions as to developers' motives. The incendiary issue of public compensation for failed promises, if not evolved through such a win-win plan as Calama PLUS, could have wiped out its viability

whole city, transforming Calama's identity from a mining camp into a proper city. The mechanisms included Andean terraced irrigation, a new forest to reduce the dust coming into the city, and Balmaceda Park, a new 16-hectare peri-urban linear park. In the form of a green belt, it redefines 10km of the city's urban limit. Water from the city's treatment plant is gathered in a cistern, and then distributed via a new aqueduct running next to the new park and feeding the trees' irrigation system across all districts.

As well as this new infrastructure, the masterplan includes a number of new public buildings in two locations. Markets, a cultural centre, a mediatheque, a mining museum and the governor's building sit along a central linear north–south boulevard. In response to requests put forward by residents as part of the participatory process, the Neighbourhood Zeus Plan on the western periphery brings

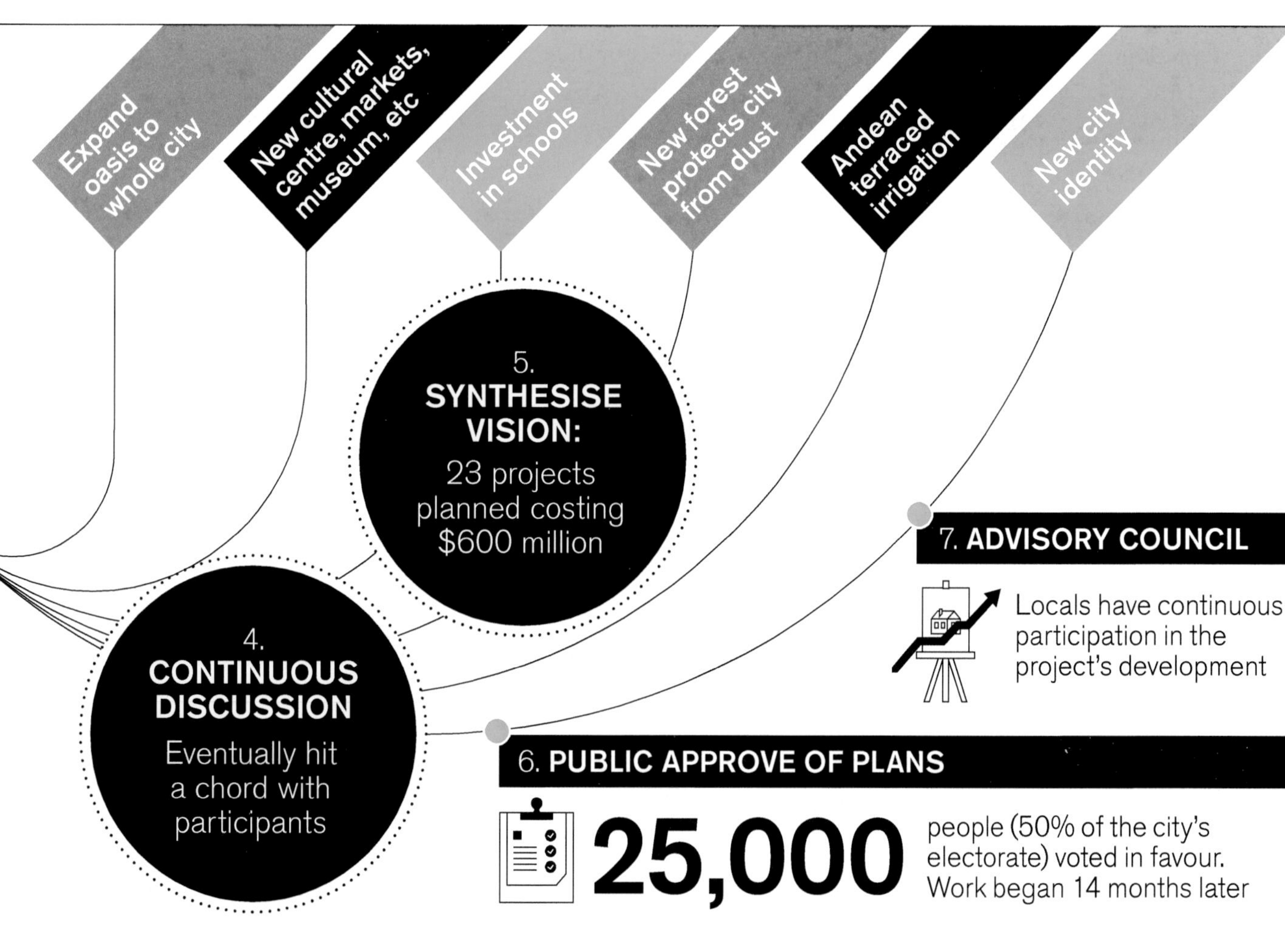

investment in seven local schools to make a network of community centres, expanding the buildings' use from 8 hours per day to 14 hours.

In April 2012 the plan was shown at a third big town meeting. 'It was not an easy task', says Aravena. 'Resentment was still there despite months of intensive dialogue', and speakers still talked of an immense social debt from the mining companies and different governments over the years. The following week a public referendum was held to establish priorities to the projects, and to give social and political weight to the project. The authorities were sceptical, but 25,000 people voted in favour, 50% of the entire voting population. Many locals had seen the failure of four urban renewal proposals driven by regional governments since 1998. However, by now, after the extensive meetings, voters of all ages knew that making Calama PLUS viable relied on the active participation of all the inhabitants and institutions, and involved both the private and the public sectors.

Investment in Calama PLUS amounts to US$600 million and the first urban improvement projects have already advanced to the implementation phase. In total, 23 have been forged. They range from urban parks and schools, to proposals on how to use scarce water resources more efficiently. There is a big focus on resource management, compost creation in schools and nurseries using grey water for the city's tree planting, and agricultural development plans to halt the desertification of the oasis. Locals take an active part in the Citizen Participation and Citizen Advisory Council. Rodolfo Reygadas, manager of the Calama PLUS consortium, which is both comptroller and quality-control body, told local media last year that the consortium ultimately works for residents. 'The community also gives continuity to the plan, because it will always be here', he adds.

The marketing of new urban plans can easily raise suspicions as to the developers' motives. The incendiary issue of public compensation for failed promises, if not dealt with through such a win-win plan as Calama PLUS, could have wiped out its viability. By contrast with Constitucíon, which had suffered from two severe tsunamis, in Calama the problem was there was too little water. But in both cases trees became a solution, as part of the system to 'domesticate' the environment. In the view of the team, this process was helped by the new urban design plans, operating as a 'magnet' – as Elemental describes it in the title of the practice's short film *The Magnet and the Bomb* (see endnote 2) –to dismantle the 'time bomb' of social and ecological unsustainability, and assist a shortcut towards equality. Calama's social mobilisation in support of Calama PLUS happened because people felt a sense of ownership of the plan.

'It was an industrial relic that no longer was viable in Manhattan', says Robert Hammond, executive director of Friends of the High Line, of the elevated freight railway line that stopped running through the West Village, the Meatpacking District and Chelsea, and Hell's Kitchen, close to the Hudson River, in the 1980s. 'It was not romantic for the people who remember it. It was dirty, really loud, and it was a sign you lived in a bad neighbourhood. When it was a working railroad, you didn't want to live next to the railroad tracks. There's a reason why you call it, the other side of the tracks.'[1]

But for over a decade Friends of the High Line, the non-profit conservancy established in 1999, fought for the railway line's preservation and conversion, fending off threats of demolition, successfully advocating for the transformation of the 2.33km-long elevated tracks area into a public park on Manhattan's West Side, from Gansevoort Street to West 30th Street between Washington Street and 11th Avenue. Section 1, Gansevoort Street to W20th Street opened in 2009; Section 2, W20th to W30th streets, in 2011; and in September 2014, the third and final section, between W30th and W34th streets, was opened to the public.

Once, before the original meatpacking district developed, with its late 19th-century abattoirs and packing plants, a farmers' market took place here. 'We started calling it the High Line district because it includes [different] places but it has its own identity.' The High Line is owned by the City of New York, but is maintained and operated by Friends of the High Line in partnership with the city's Department of Parks & Recreation, and raises private funding to support more than 90% of the park's annual operations.

Below:
Looking north on the High Line during construction at West 18th Street, 2006.

Bottom:
Looking north on the High Line under construction at Little West 12th Street, 2006. Building was also under way for the Standard Hotel bridging the park.

Friends of the High Line

Right:
Friends of the High Line displayed hundreds of its favourite entries to the ideas competition in an exhibition at Grand Central Terminal's Vanderbilt Hall, July 2003.

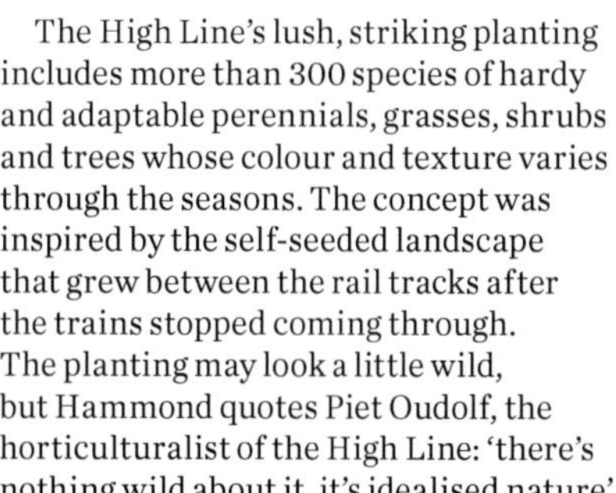

The High Line's lush, striking planting includes more than 300 species of hardy and adaptable perennials, grasses, shrubs and trees whose colour and texture varies through the seasons. The concept was inspired by the self-seeded landscape that grew between the rail tracks after the trains stopped coming through. The planting may look a little wild, but Hammond quotes Piet Oudolf, the horticulturalist of the High Line: 'there's nothing wild about it, it's idealised nature'.

Friends of the High Line was founded by local residents Joshua David, who became its president, and Hammond. 'I lived down on 10th and Washington, since 1993', says Hammond. 'I loved this neighbourhood and had always seen the High Line from my apartment.' In 1999 he read an article in the New York Times that the High Line was slated for demolition, with a map showing the entire run of connected tracks, a rare urban feature in Manhattan at the time.

Hammond assumed that the High Line already had a preservation group working on it, but on making enquiries discovered that no one was really doing anything. The head of the community board had bought it from the railway company for $10 in 1980s to use for waste transfer but 'he didn't have the resources to pull it together and the property owners sued him'. The railway organisation itself, who owned the structure and the 9-metre high space beneath it, had hired the Regional Plan Association (RPA) to do a study on possible uses. 'It was a liability for them and they wanted to get rid of it.' Hammond discovered that 22 different owners owned the land beneath it. 'They had this rail line running through the middle of their property, and could build around it, but it was incredibly expensive and inefficient to do that. So they built condos in place of the buildings they tore down to monetise it, and it was just a liability for them too.'

When Hammond went to the first local community board meeting he attended in Chelsea, he found that most of the people there also wanted to tear it down, as indeed did Rudy Giuliani, the then mayor of New York. 'The three mayors before him had also reviewed it and also favoured demolition.' Hammond found himself sitting next to Joshua David, whom he did not know at the time. 'Joshua and I exchanged business cards, and said maybe we could do something together.'

Many people told them that it was a good idea. 'But as we had no experience, they questioned the project: "how are these guys going to do it?" Well-intentioned people said, "you're just postponing the inevitable, let's just get it down."' At the time the site was mostly occupied by parking garages. 'People also thought the High Line would cut people off from the Hudson River. They worried that it would prevent the neighbourhood from continuing to develop. It had never happened before in the USA. They asked, "how would that happen in NYC? Where would you get the money? Would it work?"'

Talking further to urban planners and historians, Hammond and David found that back in the 1950s and '60s elevated walkways were heralded as the saviour of cities, but that they turned out to be 'downtown city killers' because they took people off the street, or were not well used. 'Would [the activist] Jane Jacobs have supported an elevated walkway in a residential neighbourhood? From an urban planning textbook standpoint, there were arguments against it.' The only other example the pair knew of was Paris's Promenade Plantée (opened in 1993), and they talked to the city planners there. 'It was popular among Parisians, but it was just a park, and like any other neighbourhood pocket park, they weren't trying to do anything →

Below:
Aerial view of the High Line looking north from West 23rd Street, a section of the park where the narrow railway is very close to neighbouring buildings.

Right:
Friends of the High Line presents more than 450 public programmes per year. On field trips schoolchildren learn about horticulture, urban history and design.

special. They tried to cut it off from the street with hedges.'

The High Line is 'more like a Central Park model, so when you are there, many people feel like they are are in bucolic countryside.' The American urbanist, journalist and organisational analyst William 'Holly' Whyte's seminal book from 1980, *The Social Life of Small Urban Spaces*, 'really had a powerful effect' on Hammond and David.[2] It contained all the findings from his revolutionary Street Life project (begun in 1969), for which he filmed public spaces, supported by assistants with notebooks, in order to discover more about the behaviour of pedestrians and what made particular urban dynamics so popular.

'People would ask us, you want to save [the High Line], but what is it going to do, what is it going to be?', so Hammond and David hired an architect to do some renderings; but the best tactic was to show people a beautiful set of photographs of the elevated, overgrown site, to let them conjure up their own vision of how the High Line might be. Some people envisaged horticulture, others railway history, or space for architecture. Even Hammond and David did not see the future High Line in the same way. Hammond 'loved it exactly as it looks', which has changed progressively over time, while David favoured a completely built environment. 'The advantage was that neither one of us was architects. We always said: "the community, the city, should decide what's up there, openly and over time."'

One property owner has spent almost $3 million in legal fees fighting Friends of the High Line, because he wanted to tear down the railway in order to build a FedEx depot (in 1999). In the end, 'we had to sue the city to stop it being demolished. Giuliani signed a demolition order two days before he left office [in 2001]. There were several lawsuits, but the unspoken heroes of the story were the lawyers. No one really likes hiring them. It helps developers to get things done, using legal techniques.' As Hammond and David knew that the regeneration of the High Line, including its maintenance costs, was 'going to be expensive', they commissioned a financial feasibility study from a firm called HR&A to show that the plan made economic sense.

In order to have a design concept to back up the financial feasibility study, in 2000 the pair held an ideas competition, receiving 720 entries (half of which were from international architectural practices), and staged an exhibition of the submissions at Grand Central Terminal. As part of the judging they held community input sessions. The winning creative concept came from the architectural practice Diller Scofidio + Renfro, landscape architects James Corner Field Operations and horticulturalist Piet Oudolf.

The team's wooden planking design system, which combs into the landscape,

is useable in different ways and contains a mix of perennials that change appearance from season to season, convinced the judges. Even the design team did not always agree about the project, but this creative friction enabled a fruitful process of design discussions. The team's selection and the resulting High Line, widely written about in the media and the subject of *High Line: The Inside Story of New York City's Park in the Sky,* has 'encouraged developers around to use good architects', says Hammond.[3]

When Michael Bloomberg became mayor of New York in 2001, he was much more supportive of the High Line project. But trying to get the community to support the High Line was hard. It 'took [us] several years for them to come on board, after difficult negotiations. Their preservation and planning representative always voted against the High Line because he wanted lower density and preservation.' The trouble was that there were three main things people wanted in the neighbourhood: affordable housing, low density and the High Line, Hammond explains, and 'they compete with each other. You can say, I want all three, but you can't get a lot of affordable housing unless you have more density, and preservation was another piece [of the jigsaw]. What happened is a compromise: there's 30% affordable housing, there are all these height restrictions, but the High Line has slightly taller buildings in the neighbourhood.'

Hammond admits that 'the biggest mistake we made [was] with the zoning, because it was so contentious'. It was already 'such a long shot, negotiating with the neighbourhood needs, the developers who didn't want it, and people in the city who thought it was unlikely, so we barely got this zoning through, and now it's been so successful. People like helping [to make projects like High Line happen], but they also like it being part of their vision. So if it's a collective vision, it's different than "my vision, help me build my vision" and that's not as compelling a case. "Help me build our vision, or this vision we share", is more compelling.'

Hammond says the best creator of value in Manhattan is Central Park, representing 'billions of dollars in real estate appreciation – that's where the tax base comes from', so it is a question of looking 'at the appreciation in real estate taxes in 20 years' time.' For a more direct comparison, Hammond and David looked at smaller pocket parks, not especially well known, 'that are a quarter of an acre, where, within a two-block radius has anywhere from 6-15% in added value'. The real estate marketeers the Sunshine Group advised the pair that 'the way you create value is to create a neighbourhood people really want to live in, work in, visit, shop, like Grammercy Park'.

'We said the High Line would create $250 million in added value, and would cost $100 million to build. The whole thing has cost

People like helping to make projects like High Line happen, but they also like it being part of their vision

Left:
Looking north on the High Line at Little West 12th Street, spring 2014.

$250 million [which came] mostly from philanthropists, and a lot of it had to be spent on legal fees, including the third phase. It's already created $2 billion in new development. In 2013, the predictions were that in a 20-year period, it [would] yield close to a $1 billion in terms of tax revenues for the city.' The City of New York put in around $100 million to build the High Line (it costs about $5-7 million dollars per year to run) and the Friends get about $70,000 in public funds and pay for all the gardeners and horticulturalists, and all the 453 community programmes per year. 'It's an expensive park to maintain. The quality of the plantings is more at the level of a botanical garden than a park that is much cheaper to maintain.'

'Everything was through advice other people had given us – very little of it was our idea,' adds Hammond. 'We get all the credit, but the most important thing we did was to raise the flag and to allow other people to come along to help get it done, and provide the experience which neither of us had, but an entrepreneurial background helps, bringing people together. Dan Biederman, who ran the regeneration of Bryant Park, gave me 11 things that public space needed, and only one is design-related.' Jim Capalino, a lobbyist, proved to be really helpful. 'How do developers get things done? They hire lobbyists to lobby and push. Travis Terry, who works for [Capalino] started this project in Queens called the QueensWay, where they are doing a good job.'

Hammond and David never anticipated the sheer number of visitors the High Line would bring. 'We thought we would get 300,000 people per year. In 2012 we had 4.3 million'. The new Whitney Museum of American Art – sited next to the Friends of the High Line building by the High Line at the junction of Gansevoort and Washington streets – has brought the Friends a goods lift (a real boon as previously the Friends had to 'crane everything up or carry [it] up'), refuse storage space, a programming space and public washrooms. Renzo Piano, the Whitney's architect, wanted the facilities to look separate 'but they nestle together'.

In 2015, on their premises' street level the Friends opened Santina, the High Line's first sit-down restaurant (Piano was its exterior architect). A percentage of the proceeds from Santina goes to support the High Line's maintenance and operations. The Friends have 'a licence agreement with the city since the Friends pays for a lot of the maintenance. They are giving us that space and [we'll] share the revenue with the city.'

What is successful about the High Line, feels Hammond, is that 'it is not an escape

Above:
A new section of the High Line at the Rail Yards was completed in 2014, including the Pershing Square Beams, a hot spot for children.

from the city; it's part of the city, a way of experiencing the city in a different way. When you are there, you can hear the honking, smell the streets, you see the taxis, but the elevation, the combination with nature, gives it this very different perspective. It embraces NYC, it's why so many people get their wedding photos taken up there, and cruising websites like Grindr have shots of it. It's saying, I live in NYC. It's flattering. It's that combination that works.'

Hammond loves 'how people have taken ownership of the High Line, and use it for different things'. The neighbourhood was struggling when it was developed as a park. 'Now, the biggest complaint is that gentrification is happening so quickly', he says. 'Gentrification was coming to this neighbourhood anyway, because it was going to be rezoned for residential use. The High Line speeded it up, accelerated it and increased the value.' Given that 'gentrification creates an incredible amount of new tax base for the city', the High Line gets too much credit, and blame, for all the change, feels Hammond.

The High Line is an influential model, Hammond observes. 'Public parks have the ability to transform cities.' The Lowline, an underground park along an historic trolley terminal on the Lower East Side, is being planned by James Ramsey, an architect, and Dan Barasch (now the Lowline's executive director). 'People are already doing it with community gardens. Jane Jacobs's attitude was very interesting – all you need to do is look around your own city and come up with answers.' The High Line is 'such a big example, expensive and different, but to me it inspires not just elevated or underground parks, but any kind of civic project that people can start', says Hammond. 'You don't necessarily have to have the experience or the money, or the plan of how you're going to get there, but just start it and other people can rally round.'

The community, the city, should decide what's up there, openly, and over time

Below:
Co-founders of Friends of the High Line Robert Hammond and Joshua David attend the Summer Party on the High Line presented by Coach, 19 June 2012.

ENGAGEMENT
REPLICABILITY
DESIGN DRIVEN
SCALE
IMPACT

IDENTIFY → ENQUIRE → DEVELOP → CO-DESIGN → CO-CONSTRUCT → HAND-OVER

Gap Filler

When a massive earthquake struck New Zealand's South Island in September 2010, a significant number of buildings in Christchurch's downtown area collapsed or were badly damaged and subsequently demolished, as rebuilding anew was deemed the cheaper solution. The disaster had a number of after-effects, one of which was to highlight the widespread acceptance by city dwellers of permits and bureaucratic processes prevailing, along with road closures and other restrictive measures, simply in order to survive. For many people, life became temporarily communal.

One response to the destruction was the 'activation' around the city of vacant sites where buildings had been demolished. 'There was significant pressure to act quickly, as damaged buildings were forcing the temporary closure of neighbouring businesses and dissuading people from visiting the central city', says Ryan Reynolds.[1] Together with fellow performance-studies scholar Coralie Winn and architect Andrew Just, Reynolds set up the Gap Filler organisation to 'activate' those vacant sites via a community-centred, participatory innovation lab. Starting as an entirely voluntary initiative, by late 2014 Gap Filler had seven paid staff as a result of fundraising, from Christchurch City Council and many other trusts and foundations.

Reynolds says that the city has been going through an intense rite of passage, and has had to contend with the reality of a military cordon locking people out of large parts of the city for more than two years. 'The earthquakes in Christchurch have both intensified our restrictive and repressive society, and invited the possibility and desire to change that radically.'[2]

As a small group, Gap Filler initially created on the former site of a popular downtown restaurant a temporary space for people to linger in, 'perhaps to ease the pressure for rushed decision-making and to encourage social interactions in the central city'.[3] Here the group created 'a kitschy garden picnic spot and open performance space', projecting old heritage films onto the exposed wall of the building next door.[4] It called out for performers and gathered bands, circus performers, puppeteers and poets. 'It became a positive feedback loop: our spatial intervention attracted social activity, which further changed the place and encouraged more social activity.'[5]

With support from Sustainable Habitat Challenge (SHAC), on a vacant corner site Gap Filler built itself a sustainable off-grid office that, thanks to specifications that were within the limits of Council approval, did not require any building permits or consents. The vacant lots it works with represent the opportunity for design research, for prototyping

Right:
The yellow pavers used instead of traditional signage draw people to Gap Filler's Think Differently Book Exchange, Christchurch, New Zealand, 2011-14.

Below:
Student volunteers weeding and tidying up the site of the Think Differently Book Exchange on the corner of Kilmore and Barbadoes Streets, Christchurch.

A positive feedback loop: spatial intervention attracted social activity, changed the place and encouraged more social activity

community spaces that do not require planning permissions, that are flexible and can evolve through time, and that engage people as both makers and users. The projects are simple and singular. For Gap Filler's seventh project the group salvaged a large fridge and placed it at the back of a corner site, then built a path to it with paving stones. People were invited to donate books that had changed their way of thinking. Gap Filler stocked the fridge with the books and left it unlocked, with a sign inside saying 'take a book, leave a book'.

The Dance-O-Mat, the group's 15th project, featured a jukebox made from a launderette washing machine that when activated with a coin connected to an iPod, and a sprung wooden dance floor. This became a magnet for impromptu activities such as birthday parties and dance classes, and was used for around seven hours a day as many of the dance studios in the city had been demolished; it even attracted Prince Charles during a visit to the country. This 'reframing of space encourages, and makes comfortable, otherwise aberrant activities', says Reynolds.[6] Another project, on the first-year anniversary of the 2010 earthquake, was the open-air Cycle Powered Cinema.

Reynolds explains that, while the term 'gap filler' implies a →

Above:
Members of the public help themselves to books from the Think Differently Book Exchange, Christchurch.

↓ makeshift physical structure or solution that may last only for a short period, the group does not regard the Dance-O-Mat in that way, quoting the sociologist Richard Sennett who pointed out that many permanent urban developments and buildings have short life spans. 'If you plan a spatial product to be permanent, it quickly becomes outmoded', Reynolds adds. 'If you plan it to be temporary, it is almost inherently more flexible and adaptable, a work-in-progress – and hence is actually more suitable (in some regards) for long-term evolving use.'[7]

In an email exchange discussing their co-authored essay on the 'performative' and scenographic aspects of Christchurch's urban landscape,[8] Dr Reneé Newman-Storen of Perth's Edith Cowan University commented to Reynolds that she did not see the projects as 'just a temporary fix before the big guys come in and enact a masterplan', but as interventions that 'engage with the public to ask them what city they want and how they want to remember, or even memorialise, who they once were'.[9] As part of his email response, Reynolds remarked that 'perhaps Gap Filler is successful by being open to these ruptures, the unstable and the changing'.[10] Newman-Storen concurs: for her, 'Gap Filler is about embracing the symbolic space of the city and its inhabitants'; in turning spaces that are personally known by the community, yet are not considered useful post-earthquake, 'into something that can be seen, used, felt and loved again', Gap Filler opens up a reassessment of their value.[11]

In the aftermath of the more catastrophic earthquake that hit Christchurch in February 2011, Gap Filler continued to create events. It has engaged in more than 40 urban interventions that have lasted from a few days to two years. The group perceives its role as having a dual purpose: community-building, involving local people and organisations in the creative reactivation of their damaged neighbourhoods; and igniting experimentation and innovation in the renewal of the whole city. 'We lower the barriers, by handling the legal constraints and liability insurances, to help ideas become reality.'

Gap Filler is now among the leaders of the Transitional City movement in Christchurch, promoting the value of local, bottom-up, small-scale temporary activities in the midst of the major top-down masterplan being carried out by the government. Its symbolic work is mirrored by an expanding number of new programmes of a similar, improved type that are developing around New Zealand. 'Gap Filler's projects seem to fulfil people's longing for the ability to intervene and determine their (and their city's) outcome.'[12]

Top:
Members of the public having a dance on the Dance-O-Mat in the first days at its first location, St Asaph Street, Christchurch, February 2012.

Right:
Prince Charles dancing with a local woman at the Dance-O-Mat, Christchurch, during his visit to New Zealand in November 2012.

Gap Filler: linked activation interventions

In response to an earthquake, a range of linked creative pop-ups were produced in Christchurch for community benefit to bring life and vibrancy back into the city

Community-centred experiences: each project injects life into a vacant site

40+

projects around Christchurch, New Zealand

INTERVENTIONS

- Project sites
- Book exchange
- Dance-O-Mat

EVENTS

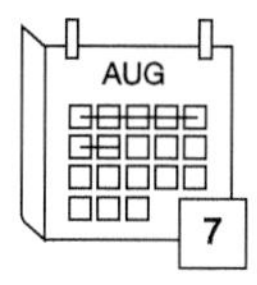

Events range in duration from one day to nearly two years

DANCE-O-MAT

5x7m public dance floor with a jukebox. Was very popular and used by all kinds of people

1. Used 7hrs a day
2. Used for birthday parties and socialising
3. Used by those who lost their dance studio

BOOK EXCHANGE

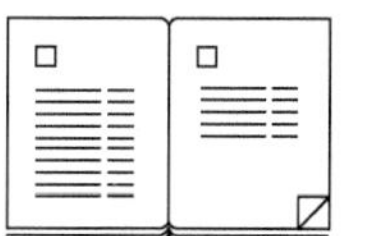

24/7 free book exchange with the theme of 'Think Differently'

FACTS

Active even after all the books were stolen, twice

Popular resource for both locals and tourists

ENGAGEMENT
REPLICABILITY
DESIGN DRIVEN
SCALE
IMPACT

IDENTIFY → ENQUIRE → DEVELOP → CO-DESIGN → CO-CONSTRUCT → HAND-OVER

Herkes için Mimarlik

In 2013, at Gezi Park in Istanbul, Turkey, the enactment of social inclusion through extensive self-organisation and of the 'right to the city' – first evoked as a set of ideals in 1968 by the French philosopher and sociologist Henri Lefebvre – demonstrated the power of ordinary people to act to create and protect their own social space.[1]

In the face of top-down development plans protestors at Gezi Park asserted the use value of urban space rather than its exchange value. Their actions also echoed the central points of protests made against inequality in recent years at Tahrir Square in Cairo, Puerta del Sol in Madrid, Syntagma Square in Athens and Zuccotti Park in New York.

Gezi Park is a small urban park next to Istanbul's Taksim Square, at the heart of one of the city's major leisure districts, and one of the few remaining green spaces in the centre of its European side. In 2011, right before the elections, the Turkish prime minister, Recep Tayyip Erdoğan, and the mayor of Istanbul, Kadir Topbaş, announced the Taksim Square Pedestrianisation Project. This top-down proposal entailed taking vehicular traffic underground into tunnels and removing all of Gezi Park's trees and benches and its children's playground to make way for a shopping mall, as well as rebuilding military barracks demolished in 1940, on the basis that Taksim Square had no special qualities as an urban space and that Gezi Park was not being used by anyone. Many NGOs and other platforms of this kind were immediately alarmed, as citizens had not been consulted and moreover, the plans threatened to erase a vital public space in the centre of the city.

The events staged in Gezi Park in 2011-12 by Herkes için Mimarlik (HiM), an Istanbul-based non-profit, independent architecture organisation, showed people who used Taksim Square, but had not yet experienced the park itself, that it is a calming, but also lively, 'common' place in which to spend time. Through numerous workshops HiM scrutinised the claims that the Square was not of value as urban space and that no one used the park, maintaining that '*herkes*' ('everyone' or 'all') – needs to have a voice.

The debates created momentum for a new type of festival at Gezi Park, including picnics, which ran to ten different events. There were performance arts, games and workshops for children, and everyone was invited to comment on the plans for the park. HiM felt that it 'accomplished a major task of urban spaces, which is to bring different kinds of people together'; it successfully made Gezi Park 'a trademark platform which brings together people interested in the future of urban spaces'.[2]

HiM is a young organisation, founded in 2011, devoted to solutions to social

Top:
One of the Gezi Park Picnic Festivals, Istanbul, 2011-12, organised by Herkes için Mimarlik.

Above:
Aerial view of Taksim Square, Istanbul, Turkey, with the edge of Gezi Park to the left, 2011.

problems in Turkey and further afield. As denoted by its name, which translates as 'architecture for all', the group is a mix of young architects, urban planners, civil engineers and sociologists, a social platform that now numbers around 70 people. It promotes participatory design processes, and seeks social change through these, in both urban and rural contexts. All the while, it tries to establish a common ground between the financial and administrative sectors so that sustainable design solutions to challenges within the built environment can be found and implemented.

At the same time, 'when architecture is removed from architects', they need to find new roles, said Yelta Köm, one of HiM's members. The Gezi Park festivals demonstrated the shift of the group towards social activism. The oasis at the heart of the park became surrounded by ever more barricades; inside grew an encampment that included a library, medical supply stations, and places designated for performances and speeches. HiM publicised its events, which expanded to encompass an audience of 500, through social media. The question was whether the group could actually change entrenched existing frameworks.

It tried very hard. HiM created an online petition to save the Park, calling for an open and democratic process for the decision making. It also made an archive of photographs and drawings of the 'event architecture' to document the makeshift shelters, which included a speakers' stage, a barricade made of benches and a communal dining table created using makeshift materials. Each 'unique structure' the group noted at Gezi Park during the protests had 'its own in-situ design and implementation process', and its ephemeral nature made it vital to document as a 'collective memory'.

In May 2013 the demonstrations spurred by the eviction of protestors against the park scheme became the largest scenes of public unrest in recent Turkish history. Under the slogan 'Taksim is Everywhere. Everywhere is Taksim', their actions revealed the depth of feelings against the government's displacement plan. The police crackdown and the clashes that occurred (Gezi Park was violently cleared on 15-16 June) led to eight casualties and over 8,000 people being injured, more than 100 of them very seriously. Eventually then-president Abdullah Gul announced that the redevelopment plans had been suspended. Since that time there have been numerous protests and democracy forums set up in Turkey, including against Istanbul's proposed third airport project, a third bridge over the Bosphorus and other construction projects planned for the city's few remaining green areas.

HiM remains tireless in its development of projects dealing with social problems throughout Turkey, designing participatory processes with a wide range of actors. While common ground between all involved parties on a spatial project – clients, administration and users – is so often elusive, that remains their aim, in order that architecture can be practised collaboratively. HiM 'aims to be a long-term architecture researcher, practitioner, school and student', arguing that this is possible only by 'establishing a social architecture that all parties of society can benefit from'.

As part of a rural revitalisation initiative, HiM's Caka Design Workshop held in a village on the shore near the Black Sea port of Ordu brought together locals, students and new graduates of architecture, landscape architecture, urban planning, civil engineering and sociology to find solutions in refurbishing school buildings abandoned for the last 25 years. HiM's workshops in Istanbul, conducted mostly at the SALT Galata cultural centre, cater for a wide range of ages and different social groups. Scene, a one-day workshop for primary school pupils, asked small groups to animate a television scene; Parkur focused on creative learning and critical thinking about the interaction of architecture and social culture; another workshop realised a travelling library.

Participants in HiM's workshops have attested to the fact that 'the architecture we learn at school does not really find its place in the real world ... mostly because of the gaps in the practice and disconnection from the social aspects'.[3] In the context of contemporary Turkey's deepest tensions between old and new forces, and top-down and ground-up movements, HiM's amelioratory activities are playing a vital role in bringing about a cultural platform for 'herkes' (everyone) based on the responsible reclamation and use of civic and rural resources through participation, education and sustainable design.

Below:
Musicians at one of the Gezi Park Picnic Festivals, Istanbul, 2011.

ENGAGEMENT
REPLICABILITY
DESIGN DRIVEN
SCALE
IMPACT

IDENTIFY → ENQUIRE → DEVELOP → CO-DESIGN → CO-CONSTRUCT → HAND-OVER

Right:
METI School, Rudrapur, Bangladesh, 2006. Earth, straw (ground floor); bamboo (first floor). Design: Anna Heringer; technical plannning: Eike Roswag.

Anna Heringer

What is lost when sustainability falls into the domain of advanced technological solutions? A lot, says the German architect and UNESCO Chair for Earthen Architecture Anna Heringer, because these solutions are 'exclusive, which isn't sustainable.'[1] Her vision of sustainable architecture involves rammed earth, sourced and worked on locally. Working with it reclaims cultural resilience through earth's tactile and versatile qualities, as well as providing local labour opportunities that standardised alternatives do not support. 'For me, architecture is a tool to improve lives ... to build up communities, [and] the self-confidence of the people and [their] skills as well as offering work opportunities, caring for beauty and cultural identity, as this is very strongly linked to dignity.'[2]

Together with colleague architect Eike Roswag, who did the technical planning, Heringer designed the METI (Modern Education and Training Institute) Handmade School in Rudrapur, northern Bangladesh. The two-storey primary school was handmade in four months using local earth and bamboo, with ceilings made of sari fabric. Heringer first visited Bangladesh in 1997 as a gap-year volunteer with a German NGO. One of the most densely populated countries in the world, like many other nations it has turned away from earth, perceived as a 'poor' material, in favour of expensive imported materials and energy-intensive bricks. But the METI project, which won an Aga Khan Award in 2007, enabled locals to value earth as a building material once again.

The bright, uplifting environment of METI, which includes imaginative, cave-

like learning and playing spaces, was realised with support from Dipshikha, a Bangladeshi NGO that helps the rural population in its sustainable development to learn how best to develop its village community through all its resources, improving educational facilities. Heringer and the design team, which included student architects, carried out a number of tests and experiments before construction began. As well as employing local craftsmen and using volunteers from Europe, the team involved the future users in the construction: teachers and the young schoolchildren, who then felt they had built the structure. This method of working meant that the local workers could learn how to build stronger walls and use measurement tools – and the visitors could understand how to take advantage of the water buffalos in their mixing processes.

Right:
Left to right: Shushen, the architect Anna Heringer, Stefanie and Ghogen work on the construction of METI School, Rudrapur, Bangladesh, 2010.

Left:
METI School's cave-like spaces attached to the classrooms serve as retreats and play areas for the students.

> **For the construction, the team involved the future users – the teachers and schoolchildren**

In a later project in Bangladesh, Heringer advocated two-storey houses so as to save land for food cultivation. Once again, she involved students in the team, and she encouraged locals to try new things. This project included the construction of a complex with teachers' flats and a school. In line with Heringer's policy of benefiting the region and contributing to more equality, it put funds into the locals and craftsmanship, such as basketmaking, rather than into industry. Heringer's choice of materials and her collaborative building methods are focused on improving local building techniques and advancing their sustainability.

In the USA, where rammed-earth projects are few and far between, Heringer has helped to change people's views of sustainable development with MudWorks, a demonstration project at Harvard University's →

Graduate School of Design, in Cambridge, Massachusetts. Positioned on a piece of windy, disused university land, the 2012 project – which required 50 tons of earth – symbolised the potential for creativity using rammed earth. Heringer and her collaborator, the artist and architect Martin Rauch, built the structure with a team of 150 students, Loeb Fellows and members of the public, in just seven 12-hour days.

'Those 12-hour days were spent shovelling 50 tons of earth into wooden forms resembling giant cake moulds, and packing the dirt down layer by layer with hand-held and electric-powered ramming tools', observed Inga Saffron, who worked on the construction. The earth from a Boston supplier was wetter than Heringer was used to, and the ramming tools were far more powerful, so they had to source gravel to lighten the

mix, she explains.[3] Few people in the USA are familiar with rammed earth projects, and the team involved with MudWorks got a thorough training in various earth construction techniques, from rammed earth to mud plastering.

As getting a city permit to give MudWorks building status would have taken a long time, it was deemed an art installation. The structure's open-plan arrangement, with small niches and benches inside, made this previously unloved spot a magnet as a meeting point for students and professors, but also for children and skaters; homeless people went to sleep there at night. Through MudWorks, the University also gained a valuable interface with the wider public.

Earth is a beautifully tactile and versatile material, and Heringer admires its wonderful sensuousness and presence, the connection it signifies, as well as its adaptability through the addition of

Left: Constructing MudWorks gave training in different earthen building techniques, from mud plastering to rammed earth, Gund Hall, Harvard University, 2012. Design: Anna Heringer, Martin Rauch and the Loeb Fellowship class of 2012.

Left:
MudWorks became a point of congregation for students, children, academic staff, and the public including homeless people.

colour, and the layering and embossing effects possible. 'It's available almost everywhere in the world, apart from the North and South poles, and it has fantastic material characteristics.'[4]

More importantly, rammed earth has many advantages for people's environmental health: with its high thermal mass, it moderates temperature naturally; it can be sourced and used locally, so transportation is eliminated; it absorbs sounds and smells. It can be built jointless over a long distance; in compression, it is two-thirds the strength of comparably thick concrete; for full recycling later, it should not be mixed with cement or aggregates to stabilise it. For urban contexts in which local excavation is not possible, Rauch (who has built more than 50 rammed-earth structures around the world, including the Chapel of Reconciliation in Berlin) has pioneered prefabricated elements, such as walls.

When people are involved with the process, they can create a sense of ownership for their whole community, not just their own building

The relatively high labour intensity needed to realise an inhabitable rammed-earth structure is a huge plus, Heringer says: 'There are [some] 7 billion people on this earth. The cheapest technology is now cheaper than even the cheapest labour on earth. We need some good employment opportunities, and not just for specialists.'[5] Other architects using rammed earth have formed collaborations with local students and citizens. The Dutch firm LEVS architekten, for example, used hydraulic compressed earth blocks (HCEB) for the walls of their primary school near Gangouroubouro in Mali, realised with Enterprise Dara, students from the technical college in Sevaré and local people.

'Humankind has always been able to use the potentials and the materials that we find under our feet that are locally available to build a beautiful habitat', says Heringer. 'I think that we have to start with this knowledge again ... and reconnect ourselves to these skills, and relearn that. ... In development work we are always trying to find standardised solutions, because [they're] controllable and easy to plan, but we should really have in our mind the diversity of cultures, and we really need to be more sensitive to that.'[6] The standardised route is also much more hands-off than making context-specific solutions, Heringer believes. 'When people are involved with the process, they can create a sense of ownership for their whole community, not just their own building, because they are helping each other, while building the buildings.'[7]

Right:
Home for All, Sendai, designed by Toyo Ito, Hideaki Katsura, Kaori Suehiro and Masashi Sogabe, 2011, as part of the Kumamoto Artpolis.

The destruction wrought in Japan by the Tohoku earthquake and tsunami on 11 March 2011 left 129,225 buildings totally collapsed, 254,204 half collapsed and 691,766 partially damaged along a 400km stretch of coast in north-eastern Honshu, the main island of Japan. Nearly 1 million people were affected throughout the wrecked built environment. Recovery efforts experienced major delays: available land was limited, as flood plains cannot be used. Local councils have also had to rebuild sea walls and water irrigation systems, and there has been a scarcity of construction materials.

Home for All

The massive dislocation demanded new facilities to help to foster human bonds and restore dignity

The Japanese government was highly efficient in the immediate aftermath of the disaster, repairing within five days roads that had collapsed completely. Temporary prefabricated housing was erected within three months on sports fields, for example in the city of Soma where 7,000 homes had been lost. But these units are small, and there was nowhere for people to meet, chat and play with their children. The dislocation demanded new facilities to help to foster human bonds and restore the dignity of everyone in the community.

In the aftermath of the earthquake and tsunami, and with ongoing concerns about radioactive contamination from the local nuclear power plant, architect Toyo Ito was one of many to get involved in reconstruction relief, rallying support and considering new facilities. He came up with the idea of creating new community hubs, places that would have a healing effect on people who had lost so much, where residents could nourish their social life once again. Together with architects Riken Yamamoto, Hiroshi Naito, Kengo Kuma and Kazuyo Sejima, Ito formed a team called Kishin no Kai, which also enlisted architectural students and other volunteers.

Kishin no Kai's founders say that the project, which they titled 'Minna no Ie', Japanese for 'Home for All', 'began with the intention to empower disaster-affected individuals to get back on their two feet. Each project forms a space for those who wish to proactively start afresh

Left:
Community members enjoy the new communal space of the Home for All at Miyagino, Sendai, designed by Toyo Ito and colleagues, 2011.

Map:
Between 2011 and 2015 a total of 12 Home for All community centre projects have been built in the north-eastern Tohoku region of Japan, with more planned.

and aims to inspire "the spirit of new beginnings".[1] Several years on from the disaster, the group is now creating a global Home for All support network to build up the organisation and its vital work still further, potentially consulting for other disaster-struck areas in the world.

Beyond Home for All's role in disaster relief, Ito also sees the project as a way of reviving local culture and fostering a means for communities to contribute to rebuilding, feeding back into further ideas for ways in which contemporary architecture can support society. Impressed by the courage and resolve of the locals, he established three rules: take steps to achieve something every day, even if it is small; transcend individuality; and let the design proposals for the projects do the talking.[2] Ito interviewed elderly people in relief centres and discovered that they were disinterested in moving into temporary housing because they dreaded living in 'egalitarian and homogenous' single-storey row houses built by the government, preferring instead to be close to nature and the local community. So Ito resolved to create a communal space in which residents could gather, discuss things and collaborate on planning their future.

The first Home for All, a community centre serving temporary housing in the Miyagino district of the city of Sendai, was designed by Ito with Hideaki Katsura, Kaoru Suehiro and Masashi Sogabe and built in October 2011 – some seven months after the disaster. Part of the innovative ongoing Kumamoto Artpolis project in the southern island of Kyushu, the project was funded by Kumamoto Prefecture, and the building was made wholly of donated wood pre-cut in Kumamoto that was then transported to Sendai by truck. The community centre was constructed by volunteers from Kyushu, who also made the furniture, and local people planted a flower garden alongside the building. Everyone gathers here for meals, to have a chat or to organise activities.

The third Home for All in the series, in a shopping area of the city of Kamaishi, was designed by Ito's office and the Ito Juku architectural school, after Ito became an adviser to Kamaishi's reconstruction project and had →

↓

his own NPO.[3] A bit like a primitive shelter in appearance, the structure was robustly but simply made with a steel frame and a timber pitched roof (June 2012). The playful-looking Home for All built in November 2012 in Rikuzentakata (designed by Ito, Kumiko Inui, Sou Fujimoto and Akihisa Hirata) is a vertical structure of roughly cut cedar – residue from the seawater flooding – with a lookout platform, set around a small white building housing a stove. It received the Golden Lion Award at the 13th International Architecture Biennale in Venice, marked out for its 'humanity', exceptional quality and accessibility to a broad audience.

Other Home for All projects have included a Home for All in Kamaishi's Heita district (designed by Riken Yamamoto and Field Shop), completed in May 2012; here student helpers and a tent manufacturer helped to create a soaring roof over the central stove. In July 2013 construction began on a Home for All for fishermen, a hut designed by Ito with TeMaLi Architects to be mobile so that it could still be used if the coastline were affected by a reclamation plan.

In spring 2015 a Home for All was completed in the city of Soma, an indoor play 'park' for toddlers and young children, designed by Tokyo-based Klein Dytham architecture (KDa). The background radiation in this particular area is still a concern, and because, typically, toddlers crawl on the ground and love to ingest anything they can get their little fingers on, they are not allowed to play outside. Yet they need a place in which to run around and exert their developing muscles. All the design and supervision for the project is voluntary, so in order to add to the generous donations for the construction materials Mark Dytham, co-director of KDa, ran

Left:
Toyo Ito (4th from left) with Kumiko Inui, Sou Fujimoto and Akihisa Hirata, architects of Home for All, Rikuzentakata, 2011-12.

Left:
Klein Dytham architecture's Home for All, Soma City, an indoor 'park' in which children of up to 4 years of age can play, 2013-15.

Below:
The cross-laminated timber columns of Soma City's Home for All create the sense of a large straw hat held aloft by trees.

the Tokyo Marathon in 2014, 'sponsored' by an Indiegogo crowdfunding campaign that raised over $11,000.

As a result of Ito's guidance and support from donors and the architectural world, Home for All has at the time of writing realised ten low-budget projects in the Tohoku region and many more are in the pipeline. The teams have built housing, children's playgrounds, community centres and an NPO outpost for staff in the farming and fishing industries involved in the reconstruction effort. The land used still bore the ruins of housing, retail centres and fishing wharves. Because of what happened, says Ito, we must rethink what architecture means and for whom we make it. Its essential role is always to 'create forms of gathering spaces for people'.[4]

On the third anniversary of the disaster in March 2014, the Home for All group reviewed its purpose and status. 'Though our projects are limited in area and scope, we do have a unique opportunity to use our experiences to reflect the paradigms of society and public facility construction'.[5] Up to that point all of the projects had been executed on an individual basis, typically led by NPOs, sponsoring organisations or local residential associations. Other monies, from struggling local governments or from visiting volunteers' donations, have helped to cover the group's utility costs.

Home for All has now become a Japanese NPO in order to create and oversee a network to link all its buildings, to continue funding the activities that take place in them, and to plan further building projects. This transition has set a new course to improve the group's operations and framework. Home for All gives people relief – for however short a time – from their hastily constructed, makeshift replacement homes, in places where they come together to find comfort in one another. Each Home for All project has also triggered a new conversation between architects, builders, sponsors, volunteers and users. Through this unique undertaking, among the many positive things to come out of the disaster are a revived image of Japanese architecture's humility and capacity to respond to social needs, as well as understanding and encouragement to work towards common goals.

Elderly people said they preferred to be close to nature and the local community

Kéré Architecture

Burkino Faso, a landlocked country in West Africa, is a semi-arid land with a primarily tropical climate; in the northern Sahel region, there are both great highs and great lows in temperature and rainfall. According to the United Nations Children's Fund (UNICEF), 44.6% of Burkina Faso's population live below the international poverty line of little more than $1 a day, and the country has to meet all its energy needs through imports, so greater self-sufficiency here is a crucial aim.[1] As regards self-sufficiency in building, 'what is architecture for somebody coming from a place where infrastructure is needed, but not existing?' reflects architect Francis Kéré, who was born in Burkina Faso and set up his Berlin-based practice, Kéré Architecture, in 2005. 'It is a process together with people – how you think about a project, and come out at the end with something they really feel is their own. We see ourselves in that.'[2]

Top:
Detail of perforated wall, Mali National Park, Bamako, Kéré Architecture, 2009-10.

'More than 80% [of Burkinabés] are illiterate. Most of the people have never heard of the terms "architecture" or "design"', Kéré said in a lecture at Harvard Graduate School of Design.[3] Because of this, they build their own, but poverty means that they cannot bring in technical assistance; so when building new structures, they are inclined to copy the latest new house built in the neighbourhood. Quickly built mud houses are the norm, calling for repairs after each rainy season, and they often end up with corrugated tin roofs that make the interior very stuffy, as Kéré recalls from childhood.

Determined to bring traditional practices into creative resolution with a trained sensibility, while still at college in Berlin Kéré designed a primary school for Gando, the village where he was born. In 1998 he set up his own charitable foundation, the Schulbaustein für Gando e.V. (Bricks for Gando), raising money to help fund the making of the school, and began transferring his skills back into his home community.

Kéré had no resources to make the Gando primary school in the typically

Left:
The local community contribute their earthenware pots to be repurposed as building material for the School Library, Gando, Burkino Faso, Kéré Architecture, 2010-15.

Left:
Exterior view of sport centre entrance, Mali National Park, Kéré Architecture, 2009-10.

French imported model. Favouring mud as it both retains heat and cooler air and protects against them, he found women who were specialists in making mud floors, beating the surfaces down to make them flat before polishing; to even his surprise, the 3m-high walls produced with this material survived torrential rain. Originally the community had felt that they needed a typical French-style school made of concrete, which is expensive and is not suited to the climate, but Kéré brought them round to a more traditional mud solution. These days he is highly respected as an expert in the use and teaching of cement-stabilised reinforced mud casting techniques that are now applied in his home country.

'Getting people involved with the work is fundamental for this kind of work', Kéré avers. 'You need to teach people modern skills so later on they can understand what you are going to do, even for the maintenance.' Using local materials, mostly mud (bricks, layered) and wood, he evolved a modern articulation for building in Burkina Faso. 'We will have a better future, because we use the →

Kéré's buildings are made by working with people, and quality develops through the process

Above:
Secondary school extension, Dano, Burkino Faso, Kéré Architecture, 2006-7. View of over-hanging structure creating shading.

resources that we have.' By reinventing local building habits, well-functioning buildings geared to the climate can result. Now 'people are self-confident, they have their resources, they only don't know how to use them. They are proud, and that can deliver a lot of energy.'[4]

Kéré has strong memories of sitting in a circle in the communal space between dwellings, listening to one of the grandmothers telling stories. 'The common space was guided by the voice of the storyteller', he recounts. Interaction, in such a context, is like having 'air to breathe'.[5] Kéré explains that because most villagers cannot read and write nor understand plans, his buildings are made through a process of working with people. Things are not predetermined, but quality develops through the process. The mix of traditional Burkinabé building techniques and materials and the modern engineering-led methods he learned in Europe at the Technical University of Berlin, has enabled the educational, cultural and sustainable needs of many communities in Burkina Faso and elsewhere to be supported through his work.

The Gando primary school, which won an Aga Khan Award for Architecture in 2004, is made of mud bricks taken from local soil, with some cement (6-8%) to strengthen them. It does have a light tin roof, lightly laid on a structure of steel bars and with wide overhangs to protect the walls from rain; natural ventilation is ensured by openings under the roof, allowing hot air to flow out and cool breezes to circulate. There is also a vegetable garden.

Kéré's secondary school in Dano (2007, for ages 15-18) was built with young people trained in earlier projects by Kéré's foundation, and here they added experience of working with laterite stone, found all around the region and therefore the main local building material. This design allowed for natural ventilation with a suspended ceiling, and the teacher housing collects rainwater to save for the dry season.

For the School Library in Gando completed in 2015, local people were invited to contribute any earthenware

Left:
Classroom at primary school, Gando, Burkino Faso, Kéré Architecture's first project, 2001. Winner of the Aga Khan Award for Architecture in 2004.

Below:
Primary school, Gando. Built by local villagers, it has a perforated brick ceiling enabling maximum ventilation.

pots they did not need. The donated pots were cut in half and cast into the concrete ceiling to create holes for light and ventilation, to produce a building that breathes. For the façade and the study-area seating, Kéré chose eucalyptus wood, which is fast-growing and robust. In Burkino Faso, eucalyptus is regarded as a weed and is usually burned, but in a country suffering from desertification due to deforestation, it is a vital building material. The façade includes alcoves for shaded seating.

To keep the office going Kéré also takes on commissions in Europe and elsewhere, such as the International Red Cross and Red Crescent Museum in Geneva and the Zhou Shan Harbour development in China. All commissions require him to collect the resources of knowledge, techniques, climate, clients and society. In his own community, however, adapting Western technologies is vital, rather than copying Western models without knowing how to make them work locally. This would serve only 'to help [communities] destroy their own richness ... What is "modern" for my people is building a building where the walls survive the rainy season: that is modern for them.'[6]

1to1 Agency of Engagement

The extensive social scars of spatial segregation in South Africa are strongly evident across the country's 1.7 million informal settlements.[1] A key process in responding to these scars and healing them, says Jhono Bennett, co-founder with Mohau Melani and Jacqueline Cuyler of Johannesburg-based 1to1 Agency of Engagement, is to extend the capacities of both design practitioners and members of community-based organisations. In instigating the 1to1 non-profit platform of design professionals (initially as a student-based organisation) in 2010, Bennett was acting on his belief that there was a strong need for empathetic and experienced spatial practitioners able to rise to the complex development challenges in South Africa: the realisation of an equal-opportunity built environment in a country marked by scars of spatial segregation. He aimed to create a facilitative platform of engagement in which to learn about, share and advance successful methodologies based on alternative modes of engagement.

Bennett declares: 'While broadening my understanding of the complex spaces that make up this country, my aim is to develop additional modes of practice for myself and other spatial designers, to effectively support South Africa's redevelopment processes.'[2] He identifies the need for a new kind of design practitioner: 'socio-technical' men and women able to provide technical design solutions and services but also to play a role in large-scale social and policy processes vital for long-term sustainable development. An important skill is mentoring, so as to challenge low expectations and the slanted perceptions of a situation, and 1to1 is fostering a student league across many universities in South Africa.

Bottom:
Slovo Park residents gathering at Slovo Hall for a community meeting staged by 1to1 Agency of Engagement as part of their ongoing project at Nancefield, Soweto, South Africa, 2010.

Part of the mandate 1to1 set itself is to make today's knowledge of space, structure and policy more accessible to and useable by all stakeholders – government bodies, NGOs and other civil society members, as well as the private sector engaged in urban upgrading. Strategic dissemination of this kind by the team supports both small-scale changes as well as larger-scale development. In order to create this additional mode of practice, 1to1 trains students of spatial design disciplines so that they can work directly with members of the technical community, co-developing sustainable local solutions and applying an 'empathetic and critical ethos of practice'.[3]

Among 1to1's many project partners is the Slovo Park Community Development Forum (SPCDF), a group of residents representing the informal housing settlement outside Johannesburg, for whom 1to1 lobbies government and other

Below:
University of Pretoria students and 1to1 founder Jhono Bennett discuss the design of Slovo Hall with the Slovo Park Community Development Forum, Nancefield, Soweto, South Africa, 2012.

Part of 1to1's mandate is to make today's knowledge of space, structure and policy more accessible to all stakeholders

institutions to assist in its serviced delivery. Melani has been actively involved with SPCDF activities for over a decade as part of his social development of informal settlements. The group also collaborates with the Build Collective led by Austrian architect Marlene Wagner and the local design practices Architecture for a Change, 26'10 South Architects and Boom Architects. It also teams up regularly with Impact Hub Johannesburg, the innovation lab, business incubator and community centre in Braamfontein, part of a network of over 7,000 hubs worldwide. It also has an alliance with the Informal Settlement Network's uTshani Fund, a credit mechanism controlled by the homeless set up in 1995 by the Federation of the Urban Poor (FEDUP), the South African affiliate of the global network of community-based organizations, Shack/Slum Dwellers International (SDI).

For FEDUP – for whom Bennett worked for a year – 1to1 provides design support, internships and links to mentors and other development partners. A vital bond has been made with the Universities of Johannesburg and Pretoria, through which students become part of a larger collective from universities across South Africa of architects, planners, engineers and people working in other spatial disciplines. These links expose students to various methodologies and experiences, and to technical advice on design/build projects and the allocation of funds. This information is key to the complex process of working both with and for the residents of informal settlements.

The 1to1 group cut its teeth as University of Pretoria students with the Slovo Park project (completed in 2010), a scheme devised to open eyes to the reality of South Africa's urban poor. It not only created a new physical resource but also helped to trigger a process of community activities. Once known as Nancefield Township, and by the local council as Olifantsvlei, Slovo Park was renamed in 1995 in honour of post-apartheid South Africa's first Minister of Housing, Joe Slovo. It has struggled to gain recognition as a legitimate settlement in the face of numerous about-turns in government policy. In 2010, a research team composed of community members approached by Bennett and other students at the University began designing a plan to upgrade and develop the settlement. After a series of workshops and a participatory design and build conversion of a dilapidated building into a place where residents could meet and discuss their futures, a new community hall and civic area opened at Slovo Park later that year.

In 2012 the 1to1 team returned to Slovo Park with a group of Pretoria students, guiding them through another process of research, mapping and participatory design and build with a long-term vision. They collaborated with the community forums on an addition to the Hall, a shaded structure for meetings and gatherings. In what proved to be a moving collaboration with Pretoria Picture Company, the documentary *Waterborne*, made by Bennett, Ingmar Büchner and Alexander Melck, conveyed the persistence of the Slovo Park community members' efforts and hopes concerning sewerage service delivery; suitably, the film was sponsored by the Cement & Concrete Institute (now defunct).

The film also picked up on the lack of safe places for local children to play. In 2013 Bennett added undergraduates from the University of Johannesburg to 1to1's student team in order to realise a community playground strategy. Together they designed a robust and secure space responding to the way the children like to play outdoors. At the time of writing this was under construction; as was, in Ekurhuleni east of Johannesburg, the upgrade (with Boom Architects) of a support centre for Heartbeat, an NGO providing health and social services to orphans and vulnerable children; and (with student Shyam →

↓ Patel, in Alexandra Township) the expansion of a local gym.

Safe environments for children became the theme of What it Looks Like When it's Fixed: The Best Life for Every Child, a series of workshops hosted by the Johannesburg Child Welfare Society to forge an action plan for inner city children that would be supported by collaborative civic stakeholders. Again, 1to1 facilitated the student engagement (Dr Barbara Holtmann was overall facilitator), and is collaborating with the organisers on the project's development strategy.

What has been lacking is an integrated body of contemporary development knowledge about informal settlement communities that would be available to community leaders and members, local government, private-sector developers and NGOs. The 1to1 team has devised a new system that is accessible and easy to understand ('Blue Pro-Filing'); participation toolkits, drawing on the group's experience of devising tools and processes, are being developed.

Through critical engagement, people can address pressing socio-technical issues and tap into social capital

Bennett has also worked with the architects, activists and curators Katharina Rohde and Thireshen Govender, who say that in public space in South Africa, a recalibration to new pressures can manifest itself positively. Rohde and Govender lead PublicActs/ Johannesburg, investigating emergent conditions and devising ways of fostering reciprocity between space and society. With Liliana Transplanter and WayWord Sun of AMbush Gardening Collective, and Bennett, the group carried out an incisive, research-based spatial experiment in Mai Mai, one of the oldest markets in Johannesburg's Central Business District. Long a lively hive of self-employed artisans, the market has woodworkers, panel beaters, vendors' stalls and cooking and eating areas, and is presided over by a group who liaises with the local governance bodies. While Mai Mai is officially deemed worthy of preservation, it has also become the butt of negative attitudes by people living further afield.

The market traders longed to upgrade the food court area with new lighting, walls and gates, and to develop the market's traditional, primarily Zulu cultural identity with scope for tourism. Through a series of discussions, informal workshops and mapping exercises, the team's socio-spatial participatory research got under the skin of the issues. The team observed patterns of gathering, ownership and access. At a gathering around improvised tables constructed out of wooden market pallets, the group encouraged market elders and people using the space to talk about what it means to them, utilising communal planting and plant growth as metaphors. Participants chose familiar plants, which were planted in a soil tray embedded in a display table.

The conversations drew out a sense of the cultural values, norms and practices underlying the market and its rich history, as well as concerns marketgoers had about the development of surrounding areas. The curatorial team transcribed some of the remarks in English and isiZulu on the planks of the pallet tables, generating further discussion. Visitors were invited to collaborate in planting greenery in more wooden boxes bearing transcribed statements. The project culminated with PublicAct, a free 24-hour-long programme of events at Mai Mai. One of its experimental initiative arrayed a set of stackable plastic stools in the market, all of which were borrowed and then

returned later on, underlining for the team PublicAct's success in promoting productive democratic space.

The 1to1 team's dedication to 'active designs that rely on genuine inhabitant participation', is something Bennett describes in his dissertation *Platforms of Engagement* (2011) as 'support and infill'.[4] He observes this to be 'an undercurrent concept' in the work of many other designers, such as Teddy Cruz (see page 148), Urban-Think Tank (page 266), Elemental (see page 164) and other local South African groups including 26'10 South Architects and Asiye eTafuleni.

As regards what Bennett identifies as South Africa's 'current unprecedented growth rate in the peri-urban areas', he writes that 'spatial strategies that embrace participative and critical design will have to adapt to the increasing rural movement to metropolitan areas'. Through critical engagement, people can address pressing socio-technical issues and tap into social capital. Drawing on a wealth of experience, Bennett puts a premium on intervention that aims 'to exist in balance with its contextual networks', and in so doing, 'through a symbiotic relationship enhance both the building and its host network'.

↖

Top left:
Students from the University of Pretoria discuss with the Slovo Park Community Development Forum new additions to the original Slovo Hall to adapt to the community's changing needs, 2012.

Above:
Students building Slovo Hall with members of the Slovo Park Community Development Forum, 2010.

Left:
Students discuss the design of Slovo Hall at an outdoor meeting with members of the Slovo Park Community Development Forum, 2010.

Operation Resilient Long Island

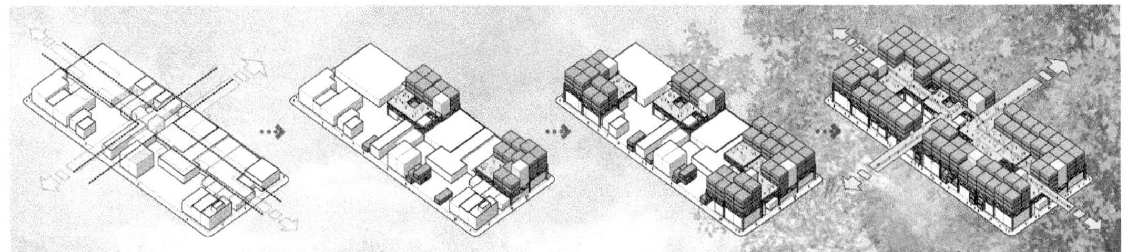

On 29 October 2012 Hurricane Sandy barrelled up the US eastern seaboard, hitting the coasts of New Jersey, Long Island, New York City and southern Connecticut. It killed more than 280 people and wreaked an estimated $65 billion of damage – the third costliest storm in US history – affecting 650,000 buildings, leaving 3 million homes without power.

The water surge created by Hurricane Sandy meant that all low-lying coastal communities became disaster zones, says Daniel Horn, an architecture student who became involved in regeneration plans.[1] Homes became fishbowls, filling up with up to 2 metres of saltwater, and the salt also destroyed the wires of the power grid. Neighbourhood-scale fires broke out after wire masts broke in the heavy winds. Cars were destroyed; streets were deluged with sand from nearby beaches, making them impassable. The severity of damage called for an immediate force for regeneration. Horn, along with fellow students of architecture, interior design and construction management at the New York Institute of Technology (NYIT)'s School of Architecture and Design – which has a significant reputation in architectural innovation – immediately set up a student-led grassroots committee to see what they could do to help.

Operation Resilient Long Island (ORLI), the group they founded, has been a key force for regeneration in the

Below left:
Adaptive Urban Habitat strategy, Mixed Paper Design Collaborative, for Red Hook, NY, 1st place, 3C Comprehensive Coastal Community design competition staged by ORLI, 2013.

Below, bottom left:
Diagrams, Adaptive Urban Habitat strategy, by Mixed Paper Design Collaborative for Red Hook, NY, 2013.

Below:
Mixed Paper Design Collaborative's Adaptive Urban Habitat strategy proposed a comprehensive air rights development strategy and radical rezoning to be built incrementally.

ORLI has strived to show others what 'meta-resilience' can be through the concept of 'bounce-up'

Left:
The Adaptive Urban Habitat design strategy by Mixed Paper Design fosters the evolution of threatened low-lying urban neighbourhoods so that they become resilient built environments.

aftermath of Hurricane Sandy. ORLI believes that urban design and planning skills are for everyone to learn and employ, because unless communities better understand the elements making up an overall structure they cannot reform zoning codes influencing the whole town. Horn, ORLI's co-chair, explains that after Sandy struck the New York metropolitan area, the student group contacted John Maguire from Long Island's Nassau County Office of Emergency Management; he put them in touch with Scott Kemins, the buildings commissioner of the city of Long Beach, New York. The group toured the Long Beach site, noting specific damage throughout the city, and set up ORLI to help affected local towns to plan and to rebuild in the future using a range of methods and means, raising awareness of viable possibilities.

In its remit ORLI included 'all subsequent natural disasters and extreme weather events'. The group envisaged that homeowners struggling to rebuild their lives would face three alternatives if their home had been more than 50% damaged: to raise the existing home above the 'base flood elevation' (BFE) newly stipulated by the Federal Emergency Management Agency (FEMA); to relocate to a new location away from water; or to demolish the existing home and rebuild a FEMA-compliant modular home in its place.

As Horn notes, the FEMA codes 'ensure life safety to citizens living in flood plains.' The snag, however, is that 'the combination of all three of these vastly different scenarios will disrupt the unique character and cohesion of once pleasant communities'. But residents were barely aware of this: nobody had considered the implications of the new codes for the overall aesthetic of the neighbourhood.

So ORLI asked what would happen to an entire community if some homes were raised and some remained on the ground, and whether a comparable community could be envisioned. The group felt it could make an impact on local town codes by focusing on community planning. In 2013 ORLI staged a global design competition, 3C (Comprehensive Coastal Communities) to crowdsource visions for planning and implementation strategies from both professionals and students. They wanted specific north-eastern coastal community urban design that would be resilient for the long-term future, and a prototype housing typology that complied →

Operation Resilient Long Island

Saving the urban fabric and the community: prototyping long-term storm-resistant building solutions and repairing, while respecting local character

IGNITES OTHER COMMUNITIES

Empowered with knowledge and confidence in solutions available

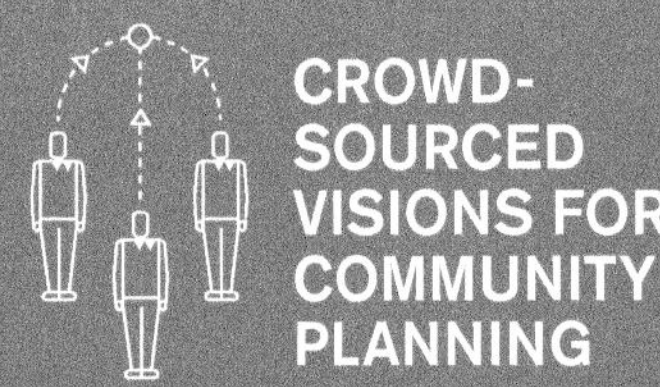

CROWD-SOURCED VISIONS FOR COMMUNITY PLANNING

ORLI held a competition for FEMA-compliant designs; more than 150,000 public votes received in two weeks

IDEAS SHARED WITH OTHER TOWNS

Helping other districts to effectively adopt FEMA codes and find designers

FEMA CODES COULD DISRUPT COMMUNITY

FEMA building guidelines for homes would disrupt cohesion of communities

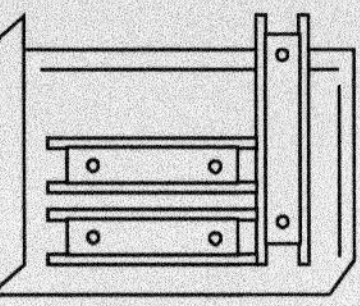

BUILT WITH A STANDARDISED KIT

Parts produced in local manufacturing facilities

DAMAGE FROM HURRICANE SANDY

650,000

buildings were affected and 3 million homes were left without power

DISASTER ZONES

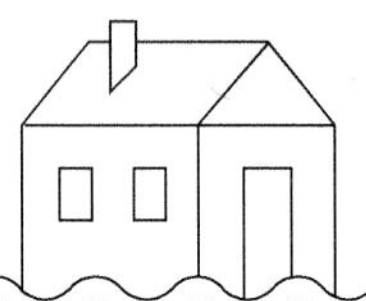

Homes in low-lying land were overwhelmed

GRASSROOTS COMMITTEE

Led by students from NYIT School of Architecture and Design

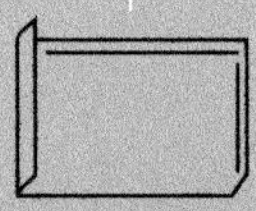

WINNING STRATEGY: BUILD ABOVE NEIGHBOURHOODS

The vision by Adaptive Urban Habitats protects future development and is contextually sensitive with FEMA's resilient design guidelines. Submissions needed to show how the new designs would integrate with the neighbourhood block to preserve or enhance the community, including considerations for landscapes, façade cohesion and zoning.

While assessing the entries, ORLI wrote that 'there is no lack of ideas, but rather a lack of understanding on how to organise new community characters. It requires hands-on community planning. Getting the residents involved more heavily in the actual planning of their towns is essential in really finding a unified character everyone can enjoy.'[2] ORLI also set up a public ballot through an online campaign that brought in over 150,000 votes in the first two weeks alone – proof that the competition had reached a global level.

ORLI received 60 submissions from 20 countries, and analysed them through five 'building blocks of resilience, each representing a unique architectural challenge' that it hoped would serve 'as a new lens to understand resilient reconstruction'. These were: New Foundations (how the house was raised); Vertical Access (how the new ground plane was accessed); Raised Entrance (where the entrance was placed); Usable Underside (what would be under the house now); and Elevated Sidewalks (how a community could exist on the new ground plane).

The 3C competition was won by Adaptive Urban Habitats, an ecologically responsive development strategy for the neighbourhood of Red Hook in Brooklyn that advocated rethinking outdated zoning, designed by Matthew Stoner, David Parker, Debby Yeh and Lukas LaLiberte. Its standardised kit of parts produced by local manufacturers can be deployed to infill vertically above existing neighbourhoods, increasing buildable space and density and protecting future development from rising sea levels and flooding, while also being contextually sensitive.

Horn explains that through the competition ORLI became a broker between a network of designers and local communities in need: the ideas generated by 3C have been catalogued and shared with local towns to help them adopt appropriate changes in their land zoning codes. It is also the first post-Sandy group to have hosted an event at which architects, student groups and non-profit organisations from Long Island, New Jersey and New York could share their work and make plans to collaborate in the future. ORLI has since established an advisory group of students from around the USA to participate in the planning process.

ORLI also set up a partnership with Waves For Water, a group that is repairing and rebuilding homes along the east coast, but most specifically in the Rockaway and Long Beach areas of Long Island, and together they are creating a series of charrettes on innovative construction technology for the restoration of damaged homes. ORLI has also coordinated efforts with the Pratt Disaster Resilience Network, a similar group based at Pratt Institute's School of Architecture.

In April 2013 the New York Rising Community Reconstruction Program was created by Governor Andrew Cuomo to provide rebuilding and resiliency assistance to communities severely damaged by Hurricane Irene, Tropical Storm Lee (both 2011) and 'Superstorm' Sandy, drawing on lessons learned from past recovery efforts; the programme later included the summer floods of 2013. The following January the programme's regional groups from the south shore of Long Island – Lindenhurst, Copiague, Babylon, West Babylon and Amityville – gathered to present their plans. Each went through a comprehensive 'community asset' workshop, focusing the resilient projects for each town on locations near key assets – waterfronts, marinas, parks, schools and housing developments close to the water – in order to protect them.

ORLI's concepts are a starting point, and they are now being mobilised via a travelling gallery (inaugurated at New York's Archtober festival in 2013) and workshop project that will grow through input from each community the team visits. Alex Alaimo, ORLI co-chair, proudly states that the group 'has strived to be an example to show others what "meta-resilience" can be through the concept of "bounce-up"... We are now able to bring these ideas to communities to make a lasting impact.'

Above:
The ORLI student team, Long Beach, New York, 2012.

Marcos L. Rosa

The United Nations states that, by 2014, 80% of Latin America's population were living in its cities, with 82% in 'developed' North America.[1] Latin America's huge cities have complex local histories and an 'informal' sector that needs more innovative, engaged collaboration responding to long-recognised problems ranging from inadequate waste disposal and inadequate, ineffective public transport, to urban violence and ethnic tensions as well as limited local cultural resources.

Right:
Collective retrofit, for the tenement housing Edificio União, São Paulo, 2009-10, Marcos L.Rosa and Kristine Stiphany, with the building's residents.

In the last two decades, research on community building in such cities as São Paulo and Rio de Janeiro in Brazil, has already shed light on potential adaptation to regulations and policymaking in the future. The potential to change the city thanks to fresh situational knowledge cannot be overestimated. People's perception of these cities' informal settlements, poor and derelict areas known as favelas, have changed since the 1990s. 'There is a perception by residents, and outsiders, that aspects of the favela give them a potency, rather than a weakness, which can be perceived in the work of artists, architects, film makers, photographers, educators, sociologists among many others', says Brazilian architect and urban planner Marcos L. Rosa. 'This involves an understanding of another way of making the city, of sharing space, of creating local economies, all of which are expressed in the urban landscape these activities produce. That discourse collides in Rio, a city that is changing fast, preparing for the Olympic Games of 2016, which is to a great extent missing the chance to incorporate that knowledge in the way it is intervening in the city. On the other hand, pioneering slum upgrade programmes have experimented with alternatives for rebuilding favelas since the 1980s, representing a change in attitude from tearing down to upgrading what is already there. The documentation of those experiments acknowledges the social intelligence of it and is recognised worldwide.'[2]

Rosa focuses his work around 'proactively acting on the city, reading it through a more anthropological approach, and testing it 1:1 scale through collective research groups. I have an interest in designing processes and generating tools that architects and planners can use in their practice.'[3] In the book *Microplanning: Urban Creative Practices*, Rosa discusses 18 projects he identified in São Paulo. All of them experimental, micro-scale and bottom-up initiatives, largely undocumented to date and born of local alliances, they aimed to create a positive impact on urban space and community well-being, Rosa calling them 'cross-cuts of utility infrastructures and community initiative designs'.[4]

Rosa's work in São Paulo in 2008 enabled him to conceptualise and develop a research platform based on the process for the Deutsche Bank Urban Age Award, and led to him co-editing the book *Handmade Urbanism* with Ute Weiland, co-director of the Alfred Herrhausen Society that co-organises the Urban Age series of conferences with LSE Cities.[5] He then curated the 2013 Deutsche Bank Urban Age Award, held in Rio and won by the Plano Popular Vila Autódromo, a project that created a platform for dialogue between the community, the city authorities, the Federal University of Rio de Janeiro (UFRJ) and Fluminense Federal University (UFF). As part of his fieldwork

in Rio, carried out with designer Bruna Montuori, Rosa conceptualised and coordinated a collaborative mapping of local initiatives which were given support to promote their visibility, through an online platform.

The book *Handmade Urbanism* focuses on participatory modes of practice employed by local people facilitating urban change, making creative use of their resources and bringing together different stakeholders. It also led to exhibitions in São Paulo and Rio displaying kits, or 'mobile supports for collective action'. These were assembled to help enable different uses of space including soft urban infrastructures (mapped that year), such as temporary playgrounds and public spaces, kite workshops for children, support for urban agriculture and street art. A series of workshops in communities used a foldable poster designed by Rosa with Julia Masagão that transforms into a child's stool, so as to help forge participation and focus on the principle of 'making'. New urban furniture – simple, familiar artefacts – work well to enliven environments.

Rosa refers to the sociologist Richard Sennett's themes of the 'maker' and the empowerment of the craftsman, and the impact on community buildings. It 'points to the idea of allocating funding on a small scale, often to self-driven projects providing new platforms that allow the city to develop differently, based on a multiplicity of small-scale, self-organised actions rooted in social networks that ultimately create and manage improved urban sites.'[6] This approach is very valid as it is currently strongly demanded by communities.

'Community initiatives can seem very humble, small in size', but networks of local actors involved in collective practices are in fact quite complex, Rosa says.[7] At issue is how we connect the micro and the macro scales. How do we think about replicating projects of this kind, Rosa asks, referring to the architect Aldo van Eyck's first playground in the Netherlands in 1947, which was later implemented several hundred times in Amsterdam in typologically similar sites but in ways that revealed the sites' differences.

Social networks embody the sharing of responsibility and participatory politics made on the ground and by the people. Rosa quotes Marxist philosopher Henri Lefebvre's 'Theory of Moments', speculating on the value of everyday production.[8] Networks' combined effect on local empowerment through new platforms 'allow for the city to develop differently' on a 'human scale' with 'design that becomes user-oriented, based on a multiplicity of small-scale, self-organised actions rooted in social networks that ultimately create improved urban sites'.[9]

Rosa cites networks such as Agência de Redes para a Juventude and entrepreneurship programmes Sebrae and Petrobrás, among others, that have helped to fund locally based projects to improve local facilities and public space and offer cultural activities. The Agência recently published online a methodology of 'agency to inspire youth empowerment', including an introductory text by the writer, anthropologist and political scientist Luiz Eduardo Soares titled 'The art of changing people and places'.[10]

Many of the projects Rosa mapped in Rio – initiatives facing lack of quality educational services, or limited access to culture and →

Left:
Boy at the Deutsche Bank Urban Age Award's foldable poster and stool-making workshops with the local community, Julia Masagão and Marcos L. Rosa, Rio de Janeiro, Brazil, July 2013.

Edificio União, São Paulo

Creating fair housing close to city centre by retrofitting an uncompleted high-rise

1. **PLAN TO ADAPT STRUCTURE**

Cleaning abandoned concrete frame and installing necessary amenities

2. **MEDIA TRIGGERED INTEREST**

30 engineering trainees offered to help out

RETHINKING THE STREETSCAPE

The design improves the public realm by creating a semi-public area in the setback from the plot edge

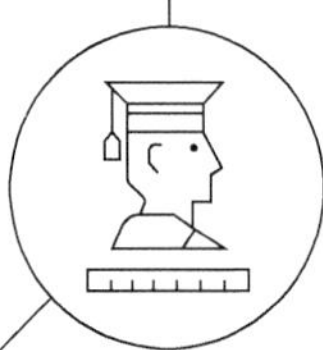

3. **BUILT JOINTLY**

Students from the faculty of architecture got involved, along with members of the community

42 FAMILIES HOUSED

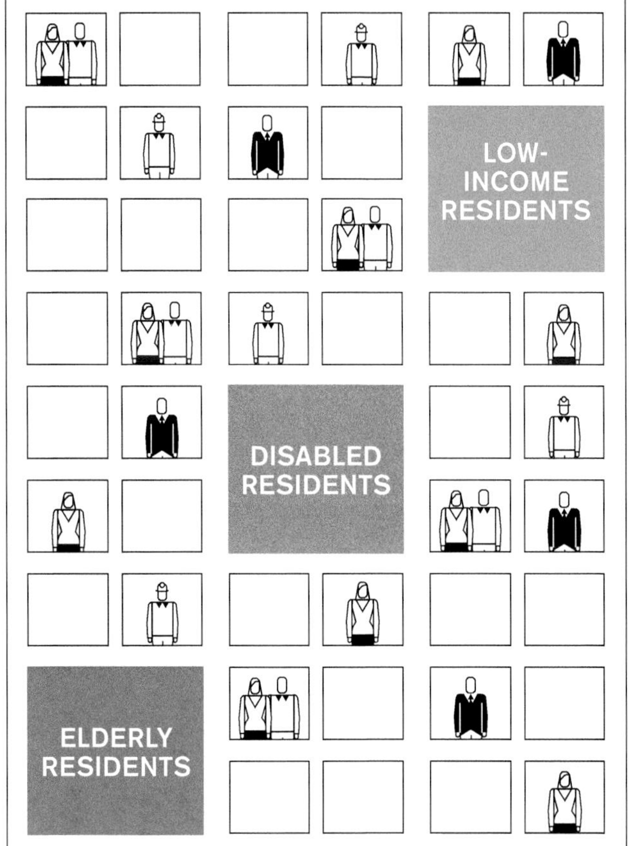

MIXING URBAN POPULATIONS

Helps to combat São Paulo's high inequality and segregation

USING EXISTING BUILDING STOCK

Reduces public spending and maximizes value for landlords

MORE CENTRAL LOCATION

Closer to residents' jobs and the city centre: less commuting

ALTERNATIVE TO SLUM DWELLING

Better quality of life, more dignity and less violence

leisure activities, for example – were temporary but nonetheless revealed a capacity for 'receiving new articulation... hosting new activities and fostering human contact'.[11] They also often did not fall into traditional identities of the informal.

Rosa has also observed others focused on spatial inadequacies: lack of basic infrastructure, of quality open space, of urbanisation programmes and of alternative transportation modes. With 'their own means and hands' residents recognised a problem and actively found ways to solve the immediate difficulties. They recognised 'chances in challenges, making creative use of existing resources, and forging partnerships and relationships to achieve predefined goals that address their daily needs and, eventually, ensure an improved quality of life for communities'.[12]

For the collective retrofit of the Edificio União block of tenement housing in the centre of São Paulo, together with architect Kristine Stiphany Rosa took on board as a building adaptation scheme a high-rise, concrete-frame shell structure. Dating from the 1970s, it had remained uncompleted and had been squatted throughout the 1980s. Since then, residents partnered with a series of institutions and professionals, including the University of São Paulo's Faculty of Architecture (FAU-USP), engineering companies and photographers. Those partnerships were fundamental to establishing the residents' priorities and organising a working plan, which has been carried out since then.

Rosa and Stiphany's design initiative, developed with the community in 2009, gives continuity to the resident-led conversion of the block into homes for 42 families, with new kitchens and bathrooms and basic plumbing, electricity, water supply, sewerage and waste disposal. Residents cleaned the site, installed a collective power grid and security gates, and improved three of the façades, and added the name of the building to the front façade to give a sense of ownership and pride in where they lived. In 2010 Rosa and Stiphany's design proposal won first prize in the national Innovation Alcoa Prize, after the project had won the Deutsche Bank Urban Age Award in 2008 and became a successful alternative to conventional social housing practices in the city.

The media coverage triggered the interest of engineering firm Método, which organised a team of 30 young trainees who became involved in further improvements to the site and building with the residents. Together they collaborated on reimagining the building's foyer, and creating new linear furniture for the garden and a 'second skin' on the façade to give protection from the sun.

Their design derives from uses made by residents to adapt the structures to their needs, and from the observation that their everyday activities carried out demanded support. Five different façade modules were then designed and presented to residents, who could choose which ones best suited their individual needs.

Social networks embody a sharing of responsibility and participatory politics made on the ground

The building differs from other gated communities by blurring the boundaries between public and private through its setback from the plot's edges, creating a semi-public street where everyday activities unfold from the residential units. The proposal assumes that the façade will be the result of the collective narratives and choices, and that its final form and image will be finished only with the participation of all residents.

People generally want to live closer to their workplaces in the city centre, an area best served by infrastructure, and the Edificio União project allowed residents to remain near their jobs, schools and social amenities. Carried out in tandem with students from FAU-USP and the local community, the project set in motion a process that empowered dwellers to make choices and understand design as part of that.

Retrofitting projects such as this can have a strong impact, and help to integrate top-down and bottom-up worlds of cities. Rosa believes that design, and what it might mean in community contexts, can be advanced through close observation of informal living patterns. By engaging with processes driven by collective intelligence – by listening, testing and 'creating different modes of participation', which 'is what architects train to do'– design serves to enrich understanding and outcomes.[13]

Left:
Aldo van Eyck, Amsterdam playground, 1947, photo by Marcos L. Rosa. Playgrounds: Reinventing the Plaza exhibition, Madrid, 2014.

Right:
Northala Fields park, Marko and Placemakers, for Ealing Borough Council, 2000-8. Four conical earth mounds are made of construction rubble obtained in a recycling deal that financially supported the project.

Marko and Placemakers

There is no single answer to the question of how to develop the character of neighbourhoods in a way that is socially equitable, but the process almost always involves negotiating the contestatory realms of public and private sector, community members and media through a custom-designed approach to urbanism. Marko and Placemakers, founded by Igor Marko in 2013 in London after the demerger of his previous architectural practice FoRM Associates, are adherents to this way of working, bridging the boundaries between urban design, architecture, art and engineering. The words 'animated, connected, inclusive, contextual, green', which appear on the practice's website home page indicate a studio dedicated to transformative local urban value.

With colleagues Petra Havelska, Francis Moss and Jorge Martín, Marko constantly explores new methods of urban design and regeneration, including scenario-based methods, mapping and visual ethnography to open up the psychogeography of a place. The practice's highly commended submission to the RIBA Vauxhall Missing Link design competition (2013), for example, strengthened the neighbourhood's identity by discovering its potentials through the narratives of people who live, work and play there, going far beyond a mere rebranding of the area to the achievement of environmentally, economically and socially sustainable change.

The value of transformational placemaking resounds at north-west London's Northala Fields (2000-8), a part of the much larger Northolt

and Greenford country park. The project, commissioned by the London Borough of Ealing through open competition for a wasteland site, is that Marko calls 'an exemplar of people-led sustainability'.[1] A magnet for crime and antisocial behaviour, the land had been a cause for increasing concern by the Labour-led borough council. Not really knowing what to do with the site, but hoping it could somehow become an asset for the area, and also provide a barrier to the noisy A40 road on its north end, the council elicited proposals from artists. This has led to one of the largest examples of land art in Europe, garnering numerous awards.

The winning design proposal by Marko and artist Peter Fink (as FoRM Associates)[2] featured four conical earth-covered mounds composed of construction rubble taken from many different development sites around London, such as the old Wembley Stadium and Heathrow Terminal. This tactic enabled the bold project to become financially feasible: the developers of these sites were charged £70-£80 per lorryload to deposit their rubble on the local council's land at Northala Fields, and over six years the vast amount of waste required to make the mounds generated income of £6 million to the council, covering the project costs, and enabling investment in the park's varied facilities, run by a charity. Such a sum was a boon to the borough council as it had very little funding for public space projects, and creating Northala Fields by this means brought 'a previously unimaginable solution', says Marko.[3] The developers were more than happy to take their construction waste to the site, where a waste recycling plant was set up on site to process the rubble, as then they needed only to haul it 10 miles or so, rather than being obliged in any case to transport it, at a considerable cost, to a remote landfill site as far as 100 miles away.

More soil was needed to create the topsoil for planting on the mounds, and this was created by using soil excavated directly on the site, creating the fishing ponds and a model boating lake.

Creating the park also involved a very engaged public consultation process over two years. Realising how much there was to gain by empowering the park's users and fully integrating them into the development process, Marko now sees them as 'the biggest advocates of the park'. It was a rewarding →

Marko strongly recommends engaging with the public very early on and being honest about intentions

Left:
An extended-family get-together, Northala Fields Park, designed by Marko and Placemakers, which since opening in 2008 has become a vital community resource.

ENGAGEMENT
REPLICABILITY
DESIGN DRIVEN
SCALE
IMPACT

IDENTIFY → ENQUIRE → DEVELOP → CO-DESIGN → CO-CONSTRUCT → HAND-OVER

Regeneration of the Northala Fields

INITIAL PROBLEM

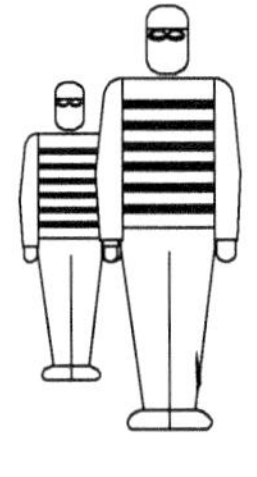

In 2003 before construction began the fields were unmanned and a magnet for crime and antisocial behaviour

OPEN COMPETITION

Ealing Borough Council selected the design by architect Igor Marko and artist Peter Fink as the winner

CO-DEVELOPMENT

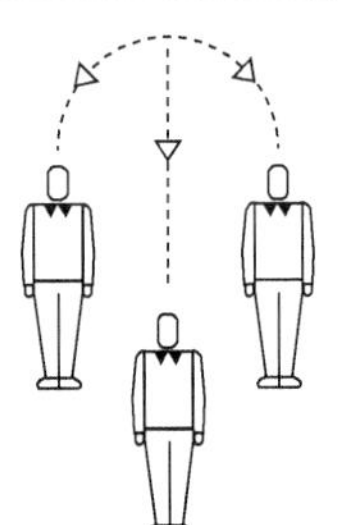

Public closely involved in consultation spread over two years

> **The engagement process meant that as designers we could always test ideas in discussion and make them better suited for people's needs**

process for the practice, and Marko strongly recommends engaging with the public very early on and being honest about intentions, which is most likely to encourage people to be part of the process. As a result, many local residents were closely involved in the design of the site, with the Northolt and Greenford Countryside Park Society members being key players. The fishing and boating lakes concept, in particular, came directly out of the consultation, and were joined in the final design by sports pitches, a natural amphitheatre, and children's play spaces with views across the city.

The resulting topography reduced visual and noise pollution from the busy A40. The other part of the design intention in creating the mounds was 'to introduce a new topology that would encourage movement and fitness. When people are in the park they naturally incline to climbing up the mounds to get the "reward" of the view, similar to Primrose Hill, in north London, for example', says Petra Havelska, the practice's co-founder.[4] The whole of

CONSTRUCT

£6m

earned by using waste materials; this was reinvested

65,000

lorryloads of waste material used to construct the four hills

SOLUTION

Since the park opened, it has become more and more loved. New recreation opportunities have been created. People feel like the park is theirs

For sustainability, additional woodland and meadow types have been added

Hills reduce visual and noise pollution from the busy A40 road

ENGAGEMENT REPLICABILITY DESIGN DRIVEN SCALE IMPACT

London can be seen from the towering grassy mounds, each with footpaths leading to the summits. As landscapes with unique gradients, they induce an immediate, child-like attraction, resonating in the unconscious as familiar, recalling other man-made mounds at prehistoric sites such as Silbury Hill near Avebury.

Northala Fields offers a dream of a place, full of diversity, for young people who might otherwise hang around the streets as well as for all sections of the community, while being of enhanced ecological value; each mound has its own soil conditions supporting wildflower and grass-seed mix to create four distinct habitats. The design of the mounds also deals with flood risk through the maximisation of soft surfaces for water attenuation: unlike hard surfaces, they absorb water easily. The fishing ponds and model boating lake are also part of a water regulation system. Northala Fields is part of the All-London Green Grid plan of interconnected green infrastructure systems promoted by the Greater London Authority (GLA).

Marko says that it was through the consultation process that the idea was developed of introducing six interconnecting fishing ponds and a model boating lake, where classes and events by the charity Get Hooked on Fishing are staged. After completion, the surrounding communities' support took the form of an active engagement in organising activities and programmes for their 'asset'. 'The engagement process meant that as designers we could always test ideas in discussion with the people and make [the ideas] better suited for their needs', Marko explains, and he also appreciates how motivating it is to return to the site years later to 'see that the park is becoming more and more loved and cared for by the people'.[5]

Locals lobbied when, a year before completion, the new Conservative administration looked to cut the park's £5.5 million budget raised at no cost to the taxpayer, and divert funds elsewhere. Along with project leaders and some local politicians, residents defended the self-funding legacy project. In letters to the local newspapers, local community members pointed out that some of England's most deprived children lived in the borough, which lacks many of the cultural and leisure facilities of others. As Havelska notes, 'by then people felt so much that the park was "theirs" that they campaigned for its completion and we as designers were recommissioned to successfully complete it'.

For its other recent urban framework at Vauxhall, in south London by the River Thames, the practice's framework plan strengthened neighbourhood identity through a riverside walk, an arts quarter and the linking of all the green spaces and the city farm. It fostered collaboration and economic opportunities in the area through many social media forums and activities, such as recycling and composting, tackling practical issues at the local level, without alienating local residents. Marko and Placemakers' tactics lie in both revealing and developing the character of neighbourhoods. At Northala the sense of local 'ownership' built through the process becomes a decisive force for positive change in its own right.

MASS Design Group

In Rwanda, the complex mix of factors and events that erupted in the 1994 genocide by Hutu extremists of Tsutsi people, led, over the course of 100 days, to some 1 million people being brutally murdered. But to this day Rwanda retains its identity as a 'garden country' with 'bucolic' landscape in the eastern 'mountain and highveld' part of Africa, as architect David Adjaye describes it.[1] Kigali, the capital, with a multicultural population of 1 million, typifies this 'land of a thousand hills', being set on one surrounded by rolling, lush green landscape. There has been widespread acknowledgement of the amazing recovery Rwanda, Africa's most densely populated country, has made since the mid-1990s. Within hours of arriving in Kigali for the first time, writer Kit Buchan was 'struck by how attached' she already felt 'to its resilience and ambition'.[2]

Left:
The walls of the Butaro District Hospital in Burera, Rwanda, designed by MASS Design Group, are made of local volcanic rock, a first-time use here, 2008-11.

Rwanda now has a vision plan – Vision 2020 – launched in 2000 by President Paul Kagame following the Urugwiro Village dialogue in 1997-98, to bring about an economic and social transformation that would build sustainable security, fight poverty, bring back people's dignity and engage with other development partners. The plan established a time frame to introduce a science, technology and knowledge-led economy, and consultation with all sectors of society has helped to establish far-reaching policies in these fields. A national strategy for climate change and low-carbon development was developed; Carnegie Mellon University, based in Pennsylvania,

USA, opened a branch in Rwanda, and this is setting up a local Global Climate Change Observatory with the Massachusetts Institute of Technology.

In Kigali, which has not had much exceptional architecture, there has recently been a building boom, adding new banks and hotels, structures up to ten storeys. Since 2011 what sounds like an all-too conventionally zoned masterplan has been developed by the Singapore-based building consultancy practice Surbana and OZ Architecture (Denver), to create new areas and densify others. The aim is to enable the city's population to be trebled and to further establish Kigali's identity as a regional centre; the plan is reportedly based around pedestrian-friendly urban space. Other foreign architects are working in the city on mixed-use buildings; one of these is Paris-based O'Zone Architectures, in conjunction with local developer Habi. In 2011 Kigali saw the opening of the Umubano primary school for over 300 vulnerable or orphaned children, designed by the MASS Design Group whose headquarters are in Boston, Massachusetts.

In 2012 there were only 30 registered architects in Rwanda, all trained outside the country.[3] The first class of architectural students at the Faculty of Architectural and Environmental Design (FAED) at Kigali Institute of Science and Technology graduated in 2009. FAED was born out of the 2008 Urban Forum discussing Rwanda's widespread changes, including Kigali's shift from provincial town to modern capital city. The lack of skills and resources has led to overseas architects being encouraged to work in the country. But urban development leaders and politicians are also keen to encourage home-grown talent, to build a sense of local ownership, character and pride.

MASS Design Group, founded by Michael Murphy and Alan Ricks in 2008 and by far the best-known international practice working in Rwanda, is a non-profit design firm based in Boston and Kigali; the practice is also very active in Haiti. MASS was set up to improve lives, mobilising architecture to do more to contribute to peace, and much of its built work has created health-care facilities as community assets – public health is a field in which Murphy and Ricks are experts. One of their videos about MASS's work shows a Post-it note with a single message: 'We have to be more creative about how design can improve people's lives.' For MASS, 'a building is a vehicle for social change', a community asset.[4]

While Rwanda has one of Africa's fastest growing economies, 'the country is still rebuilding – →

Above:
The Butaro Doctors' Housing, Burera, MASS Design Group, was made almost entirely from local materials, and by 100% local labour, 2011-12.

↓ **Below:**
Night view of the Butaro Doctors' Housing, MASS Design Group, which accommodates eight doctors on-site at the District Hospital, 2011-12.

philosophically and physically – after a genocide that decimated 20% of the population', says writer Meara Sharma.[5] In one of the MASS videos, Dr Agnes Binagwaho, the country's minister of health, says that Rwandans 'dream of a beautiful future ... a beauty that provides you with dignity', and that the transcendent qualities of community-oriented architecture help to nurture that guiding quality. It is vital that buildings reflect patterns of community living. 'If we make spaces that make people feel uncomfortable, we are taking away their dignity', says Amelie Ntigulirwa, one of the architects at MASS's Kigali office.

MASS has committed its energies to working in the rural district of Burera in the Northern Province, one of the country's most impoverished. It has completed three main projects at Burera on what is now known as Umusozi Ukiza – the 'Healing Hill': the 140-bed Butaro District Hospital (2011); doctors' housing (2012); and the Ambulatory Cancer Centre (2013), a holistic health-care facility that will have its own housing and a teaching hospital extension. These were made possible through the partnership between social justice and health organisation Partners In Health (PIH), founded by the physician and anthropologist Paul Farmer, who lives in Kigali, and the Rwandan Ministry of Health. Since 2005, they have worked together to extend health care throughout rural Rwanda, especially in the Burera district whose population of 340,000 had limited access to care.

The MASS-designed buildings are constructed by local labourers from local materials such as mud, volcanic sand and rock, usually regarded in the area as worthless. 'If architecture is only thought about as a commodity, we fail to acknowledge all the other indicators which may create impact', says Murphy. The MASS intern Jeancy Mulela feels that it is vital to engage local people, 'because they are the first to benefit from new input, and to receive new methods and theories of construction'. It 'gives them the opportunity to express themselves and make themselves known'. The garden landscapes of the hospital, conceived to be transformative, to help heal people, are tended by master gardener Jean Baptiste.

The design of the hospital, where the intention was to minimise risk of airborne diseases, called for an immersion in the community of doctors, nurses, staff and community. In addition, some 4,000 people were trained and hired to help to excavate, construct and manage the scheme. The learning curve the local builders underwent involved them using the local volcanic stone. This is everywhere to be seen on the fields, and it is regularly cleared away by farmers who regard it as a nuisance. MASS wanted to show off the stone's beautiful deep-grey colour and its porous texture. 'After multiple mock-ups, the masons grew excited ... and as they progressed

> In its community work MASS sees capacity sharing, a blending of ideas, and that's where innovation happens

Left:
Butaro Ambulatory Cancer Centre, Burera, MASS Design Group, with doors that swing outwards, fresh air and a view of nature, 2011-13.

Bottom left:
Excavating the hillside for building work at Butaro District Hospital, Burera, Rwanda, MASS Design Group, 2008-11.

through the various buildings on the hospital campus their work became more and more refined', says the MASS team. The group adds that when the masons recognised 'how their skill had advanced as they worked, [they] eventually offered to replace their initial work out of a sense of pride'. These men are now widely sought after in other parts of the country. In their community work the MASS team members increasingly see 'capacity sharing, a blending of ideas, and that's where innovation happens', says Ricks.

The experience also taught MASS that the new health facilities relied on the best staff, both native Rwandan and foreign expatriates, hence there was a need for local housing. Four two-bedroom houses now sit five minutes' walk from the Hospital. The buildings were constructed with compressed stabilised earth blocks (CSEBs) made with soil excavated from the site. This minimised the use of cement, and meant that no transportation of materials or firing was necessary. It also created jobs in block production. The on-site earth-block workshop began life in a training phase; ten newly trained community members then led a full-time block production crew who over three months made 29,000 blocks.

Everything for the buildings – cypress and pine furniture, metal light fixtures, doors made with pieces left over from the muvura-wood roof trusses, the second layer of local volcanic rock on the walls – was customised by local masons, carpenters and artisans who were trained and provided their own local knowledge. A total of 275 locals received training in all these areas, and also in terracing for Rwanda's agricultural hillsides; their expertise was then marketable around the country. The other key feature about the process was that MASS implemented rotational hiring, so that over 900 individuals could be employed in total; this fostered an even greater sense of community ownership and extended the distribution of funds locally.

'One of the things that I've learned over the four years that I've been working on projects with MASS in Rwanda', says MASS senior director Sierra Bainbridge, 'is that the relationships that we have and that we build with people, as we move through these projects, are some of the most important results, and also allow for the work to build into a movement.' Bainbridge's colleague Amelie Ntigulirwa understands how this happens: 'The more you bring people together, the more they have something in common, and once you have something in common, you fight to protect it.'

SENSEable City Laboratory, MIT

Technology is the answer, but what is the question, the British architect Cedric Price once asked, anticipating today's feverish debates about where technology's civic responsibility lies. Carlo Ratti, the architect founder in 2004 of the SENSEable City Laboratory at the Massachusetts Insitute of Technology (MIT) Department of Urban Studies and Planning, recently argued in an article written with research fellow Matthew Claudel that 'governments should use their funds to develop a bottom-up innovation ecosystem geared towards smart cities'. And this ought to be done without them playing a 'more determinist role', nor oversubscribing to the proprietary offerings of technology multinationals.[1]

The Lab evaluates and anticipates shifts in the built environments of cities, focusing on a greater creative relationship with electronic sensors, mobile technologies and their users and advocating citizen power and a better understanding of systemic thinking. Its earliest multidisciplinary project was the Copenhagen Wheel, a hybrid 'e-bicycle' that doubles as a mobile sensing unit controlled by smartphone. It was launched in 2009 at the United Nations Climate Change Conference – the 'Copenhagen Summit'. The bicycle's sensing unit tracked not only the user's effort level but also data about the cyclist's surroundings, such as road conditions, levels of carbon monoxide, NOx gases and noise, and ambient temperature and relative humidity.

Among the many projects the Lab is engaged with, one examines cities' effects on social relationships by studying patterns of mobile phone calls and their impacts on 'smart' urban space. Its first project of this kind was New York Talk Exchange, exhibited in curator Paola Antonelli's riveting Design and the Elastic Mind exhibition at the city's Museum of Modern Art (MoMA) in 2008. This analysed all the call data, and also all the internet interaction of specific locations in New York with the rest of the world, assessing connectivity patterns. It looked at which other places around the world people in New York interacted with, at what scale and at what time of the day, and asked how this geography of talk corresponded to what we know about the city.

New York Talk Exchange triggered many academic papers and a dissertation by team member Francisca Rojas. 'She saw a different story of globalisation in this data', says Dietmar Offenhuber,

Left:
Map of the recorded traces coloured by waste type, Trash Track project, MIT SENSEable City Lab, 2009.

Below:
Trash Track project, MIT SENSEable City Lab, 2009. Project leads: Dietmar Offenhuber and David Lee.

> **The Lab anticipates and evaluates shifts in the built environments of cities, advocating citizen power**

research fellow at the Lab. 'Normally we always talk about globalisation as the integration of the financial system, or large corporations, for example. But [Rojas] found in the data that there's also a component of migrant workers and migration'.[2] It turned out that among New York's most active neighbourhoods were those containing large numbers of immigrants from the Dominican Republic, 'who were in almost constant telephone contact with their countries, with their families back home'.

Rojas conducted interviews with these people, who would typically buy call cards that allowed them unlimited use of the phone. There are 'lifestyles where telecommunications and digital technology has a very different role and meaning', she says, 'not any longer a tool for upper middle-class male thirtysomethings, but an essential tool for this kind of demographics to stay in touch with their families.'[3]

The Lab's Trash Track, shown in 2009 at the Architectural League in New York and at the Seattle Public Library as part of the exhibition Towards the Sentient City, used custom-designed electronic tags to track waste. It encouraged people 'to make more sustainable decisions about what and how much they consume, and how it affects the world around them', Assaf Biderman, associate director of the SENSEable City Lab, said at the time of the launch. 'The project represents a bottom-up approach to managing resources, promoting more informed decision making in the public through the use of pervasive technologies and information.'[4]

Offenhuber, Trash Track's first project architect, calls it 'an initial approach making a procedural or invisible infrastructure, making public services a bit more tangible and experiential [...] in the same sense that [the urban theorist] Kevin Lynch talked about the legibility of the built environment as a quality of global cities. That has to be even more the case for infrastructures and public services.'

The Lab's work on bottom-up informal systems takes place in various countries – for example in Brazil, which has an innovative policy of →

Below:
The Trash Tag created by SENSEable City Lab for Trash Track.

self-organisation. New legislation there has required that businesses of all kinds cooperate with the informal sector on recycling measures. While Offenhuber admires this policy, he sees its effects as limited. 'Because the cooperatives have to scale up, and are entirely organised based on tacit knowledge embedded in their practices, they don't really have any formal planning.' He does not want to force them to adapt their traditional business practices, but aims to 'reach a condition where the community, the people who have waste for recycling or donation, the waste collectors and the companies and the municipal governments work together and contribute information in order to make this system work'.

Participative co-design planning processes with the local community have 'a certain requirement for legibility on the residents' side. The businesses need some kind of contract they can rely on, the cooperatives need a way to assess the whole logistics because this gets very complex in the end.' Offenhuber sees it as 'not just an environmentalist position, but one of accountability'. He explains that 'people wanted their infrastructures to be more accountable, more legible. They distrust the city sometimes, because of all these hazardous-waste disputes, so they also see all these recycling laws very critically – "All this separation, telling us we have to engage. But do we know whether they do their part?"'

In downtown São Paulo, waste collection is done manually but also by truck. Here, a 20-strong Lab team also used location-based technologies, not as a means of passive observation of how the system behaves but as an active tool for coordination. 'This means that each collector would get a GPS logger and afterwards, we would sit together and show them the map that they'd generated, discuss why they would take a certain route.'

For ten days the team mapped movements of manual and truck collection to detect their respective advantages and disadvantages, and then staged a participatory design workshop in which they considered

Above:
Trash Track, SENSEable City Lab, 2009. Project leads: Dieter Offenhuber and David Lee.

Right:
The Copenhagen Wheel, MIT SENSEable City Lab, 2009.

how these technologies could be used to coordinate the collection activity to support collectors in their work. 'We were showing them something, and trying to provoke them with a certain technology', says Offenhuber. 'But if they think it's not worth their time, even during the interviews, then we are out of the picture.'

The team made a proposal: 'to let the residents use their phones to send messages to the cooperative to tell them that they had material to collect'. Offenhuber admits that there was concern that 'it would raise unrealistic expectations. That once the residents clicked a button and requested a pick-up, it would be very difficult for the cooperative to be there on time, given the traffic and all the different constraints there. So it became a design and wording problem – how to design this so that it doesn't raise these expectations.' At the time, 'residents had to come to the cooperative with their material, and that was quite inconvenient for them. But on the other hand it gave us face-to-face exposure and this is very important for them to build the trust. All these become design questions, not so much technical questions.'

The team found that all those issues 'validated the methodology', because they 'showed that it's not just a technical problem. That all those interviews and experiments and participatory workshops are necessary; otherwise you do not end up with a system that anyone will use. You have iterations – you cannot design it clearly on a piece of paper. You have to go there and talk to people.'

Offenhuber recalls that in one of his last books, Lynch reflected on the impact of the image of the city and maintained that it had 'become a trend to use this terminology of "nodes" and "paths" and "networks". But all he wanted was for the urban designers to listen to what the people have to say about a specific area.'

Trash Track is a bottom-up approach to managing resources

In the 1980s when the technology did not exist to collect today's range of observational data, all we had to predict certain activity on an urban scale were simulation models, says Offenhuber. He states that one thing the Lab is known for is that 'early on it started exploring data sets as a proxy for understanding urban activity and urban interaction'. It did this 'without the need to simulate and model it from a very abstract point of view, but rather by looking for patterns and trying to draw conclusions on what this can tell us about the activity of the city'. Ultimately the Lab is 'not so much focused on methodology itself, whether it is visualisation or participatory design. Those for us are all means we use, but we don't use them as the main research goals. We are more interested in the city and real problems that call for these kinds of tools.'

Muf Architecture/Art, J&L Gibbons

Although the extent of inequality in larger cities cuts deep, regeneration projects are often little more than processes of displacement. The starkness of these findings, reported by writer and director of the think tank Martin Prosperity Institute Richard Florida in The Divided City and the Shape of the New Metropolis, demonstrates that the innovative roles played by creative adaptive planning are increasingly important, but harder to sustain.[1] Florida and his colleagues studied American cities, but because class and income differentials are so inscribed on the geography of London, and especially in its poorest boroughs, their observations apply there as well. The borough of Hackney in east London, which has seen inward migration since the 18th century, has a richly diverse population, 25% of which is under 20 years of age. Dalston is one of many of Hackney's 19 wards that, lately, have seen an influx of younger creatives and City workers. But, like many other east London districts, the borough is still in the top 10% of the most deprived areas in England.[2]

Above:
Outdoor activities at Gillett Square, Dalston, east London, one of the Making Space in Dalston sites (2009-12), Muf Architecture/Art, J&L Gibbons, Objectif and Appleyards.

Right:
Eastern Curve Garden, Dalston, Muf Architecture/Art and J&L Gibbons.

Dalston, with a population now reaching around 11,000, has 57% less green space than other parts of Hackney, and no public parks, as opposed to 56 elsewhere in the borough.[3] Regeneration has been under way in Dalston for many years, beginning in 1993, at Gillett Square, close to Ridley Road Market which has been there since the 1880s. Since 2010 the area has benefited from the reopening of Dalston Junction station on the Overground line, a recently amalgamated London orbital rail service that serves many underprivileged areas.

A pioneering scheme for Gillett Square by the local community economic development agency, Hackney Co-operative Developments, and others, was kicked off after a team of architects including Hawkins\Brown was commissioned to create a new town square with affordably rentable market kiosks, a library in a converted derelict factory and the Vortex jazz club. Their designs found a satisfying, permanent solution to the lack of open space, the heavy local traffic, and the cramped, hostile and dangerous environment for pedestrians at Gillett Square. The square is now a highly successful community-led public space in which events are held regularly.

In 2009, Muf Architecture/Art and landscape architects J&L Gibbons published Making Space in Dalston, a strategic design and engagement study on 10 related themes for improved public space carried out for the Borough of Hackney and Design for London, the development unit of the Greater London Authority (GLA). 'All buildings in the UK

have a planning classification according to use. We see the public realm as an extension of D1 use [non-residential institutions], as the potential site par excellence of non-monetary exchange – a place of protection and of exploration, learning and rest', says Liza Fior, co-founder of Muf Architecture/Art.[4]

Fior recalls how the late Katherine Shonfield, a planner and collaborator with Muf Architecture/Art, described the public realm as the place in which to experience democracy. 'We endeavour in all our projects to make spaces where more than one fragile thing can coexist at a time; truly public spaces where you can spend time without having to buy anything; spaces for play which are not playgrounds, where there is space for reverie and exploration.'[5]

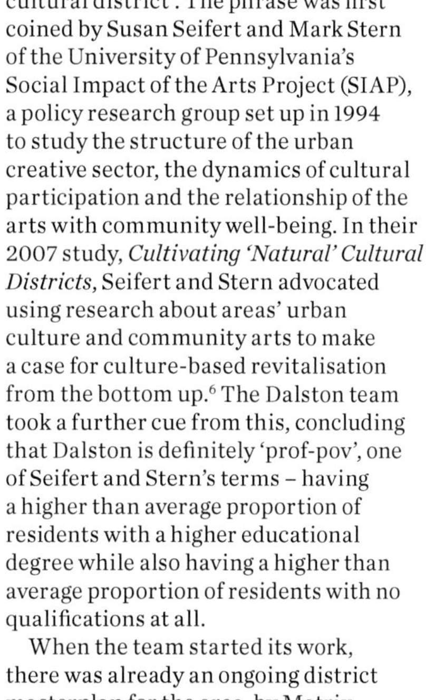

The study team felt strongly that Dalston fitted the definition of a 'natural cultural district'. The phrase was first coined by Susan Seifert and Mark Stern of the University of Pennsylvania's Social Impact of the Arts Project (SIAP), a policy research group set up in 1994 to study the structure of the urban creative sector, the dynamics of cultural participation and the relationship of the arts with community well-being. In their 2007 study, *Cultivating 'Natural' Cultural Districts,* Seifert and Stern advocated using research about areas' urban culture and community arts to make a case for culture-based revitalisation from the bottom up.[6] The Dalston team took a further cue from this, concluding that Dalston is definitely 'prof-pov', one of Seifert and Stern's terms – having a higher than average proportion of residents with a higher educational degree while also having a higher than average proportion of residents with no qualifications at all.

When the team started its work, there was already an ongoing district masterplan for the area, by Matrix Partnership, that proposed a series of strategies for the public realm aiming to improve land use and also specifically to create neighbourhood-based building energy systems. The Making Space for Dalston study was distinct, however: while it was equally focused on improving the public realm, it was also driven by the team's fresh research and interaction with a huge range of local people to identify existing social, cultural and physical assets, placing as much importance on the process of engagement as on the delivery of strategies. Regular stakeholder meetings were held with a guest list as wide-ranging as possible, and included on the steering group participants from the Design for London urban design office of the GLA, representatives from the local businesses and organisations, and Transport for London, the London transport agency.

> “
> **The public realm is the place in which to experience democracy**

The mapping carried out by Muf and J&L Gibbons was widely inclusive, partly so as to gather publicity material for all the local activities and put it on a webpage, along with all the existing arts and cultural venues identified – 700 of them. Dalston's cultural diversity is matched by its long history of social activism, with proudly independent enterprises such as the Rio Cinema, and Bootstrap, an agency helping small businesses. All 700 venues were incorporated into a new map showing their adjacencies.

All the different types of existing open spaces – public and semi-public, even extending to small urban agriculture tracts and city farms – were also identified and assembled →

in a diagram. On heritage walks with a mix of local bodies people identified what was of value, from buildings as artefacts to buildings as repositories of social history, and a composite map of the mutually agreed results was created. The local Youth Forum was commissioned to document all the disused shops.

This intelligence enabled the team to devise a pieced-together discontinuous park for the district, and to formulate plans for costed, complementary design projects – ten in total – to bring better-quality public space to the neighbourhood without sacrificing its existing qualities. For each proposed project an action plan was devised for amenity space and a programme of cultural activities, and, together with the stakeholders, a Rolling List was compiled. The List enabled all the projects to be considered in relation to issues of possible partners, delivery agencies, property owners, additional equipment and resources needed, their size and potential to act as host spaces, the costs, funding possibilities, long-term management and who was involved in the consultation in each particular case. A number of the proposed projects went ahead as a result of the study, and the financial department of the GLA began fundraising for some of the others.

Some £1 million for the initiative was earmarked as part of the Mayor of London's £220 million budget for the 'Great Outdoors' public realm improvement programme. As the team proceeded with implementation from 2009, it resisted a top-down approach;

Far right:
Eastern Curve Garden, opened in Dalston in spring 2010, with oak timber open-sided barn by Exyzt for community uses, built with local young-adult apprentices.

Right:
The Eastern Curve Garden, Dalston, by Muf Architecture/ Art and J&L Gibbons, 2010, encourages young people to participate and gain work experience.

instead, it continued to work very closely with local residents, businesses and organisations, encouraging these local partners to take ownership of the projects. The regenerated Gillett Square was the site of one of these projects, with new street signs designed to evoke the area's historic signage that had been documented during heritage walks. There was also an imaginative design for a new supervised, pack-away playground, with sound and projection equipment, which when not used was stored inside a large mirrored container. These facilities enabled residents to make more effective use of the public space, which was no longer a hazard.

Other projects included a decluttering of the High Street and a green wall for the Princess May School. In response to local desires for the opportunity to 'grow their own', a new orchard and vegetable garden was created for the Somerford Grove Estate, which lacked any kind of green space. The Eastern Curve Garden, completed in spring 2010, transformed a piece of abandoned railway land into a much-loved community garden. Here,

on a site owned partly by developers Criterion Capital, who offered a temporary loan, and partly by Hackney Council, a new wooden pavilion designed by the architectural collective Exyzt was created for hosting community events, and a rainwater collection system was set up. The Garden works with young people through local organisations, schools and charities, offering a communal space where people can join the gardening activities, as well as make furniture at on-site community workshops, or play music.

The sociable, safe and welcoming atmosphere of the space, open to everyone, is unique, bringing local residents seven days a week. 'The Dalston Eastern Curve Garden is a perfect example of a small budget [creating a] big impact', said local resident and Garden manager, garden designer Marie Murray of GrowCookEat in 2011. 'We're in an area severely lacking in public green space that can feel very frantic with traffic and noise. The Garden is a peaceful oasis where people can connect with nature and meet their neighbours in a relaxed way.'[7] As Johanna Gibbons of J&L Gibbons puts it, 'the contact with nature when the majority of people live in cities, is very important. The open area at the bottom is tucked away, and then the tree density increases towards the top. You need to have those differences, combining it with planting. You can't just have big open spaces. The connection with health and well-being needs to be stronger. You never see kids ripping up plants. It's a whole attitude about being civil and caring.'[8]

However the civic pride and feeling of a comfort zone the Garden induced was put under threat in 2013. Plans by Criterion Capital for the replacement of the Kingsland Shopping Centre from the 1980s into 14-storey apartment blocks with 445 units, a new shopping mall and a Sainsbury's supermarket, showed the Garden replaced by a planted thoroughfare designed by Matrix. This proposed 190,000sq m scheme alarmed local residents: campaigning group Open Dalston pointed out that a garden such as the Eastern Curve needed to receive income to be sustainable, and that 'an undifferentiated thoroughfare' was not appropriate.[9]

In early 2014 at a packed meeting at Stoke Newington Town Hall, at which members of the public were not allowed to speak, the developers and Waugh Thistleton Architects presented their plans. They proposed joining part of the garden to another piece of land, to accommodate the thoroughfare, increasing the amount of green space, but Murray and business partner Brian Cumming were not impressed. 'Dalston's changing so much and the garden's one of the things people love about the area. It delivers on lots of policy objectives that Hackney Council has got. To get rid of it seems short-sighted and unimaginative. It does not continue to exist as a garden when it's a walkway', commented Cumming at the time.[10]

The town centre of Dalston was identified as one of the locations for new housing development as part of the Olympic legacy, but seemingly a clash of objectives here, and the drawback to agreeing a 'meanwhile' use (see Canning Town Caravanserai, page 118) has made the Garden's future an uncertain one. The Making Space in Dalston team was from the first acutely cynical about tactics that lead merely to an 'ephemeral city', and not to deeper-level city-making. The hope for the Garden, should this urban oasis be co-opted into a public walkway, is that an alternative piece of land can be found and that the Garden's managers will be supported by community members in negotiating the best possible terms.

Looking at the Making Space in Dalston initiative as a whole, the incisive way that it considered both the hard and the soft aspects of proposed plans with their diverse interdependencies, involving so many local people from the very beginning and consistently and intelligently throughout, it is clear that the team was able to use the credibility of their integrated study as genuine leverage for positive physical, cultural and economic change, and for forging new partnerships of many kinds in the process. Given the pressures of potential displacement imposed by regeneration on urban districts, it is understandable that, more recently, Fior has pointed out that 'the attempt to salvage the possibility of the city as a shared platform for the best and worst of times and those in between, becomes ever more heroic.'[11]

The attempt to salvage the possibility of the city as a shared platform becomes ever more heroic

Neighborland

There is a huge amount of room for improvement in the ways in which city leaders and organisations collaborate on participatory placemaking with citizens. Some excellent web-based platform and design tools are emerging that enable organisations to collaborate with residents on local public space issues, but to date not many bodies have adopted these kinds of tools because of their cost, and also because of lack of training. The US-based Neighborland platform shows how easy it can be to use these media, and its track record demonstrates the rich cultural benefits of tools in action. They help local people deal with what many find a stultifying legal and political status quo.

What if residents had better tools to shape the future businesses in the area, and beyond?

The Neighborland platform came about as a consequence of 'I Wish This Was', a 2010 project by the public installation artist and social activist Candy Chang, a New Orleans resident and co-founder of Civic Centre, an art and design studio in the city. 'In New Orleans people talk about planning fatigue. After [Hurricane] Katrina [in 2005], lots of people went to lots of community meetings, and put lots of stickers on lots of maps. Lots of times they didn't see any noticeable change. So I thought, what if residents had better tools to shape the future businesses in the area, and beyond? Where better to ask for civic input than on the very space that we are trying to improve?'[1]

The many neglected buildings around the city resonated with Chang. On many of them she posted vinyl stickers printed with the unfinished sentence 'I Wish This Was ...', hoping that people would express their wishes for these structures. The response was huge – practical, funny and moving. 'It led to bigger questions, like what if residents had better tools to shape their neighbourhoods? We're the ones that know the businesses we need, what things need fixing. [It's] like a lovechild of urban planning and street art.'[2] In 2011, Chang turned the façade of one neglected building into a blackboard for responses to 'Before I Die I want to ...' The resulting dreams were posted online, triggering more than 500 similar participative walls in over 70 countries around the world.

Judging by the ubiquity of billboards, 'it seems easier to reach out to the entire world than it is to your neighbourhood'.[3] Believing that there are many things in neighbourhoods that could be shared – memories, hopes, skills – reflecting personal well-being and helping people to lead better lives, Chang set up Neighborland with product designer Dan Parham and principal engineer Tee Parham, initially creating a website with support from New Orleans's Tulane University. Today its collaborators include the Rockefeller Foundation, GOOD Ideas for Cities, the San Francisco Planning Department, SPUR and New

Left:
Let the Food Trucks Roll community meeting staged by Neighborland, Ashé Cultural Center, New Orleans, 25 July 2012.

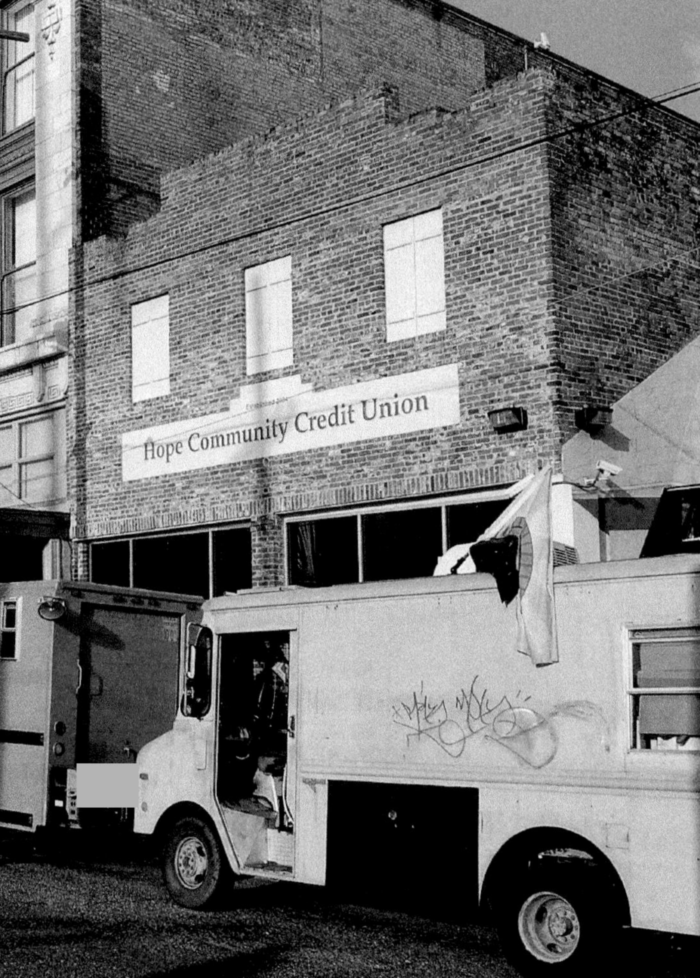

Below:
The crowd at the Let the Food Trucks Roll community meeting, 25 July 2012.

York's New Museum of Contemporary Art. Not only has this design-led team invested creatively in building versatile tools for public space, but also they use them as part of a clear programme of participatory placemaking.

Neighborland's step-by-step advice is simple. Define the issue and solution. Identify stakeholders. Find a guerrilla bureaucrat. Form a coalition. Choose a leader. Show a clear path to action. Execute your campaign – ask a question (for example, via a mobile whiteboard on the street, or the kinds of stickers Chang is famous for), collect ideas, vote and share, take action. Learn from losses and celebrate wins. Grow your network. But it is the incorporation of online tools linking to large displays in public space where people can express their ideas and give feedback, that gives a unique reforming dynamic to Neighborland's activities. Not only is the process a fun and accessible way of playing a role in community affairs, so helping to overcome public participation fatigue that can beset such programmes, but also it culminates in data that can be used to support an issue and raise awareness about it, to open doors for funding, or to change legislation. As part of this, Neighborland also educates people reflexively through the results of their own ideas and information inputs, encouraging them to take affirmative action.

There are now online tools on Neighborland for more than 100 projects, 350,000 individuals and 100,000 ideas and actions, and they are expanding fast. The design includes an SMS and Twitter input, as well as scope to embed Neighborland into other websites, through a Read/Write API (application programme interface). Online citizen subscribers can post their questions, ideas, proposals and actions, and register their support →

ENGAGEMENT
REPLICABILITY
DESIGN DRIVEN
SCALE
IMPACT

IDENTIFY → ENQUIRE → DEVELOP → CO-DESIGN → CO-CONSTRUCT → HAND-OVER

Above:
Members of the New Orleans Food Trucks group, at New Orleans City Hall, 5 February 2013.

for others people's ideas and information resources. At key turning points in projects, email notifications about activities are sent to people particularly invested in them. All this activity is measured and displayed on a dashboard, and exported into Google Analytics.

From this intelligence, Neighborland designs comprehensive, easy-to-read reports supported by diagrams. The data is gathered from many projects and locations, creating insights into the most pressing issues facing cities. The picture of problems and opportunities facing New Orleans, for example, has built up incrementally. Among the everyday issues in the city is the need for bicycle lanes, and in this respect the diagrams show that the boundaries between 'categories' are becoming cloudier – the bike lanes are as much a public safety issue as they are an environmental one, for example. The diagrams also show those ideas which resonate with the largest number of residents: the scope for recycling a particular material, for example, or improving transport facilities.

By building a large pool of ideas, resources and data in an accessible form, Neighborland and its collaborators have been able to use and apply its online design platform tools itself to lobby for change. The various groups Neighborland has worked with include the National Gardening Association, the League of Awesome Possibilities, RIDE New Orleans, the Greenbelt Alliance (which was forging a plan for the sustainable development of the San Francisco Bay Area that would influence the city's 2014 masterplan), and the New Orleans Food Truck Coalition (NOFTC).

The NOFTC, founded by food truck owners – vendors, restaurateurs, community activists, neighbourhood organisations, consumers and others – has been promoting food truck and other mobile vendors in the city. It has paid off, and from being near non-existent in 2008 the young industry is now burgeoning, in line with the growth in popularity of food trucks across the USA (it is estimated

Below:
Residents participate in the Good Ideas for New Orleans event, New Orleans Museum of Art, 12 July 2012.

Right:
Screenshot of Neighborland's mobile app inviting ideas to improve New Orleans, 2014.

that 2013 sales were nearly $700 million, about 1% of all US restaurant sales).[4] In New Orleans, projects include the St. Claude Food Truck Park, which pops up regularly, with several trucks, picnic tables, live music from local bands and youth programmes. NOFTC's argument is that food trucks are an important source of entrepreneurial activity, and that they enhance the culinary culture of the city and enliven the streets as well as providing food options in areas that are underserved.

NOFTC's campaign fought for reform of the outdated legislation from the 1950s, restricting food truck lots close to where people live and work to three days a week and with constraining spatial requirements around each truck. The campaign – based around an issue that several organisations had been working on solving for a while – attracted more locals' support online than any other idea posted on Neighborland before. Meetings led to a coalition, supported by the Institute for Justice, a public interest law firm that has widely advocated for mobile vendors, events and rallies.

After one year of work, raising public awareness on the benefits of food trucks to neighbourhoods and local

neighborland.com

MADE IT HAPPEN

1611 neighbors want food trucks in New Orleans.

Me Too

Suggested by New Orleans Food Truck Coalition

Mission

The New Orleans Food Truck Coalition (NOFTC) supports the growth and success of food trucks

We're just making it easier for passionate individuals and organisations – people who want something – to come together

economies (including a public debate at New Orleans's city hall), in 2013 the municipality passed an ordinance allowing for better regulation of mobile food vending. Neighborland made a stab at estimating the net economic impact of the result, and gave thought to how the social impact could be measured. As it continues to work more closely with different organisations, Neighborland will continue to consider, and share its thoughts on, a new framework for measuring both the economic and social impact of civic engagement.

As Alan Williams, Neighborland's community manager, says, 'a lot of people are meeting each other for the first time ... people who are interested in one of these challenges, whether it is food access issues, or bike transportation issues, or making their neighbourhood a nicer place.'[5] Chang notes that 'in every city there are passionate organisations and individuals in the community, people who want something, but don't know where to begin. With Neighborland, we're just trying to make it easier for all these people to come together.'[6]

Partizaning

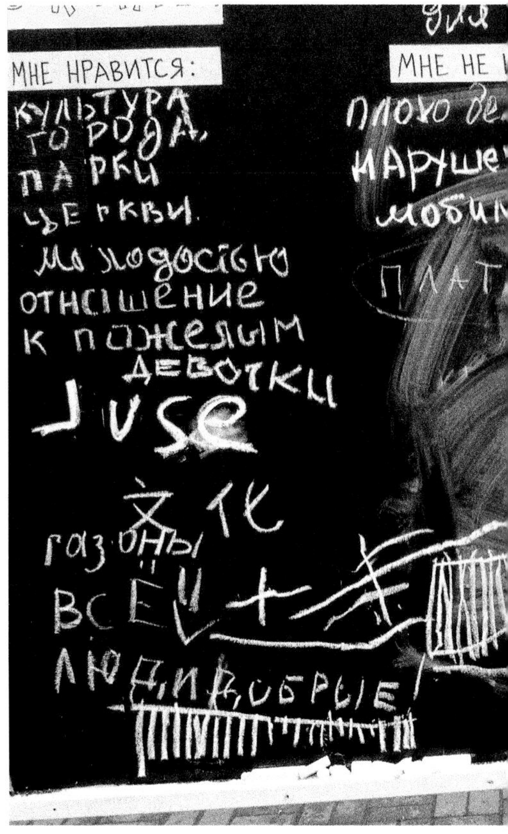

Russian cities today are 'struggling with remnants of Soviet-era urban planning and the development of a neoliberal form of the city', says Shriya Malhotra, an urban researcher and artist. In 2001, Malhotra was one of the founders, along with artists Igor Ponosof and Anton Polsky/MAKE of Moscow-based Partizaning (meaning 'guerrilla' in Russian), a group of artists and art historians engaged in creating art for public spaces. Many plans by Russian architects and urban designers in the 20th century, while distinctly top-down in manner of implementation, promoted social equality through new infrastructures and better circulation. But, 'although highly organised, these plans were not created for people to experience life in the city'.[1]

A lot of things bothered the group's members about the way in which cities in Russia were developing. Since the collapse of the Soviet Union, the growth of the Russian economy, the subsequent privatisation of urban space and the ensuing construction boom, a lack of vision has placed a strain on natural resources and had led to Moscow, in particular, being overwhelmed. The capital's traffic congestion, the haphazard parking in public places, the lack of cycling infrastructure, and the lack of relationship between the government and citizens led Partizaning to ask: 'How is this shift to a capital system possible without removing all ideals of social equity?'

Russian cities have a unique and complex identity, Malhotra feels. After the Russian Revolution of 1917 that led to the formation of the Soviet Union (dissolved in 1991), 'all land was nationalised and socialized, transferred to state or local authorities. The houses once belonging to the bourgeoisie were divided into accommodation for the proletariat.' While urbanists wanted a controlled expansion and urban planning, with garden suburbs, 'dis-urbanists' preferred to 'dissolve the difference between town and country'. In the 1970s the dominant vision of the urbanists, for 'top-down, functional planning' created 'microrayons', state-constructed high-rise blocks of apartments with schools and doctors' surgeries near by, and built on land interspersed with work zones, chequerboard style. Although microrayons were intended to be connected to local transport, in most cases services of trolleybuses and buses became available only later, and the distances from home to stops were relatively long.

Partizaning advocates that local people adopt a sense of creative responsibility for the processes shaping their cities, and promotes their resistance to normative planning of today's privatised urban spaces. The group combines endeavours in activism, urbanism, contemporary art and street art, collaborating with sociologists and geographers. More specifically, as Malhotra says, that means 'public art practices which strategically

Right:
The Partizaning Lab team – Anton Polsky, Shriya Malhotra and Igor Ponosov – at the Moscow Architecture Biennale, 2012.

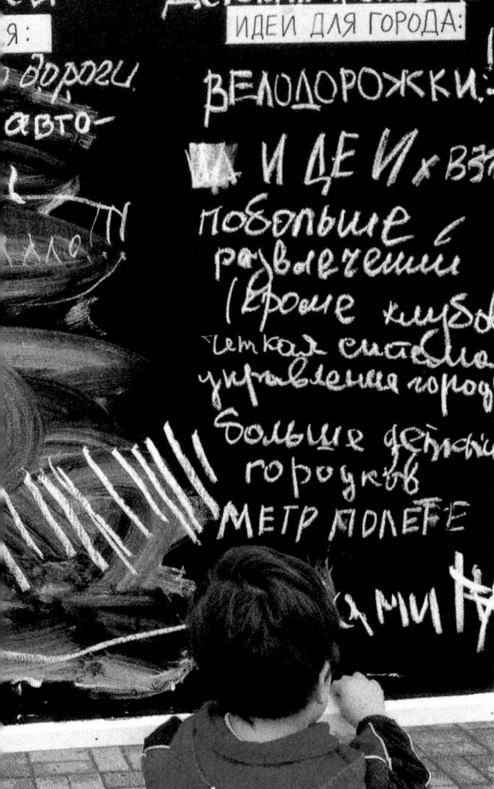

Left:
Partizaning used this chalk board as a research intervention, asking people what they liked and disliked in their city, and for ideas for the Russian city of Kaluga, 2013.

challenge, shape and reinvent urban and social realities. Our work straddles the worlds of art and urbanism: we work in the city and with the public but use artistic venues as just one forum for sharing our ideas.' Most of Partizaning's recent interventions strongly promote the practice of self-organisation and 'flat management' or 'horizontal organisation', as well as the idea that solving most urban problems requires neither government nor leaders.

Since 2008, three years before Partizaning was founded, members have used an old shipping container as a studio and store for its equipment, which has been set up at various locations around Moscow. The group styled its website as an online project in Russian (2011) and English (2012), documenting examples of its urban interaction and participatory activities. These have included Public Mailboxes (2012), a project for which 15 post boxes were set up on walls in various neighbourhoods of Moscow, into which people were invited to post letters outlining what they wanted to change locally. The resulting letters were shared with participating municipal authorities, and were included in an exhibition at the Vostochnaya Gallery.

The practice of creating guerrilla crossroads (marking the road in places where there is no crossing but many people cross out of need), part of the Partizaning repertoire, has also spread to other Russian cities. These guerrilla crossroads have received a lot of press coverage, causing government to recognise the need for them and to take action to create official crossings. Partizaning's promotion of pedestrianisation has also highlighted the fact that, because there is a lack of parking garages in Moscow, many drivers park on crossroads and other public places. Artist Kirill Kto took some of the pavement bricks introduced by the city's new mayor, Sergey Sobyanin, to replace asphalt surfaces, and lined them up on the ground where parking blocked the passage of pedestrians.

Visuals mocking the 'Absurd Parking Lot', highlighting drivers' habits of also parking in parks and playgrounds, were included in the exhibition 'Sobyanin, Baby Come on' (December 2012-January 2013), again at the Vostochnaya Gallery, the venue for Partizaning's art research and urban interventions projects to date. The title of the exhibition referenced Moscow's mayor, who had started to promote public transport, cycling and improvements to pavements in Moscow, to encourage him to keep up the good work. Partizaning saw these outward signs of positive improvement as just the beginning. 'Our goal is to create a new society, where the boundaries between public and private, rich and poor, art and non-art, the author and the audience, professional and personal life will repeatedly be called into question', posted Polsky on Partizaning's website.[2]

The array of items in the exhibition showed how prolific Partizaning had been, constantly producing →

Partizaning advocates that local people adopt a sense of creative responsibility for the processes shaping their cities

> Partizaning calls its philosophy a 'new collectivism', promoting a shared common or public good in the city and engaged way of life

intriguing and useful artefacts: signs and posters, new cycling maps and a how-to guide for making a bench, for example. It has also taken advertising billboards and graffiti that it removes from walls in streets, using their imagery on fabrics for bags. The group has co-opted official languages of orientation and warning signs used in public spaces, creating its own signs and posters in order to reveal the reality of the condition public spaces and government plans.

Over the years it has also staged numerous workshops to redesign public space, many of them held as part of international events – such as the 10th Architecture Biennale of São Paulo, Brazil, in 2013, and the Kunstvlaai Festival of Independents, the Netherlands' largest forum for alternative, experimental and non-commercial art – but also in Moscow, for example at the Delai Sam marathon, a grassroots summit of civil activists, urbanists, street artists and environmentalists.

Partizaning has from the first pursued its manner of working 'illegally', through unsanctioned urban interventions, using the idea of vandalism but transforming it into something productive: the painted pedestrian crossings, the addressing of car domination, the development of alternative cycling infrastructure and the inviting of people to join the group in public dialogues about urban planning. 'Some things have changed in Moscow, and now there are several official programmes to improve the city', said Malhotra in 2014, assessing the advances, although 'very often programmes do not work in Moscow, because it has a unique situation with a mix of socialistic and capitalistic traditions.'[3]

But overall Malhotra feels that Partizaning's interventions have had an impact. Moscow's government has started to create an official cycling infrastructure, and some of Partizaning's activists now work in the city's transport department, in official roles for public spaces or with cultural institutions. But the suburb and dormitory districts have not changed. For one of its projects, Cooperative Urbanism, the group concentrated its work on the outlying districts of Moscow but '[we] found that our changes were not effective.' The soulless highways, and the lack of cultural institutions and comfortable public spaces continue to exist, says Malhotra.

In 2013 Partizaning set up its Partizaning Laboratory to experiment with new ways of changing the city, cooperating with official organisations such as the Moscow Youth Multifunctional Center. It started research and talks with the local community of Moscow's Yaroslavsky district. 'We have worked a lot, but nothing much has changed, because the bureaucratic system still works and it is not possible to push something officially', Malhotra explains. 'We continue these experiments, but it's hard, because people need quick changes and many activists and experts try to use western practices, but these do not work. We realised that we needed an alternative way of doing things – mainly by using creative methods in public spaces and leveraging the power of the media to ignite discussions for change.'

Although Partizaning has worked internationally in such cities as São

Paolo, Berlin, Dusseldorf, Amsterdam, Helsinki and St Petersburg, after three years the group concluded that it needed 'a better analytical and research-based approach understand the urban communities and their issues in the different contemporary cities we live in', Malhotra says. 'We have been encouraged by the fact that people realise that quality of life is not just up to governments and authorities, and that there is power in simple, transformative everyday acts which can also have a wider impact.'

Since mid-2014, two members of the collective, Malhotra and Anton Polsky, no longer live in Moscow. Malhotra is now based in Delhi, India, where she is researching the ideas and traditions of DIY, creating interventions and starting a PhD. Her work also examines gender in spaces – a major issue in Delhi – and matters of transport and migration. Polsky is pursuing a master's degree in political science and sociology in St Petersburg. Igor Ponosov continues to live in Moscow, where he is working with a growing circle of active residents across the city.

Although all three now live and work in different national and international urban contexts, they remain in constant communication. Together they are focusing on improving their respective research capacities, which Malhotra says will help their collective methods. For his part, Ponosov says: 'the most important thing for us as creative activists is not to be experts, but to make new trends and share artistic messages, sometimes crazy, to change the city, country and world we live in. And we are trying to do it in our separate cities and ways.'

Each of the three is finding shared and resonating situations in the cities in which they live or to which they have recently moved, but also in those cities' histories. 'We have been very inspired by activist artistic movements, and find the same ideas of failures and lapses in governance and apathy among the general population in Russia, India and many other countries', Malhotra explains. 'We also find that DIY traditions exist in Russia and India in an interesting manner', based on the polarization between extreme wealth of a few and the limited resources of the majority.

Partizaning has in the past described its underlying philosophy as a 'new collectivism', promoting 'a shared common or public good in the city, a way of life and living that is engaged and not rooted in consumption or profit making', Malhotra says. This idea about collective forms of living is 'in response to, and resists, the capital-led urban development trajectory which most cities inevitably follow', and the three founding members of Partizaning use this philosophy and ethical approach when discussing political and socially artistic ideas in Moscow, St Petersburg and Delhi.

'We believe ideas of collectivity and thinking in groups can be socially transformative in a positive manner, for the common good, from the bottom up, in any city', maintains Malhotra. She emphasises the historical lineage of this ambition. 'This is an idea that already exists and has taken shape in many places, particularly those with a socialist tradition and limited resources where people have always had to make do.'

Left:
A collaborative workshop series, Collaborative Urbanism, involved building street furniture in a parking lot, with the Norwegian group TYIN (see page 262).

Below:
A public mailbox created for a project with the Department of Libraries, Moscow, 2013, for which Partizaning asked people to share their opinions about the future of public space.

ENGAGEMENT
REPLICABILITY
DESIGN DRIVEN
SCALE
IMPACT

IDENTIFY → ENQUIRE → DEVELOP → CO-DESIGN → CO-CONSTRUCT → HAND-OVER

PITCHAfrica

Above:
Early morning roll-call in front of the front facade of the Waterbank School at Uaso Nyiro Primary School, sometimes used for film screenings, 2012. Architects: PITCHAfrica/ATOPIA.

Below:
Computer model of Waterbank School with classrooms, central hall (reservoir underneath), teachers' rooms and gardens on three sides. PITCHAfrica.

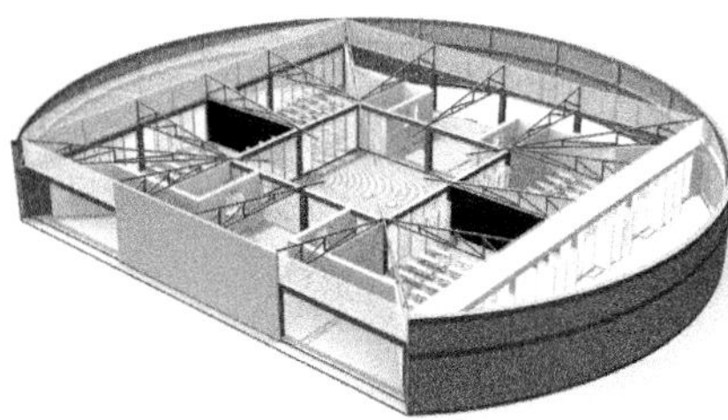

The Waterbank initiative by PITCHAfrica for poverty-stricken, semi-arid regions of Africa aims to change the design of school buildings globally by using harvested and stored rainwater as a catalyst for social, economic and environmental transformation. As an alternative to the four-classroom, barrack-style school building common throughout the developing world, the Waterbank school is simply constructed for the same cost, with the same local materials and expertise. But it provides twice the accommodation and has a wide range of life-changing capacities and amenities, creating a vehicle for environmental education.

UK architects Jane Harrison and David Turnbull, the founders of PITCHAfrica, do not call what they do 'humanitarian' architecture. 'We start the questions much earlier in the process, and the models that emerge can be replicated.'[1] The very nature of the contexts in which they operate demands an innovative approach: 'We are working with minimum resources in parts of Africa where we have to use great ingenuity to get things to work', says Turnbull.

Harrison and Turnbull, who also lead the Princeton, New Jersey-based architectural practice ATOPIA Research, started PITCHAfrica as a non-profit social enterprise organisation after the 2004 Indian Ocean earthquake and tsunami in Sri Lanka, looking at developing water resources and aligning their activities with sports. '[Water] is not used that way typically', says Turnbull, but 'as a social or political tool, it is very powerful.' After doing yield calculations they realised that storing water under the surface of small football stadia, with localised tank reservoirs, would be very efficient. So as to include girls and women, who in Africa do not usually play football, they also make adaptable versions for volleyball courts.

The duo are developing 'dynamic infrastructure' for social and environmental situations facing challenges. Through such means, essential social, economic and environmental processes can be integrated with the physical design and structure of buildings. This creates an active platform and gathering spaces for community engagement, as well as giving social and environmental support and scope for transformation – 'seeds for ways of thinking, in a way', says Harrison.

The flagship project is PITCHKenya, a loose cluster of buildings for the Endana secondary school as part of their 10 acre Waterbank Campus in rural Laikipia, in Kenya's Central Highlands. The school, which has some 300 students, has a rainwater-harvesting football and volleyball stadium that is home to the Samuel Eto'o Soccer Academy. It follows the completion in early 2013 of the first Waterbank school, a primary school also in Laikipia. This was named the 'Greenest School on Earth' by the US Green Building Council in 2013 for its deployment of facilities in one of the world's poorest areas. It was built for less than $100 per sqare metre, the same price as a typical linear four-classroom school building, but with twice the volume. The extra facilities thus enabled include a 150,000-litre reservoir, teachers' rooms, sheltered gardens for growing food, a courtyard that can hold the whole school population and is used for morning roll-call and special events, and community spaces. Walter filtration systems are integrated in the perimeter wall.

The site includes 4 acres of irrigated conservation agriculture and seven new low-cost buildings, which all harvest, store and filtrate rainwater, collectively gathering more than 3.5 million litres of water for use by the community each year. Using urban waste such as recycled plastics and decommissioned parachutes as rainwater harvesters, the architects are asking questions about how they might measure social benefits in relation to the environmental costs.

The campus clusters classrooms, a canteen and staff housing with good light and cross-ventilation, that overlook a central, grey-water recycling demonstration garden planted with fruit trees. The girls' dormitory also has a garden, central reservoir and night-time latrines. Kenya →

PITCHAfrica is developing dynamic infrastructure to meet social and environmental challenges

Left:
End of year prize giving in the central courtyard of the Waterbank School building at the Uaso Nyiro Primary School, the first of its type, built in 2012.

66

PITCHAfrica has new plans for a future urban district in West Africa with high-yield rainwater harvesting

Above:
PITCHKenya/ The Samuel Eto'o Laikipia Unity Football Academy, School and Environmental Education Centre, Endana Secondary School, Laikipia, Kenya, 2014. Architects: PITCHAfrica/ ATOPIAResearch.

Top:
Aerial view of PITCHAfrica prototype constructed in the Port of Los Angeles to coincide with the World Cup in South Africa, 2010. Graphics explain the design fundamentals and the structure's potential for hybridity. PITCHAfrica/ ATOPIAResearch.

↓ is a culture in which almost 60% of young women of secondary-school age experience sexual abuse, and the building's plan and form creates a protective setting for the teenage girls.[2]

As the school designs have evolved, Harrison and Turnbull have looked at the impact of each assembly – for example, the feasibility of different material systems for the frame and the masonry, for example. PITCHAfrica's long-term plan is to continue working with organisations and communities in East, West and Southern Africa, and beyond – anywhere where annual rainfall is adequate to address the water needs of a particular community – and to shift in scale to urban contexts.

Harrison and Turnbull are also developing manuals for communities throughout the African continent, covering rainwater harvesting, water filtration and how to achieve optimum yield. These provide communities with the information required to build Waterbank schools of their own, using techniques that are regionally appropriate and resilient.

PITCHAfrica's work continues to be recognised by awards, for example the Danish INDEX Design to Improve Life awards, 2015. Further Waterbank school-building types are now under construction in Kenya's Central Highlands, in partnership with the Zeitz Foundation, and with funding from the Samuel Eto'o Foundation and a variety of public and private donors.

Harrison and Turnbull chose to focus on schools as a building type that could be transformed into a vehicle supporting the resolution of tensions across the region. Not only are they more protected buildings in the community, but they are attracted by the notion of the commons in such contexts – 'like Actor–Network–Theory in reverse', says Harrison, with the object itself as the catalyst.[3] 'It's very important as water is increasingly privately owned. Rain is the last manufacturer of the commons.' Moreover, 'while very specific issues are [still] not addressed, there is tremendous potential for replicability [of the PITCHAfrica school types]'.

The arrangement of building typologies can be adapted, taking in latrines, dormitories, canteens and kitchens, as well as fruit and vegetable patches to encourage the growing of food. Thinking about such issues has led Harrison and Turnbull to found PITCH USA, in order to tackle other vexed problems, for example of obesity, closer to home. Meanwhile in 2014 they began talking to potential funders about creating in West Africa an urban district with high-yield rainwater harvesting, which would contain housing, retail, light industrial and institutional building types. The district's design aims to deal with issues of rural-urban migration, congestion, resource starvation, and the close tie between poverty, gender inequality and, of course, access to water.

PITCHAfrica

Waterbank initiative aims to change the design of school buildings so as to transform the surrounding community

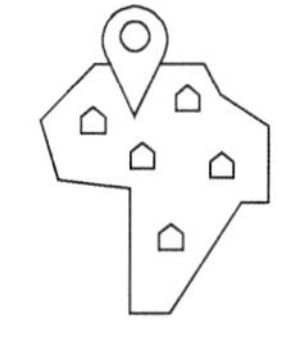

REPLICABLE

Waterbank schools can be built throughout Africa

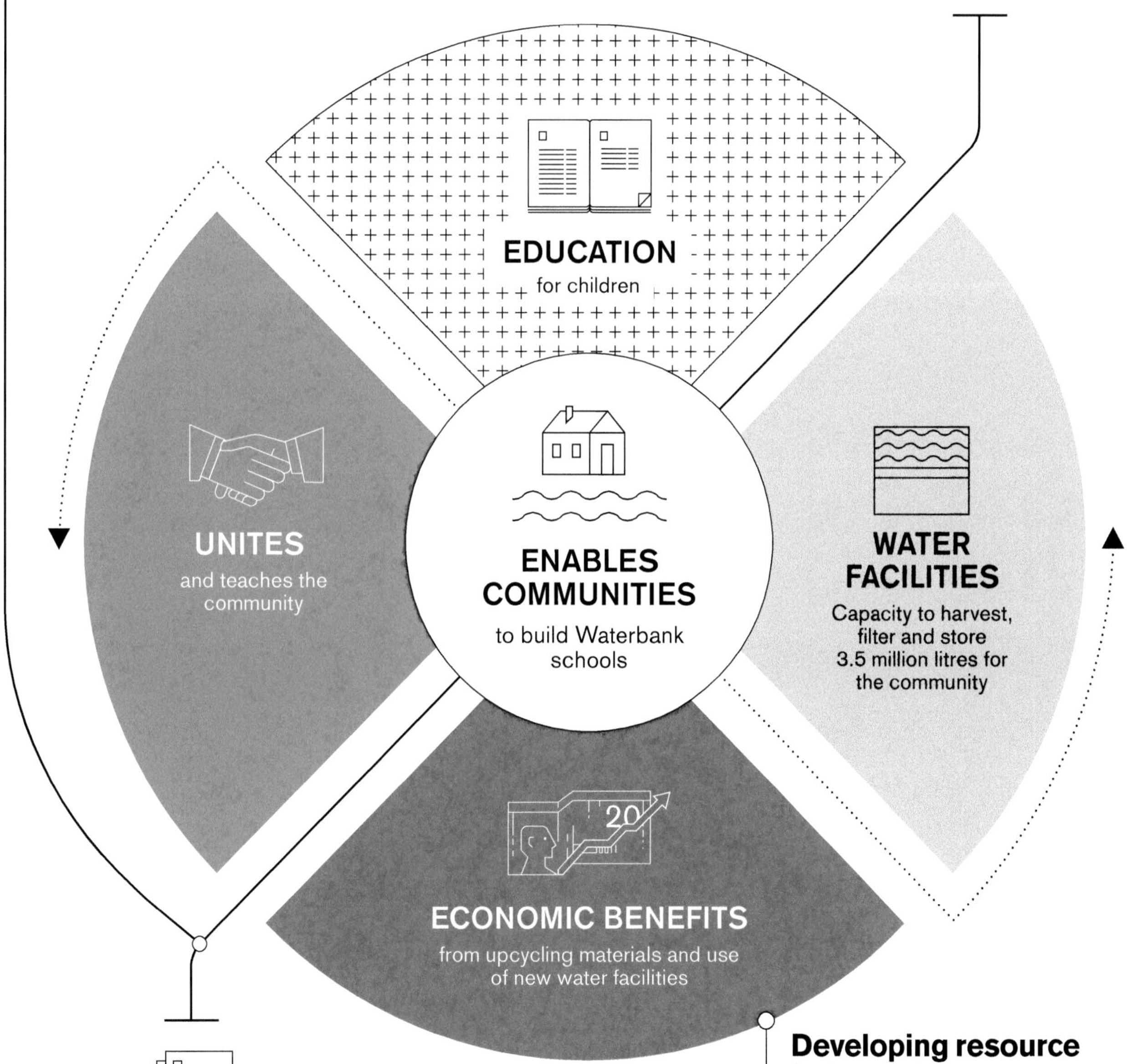

EDUCATION
for children

UNITES
and teaches the community

ENABLES COMMUNITIES
to build Waterbank schools

WATER FACILITIES
Capacity to harvest, filter and store 3.5 million litres for the community

ECONOMIC BENEFITS
from upcycling materials and use of new water facilities

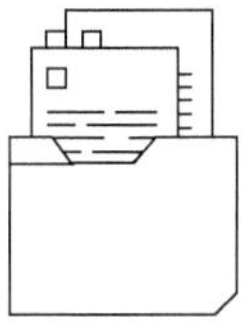

CONSTRUCTION MANUALS
from PITCHAfrica empowers African communities

Developing resource independence

The concept is to provide a modular and regionally appropriate all-in-one alternative infrastructure for rainwater harvesting, education and sports

In the face of harsh economic decline, in shrinking cities, contending with both severe loss of industry and population, a convincing approach to placemaking is one that combines numerous forces to create a versatile set of tools through deep cross-sector collaboration, in order to bring about broad-based beneficial economic and social change.

To foster community identity and build resilience at street level, the 'soft' tools of social capital are of primary importance, but their use does not mean dispensing with a masterplan framework. Through a complementary approach, tactical urbanism demonstrating change in the short term can serve as a catalyst for a strategic longer-term strategy, so long as both are conceived with adaptability in mind and are based on an inclusive placemaking ethos. In this respect, networked creative leadership is vital, to help enable the tasks in many diverse contexts to be grown from each location.

'Most of our work around the world is looking to create change in planning culture city-wide', says Ethan Kent, senior vice president at Project for Public Spaces (PPS), the pioneering non-profit planning, design and educational organisation founded by his father in 1975, and based in New York, with whom he has worked for more than 16 years.[1] PPS is devoted to helping people to create and sustain public spaces that reciprocally in turn become local community assets by spurring regeneration and catering for common needs. All PPS collaborative placemaking projects and events – thousands of conferences and placemaking leaders have been convened over the years – engage with these issues. In 2014, more than 30,000 people participated in PPS's training programmes and lectures globally.

Project for Public Spaces

For PPS, placemaking represents an integrated means to tackle sustainability, local economies and public health. PPS's reach is global. In 2013 it founded the cross-disciplinary network Placemaking Leadership Council, which today has over 800 members from more than 40 countries that come together in yearly meetings. The coalitions it has formed with equally pioneering public, private and third sector bodies – ranging from the National Endowment for the Arts, the Citizens' Institute on Rural Design (CIRD) and Community Matters, to the Environmental Design Research Association (EDRA) and the Metropolitan Policy Program of the Brookings Institution – demonstrate the strong convergence of affinities in values. Their priorities include urban equity, community engagement, local economies, public health, historic preservation, transportation, land use, local food systems, climate change, sustainability and smart growth.

On the ground, PPS's work in promoting pedestrian-friendly, healthy urban spaces, public markets and local place governance has roots in Fred Kent's earlier career as a placemaker. His intention in setting up PPS was to develop

Top centre:
Over 250 events were staged at Campus Martius Park, Detroit, including outdoor yoga and zumba classes, PPS, 2013.

Bottom left:
Campus Martius Park was transformed into a seasonal sandy beach with deckchairs and sunshades, a bar and grill and a big shared table, PPS.

the work of the urbanist, organisational analyst, journalist and author William H (Holly) Whyte, with whom he (along with his son Ethan, as a teenager) collaborated on Whyte's major Street Life research project from 1969, taking place over 16 years. Fred regarded Whyte as a mentor, a figure complementary to that of Jane Jacobs (see The Rise of Bottom-up Placemaking, page 18), and practically the inventor of a bottom-up approach to designing public spaces.

PPS's research, through direct observation, interviews, surveys and workshops, was inspired by Whyte's investigative approach. The Kents and their colleagues look upon Whyte's 1980 book *The Social Life of Small Urban Spaces*, to which it acquired the rights after the book went out of print, as a seminal work highlighting his ethnographic, on-the-street analysis of the essential requirements for successful social urban space – pedestrian-friendly, bustling, efficiently planned and offering plenty of places to sit.[2]

Ethan, who studied sociology, environmental studies and economics, and did his graduate work at Antioch University Seattle's Center for Creative Change in Environment and Community, has worked on hundreds of PPS projects, most visibly in New York where he co-founded the NYC Streets Renaissance Campaign in 2005. The campaign challenged transport policy favouring the car, in order to emphasise the public amenity and identity of streets through pedestrian and bicycle use. It was launched at the Municipal Art Society (MAS) with an exhibition, Livable Streets: A New Vision for New York, exploring the problems and potentials of the city's streets and showing examples of how global cities are tackling these issues.

'We treat people as experts', says Ethan, who explains that PPS is keen to 'move away from the silos [of isolated specialist knowledge]' which fail to serve the human scale aspects of cities. 'People can deliver place capital.' PPS's work – which has been carried out in more than 3,000 different communities in 43 countries and all 50 US states – typifies the variety of placemaking tactics it applies; many of these are about 'thinking small in a big way'.[3] Placemaking can become more reflective of local knowledge in many ways, and PPS creates opportunities for empowering participation in the design and creation of place, believing that it is the essential ingredient for successful environments. Rather than simply consulting the public, PPS creates a platform for the community to participate in and co-design new environments that reflect their detailed knowledge, and providing insights of a kind which independent design professionals such as architects or even local government planners may not have.

PPS uses a placemaking method it calls 'place performance evaluation' – or Place Game, for example. Community groups are taken to proposed development sites, where they use their knowledge to develop design strategies that are potentially of benefit to the community. Irrespective of whether the participants are schoolchildren or professionals, the exercise 'produces dramatic results because it relies on the expertise of people who use the place every day, or who are the potential users of the place', says PPS.[4] This approach successfully engages with the ultimate idea of participatory design, which intends that various stakeholders who will be the users of the 'end product' be collaboratively involved in the design process. PPS also helps to redemocratise places under threat of private interests, by working to improve citizens' power and skills. Facilitating the expression of values of place is key to this process.

The city of Detroit ('Motor City'), in Michigan, where PPS has been actively engaged for the past 18 years, filed for bankruptcy on 18 July 2013, the largest of its kind by a municipality. In 1950 Detroit's population topped 1.85 million, making it the US's fourth largest city at the time, as the automotive industry had been drawing influxes of people to work there, and in suburbs such as Dearborn, for the Big Three: Ford, Chrysler and General Motors (GM). But numbers diminished during successive crises – energy (1970s) and economy the →

We treat people as experts. People can deliver place capital

following decade, after which its debt rating was lowered in 1992.[5] Federal bailouts did not prevent the bankruptcies of Chrysler and GM, in 2011 the population fell to 713,777, a total evacuation of more than a million residents, a 25% decrease since 2000.[6] However, like many other US cities, in spite of its challenges Detroit is reviving from its core, and that means the downtown area and two of its prime waterfront spaces, RiverFront and the Belle Isle island park. Today, more than 10% of the city's workforce are engaged in research and development in advanced industries.[7]

In 1998 PPS started working on the revitalisation plan for Detroit's six-block, 17-hectare Eastern Market, in operation since 1891 and the largest public market district in the US. Its planning and provision of capacity-building services was completed in 2006, when the market transferred from city ownership to a public-private partnership, and the plan has grown very successfully. Since spring 2012, PPS has collaborated on planning for another significant downtown location in need of support, the 4,900sq m Campus Martius Park, with the Downtown Detroit Partnership (DDP) the city council, the Detroit 300 Conservancy and Rock Ventures/ Opportunity Detroit, the development arm of the mortgage lending firm Quicken Loans (CEO Dan Gilbert), whose 8,000 staff work downtown, which owns many of the buildings downtown. PPS had in fact worked on plans for the making of the Park, which became a leading public space, inspired by and named after the publicly owned area of ancient Rome, from 1999 until its opening in 2004.

Campus Martius 'was always envisioned as a grand central meeting place, but also to be a catalyst for economic development', said Bob Gregory, DPP's senior vice president. But, 'because the area was so devastated, with all the empty buildings and vacant land, we needed to jump-start that core district. We wanted to create a space that wasn't just beautiful, but had the ability to activate the area 365 days a year.'[8]

The group's plan – Lighter, Quicker, Cheaper (LQC) – stems from PPS's perception of the larger story of current placemaking in Detroit 'as a broad narrative for how everyone is helping to "make" the city in a lighter, quicker and cheaper way', focusing on reintroducing people rather than ålong-term planning, and on helping to drive economic growth in a city with almost 20% unemployment.

In the summer of 2013, the team activated spaces at Campus Martius Park. A sandy beach appeared with deckchairs and sunshades, styled in the fashion of those at lakeside resorts in upstate Michigan. Amenities such as a new pavilion for domino players and street furniture were introduced. New lighting added a fresh aura to the place. An ongoing cultural programme with hundreds of events was instituted across the downtown area: concerts, outdoor films, pop-up market stalls and festivals. Many of the events also took place in Capitol Park, Grand Circus Park and Paradise Valley, where these types of activities had rarely been held before; others took place at the RiverFront, which has been transformed over the last 12 years with new public walkways and parks still in development, and at the historic Belle Isle.

PPS's concept plan for a totally new, multi-use, 24-hour urban park aimed 'to take the areas around it to the next level', as Kent explains, and the plan has paid off, with more than $1 billion in property investment made in the surrounding areas since the LQC initiative began there. This is clearly an approach that centres on public-private partnerships. 'This focus on improving the city's public realm is a remarkable shift in thinking from within corporate America, where insular suburban office parks have been the model for so long – and still is, looking at what tech giants like Facebook and Google are planning in Silicon Valley', says PPS.[9]

The initiative was part of the overall downtown placemaking plan with Rock Ventures/Opportunity Detroit, which since 2012 has improved a network of public spaces in the central business district in tandem with the various LQC initiatives. More than 900 residents

Right: Community programming at the Campus Martius seasonal beach including sandcastle building and informal play activities, PPS.

Bottom right: Bird's-eye view of the award-winning Campus Martius Park in the heart of downtown Detroit. The park attracts more than 2 million visitors each year.

were approached for ideas through focus groups, interviews, workshops and pop-up events. PPS sees the downtown's revitalization, building on its cultural history, as a model for other neighbourhoods, such as the deprived Joy Street, for which it created the Sowing Seeds Growing Futures Farmers Market.

The family of LQC initiatives need to be seen in the context of Detroit Future City (DFC), a masterplan framework for the city over the next 50 years, developed by the Detroit Works Project; this framework is strongly based on involvement with and input from local people, based on a number of areas: neighbourhoods, city systems, land use, public land and civic engagement. Short-term tactical urbanism and longer-term masterplanning are often seen as poles apart, with the former as ephemeral pop-up activities, and the latter as rigid and hugely drawn out, with apparently not much to offer each other.

However, 'one of the key benefits of taking a LQC approach to demonstrating elements of the Detroit Future City in neighbourhoods across Detroit is that the city would be able to build support for the plan while simultaneously learning, through how people interact with local interventions, what works and what doesn't before making any capital-intensive changes to the city's infrastructure or layout', says PPS. The advantage of the LQC plan is that it was realised within one year. Being fast-track, it gave people quick and noticeable results in a re-envisioning process involving their views. It also has the capacity to 'tap more directly into each neighbourhood's social infrastructure, developing local leadership within a larger framework of civic revitalisation efforts'.[10]

One of the major philanthropic foundations funding the DFC has been the Kresge Foundation, with whose support PPS has been working since 2011 on several neighbourhood food markets, reconceiving their identity as anchors of communities and partnering with the Detroit Community Markets (DCM) network. 'We will work with neighbourhood residents, community-based organisations and the Detroit Future City office to ensure that we are investing in our neighbourhoods', wrote the Foundation's president and CEO, Rip Rapson, in a local paper in 2014. Rapson fully supports the advantages of incorporating a complementary LQC approach into the DFC, and the Foundation is doing this 'through the creative re-purposing of blighted land, the strengthening of places that anchor a community's identity and build social cohesion, the incorporation of art into a neighbourhood's daily life' and 'the development of new preschool development opportunities.'[11]

Three of the criteria for joining PPS's Placemaking Leadership Council are engaging in holistic thinking and operating, understanding that placemaking is a process rather than an outcome, and undertaking on-the-ground projects with other networks and organisations. 'The term "silo-busting" gets your feet tapping', the group states on its website.[12] In 2015, as it reached its 40th anniversary, PPS released new guides to placemaking based on its globally promoted bottom-up activities. Significantly, and in line with the founding ethos inspired by Whyte's work, the first was Streets as Places. 'Since streets are the most fundamental public spaces in communities, but also one of the most conflicted and overlooked, the goal of this agenda is to help people to see streets as vital public spaces and essential factors in the social and economic fabric of communities.'[13]

Project H Design

A flat, swampy area with only 20,000 sparsely distributed people, Bertie County in North Carolina, USA, is hardly thriving. The poorest and most rural county in the eastern part of the state, its nine townships contain many buildings that are unoccupied or in disrepair. High unemployment, relatively few educational opportunities, high obesity rates, lack of access to affordably priced fresh food – in 2007 its problems abounded. It was blighted too, by a lack of facilities, and had no pool of qualified teachers to draw on. So it was tough for Dr Chip Zullinger, brought in that year as local superintendent of education, to see a way in which the school district, no more distinguished than the rest of the place, could be repaired to raise the fortunes of its citizens. While 20% of the American population lives in rural districts, these areas receive only 6.8% of philanthropic funding.

Above: Studio H instructors and construction managers discuss truss construction on the job site of the farmers' market, Windsor Super Market, Bertie County, North Carolina, 2012.

But then Zullinger met Emily Pilloton, founder of the non-profit design and architecture agency Project H Design, and author.[1] Pilloton's prolific Project H programmes of design/build workshops include professional development for teachers, team-building challenges for schools and non-profits, and customised 'boot-camp'-style training. Today the programmes have grown to cater for over 275 students attending workshops that run full time throughout the year, and Pilloton has hired two more teachers.

Zullinger invited Pilloton and her then collaborator Matthew Miller to Bertie County in February 2009. The county was 'in dire need of fresh perspective, of pride and connectiveness, and of creative capital', said Pilloton.[2] Given a key role as educators, she and Miller triggered what proved to be a remarkable experiment in teaching the county's students to develop their creative capital and their citizenship through hands-on experience. They designed an entire curriculum for the students' needs. The way out of the rural ghetto started to look more like a light ahead than a dark tunnel.

Pilloton and Miller set up homes in Bertie County in 2010, instituting Studio H there as a high-school design/build curriculum that included student-built architectural projects for local community benefit. They set in motion a 'Connect Bertie' graphic campaign envisioning how the county's school system could help with community development, so that there was a wider awareness and a vivid reminder of the new initiative. First they carried out a series of renovations of characterless computer labs into more engaging and accessible convivial spaces for learning technology

Below left:
Students with Emily Pilloton (second from left) receive key to city, Studio H's Windsor farmers' market, Bertie County, North Carolina, 2011, Project H Design.

Below:
Farmstands made as part of Studio H, Bertie County, North Carolina, for small town centres, where farmers could sell their goods, 2012, Project H Design.

Left:
The grand opening of the student-built Windsor farmers' market welcomed dozens of vendors and hundreds of visitors, Bertie County, North Carolina, 2011, Project H Design.

skills; they also created with the students an outdoor learning landscape they shared with the teachers, which proved to be a great leveller, bringing out playfulness irrespective of age.

The design team developed hands-on 'shop classes' (industrial arts classes traditionally seen in the USA as a blue-collar vocational training path) that saw the 13 students involved learn and then apply core making skills to a multitude of neighbourhood projects needed by the local community: a chicken coop inspired by the geometry of Buckminster Fuller's geodesic dome; a 185sq m farmers' market; and a network of roadside farmstands for outlying small towns, where farmers could sell their goods and which could also be used as meeting points. As homework, the students were invited to do ethnographic research about the projects' uses – what kind of food people buy, for example – and were later paid during the summer break to be project construction staff. In Project H's hands the usually poorly funded 'shop class' was infused with a more critical and practical studio process for things that the community needed.

'Learning to design and build will open up new opportunities', said one of the students taking what became a one-year curriculum. 'It makes the youth the biggest asset and untapped resource in imagining a new future.'

Reinventing 'shop class' with a more practical studio process for things the community needed

Pilloton and Miller's Project H at Bertie County, documented over a year in the insightful documentary *If You Build It* directed by Patrick Creadon, shows how versatile their design philosophy is.[3] Assigned a social role of this kind, design opens doors and lifts the spirits of young people who had been keen to leave a place, and were fed up with the narrow curriculum that included online physical education classes.

In spite of the overwhelmingly positive student feedback and the plaudits heaped upon the documentary, the programme in Bertie County fell victim to economic cuts in 2012. However, many of the 'veterans' of the project talk of returning to give back to the community after they graduate. 'We feel that this could work in other places', says Pilloton, whose book *Tell Them I Built This* expands on the experience.[4]

Studio H is now based at REALM Charter School in Berkeley, California, the cornerstone of Project H. Among other Project H initiatives are the Learning Landscape, an educational playground environment promoting more engaged outdoor learning through game play; therapeutic spaces for children in foster-care homes in Austin, Texas; a school curriculum on local food production and waste in New York; and a homeless-run design enterprise in Los Angeles. 'I strongly believe in the power of small places', Pilloton says, 'because it is so difficult to do humanitarian work at a global scale ... When you zoom out that far, you lose the ability to view people as humans.'[5]

Rural Urban Framework

The village – whether rural, urban or 'rurban' – is a changing and diversified community condition that for many reasons demands an especially thoughtful intervention. Many villages are precariously unsustainable; others are in transition due to their blurred relationship with cities of which they are part: either physically through proximity, or culturally, as a result of rural-urban migration. And some rely heavily on government policies and support from third parties. All this is being experienced in China. There, the extensive work with some 20 villages by Joshua Bolchover and John Lin, architects and professors at the University of Hong Kong (HKU), has ranged from small interventions to the design and planning of entire communities in a number of contexts.

Bolchover and Lin's projects, undertaken through the research and design collaborative they direct, Rural Urban Framework (a non-profit entity within HKU), are 'not one-stop solutions, nor should they be heralded as altruistic archetypes. If anything they are experiments, designed to be robust enough to withstand and adapt to the rapidly changing context.'[1] Their initiative began after they took an eight-hour drive to a project site near the border of Guangdong and Guanxi provinces in 2006. The mix of remote farmland and built fabric, incomplete, part abandoned, part in transition, spurred them to begin categorising the diversity of conditions they experienced, and to investigate further the cultural, social and economic processes from which the rural urban originated. The duo work with charities and government organisations, developing projects in an array of rural villages, as featured in their book *Rural Urban Framework: Transforming the Chinese Countryside*.[1]

Many rural villagers in China are migrant workers largely based in the big cities, who send money back home to the countryside, intending it to be used for the expansion of their family houses. Still closely attached to their roots, many workers expect to return permanently to the village conurbation at some stage. Consequently, while the population of many villages is declining, they continue to densify. Issues of whether to extend or rebuild entirely are reliant on local politics, and it is not easy to find consensus. 'This may not be surprising given the gradual de-collectivisation of farming since the Mao era', say Bolchover and Lin.

The duo's research has shown them that urban villages have come about in China due to policies very different to those applied to urban land use, for example in developing cities such as Shenzhen in the Pearl River Delta, where in fact the villages are enclaves with the generic city surrounding them. The factory village, in this region, on the other hand, appeared much earlier, in the late 1970s when industrial production became globalised. Village fields were given over to factories, and a myriad of mixes of factories and worker dorms now exist as a patchwork.

At Taiping Village, a factory village in Guizhou Province, there was a 300-year-old bridge, and a collaboration between Rural Urban Framework and NGOs from Hong Kong and mainland China, the local government, architecture schools, students and villagers helped to regenerate this significant spot as a new public space. Precast concrete blocks made in a local factory were laid to make the arch in a traditional way; pavers were designed and constructed in a variety of forms to create surfaces, planters and

seating. Instead of contractors, students and villagers worked together for two weeks to position the pavers and added planting, some of which was donated by villagers. Soon the bridge became regularly used by students from a new school nearby.

In trying to bridge 'traditional and modern techniques', Bolchover and Lin realised that preservation and renovation lie very close to each other, and in Chinese villages can be understood only in the context of the recent changes in the country's dynamics; in Taiping Village, the construction of a highway and new shops next to it has taken the focus away from the river as 'the main infrastructure' and location of commercial life. By understanding these changes 'in relation to the past, architectural interventions can act to preserve continuity between past and present, while anticipating future transformation', say Bolchover and Lin.

The traditional rural Chinese village model – for example in Guangdong Province in the Pearl River Delta, with its single-storey mud-brick houses closely clustered together – is now regarded as unsafe and unsanitary. In many villages major reconstruction efforts have taken place, making them look modern, as well as uniform, in an attempt to play down wealth disparities. The government provides some funding (usually around 20% of the reconstruction cost of each family house), and provides basic infrastructure and services. Each family then has to finance the rest, with only basic guidelines to assist uniformity in heights of storeys and patterns of façade tiling, rather than spatial planning ordinances. If families can initially afford to build only one storey, they can add more in time. It often takes families more than ten years to complete a four-storey building.

At Shui Wei Dong Village, a farming community in Guangdong Province, the aim was to rebuild 110 local houses, each in a 70sq m plot sitting on a grid proposed by the villagers themselves. Through the rebuilding, new foundations would enable four storeys so that families that had been separated by lack of space and were living in individual houses, could be reunited under one roof.

Bolchover and Lin's challenge here was 'to persuade the villagers to find a balance between their individual and collective needs'. As there was no planning coordinator, →

Below left:
Presentations to villagers, Luk Zuk Community Centre, Guangdong Province, China, 2011-ongoing. Architects: Rural Urban Framework.

Above:
Villager examines models of proposed village house reconstruction, Guangdong Province, China, 2012-13. Architects: Rural Urban Framework.

Architectural interventions can preserve continuity between past, present and future

↓ the residents 'immediately put their own space needs ahead of the common interest.' In villages such as this, it is common for plot sizes to be maximised, leaving only narrow strips of circulation space perhaps just 1-2 metres wide between four-storey buildings. This growing trend for verticality, replacing the horizontal patterns of old, is a solution that mimics the urban villages in the large Chinese cities, which are surrounded by fast-track development. In the city, the municipalities are starting to regulate the density; in the rural villages, a similar process is not taking place.

When Bolchover and Lin entered the design process at Shui Wei Dong, the village had been demolished, as a solution to the awkward situation of some villagers waiting for new houses, while others got theirs early. The proposal, with a simple zoning and some 'setback' requirements, included the design of new building types, quite collective-looking in appearance on plots of exactly the same size and allowing for family growth and reorganisation through a series of stacked, changeable floor plans with balconies facing different directions. Such flexibility can also bring density: Bolchover and Lin found that it was almost impossible to persuade all of the families to limit their building envelopes with setbacks, as they were reluctant 'to concede even a small amount for the common good – for public space, ventilation and day-lighting'.

The architects devised four types of houses so as to offer an array of different living configurations and to help maximise views out, but this strategy did not win out over government regulations favouring uniformity, so the designs did not get advanced further. Bolchover and Lin feel that such situations pose a dilemma for architects concerning where their allegiance should lie. The situation is polarised: the villagers are keen to break with the past in favour of contemporary building styles and spatial amenity, while the government wants the villages to physically represent 'collective growth and harmony'. Everywhere in China villages are urbanising to a greater or lesser degree; some, more traditional, are undergoing informal growth; others are in transition with a mix of elements. There is also a

Left:
Bridge in Taiping, Guizhou Province, China, 2007-9. Villagers and students pave the bridge as part of its renovation. Architects: Rural Urban Framework.

Below:
Women weaving in the House for All Seasons, Shiya village, Shaanxi Province, China, 2009-12. Architects: Rural Urban Framework.

third distinguishable type, the newly built village, 'uniform and consistent, the most homogenous of all, arranged in strict rows, brand new but empty'.

At the poor, remote Qinmo Village, also in Guangdong Province, Bolchover and Lin's project was a long-term one over six years, involving many different donors and stakeholders, to bring about the village's sustainability in all senses of the word. Organic farming was a strong prospect, and the Green Hope Foundation had selected the village for a new school focusing on environmental education. A new school building was to be built, with the help of the Chinese Culture Promotion Society (CCPS) and 50% funding from the local government, and the old school was to be transformed into a community centre and eco-farm visitor centre.

Qinmo is typical in that it lacks public spaces and is dense. The architects conceived the school so that it would also be a public space for the whole community, with a library and facilities for outdoor theatre. They dispensed with the standard rectangular volumes and proposed an S-shaped outline to the building, which would have a 'green' roof and views of the surrounding farmland. Instead of finishing the walls with the customary, generic ceramic tiles, the villagers agreed to paint the bricks with fluorescent paint to brighten them up.

Through the involvement of CCPS and Kadoorie Farm and Botanic Garden, the Rural Urban Framework team transformed the old courtyard-style school building for community use into a demonstration centre for ecological agricultural techniques. The centre was linked to a farm outside the village experimenting with new, profitable products, and is now also an informal hub for village children, educational meetings and camps. Former students return to the village to teach the younger children about their experiences, and through the CCPS's long-term involvement an entire education and agriculture feedback loop has been sustained, one that both promotes rural sustainability and advances educational opportunities for the children.

Bolchover and Lin are open about the challenges some projects present. Luk Zuk Community Centre, in a beautiful karst river valley in Guangdong Province not so far from Qinmo Village, may never be constructed. Its design drawings are all ready and it has been fully costed, but funding was unexpectedly withdrawn before the project could go on site. When the pair first visited in 2011 it was clear the new facility was needed: teachers' accommodation was very cramped; the river was polluted with rubbish; an ancestral hall near the river in the old, largely abandoned part of the village, was disused, despite its symbolic significance, in favour of modern buildings.

The architects vowed to turn this situation around with the arbitration of the village head. The main stakeholder, once again, was CCPS. A similar plan to the one they adopted for Qinmo was mounted, with the idea that locals would participate and thereby become 'more active stakeholders, eventually taking ownership and responsibility for operating and sustaining the building'. The design, which included dormitory space, was left open; a continuous roof and ground plane, collects, filtrates and reuses water.

Little by little the villagers became interested in documenting their waste land, and seeing its opportunity

At first some villagers were sceptical, but little by little they became interested in the idea of documenting their village land. 'They began to see the site that they had ignored and laid to waste in a different light – as an opportunity and as a way to have something for free.' So it was a massive blow when the main donor pulled out. The validity of such a model is clear from the success of Qinmo. At Luk Zuk, 'this void has, at least momentarily, become an active presence in the collective consciousness of the village.'

SERA Architects

While the first US suburbs grew around streetcar lines running into urban neighbourhoods from the mid-19th century onwards, after the Second World War suburbia sprawled. This sprawl was low-density, car-dependent and lacking in public transport or cycle paths, and its features have only partly changed since then. All energy and food is produced outside the control of local people. Waste is treated remotely, and many retail and service businesses are not locally owned.

'Not city and not country, these are one of the most highly subsidised landscapes in world history,' says Tim Smith, partner at SERA Architects, in Portland, Oregon, founded by George Sheldon in 1968 during the era of the city's downtown renaissance. 'Conceived in an era of cheap fuel, free roads, unlimited parking, cheap land and favourable housing costs, many Second World War suburbs are now on life support, struggling with a new calculus amidst ever-rising resource costs and ever decreasing subsidies.'[1]

Smith, an expert in the design and planning of sustainable communities, who joined SERA in 2002, envisages a citizen-managed reversal of this picture, through the Civic Ecology whole-systems framework for sustainable communities he has developed and successfully presented in a number of places in the USA over the last 20 years. Through this new paradigm of urban design for suburbia and what he calls 'deep community building', buildings become mixed-use and ecologically advanced, and the overall urban centre is densified, with more public streets and transport-oriented developments.

But that is not all. For this overall approach to succeed, Smith argues, it also needs active citizenship to manage the 'integrated web of energy, nutrients, resources, and financial information and cultural flows and interactions' of a place, that he describes as the 'software'

Design for a place based not just on aesthetics but on the underlying systems that animate life

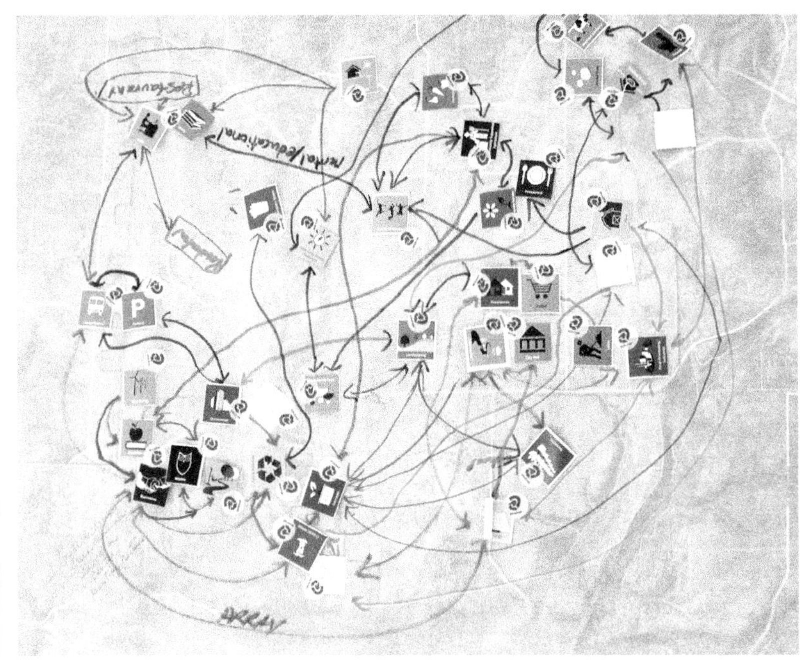

Above:
A Civic Ecology community resource flow map produced by citizens, Damascus, Oregon, 2010, during session led by SERA Architects.

of a community. This bases placemaking not just on aesthetics but also on the underlying systems that animate life in a specific context, and creates a 'living culture' to address both current and future problems.

In order to illuminate how best this can be achieved, Smith contrasts two aspects of community design for suburbia – its 'hardware' and its 'software'. In one scenario, local government, working with the private sector, improves its mobility and form through better 'hardware' – streets, buildings, parks and other physical infrastructure, built incrementally. These are typically engineering-centric, says Smith. In another, a 'software' approach introduces a 'web' of energy, food, water, waste, money and the local economy, activated and propelled through a civic public-private partnership enterprise. These are essential for suburbia's resilience, empower citizen leadership, and are conceived as 'citizen-centric'.

'An ideal scenario would integrate the two approaches', says Smith. Along with the sustainably built 'hardware', the suburban natural infrastructure would integrate next-generation open spaces and streets, rooftops for growing food, waste management, energy generation and water systems. Such a synergy of hard and soft would, he feels, 'stimulate greater density and mix of uses in support of enhanced regional mobility, a vibrant local economy, healthy social capital and enhance resilience'. The result could be a 'new public works of resilient infrastructure, a nature-works that does not just provide ecosystems services to humans, but engages citizens as an integral part of a human-nature-community ecosystem.'

Smith's vision is highly significant, for 'today's suburbs are not just bedroom communities anymore but increasingly places of employment. Almost half of the jobs in America's largest 98 metropolitan areas are more than 10 miles away from the city centre', he says, citing figures given by the US economist Edward Glaeser, in his recent book *Triumph of the City*.[2] But, 'these areas are also not entirely prosperous anymore', Smith →

Above:
Community leaders create a Civic Ecology resource flow map for their neighbourhoods. Training session led by SERA Architects and Sustainable Atlanta, Atlanta, Georgia, 2014.

Below:
Preparing for the transport and sale of materials collected through the local recyling plant, Chestnut Hill, Philadelphia.

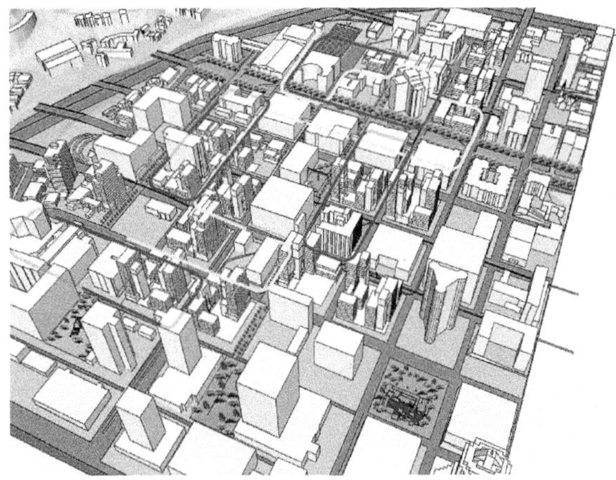

Above:
Portland State University EcoDistrict energy balancing diagram, 2010. District energy sub-loops allow trading of heat between facilities. SERA Architects.

adds, referring to the Urban Land Institute's 2012 statistics that as of 2010 the majority of the country's poor lived in suburbs.[3] As federal and municipal subsidies decline, resources are becoming scarcer. Smith is concerned that suburbs are insufficiently resilient in the face of economic pressures, ageing infrastructure, unemployment rates and housing shortages.

Nor are suburbs fully 'prepared for the sudden storm, power outage or act of terror', Smith says. 'Suburban resiliency seems like an oxymoron amidst increased traffic congestion, crime, poverty, and a host of other stresses that have appeared since the 1980s.' Once suburbs were 'viewed as place of refuge from the stresses of city life ... places to be closer to nature', says Smith, explaining that this no longer holds true.

When looking at what the precise nature of the remedial design of suburbia should be in today's resource-scarce era, Smith is adamant that design and planning teams must go well beyond raising efficiency and liveability, or imagining that giving shopping malls a makeover, or adding new visitor experience, will solve all suburbia's ills. 'Addressing the deficiency in local resource flows, particularly social capital, will be as critical to placemaking as revitalising suburban arterials [roads], retrofitting underperforming suburban malls or introducing

transport-oriented development.'

Smith wants to see suburban infrastructure fundamentally reinvented using 'lighter, less resource-intensive technologies' through a 'citizen-based, nature-works rebuilding programme', involving more ecologically sound waste treatment, storm-water management and local food production. Such an approach could draw on the EcoDistrict concept developed by the Portland Sustainability Institute (PoSI) and Smith, Ethan Seltzer and other professors of urban studies and planning in Portland State University.[4]

Taking inspiration from European models such as the eco-district Hammarby Sjostad in Stockholm, but otherwise home-grown as a concept, the EcoDistrict is a comprehensive strategy to create sustainable neighbourhoods through the integration of building and infrastructure projects with grassroots action taken by local community groups and individuals. The PoSI is developing five such neighbourhoods, including at the University, and the new governance

Left:
At Chestnut Hill, Philadelphia, a new children's playground was made with funds earned from a monthly collection and sale of recycled materials.

Below:
Public realm improvements in the Buckman neighbourhood of Portland, Oregon, SERA Architects, 2010.

model is conceived as potentially exportable to others in the state and further afield.

When talking of the social capital needed to tap what he calls 'this latent resiliency', Smith adopts the definition of the term made by public policy experts Robert Putnam, Robert Leonardi and Raffaella Nanetti in their analysis of community organisations in Italy: 'features of social organization, such as trust, norms and networks, that can improve the efficiency of society by facilitating coordinated actions'.[5] He refers to *Bowling Alone,* Putnam's 2000 study of declining levels of civic engagement in suburbs, caused by lost time due to commuting, increased online activity and other factors, and identifies it as a key systemic weakness.[6]

Nonetheless Smith feels that suburbs could become 'engines of innovation' creating 'enduring ecological, economic and social wealth'. He cites California's Silicon Valley as an example where greywater reuse and transport-oriented development have been adopted, while the San Francisco Bay area city of Mountain View has development incentives for sustainability measures within its general masterplan. Citizen engagement, Smith is anxious to point out, is not NIMBY-ism, or what he calls 'obstructionism' – 'a reaction to a lack of true civic engagement'.

Instead, 'empowering social, economic and ecological innovation, to create a sense of ownership of resources, would be the YIMC – Yes, In My Community – paradigm'. This new and more holistic paradigm should start with 'the software of resource flows' to animate community life and enable hardware to become the container for software. Smith says that his Civic Ecology framework is such a dynamic facilitator, in employing a whole-systems approach that is open, flexible and adaptive, focusing on specific community contexts, matching shared community needs with local capacities and assets, and recognising that a new social contract is needed.

Smith knows that civic engagement is not a 'one-time volunteer effort in response to a crisis but an ongoing civic duty practised by citizens and passed on as part of local civic culture'. He cites the example of Chestnut Hill in Philadelphia, Pennsylvania, a neighbourhood of 10,000 people where a volunteers' group organises the collection and →

Above:
Aerial view of the Chestnut Hill neighbourhood, north-west Philadelphia, where resident-run recycling converts materials into community capital.

sorting of materials for recycling by the local recycling centre. They found a new centre that would actually pay for some materials if they were delivered. Through this means they have supported the Chestnut Hill Community Association's activities to fund the greening of public spaces, and arranged for local schoolchildren to design an improved community park.

Smith acknowledges that today's social contract arises out of liberal democracy, consequently prioritising 'privacy, liberty, individualism, property and rights exercises through power and law'. Under this scenario, people are well 'used to electing others to do government for us, relieving us of the burden of confronting conflicts in the public realm'. But while this 'model has engendered voters and tax payers', it has not created citizens, nor does it 'offer a way for citizens to discover their shared core values and use them as a basis for creation of a resilient future'. This is not, he explains, necessarily about achieving fully self-sufficient communities, as that would be much harder to achieve and take longer. But it is about changing the existing status quo to support resilience of place through a new social contract, 'thickening up our thin democracy', says Smith paraphrasing the political theorist Benjamin Barber as advocating in *Strong Democracy,* his 2003 book about participatory politics and local bureaucracy.[7]

The suburbanising community of Damascus, Oregon (5,000 people), in the Portland metropolitan region, is one where Smith involved local people in his Civic Ecology process after joining SERA in 2002. In 2003, on being brought into Portland's urban growth boundary, Damascus began creating a new social contract for its own comprehensive plan for growth. 'In order to answer the community's question, "how will we know a good plan when we see it?", citizens crafted a series of community principles and a decade later, still refer to them whenever confronted with the need for decisions that will affect the community.' Smith could see that 'planning for new hardware (buildings, infrastructure) had the community factionalised', in some cases for years.

So in order to build collaboration on issues central to resilience, the citizens – including local business owners, representatives from local churches, local and regional government, farmers, community activists and volunteers – came together in teams to create five sets of community resource flow maps. They adhered to SERA's Civic Ecology process, known as CIVIC. Having convened (C) a local working group, they investigated

Below:
The community composter/meeting place in the Buckman neighbourhood of Portland, Oregon.

(I), to learn about the community 'with eyes it did not think it had', visioned (V) and prepared to implement (I) using SERA's resource flow mapping tool and to chart (C) progress. For the visioning process, the team was mindful of forecasting (where things could go for the local community), and instead did 'backcasting', creating a story, a narrative of vision of their community to 'paint a picture of where it would like to be' in the near-, mid- and long-term future.

Each team identified a number of 'community ecology' projects it wanted to puruse and then, over the course of four workshops, picked project teams, leaders, shared community benefits, barriers to success, community assets that might help overcome these, potential partners, and worked out implementation plans. The projects included a new community centre, a community composting and materials recovery facility, and an agriculture and food cooperative organising a new weekly farmers' market. The community teams also gave an existing non-profit organisation a mandate to serve as the civic-public-private body, with a board.

Community resource flow mapping is a tool developed by Tim Smith's practice, SERA Architects, to help enable local people of all ages to carry out systems design. SERA is exploring how to incorporate digital applications into the flow mapping exercise so that those who cannot participate live can take part online. It is also speculating on how refined versions can become public policy tools, driving decisions on a par in legal standing with building codes or zoning ordinances. 'In a citizen-empowered era, a resource flow map should be highly interactive, and we envision suburban communities with a live version in their town halls and on their websites. It could be both a policy and a web tool', says Smith.

In building social capital you create the one form of infrastructure that improves and accrues value over time

Smith feels that 'the act of designing resilient systems with strangers, casual acquaintances and even enemies, and seeing these systems realised creates a strong bond among citizens and between citizens and their community.' When it comes to making the community more adaptable to stress, and better connected on resource flows and social capital, a commitment to first rate resilient systems design is also better able to 'monitor progress and adapt as needed and more adept at identifying and taking advantages of opportunities to leverage change'.

Smith sees Civic Ecology practice as an intergenerational enterprise so that value – 'the community's DNA' – can be realised by future generations. 'Building enduring social capital is the one form of infrastructure that improves over time and becomes more valuable with use', he observes. 'Hardware, as we know, begins to wear out the minute we start to use it.'

snark space making

Right:
LOWaste for Action, 2013-14, snark space making, wearables made out of protective fabric, designed by Stefania Caputo.

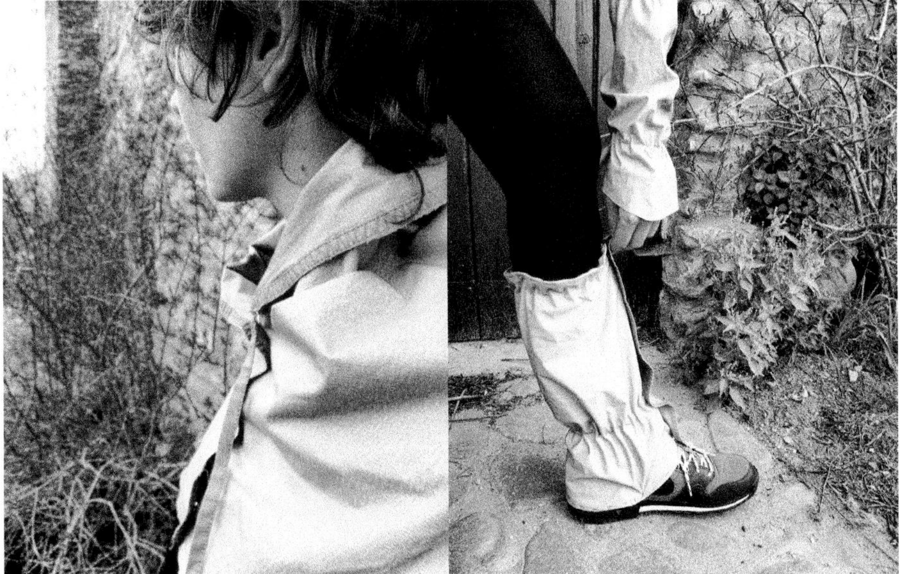

Today it is possible to mobilise an integrated mix of design tools and policies, services and processes that engage mobile-communication and geopositioning technologies. Moreover, it is necessary to do so, because all these tactics play a strong social role in urban design. Through their application on projects, deep assumptions can be shifted, even redesigned, when employed in tandem with new chains of activity: conceptualisation, interaction and the forging of new social contracts. One of the assumptions that is being challenged is the question of what exactly is 'the public'.

'The public is much more a product of the constant negotiating between subjects, places and authorities, rather than a premise', says Marco Lampugnani.[1] He is an Italian architect who along with three others in 2008 founded Bologna-based snark space making, an interdisciplinary open network of architects, planners, economists, semiologists and journalists. The four partners, each from a different discipline, had doubted whether their individual professional backgrounds were on their own the best to deal with public issues.

Snark analyses and stimulates the creative production of 'the public' through many different means, and is regularly asked by clients to 'help them in coping with their role in the public realm. They can be public administrations, companies, NGOs, or even private citizens. We offer services, but we are entrepreneurs as well', explains Lampugnani. It acts in both the public and the private sectors, at both S and XL scales, and is both socially and technologically driven.

The LOWaste (Local Waste market for second-life products) for Action project with the city of Ferrara and La Città Verde, Impronta Etica and Hera groups, launched in 2011, began from snark's premise that rubbish should be treated as a 'collective good'. During the project, which was organised over three years with the support of the Life+ programme of the European Union, the team shaped and then prototyped new upcycling chains, converting rubbish into new services and products of better environmental value. In this way, raw waste material is re-perceived as valuable. Snark began by making a call for proposals, open to anyone able to be part of some stage of the production chain, as it wanted to avoid a solely internal design-driven approach. Participants were then brought together in workshops where they designed and prototyped the chains collectively. Six potentially successful business models were developed, as well as up to 16 test products. Lampugnani explains: 'We gave back to civil society the right to do business with their garbage, enlarging their life cycles, and generating new businesses.'

Auletta, a small town in the province of Salerno in Campagnia, south-western Italy, is still half in ruins after the devastating Irpinia earthquake of 1980. Its council received funding from Regione Campagnia to regenerate the city, but decided it could not achieve this unaided, and so in 2011 asked snark to join forces with the town and RENA (a body of diverse young professionals) as project coordinator. The scheme was sponsored by the MIdA Foundation (Integrated Museums of the Environment), which manages various local sites and was keen for a new management model of post-earthquake operations as an alternative to traditional norms.

The snark team devised a management process to ensure high-quality standards, putting together a team of local stakeholders and citizens and those from further afield. The team members also designed another new type of process leading to a public tender, first with CO/A, a competition launched in November 2011 (with a deadline in January 2012). It was based on both a wiki process and 'the assumption that it was a community of people working for the common good, rather than a process of selection and exclusion', says Lampugnani. The methodology the team forged with RENA for CO/A aimed at building collective intelligence for social innovation.

To collect ideas and contributions for Auletta's transformation at both the local and regional level, CO/A crowdsourced its input through the open competition and a workshop held in early spring 2012. Here snark experimented with different levels of stakeholder interaction. The group applied blended models, such as online/offline workshops, and as a precursor to the public tender in late 2012 carried out 'design tuning' during the summer with the selected teams and local administrators.

It was snark's strong aspiration to foster a democratic process of the highest potential that would culminate in the transfer of know-how to the region. The team feels that often in Italy the collaborative process is dysfunctional, and it was keen to avoid 'fixed, self-serving, secret →

Fostering the best democratic process to transfer know-how to the region

Left:
Rifiuto a chi? (refused to whom?) advertising poster as part of LOWaste for Action, Piergiorgio Italiano, Silvia Bamonti, Susanna Mandolino, 2013.

snark space making's premise for LOWaste was that rubbish should be treated as a collective good

procedures', as Lampugnani describes it. So the open competition it created had to be different, to 'be a catalyst for social aggregation, administration, participants; society will be collaborating for a common good'.

The competition was intended to 'rehabilitate and restore trust in the concept of contest procedures in the Italian context ... protecting the participants with the principles of transparency and collaboration rather than coercion and control'. The official call for ideas stated that the competition would 'select projects and management models for the development of Auletta, from the historical centre design and reconstruction to the eventual arrangement of the work implementation'. The plan was to make accessible from the project website the full inventory of tools and materials required, and all evaluations.

Co/A had three priorities: valuing history and memory; recognising and protecting the fragility of the environment; and devising a contemporary, restorative design. The proposals needed to interweave all three, and to represent a collaborative model 'not based on hierarchy nor constraints that could potentially polarise the factors at hand'. Various project needs were defined in the open call. These included new models of temporary living space, and cohabitation between visitors and residents, that would empower residents; and the creation of devices enabling networking for area attractions and destinations through new management models of local public places such as parks.

Lampugnani sees the Auletta project as a demonstration of a way of overcoming the common polarity of 'hyper-local vs hyper-global'. Its process combined resources from the local ecosystem with international ones, he explains. It proved to be an exemplary set-up, in which planning processes, community building and engagement, and territorial marketing merged into a coherent, brand-new whole.

Furthermore, the Auletta project got the attention of politicians. Fabrizio Barca, at the time Italian minister for territorial cohesion, actively supported the project. Understanding its far-reaching impact in a field lacking such strategies, he promoted the Auletta project as a model of activities for his professional sector, enabling a new cross-sector benchmark to be fielded widely for emulation and inspiration.

Below:
CO/Auletta, snark space making, 2011-ongoing. Roundtable with all participants during the first workshop, Casa della Parole, 2012.

snark space making

Creating new methods for disaster recovery in Auletta, Italy

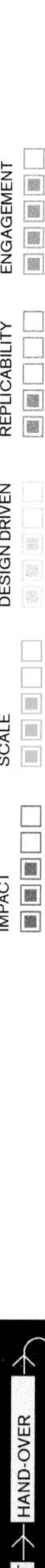

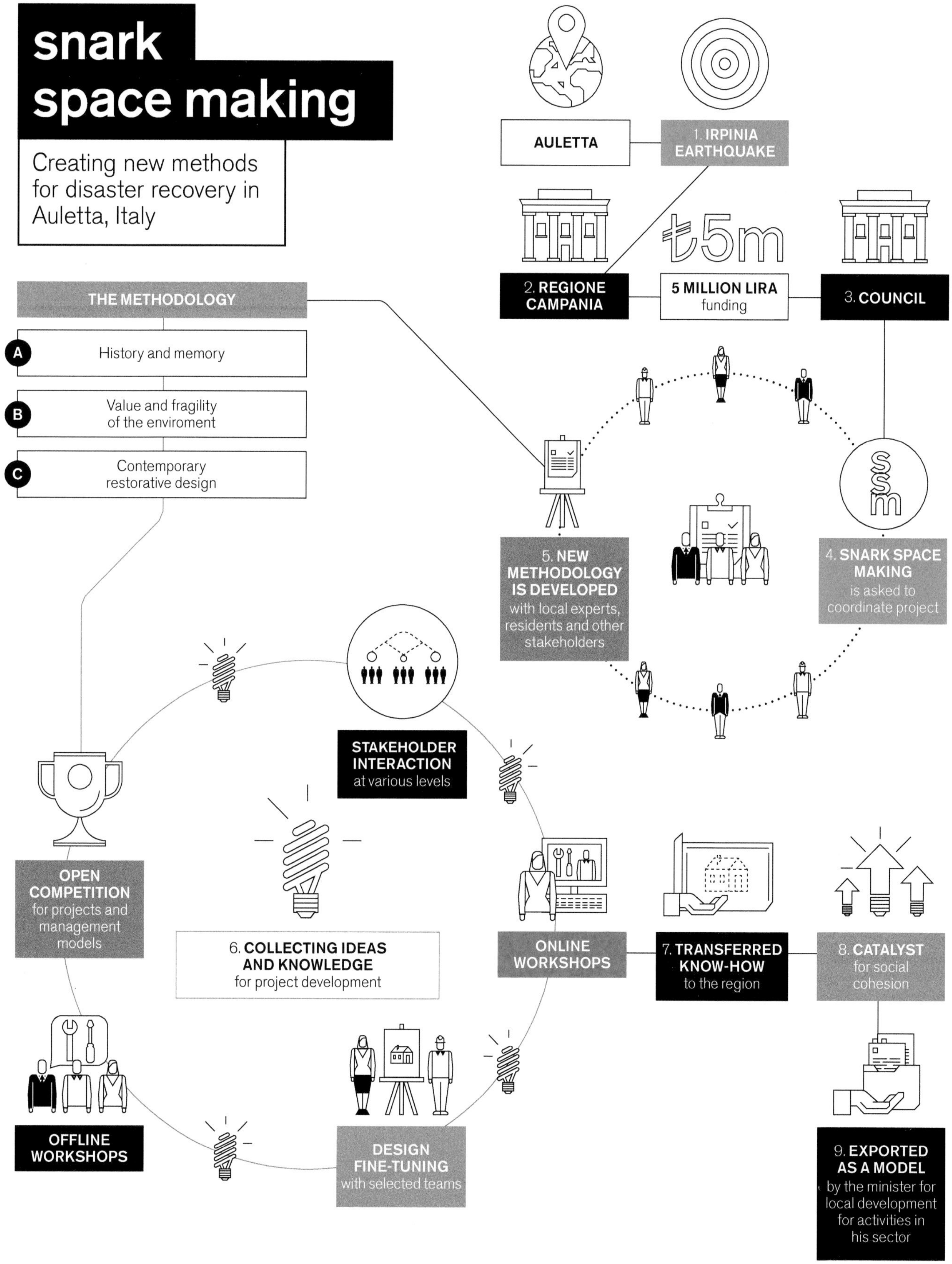
AULETTA
1. IRPINIA EARTHQUAKE
2. REGIONE CAMPANIA
₺5m
5 MILLION LIRA funding
3. COUNCIL
THE METHODOLOGY
A History and memory
B Value and fragility of the enviroment
C Contemporary restorative design
4. SNARK SPACE MAKING is asked to coordinate project
ssm
5. NEW METHODOLOGY IS DEVELOPED with local experts, residents and other stakeholders
STAKEHOLDER INTERACTION at various levels
OPEN COMPETITION for projects and management models
6. COLLECTING IDEAS AND KNOWLEDGE for project development
ONLINE WORKSHOPS
7. TRANSFERRED KNOW-HOW to the region
8. CATALYST for social cohesion
OFFLINE WORKSHOPS
DESIGN FINE-TUNING with selected teams
9. EXPORTED AS A MODEL by the minister for local development for activities in his sector

ENGAGEMENT
REPLICABILITY
DESIGN DRIVEN
SCALE
IMPACT

IDENTIFY → ENQUIRE → DEVELOP → CO-DESIGN → CO-CONSTRUCT → HAND-OVER

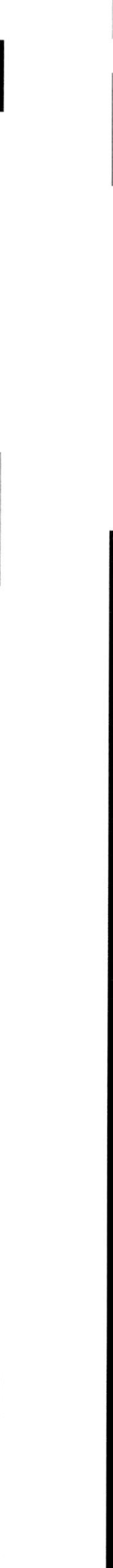

Below:
The Goodsyard site, Shoreditch, with views of the city fringe, in 2013.

Soundings

During the 19th century, the eastern edge of the City of London was chock full of small communities – traders, printer, makers and warehouses. Today the area throbs with creative industry folks, City workers, locals and visitors crossing paths. Yet the massive site of the former Bishopsgate railway goods yard, which sits on the borders of Shoreditch, Spitalfields and 'Banglatown' (the Brick Lane area famous for its curry houses), had since the 1960s been left derelict after a fire.

The area is now undergoing massive redevelopment. In 2010 Shoreditch High Street railway station opened, and the joint venture developers, Hammerson and Ballymore, have been evolving plans for the 4.2-hectare site (now called the Goodsyard) with a £800 million mixed-use scheme. Part of the site has been leased to BOXPARK Shoreditch, a pop-up shopping mall of fashion, arts and lifestyle brands, made of out of refitted shipping containers, and to Powerleague for one of its five-a-side football centres.

The Goodsyard Interim Planning Guidance (IPG) framework was adopted in 2010 by the London boroughs of Hackney (on the west side) and Tower Hamlets (east), and the Mayor of London. Through its mix of planning policies and urban design principles, the IPG informs both the masterplan for the site developed by architects Farrells and the community consultation for the development proposals undertaken from 2013-14. The redevelopment aims for up to 2,000 new homes, plus work spaces, shops and leisure facilities and 1.8 hectares of new public open space.

A key part of the process has been the public consultation undertaken by 'community engagement experts' Soundings, who employed tested principles of co-design and dialogue in the creation of public space prototypes. Apart from Farrells, the masterplanning team included architects PLP (residential), FaulknerBrowns (retail), and the design studio Spacehub with Kinnear Landscape Architects, Chris Dyson Architects (also restoring the Sclater Street cottages) and Studio Weave (park and landscaping). This mix reflects the focus of the design principles adopted, which advocate new links through the site and a range of housing and community facilities. The principles include the reuse of historical structures that underpin the character of the area, and the creation of a sustainable development solution.

Soundings, founded in 2007 by architects Christina Norton and Steve McAdam, and Fluid, its sister company grounded in spatial and planning intelligence, are together a powerhouse of architecture and participatory urbanism. Their impressive track

Below: Thinking, Talking, Shaping the Goodsyard, Bishopsgate Goodsyard, CGI of London Road.

Below right: Thinking, Talking, Shaping the Goodsyard, pop-up consultation event, 2013, Soundings.

record demonstrates that, with 'wider understandings of people, place, history and economy', the spatial and the urban can be reunited.[1] Norton and McAdam believe that change can be driven – and ownership built – by a narrative approach, with proposals driven by process and context, and by space developing as a consequence of multiple voices and demands.

A three-stage consultation on the concept, draft and final masterplan for the Goodsyard was carried out by Soundings from April 2013 to June 2014. This very thorough, creative and well-documented process, in which Soundings acted as an impartial voice, began by involving the community in agreeing local priorities and masterplan principles, and went right through to fine-tuning the masterplan – a tool that does not often reflect community values – before it was submitted for planning approval.

At each stage Soundings made transparent records of the process, its findings and the recommendations for the masterplan, culminating in a Statement of Community Involvement. This was a public planning document with a comprehensive account of the entire consultation process and its impact on the masterplan. The team worked with the community throughout, also identifying ways in which local involvement could continue after the planning application was submitted.

Through a new Goodsyard website, Soundings could keep everyone up to date with events, consultation reports and findings. The proposals for the final masterplan were also displayed in an exhibition, with background information and snapshots of the site explaining why the project was happening. The wide-ranging discussions through the consultation process crystallised a shared set of community aspirations that were expressed in both macro terms – for example, knitting old and new together – and micro terms, such as recycling removed materials.

Specialist guest speakers joined the throng. The planner Finn Williams argued that 'public spaces begin on the street corner, and having that relationship to buildings is what makes the space alive'. Dickon Robinson, adviser on housing and sustainable urbanism, asked: 'Is this property development or is this urban regeneration?' Architect and urban designer Amanda Reynolds asserted that 'streets should be place making not space taking'.

The first workshop in late 2013 looked in-depth at aspirations for the park above the arches of the old Braithwaite Viaduct and its landscaping. Popular ideas for the park were 'a green retreat with a natural character and sense of escapism', with scope for 'natural play and exercise' and potentially linking with the Spitalfields City Farm; accessibility was a priority. Also discussed were community benefits and facilities more generally: affordable housing, jobs and training. Rather than building new facilities on site, people felt it would be better to link up with, support and contribute →

"

Is this property development or is this urban regeneration? Streets should be place making, not space taking

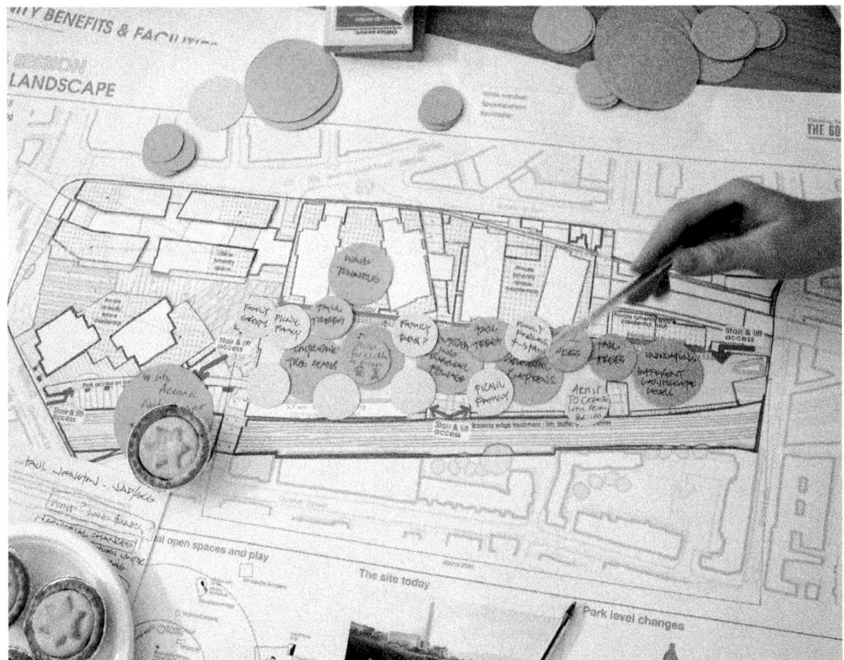

Left:
Thinking, Talking, Shaping the Goodsyard, community workshop to explore design ideas and refine a brief for a new park on top of the historic railway arches, 2013-14, Soundings.

to existing facilities in the area, for there to be a trust or group to look after them, and for affordability to extend from housing to business space.

More detailed examinations of aspirations for the park registered an interest in ecology (48%), escapism (21%), play (19%), education and maximising space. A word-pairing activity by participants matched up activities, built associations and made people think further about how they might use the park. Working in groups, people used playing chips representing the park's elements, activities and landscaping to prioritise desired aspects, and also to resituate activities better suited outside. Soundings then assembled priorities and summarised the chief suggestions; this became the basis for a thorough overview by the developers, covering affordable housing, 'meanwhile uses' of land, specific spaces for start-up businesses, management and maintenance of the park space, and so on.

Above right:
Charrette with key stakeholders and public open reviews debating and developing a set of community principles for the masterplan, Thinking, Talking, Shaping the Goodsyard, Bishopsgate Goodsyard, 2013-14.

These discussions and activities were a precursor to the final debate on the identity of the community facilities. The debate focused on the lessons to be learned, for example, what is provided, what works, what does not and why (under-resourced, for example) and what could be improved (bad history of delivery/low level of trust). When they discussed their common vision, better community integration came top of the list, along with and affordability and improved governance – including a new social enterprise for the park. People stated a clear preference that these high scorers link with and support existing facilities, systems and training in order to help support local employment and ensure affordability.

The feedback reverberating from an Ideas Week recorded by the Soundings team was full of suggestions: 'Retain the distinct and vibrant character – don't expand the City'; 'Keen to see things happen so long as there is real local involvement and benefit, and a sensitive approach'; 'A green retreat'; 'Interim uses can feed into the development'; 'Keep it low....'. There were PechaKucha talks on the key themes, and detailed responses to the masterplan revealed possibilities for a better, and more integrated design.[2]

Will these possibilities be realised? At the time of writing, public consultation continued from a marquee outside the railway station. Ballymore and Hammerson submitted their planning applications for the Goodsyard scheme to both Tower Hamlets and Hackney councils, as the development crosses borough lines, requiring permission from both councils. The East End Preservation Society - founded in 2013 by people keen to protect this part of London from the negative effects of gentrification, new developments considered to be outsize, and the loss of old buildings - has launched a campaign against the application. The number of affordable housing units as part of a total of 1,464 set by the developers is as yet potentially no more than 10%, and construction on the site may result in seven buildings of up to 46 storeys. Two-thirds of those consulted in 2014 had been against the heights, leading to some lopping off on two of the proposed buildings. The park, however, will be realised and will cover nearly 1 hectare.

The refreshingly multi-modal methods employed by Soundings allowed many locals to articulate their views, contributing to findings and analyses derived from a host of activity genres – pop-up events, one-to-one meetings, group sessions and 'walk and talk' events – some of them impromptu, others semi-formal outreach. Each was a highly valid way to help to create physical and social capital and better places to live; synthesised, they work to mobilise a lasting dialogue.

Improving consultation methods for masterplanning

Designing multi-step entries to a concerted approach for the development of the London Goodsyard

COLLABORATIVE VISION

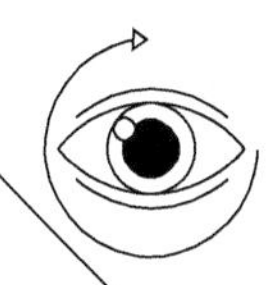

Three-stage consultation was put in place to co-create the concept and masterplan for Bishopsgate Goodsyard in Shoreditch

MULTI-MODAL COLLABORATION

Throughout the consultation process, analysis was gleaned from various types of impromptu one-to-one and group activities

CONSULTATION STAGE ONE

1

TRANSPARENCY

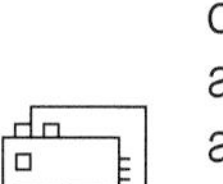

At each stage, records were collected in a public planning document, creating a comprehensive account of the entire consultation process and its impact on the masterplan

CONSULTATION STAGE TWO

2

COMMUNITY REVIEW

Local prioritories and masterplan principles were agreed upon: it would be best for the Goodsyard to link up with existing facilities in the area and support them

DRAFT MASTERPLAN

Ideas Week led to a community review and discussions of the concept. Community members were interested in more integration, and in systems and training to support local employment and affordability

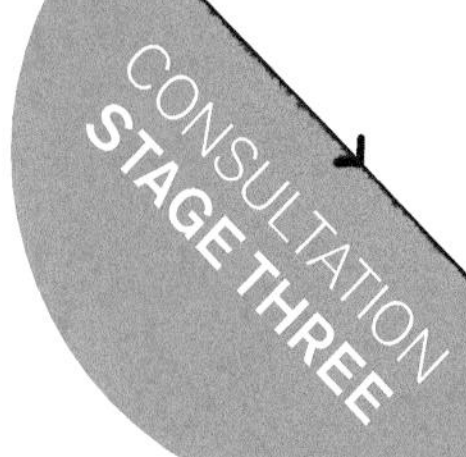

3

FINAL MASTERPLAN AGREED

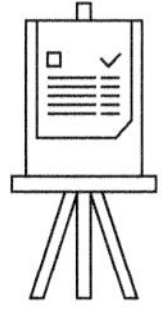

Two-thirds of those consulted in 2014 were agaisnt the height of new housing buildings. This led to 8-12 units being lopped off

PLANNING SUBMISSION

Strategic Design Scenarios and La 27e Région

'The dead ends of the ideology of "new public management" of the 1970s adversely affected the public sector in France by attempting to rationalise every decision public managers made, operating the public sector like a factory', says François Jégou, founder in 2002 of the Brussels-based sustainability innovation lab Strategic Design Scenarios (SDS).[1] One of SDS's longest-term and most locally impactful collaborations as scientific partner, has been with La 27e Région, a Paris-based non-profit public innovation lab set up in 2008, Citizen participation was not promoted in the 1970s, Jégou explains, and the notion of co-design was unheard of as a practice of public departments, which were organised in traditional vertical silos. In the 21st century, such an approach really is a dead end.

SDS is what the European Union has called an 'agile structure', drawing on Jégou's 20 or so years' experience in strategic design, new product-services definition and participative scenario-building. Its collaborator, La 27e Région, is led by a team of eight people with design, social, political and administrative skills, who work with an international network of 40 service designers, sociologists, architects, urbanists, anthropologists and researchers. It is supported by the 26 French regional governments through the Association des Régions de France, as well as the European Union, Caisse des Dépôts (a public financial institution that subsidises activities of public interest) and the Next Generation Internet Foundation (FING).

'We aim to create a shift in administrative culture to improve the quality of public policies, and radically change the way public policies are designed and implemented', says Jégou.[2] Both SDS and the 27e Région lab are focused on reshaping public administrations, re-energising them to be more user-driven and to embrace the opportunities offered by social innovation, service design, social sciences, open source, sustainable development and DIY.

Through the lab's ways of working, the administrative departments become engaged, many for the first time, in horizontal practices: using creativity as a way to find solutions; embracing citizen participation, co-design and hands-on workshops led by users and stakeholders; and envisioning and 'experience prototyping' during the administrative

←

Left:
La Transfo, 2011-14, helped four regional councils build their own embedded innovation labs, La 27e Région.

in rural Burgundy, a nursing home in Auvergne, Provence-Alpes-Côtes d'Azur and public space in a neighbourhood of Lille. Working with a range of residents, plus politicians and civil servants, SDS developed future visions through a range of sustainable projects responding to local economic and social issues. These built a better understanding of design's potential to find new solutions to existing problems.

As part of its work, the 27e Région's 'Opening up colleges' project encompassed education but also employability, social development, sustainable food, environment, culture and citizenship in a global context of drastic cost cutting. Central government was in charge of the pedagogic side, and the hardware delivery (buildings, computers, catering, books) could have ended up being very top-down. La 27e Région says the main risk for the regions is that critical attention process. The lab promotes these practices as part of a new culture 'that politicians must put higher in their agenda in order to find new solutions in fields like democracy, sustainable development or poverty', says the team.

'We think we can help them (the staff members of the administrative departments) become more efficient ... and more democratic', says one of the 27e Région team members.[3] The goal in the medium term is to empower the regions and their partners, and 'to encourage them to create and embed their own design labs'. To date the hub has carried out more than 15 hands-on 'action research' experiments in partnership with nine regional administrations, through two programmes: 'Territoires en Résidences' (2009-10) and 'La Transfo' (2011-14). A third, 'Re/acteur Public', brings together national state administration and local governments to try to expand the values, processes and methodologies of the earlier two programmes. Around 200 politicians and civil servants have so far been involved in La 27e Région's action research.

Territoires en Résidences involved 12 local 'experiments' staged like 'micro-labs' by cross-disciplinary teams, each led by a designer; each lasted three months, with three weeks of total immersion for the teams. Locations included neighbourhood schools (for example, in the eastern town of Annecy and at an agricultural school in rural northern France), a university, a station

Above:
La Transfo Bourgogne, 2011-13. One of the forum events on scenarios for the future of rural villages, La 27e Région.

Right:
La Transfo Bourgogne: the future of rural life, Forum of future villages, a 2 day event with local people exploring possible scenarios, Dijon, 2011-13, La 27e Région.

to 'the technical performance of the buildings – including environmental standards – or even the educational excellence' becomes limited. Consequently the team proposed focusing on the 'software' – 'the future of the school as a human ecosystem'.[4] It put emphasis on considering quality of life, empowerment of pupils, approaches to social responsibility and sustainability, and partnerships with the wider community and between colleges, both within the region and in other regions.

One facet of this project took place at the ENSCI Les Ateliers design school in Paris, where for one term a group of students undertook an experimental studio exploring the redesign of public services and how this could help to change public policies. The ideas generated included a College Memory system, college apps and a Diffuse Pupil House. What would an open college mean? What would a college as a local resource be? ... 'The purpose [of the project] was to distinguish signals from field noise and to propose more generic visions fully rooted in reality, with a broader point of view', says the team in its concept book, *Design des politiques publiques*, containing case studies, interviews, testimonials and visuals. 'Schools, through project-based and action learning, can play the role of active agents supporting local sustainable social change.'[5]

On the back of this successful project, in 2011 La 27e Région launched its second programme, La Transfo, with five regions: Bourgogne (rural life), Champagne-Ardenne (youth policy), Pays de la Loire (prospective) and Provence-Alpes-Côte d'Azure (youth employment). The aim was to help the regions to prototype their own design labs within three years, building their own design visions, strategies and tools. The same methods of participatory action research were applied – and the same ethos: 'action and research must be conducted with civil servants and elected representatives, and not for them.'[6]

With its focus on co-creation, the 27e Région framework calls for an 'inside-outside posture'

Above:
La Transfo Bourgogne, multidisciplinary teams work with civil servants using ethnography, co-design, prototyping and social innovation.

Jégou and his colleagues describe their framework of co-creation activity for La 27e Région as 'friendly hacking'. Hacking, as in the 'intent to challenge the robustness of public policy instruments and services, and to identify and acknowledge weak points to allow for improvement', is seen as friendly, innovative, curious and playful. Jégou acknowledges that there are tensions and risks to all co-creation processes, but says that the framework 'appears to be an effective way to implement innovation in the very specific context of public administrations'.[7] With its focus on co-creation, the framework calls for an 'inside-out posture' that gives civil servants the opportunity to feel like 'quasi-new employees' and 'external observers' at the same time. It also calls for 'neutral activism' on the part of La 27e Région in order to get people of different statuses to work together, in a way that defends freedom of speech.

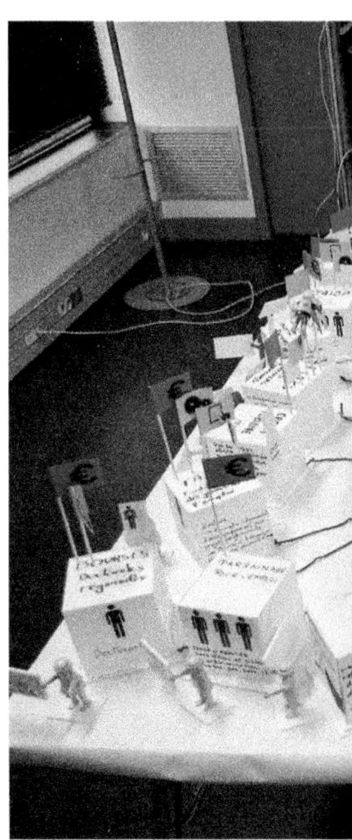

The Rio+20 United Nations conference on sustainable development was both the pretext and the occasion for SDS to look at what it had done so far, and for conducting local foresight activities to envision and outline the possible evolution of Agenda 21, the UN's voluntary 1992 action plan, at a local level throughout France via an envisioning toolbox for local sustainable transition. 'Often a forward-looking posture is lacking in Agenda 21', explains Christophe Gouache at SDS. With project partners including the French ministry of ecology, sustainable development and energy, SDS undertook a participative action research process, experimenting in five different French regions at departmental, city and regional levels, which help to refine a new toolbox, Visions +21, based on stakeholder inputs; the end result included animated videos presenting the participants' vision of the future.

Jégou and SDS continue to be active in various fields and research projects from sustainable community living in China, India, Brazil and Africa, to other European research projects, diffusing social innovation to support sustainable transition and exploring the future of innovation. His latest publication, *Sustainable Street 2030,* for the Corpus Project, asks what everyday life would be like in a fully sustainable society. What foods would we eat, how would we move and work, and how might we take care of one another? [8]

Able to juggle the intricacies and demands of his unusual, self-crafted role, Jégou is Europe's leading theorist for social change towards sustainability enabled though multi-disciplinary design and 'action research'. SDS is a hive of visualisation and stimulation through video animations, exhibitions, online platforms, mapping, 'enabling kits' and field labs. This is the arsenal of scenario building, stakeholder engagement, new solution definition, and evidencing through visualisation and simulation, storytelling and tools development. It is a body driven by deep-rooted values about the responsible adaptation of society through participatory processes (not in any way a marketing agency). In the areas of sustainability and public services today, there is a great need to shift daily practices and to support new momentum at the neighbourhood scale, and beyond to that of the city and the region. In these efforts, the creative scope for a larger collaborative approach – co-creation – is immense.

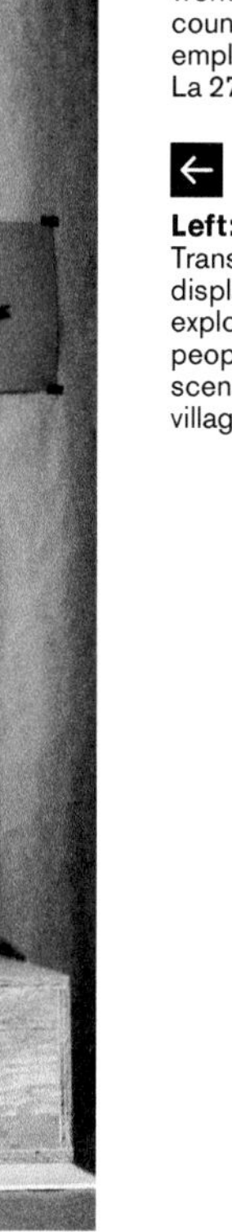

Above left:
Transfo Provence-Alpes-Côte d'Azur, workshop with regional council on youth employment, 2012-14, La 27e Région.

Left:
Transfo Bourgogne, displays from the forum exploring with local people possible future scenarios for rural villages, 2011-13.

Self-sufficiency, not reliance on any outside system, brings freedom to determine results. Freed from the need to fulfil bureaucratic requirements, design practice is radicalised. In the context of the rural hinterland of Mumbai, India, self-sufficiency has helped to shape the methodologies of Studio Mumbai, founded by architect Bijoy Jain in 2005. The studio's relationship with local materials, resources, techniques, climate and patterns of use has been generated through a responsive sensibility towards idea and form, drawing and construction, resources and site.

Studio Mumbai

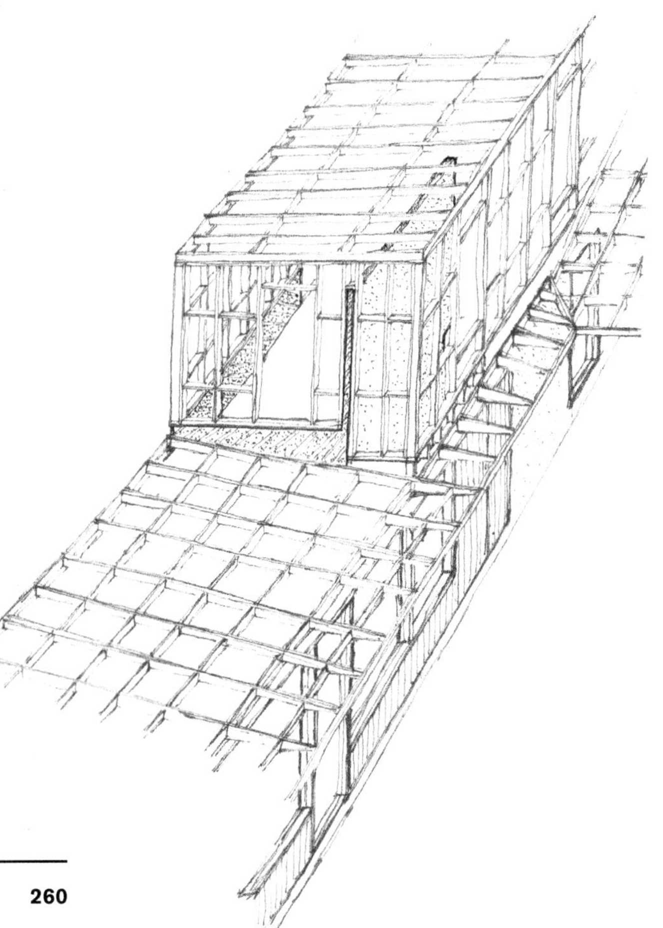

Jain comes from a small village outside Mumbai. Here he became familiar with the emotions arising from the processes of construction, emotions that are shared across cultures. He came to regard them as even more important than the objects being built. 'Architecture is an ideal of a community: architecture constructs these emotions, and the construction is in the place of overlap, something that joins us.'[1] Jain describes Studio Mumbai, now 40 strong and with about 100 staff members on site realising projects, as 'a human infrastructure of skilled craftsmen and architects who design and build the work directly'. This entails an iterative process exploring ideas through large-scale mock-ups, models, material studies, sketches and drawings.

Studio Mumbai won the BSI Swiss Architectural Award in 2012. This accolade recognised the studio's three significant projects: Palmyra House (2005), which brought the practice instant fame, and Copper House (2010), both in the state of Maharashtra; and Leti 360⁰ Resort (2006) in the foothills of the Himalayas in Uttarakhand. The award also acknowledged the practice's 'commitment to a collective working method through which a search for a relationship with history and the memory of place is conducted', as described by Mario Botta, chairman of

↑

Above:
Full-scale mockups for the Copper House II project at the Studio Mumbai workshop, 2011-12.

Left:
Copper House II, Chondi, Maharashtra, India, 2012, guest bathroom wall detail. Studio Mumbai.

Above:
Copper House II, Chondi, 2011-12. Wood frame construction of the bedroom on the first floor. Studio Mumbai Architects.

the BSI judges. Crucially, this evolves into 'a contemporary language constructed on embedded layers of knowledge, rather than sinking into nostalgia'.

India, said Jain, speaking at the launch event for the 2012 BSI award, is a country with 120 different languages, along with a myriad of food cultures, clothing styles and even bone structures. He maintained that 'it works because of the chaos, which prevents the system from completely taking over'. In his home city of Mumbai, a fast-spinning symbol of India's new economic, cultural and social geographies, his collective ethos and critical awareness of this flux are greatly needed. Globalisation needs to be embraced in a way that retains local identity, and design and construction as activities possess the potential to withstand its homogenising forces. 'Building, like a body, can extend itself; that's the core value of what we can do, to transform.'

The design encourages dialogue and this produces a choral work

Jain's collective process has made him a community pedagogic leader, producing a rich body of methodological ideas that future generations can draw on. As is the case with Francis Kéré (see page 188), MASS Design Group (page 208), PITCHAfrica (page 228) and other practitioners, Jain's concern lies with the role and identity of craft within the construction process, as well as its relationship with climate, geographical context and local resources. Recovering local traditions and materials is part of the close communications between Studio Mumbai and the craftsmen, artists and tradesmen.

As with all earlier Studio Mumbai projects, carpenters played a fundamental and creative part in discussions about the making of Copper House II (2012), in rural Chondi, Maharashtra, a second home for clients who live in Mumbai. 'Once the conceptual framework was established, [the carpenters] were asked to make study models and sketches to come up with solutions for various issues identified during the discussion.'[2] They were going to be building the project on site, so they drew numerous detailed sketches to understand and be able to discuss critical details. 'Everyone would maintain a sketchbook at site and in the workshop (at which various full-scale mock-ups were made) that became the way of communication between the parties involved.'

The site of Ahmedabad House (2014), in a very dry region in Gujarat, led Studio Mumbai immediately to consider making pressed-earth bricks (with just a small amount of concrete added) for the building on site. For this they used the earth dug out for the foundation, which mimimised impact on the site: no trucks moving in and out, for one thing, which was helpful considering the huge peacock population at the site. 'For the natural life around, the site has barely changed as the building simply rises from the earth', says Jain.

As part of the conversations and interaction between the architects and carpenters, 'the narrative process overlaps with personal memories and traditions', writes Studio Mumbai. 'The description of the idea is like telling a story, because getting to know each other fuels the imagination. The design thus encourages dialogue and ... this produces a choral work.'[3]

TYIN tegnestue Architects

In such countries as Thailand, Myanmar (Burma), Haiti and Uganda, poor and underdeveloped areas are contexts with few design choices, where architecture, to have any validity, has to get out of its 'comfort zone' to make a difference from the bottom up. 'Solutions to real and fundamental challenges call for an architecture where everything serves a purpose – an architecture that follows necessity', say Andreas Gjertsen and Yashar Hanstad, founders of the Norwegian architecture practice TYIN tegnestue Architects (2010).[1] Their team focuses on enabling community self-sufficiency and proactivity in design and build through their specialist skills in these countries. It actively involves local people in TYIN's projects, in order to 'establish a framework for mutual exchange of knowledge and skills'.

One example of this framework is Klong Toey Community Lantern project (2011, and TYIN's second realised in Thailand), carried out in Klong Toey, in the river port area of Bangkok; it is the city's largest, and one of its oldest, neighbourhoods of informal dwellings. More than 27% of Thailand's population of 65.5 million live in slums, in a context largely free of planning.[2] More than 140,000 people are estimated to reside in Klong Toey, mostly in substandard dwellings and without rights of tenure or government support, and the area also suffers from a lack of public services – healthcare, sanitation, electricity and affordable education. Crime rates are high, as are levels of unemployment, and there is a widespread drug problem.

In Klong Toey's maze of narrow alleyways and permanently open doors people sit outside chatting with their neighbours. But its port area is part of a masterplan that will turn it into a touristic area within the next decade, displacing the community in favour of mixed-use development. The location at Locks 1-6, where TYIN's Lantern project is situated, is part of the last phase of the plan to be developed, and has many NGOs working there.

In this vulnerable context TYIN designed and built a covered public playground and football court, intending

Bottom:
The site before the football court for Klong Toey Community Lantern, Bangkok, is built in 2011. A lot of work has to be done in three weeks. TYIN tegnestue Architects.

Below:
Klong Toey Community Lantern, Bangkok, 2011. The structure gives a new character to the street. TYIN tegnestue Architects.

it to become part of a long-term regeneration strategy as well as a larger-scale development. The architectural team gave itself a year to prepare, but ultimately designed and built the structure in just three weeks. Its process enabled TYIN to build a dialogue with the local community through interviews, workshops and public meetings. Local materials to be recycled in the building construction were retrieved, and practical trials made with the students involved in the scheme. Consequently, the Lantern design is an amalgam of many ideas and concepts, including artificial light, signifying that a better future may be possible.

The building was also designed so that it could later incorporate many features not yet existing in the neighbourhood: for example, basketball hoops, climbing walls, a stage for performances and public meetings, and seating both inside the playground and around the exterior. Apparently at first young people were the most resistant to the change this project brought with it. But the versatility of the space – ideal for playing various games and for get-togethers as well as for studying – and the engaging process of active participation, overcame this obstruction.

In February and March 2011, with the input of local architect Kasama Yamtree, the building came together, a mix of new materials and recycled timber and metal frames. The design's scale matches the size of a football field, with a building height of 5 metres, and the structure sits on a concrete base that supports its weight in the poor ground conditions. Simple, durable and with a repetitive logic, the design has a construction methodology that 'enables the local inhabitants to make adaptations that fit with their changing needs without endangering the project's structural strength or the →

Enabling local self-sufficiency and proactivity in design and build

Right:
Klong Toey Community Lantern's interior space becomes full of life and activity as soon as school is over for the day, TYIN tegnestue Architects.

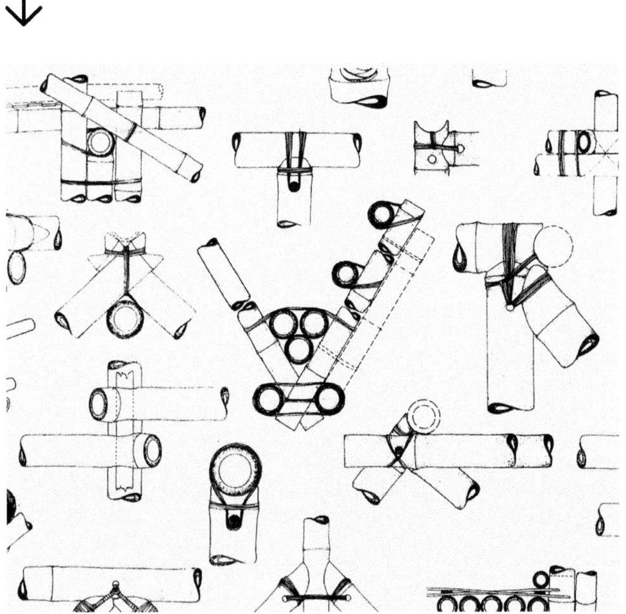

Left:
Sketches of Klong Toey Community Lantern by German students taught by the architects, one year before construction, exploring different possibilities.

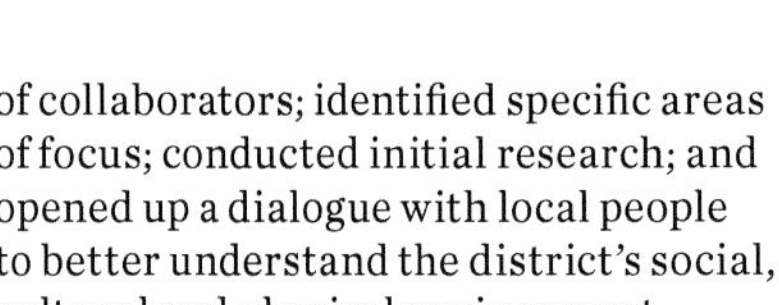

general functionality of the playground', says TYIN.

Yamtree had worked at Klong Toey for a long time before TYIN became involved, and had been advised by locals, most likely government officials, that doing anything socially sustainable there would be difficult. But this proved not to be the case. The project was also widely featured in the Thai media, becoming a model and lever for other social urbanistic schemes. As part of creating something new and useable, the collaborative process that was forged was also successful.

In spite of the spectre of big-scale masterplanning over the whole area, TYIN's aim with Lantern was to build a long-term 'cooperation channel' to assist the gradual transformation of public spaces and the revitalisation of the district. Working with the Norwegian practice Léva Urban Design and the Bangkok-based multidisciplinary design studio Apostrophy's, TYIN organised this effort in two parts. First, in June and July 2010, they created an overall group of collaborators; identified specific areas of focus; conducted initial research; and opened up a dialogue with local people to better understand the district's social, cultural and physical environment.

The groundwork went well, and each collaborative activity and temporary intervention – 'a catalyst of proximity', as TYIN puts it – became an effective instrument of communication and interaction between participants. Some of the workshops, such as that on 'designing and cleaning', were attended mainly by children, building in the process a sense of responsibility about rubbish in residential areas by setting up a competitive game collect to different items from around the streets. TYIN interviewed both residents and NGOs about their daily routines, their opinions of the place and their dreams for its future, as well as for their own. There were worries about the drawbacks of the physical conditions, and people also discussed an alternative location for the building, given that in the long run that would be necessary if the masterplan's

TYIN tried to include everyone in the activities as well as make use of all the means, to show the community that in fact it has everything it needs to improve its surroundings

final phase was implemented, but the depth of mutual support was clear.

In 2011 a larger group of collaborators was formed to create permanent structures in the locations studied. Their work generated a sense of ownership but also a genuine and constant interaction between the residents and the visitors. They staged workshops (including one about daily routes) in front of the football field, and held further interviews to better understand the options for the spaces they were working with – where and how public space improvements could be made. Small-scale improvements included rubbish bins, a shading system and benches incorporating plants. These designs involved children and teenagers working together with a local carpenter to some extent; the children themselves both designed and the built the benches.

From the beginning at Klong Toey TYIN 'tried to include everyone in the activities as well as to make use of the available means we found on the site', in order to show the community that it in fact has everything it needs to improve its surroundings. 'We are only playing the role of catalysts ... Our role was to be present and not to push people to "do something our way".' The team encouraged local residents to make the best of the limited space by, for example, growing vegetables in a 'vertical' way on walls and roofs. However, TYIN makes clear that, whatever the focus, 'the process of working, learning and exchanging has to be continuous in order to open doors for future interventions'.

Left:
Children from the community help out in the construction process, Klong Toey Community Lantern, Bangkok, 2011, TYIN tegnestue Architects.

Urban-Think Tank

Architecture, being form-driven, generally fails to engage with informal urbanism. It finds it difficult to register adequate responses to the particularly occluding nature of the high density of this sort of development, which often lacks passageways between dwellings. In Cape Town, South Africa, the practice of 'blocking out' (clustering homes in such a way that courtyards are created) was officially adopted in 2013 in order to incrementally reconfigure shacks within a community-created spatial framework. The blocking out design makes the entire ensemble safer and more productive, and it creates space for better services to be installed by government.

Blocking out has enabled settlement residents to upgrade their community, improving both the quality of individual housing units and mobility within the dense fabric of the neighbourhood. It is in effect a 'mobilisation' tool, says Rose Molokoane, coordinator of the Federation of the Urban and Rural Poor (FEDUP) and the Shack/Slum Dwellers International (SDI).[1] The blocking out concept was pioneered in South Africa as a 'best practice' in design by the NGO Ikhayalami ('My Home'), set up in 2006 by Andrea Bolnick. Together with FEDUP and SDI, Ikhayalami is a partner in the South African Alliance of community organisations.

Ikhayalami first applied blocking out in response to a major fire in Cape Town's Joe Slovo settlement. Fire, along with flooding, are huge motivators to community redesign of shack layouts.

Right:
Khayelitsha Township, south of Cape Town's city centre, home to an estimated 400,000 people, 2012.

Below:
First in-situ prototype, the Empower Shack, 2012-, developed by Urban-Think Tank with South African NGO Ikhayalami and Phumezo Tsibanto, a community leader.

Conventional approaches to dealing with informality are both unsustainable and very slow to meet needs. Bolnick says that Ikhayalami's work 'is premised on the realisation that informality is part of the modern urban fabric, will remain a reality for the foreseeable future, and calls for ingenious adaptations'.[2] The NGO gets local government and businesses to help individuals and families pay for a new shack in the same location; it also negotiates with neighbours on the creation of access pathways and communal courtyards, thereby benefitting everyone's quality of life.

Alfredo Brillembourg and Hubert Klumpner – co-founders in 1998 of Urban-Think Tank (U-TT, an NGO) and holders of the Chair of Architecture and Urban Design at the Swiss Institute of Technology (ETH) in Zurich where Klumpner is Dean – regularly visit residents and community leaders, as their raison d'être is purpose-driven social architecture in the Global South: for example in Venezuela (Caracas, where they have made significant research-based improvements to the barrios) and in Brazil (São Paulo, similarly, in favelas such as Paraisópolis). Indeed, U-TT has spawned a whole arsenal of experimental research and teaching methods focused

Left:
Empower Shack's summer design-build workshop led by the Urban-Think Tank chair at ETH Zurich, Swisspearl factory, 2013.

on raising awareness of the informal city from humanitarian, theoretical and design perspectives. Brillembourg and Klumpner founded the Sustainable Living Urban Model (S.L.U.M) Lab at Columbia University in New York as an interdisciplinary communication and network platform to share empirical research and practice knowledge, and it is now integrated into their curriculum at ETH Zurich.

After attending the Design Indaba conference in 2012, Brillembourg and Klumpner took the opportunity to have a closer look at blocking out with Bolnick at Cape Town's Pilippi township. 'In the long term, blocking out fosters civic engagement and a deeper intersection between bottom-up community improvement and top-down development strategies', they say.[3] After the visit, the image that stayed in their minds was a single two-storey self-built shack which the residents were planning to dismantle – even though it gave them more space than the more usual single-storey construction – as they felt that its construction quality was inadequate.

This need to improve the quality of prototypes triggered U-TT's motivation to develop a participatory design system for a two-storey, self-built dwelling that promotes the advantages of 'blocking out'. The Empower Shack, as they called it, would also nurture local agency and increase the urban density of local townships. The duo instituted a two-week Empower Shack design-and-build workshop to develop an innovative and replicable shack prototype for Cape Town's Khayelitsha township, the third largest in South Africa. The workshop was attended by 24 international students, and participants from ETH Zurich's architecture department took part in a summer school supported by Eternit (Schweiz), a manufacturer of corrugated fibre cement panels.

'With a population of over 50 million and the continent's largest economy, South Africa is often seen as a source of relative stability and prosperity in the region', says U-TT.[4] But it goes on to point out that economic inequality remains high. About 1.7 million households – approximately 7.5 million people – live in 2,700 informal settlements around the country; overall, even though the government has built 2.7 million to date, some 2.5 million houses are still needed.[5]

U-TT describe the government's record on housing delivery as laudable, but such is the scale of need, informal settlements will remain in the near future. In response to this fact, the authorities have begun to shift focus to incremental upgrading: between 2010 and 2014, 400,000 households in informal settlements were improved in terms of quality of life through wider provision of basic services and more equitable land tenure agreements. In Khayelitsha, working in partnership with Ikhayalami, U-TT explored both the complexity of living conditions in informal settlements, and the social role of architects in helping to address the economic, ecological and security challenges faced by residents.

The two-storey Empower Shack U-TT developed with Ikhayalami at Khayelitsha was for community leader Phumezo Tsibanto and →

Empower Shack is a participatory self-build system nurturing local agency and increasing township density

High design capabilities help slum upgrades

2.5m

Number of houses needed for South Africa's informal settlements. Economic inequality remains high

1.5m

Houses currently in South Africa's informal settlements, holding 7.5 million people

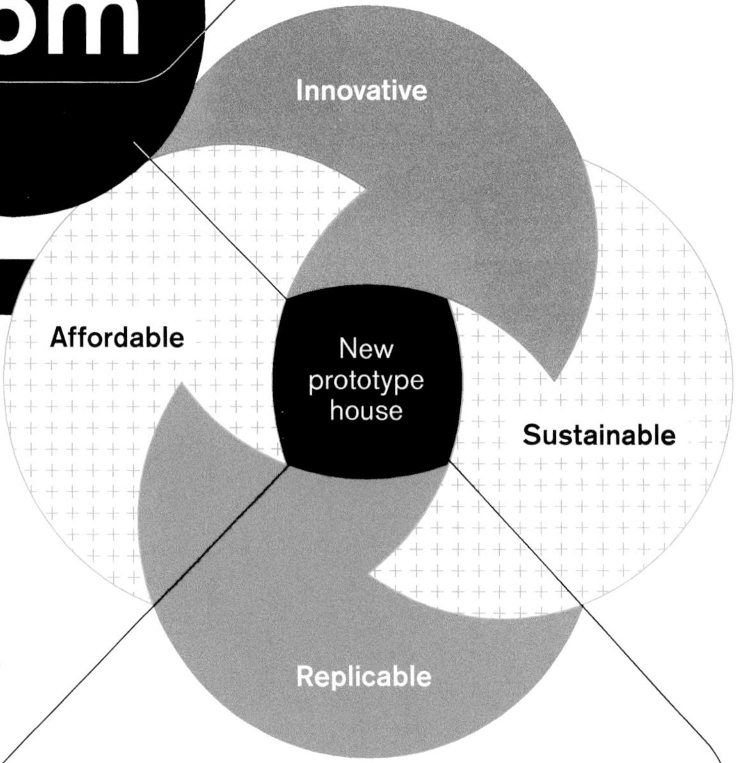

Innovative

Affordable

New prototype house

Sustainable

Replicable

PROCESS

1. **ANALYSIS**
Common slum dwelling problems

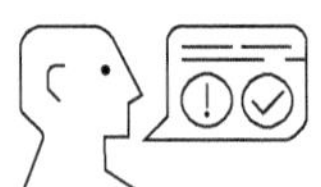

2. **VISIT DWELLERS**
Understand their key issues

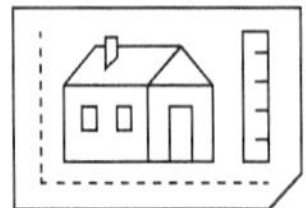

3. **DESIGN PROTOTYPE**
Laboratory with studio + students to design a house

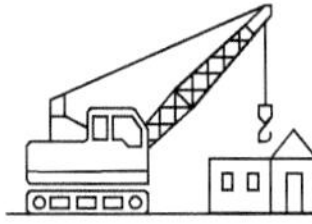

4. **CO-CONSTRUCTION**
On-the-ground construction with locals in the townships

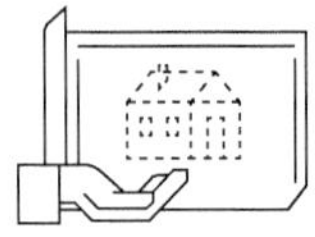

5. **HAND OVER**
Open-source design solution exemplifying methods for slum upgrades throughout South Africa

SOLUTION

Addresses residents' economic, ecological and security challenges

his family, who had lived in a shack there for 28 years. Tsibanto took part in the summer school staged by U-TT. Under South African law on prescription, within two years he would be entitled to own the land on which his dwelling stands. Local architect Heinrich Wolff, who participated in the workshop, felt that advancement on security of tenure needed more attention.

Local community members are happy with the Empower Shack as a work-in-progress. It is quick to build, simple to construct as well as to demount, easy to transport and affordable, and it offers a vast upgrade on previous living conditions. The design, inspired by Walter Segal's self-build housing system that uses materials that are readily available and simple to work with, is structurally stable and efficient. The Empower Shack is built on stilts so that it can mitigate flooding, and is made of fire-retardant materials such as an L-section steel frame and structural insulated panels (SIPs).

Ikhayalami produced and pre-cut parts of the prototype in its factory, while other elements were made on site. With input from the climate engineering firm Transsolar, roof-mounted solar panels provide energy for the inhabitants, and thanks to a 'Feed in Solar' tariff model, surplus energy can go towards paying for some of the capital costs of building the Shack's core infrastructural unit.

As a prototype the two-storey Empower Shack provides increased living space for township residents. But it also opens the possibility of on-site working areas or commercial enterprises on the ground floor, and more widely helps to generate a better urban fabric forged through controlled densification. Along with the materials research, U-TT carried out comparative analysis of pre-existing two-storey shack typologies in the township through interviews and measured drawings. This revealed that, of the six cases examined, half placed owners under stress due to the shacks' construction flaws and use of inadequate materials. Others were successful: they had a garage, a shebeen (informal tavern) and an arcade for local youth. One owner had achieved a rebuild after a fire, but wanted to remake her home on more advanced lines.

Another objective behind U-TT's collaboration with Ikhayalami is to develop a 'back-end' architectural programme, so that once information is submitted, there is the capacity to provide a range of layout options. 'On a community scale, such a system, if arranged in clusters around shared space and infrastructure, would encourage the formation of reciprocated social contracts', says U-TT. A wider aim is to encourage the local community to embark further on its plan to carry out a blocking out project of the settlement. Within months of the completion of his Empower Shack, Tsibanto had received numerous requests from fellow community members for advice on how to construct a shack on similar lines. This impetus has led him to instigate a neighbourhood upgrading project.

Brillembourg and Klumpner argue that the future of urban development lies in collaboration among architects, artists, private enterprises and slum dwellers around the world. 'People living amidst conditions of everyday scarcity in cities frequently demonstrate an innate capacity to refashion the built environment', they remark. Furthermore, 'using the limited resources found within their reach, [these people] address to varying degrees the failure of urban governance and resource distribution that denies them spatial justice'. In spring 2014, Empower Shack was the subject of an exhibition at the Galerie Eva Presenhuber in Zurich. U-TT regard the Shack as an expansive solution of in-situ upgrading, and the process as working intelligently and creatively with residents to 'unlock existing potential'.

Brillembourg and Klumpner reckon that 'the state continues to view – and fund – housing policy through the lens of a consolidated subsidy, prioritising new, formal "turnkey" developments planned and constructed without the involvement of local communities'. However, they have advocated from the days of their earliest work, in Venezuela and Brazil, that slums should be regarded as veritable laboratories. If participatory processes are taken out of this equation, citizens' needs cannot be fully comprehended and embraced.

Below: Metro Cable, Caracas, Venezuela, connects the San Agustin barrio to the formal centre below. Architects: U-TT, 2006-10.

ENGAGEMENT
REPLICABILITY
DESIGN DRIVEN
SCALE
IMPACT

IDENTIFY → ENQUIRE → DEVELOP → CO-DESIGN → CO-CONSTRUCT → HAND-OVER

URBZ

The area of Shivaji Nagar, in the M Ward of Mumbai, is usually described only as one of the poorest and most depressed parts of the city. Now half is developed as a grid; the other half is organic, or without any plan. It grew in the 1980s around the abattoir and city rubbish dumping ground and was eventually allocated for resettlement projects by the city and the state, and slum dwellers were moved there in 1986. Today Shivaji Nagar, 135 hectares in size, is a diverse neighbourhood with a strong construction scene completing more than 2,000 dwellings per year, and a strong tradition of economic artisanal activity. Many residents have occupancy rights on this government land sanctioned for resettlement, making the area a planned resettlement colony. However, some parts are more unstable as they are still officially classed as dumping grounds, and the city's Metro project is planned to pass near the area.

URBZ rejects 'rehab' housing tactics that destroy people's connections with one another, and improves slums

In March 2014, the Handstorm project began as a unique week-long workshop held in Shivaji Nagar, attended by a group of local residents and an array of artisans, builders, designers, architects, geographers and theorists from the area and other parts of Mumbai, as well as from New York, Brazil and Europe. The workshop showcased the vast array of 'home-grown' skills available in Shivaji Nagar, and demonstrated 'what can happen when worlds that usually never meet, come together', impacting the already active self-sufficient mentality of the neighbourhood.[1]

Handstorm was staged by the URBZ action and research platform for collaborative planning and design. In neighbourhoods like Shivaji Nagar, people regularly get evicted and dislocated outside the city, or are offered tiny apartments in high-rise blocks in return for giving away to speculative developers their homes and neighbourhood, which they have developed over many generations. URBZ rejects this 'rehab' mass-housing tactic that destroys people's connections with one another and the life of the area, and promotes instead improvements of so-called slums. Its work demonstrates just how powerfully pedagogic, research-based and civic concerns can be allied to innovative and resourceful design and construction processes as part of an alternative vision of participatory urban planning.

URBZ, which is based in Mumbai's Dharavi slum, was founded in 2008 by Rahul Srivastava, an anthropologist, Matias Echanove, who trained as an urban planner, and Geeta Mehta, a professor of urban design at Columbia University, New York. A participatory practice, its team and group of advisers is made up of members from planning, architecture, design, anthropology, economics and IT. They are mostly based in Mumbai, but also in other locations including Goa, New York, Santiago in Chile and São Paulo in Brazil.

The presence of a Brazilian contingent at Handstorm was due to the establishment of URBZ Brazil in São Paulo. From here, co-founder architect and urban designer Marcella Arruda (who also has her own participatory design collective, MUDA) attended along with Ataide Caetite, a self-made home builder from Paraisopolis, the largest favela in São Paulo. URBZ had previously visited and documented some of the many hundreds of homes Aruda had built there, and is now helping him to design and build his own home.

URBZ also hones its methods through fieldwork in New Delhi, Istanbul, Tokyo and Bogotá, Colombia, through its parallel vehicle, the Institute of Urbanology. Here it works with research partners including the Laboratory of Urban Sociology at the Swiss Federal Institute of Technology Lausanne (EPFL) and the German Max Planck Institute of the Study of Religious and Ethnic Diversity. The word 'urbanology' in this context refers to the knowledge and application of incremental developmental processes and daily practices in any given location via direct engagement with people and their environments.

Echanove and Srivastava fervently believe that residents are the experts in their own neighbourhoods, and that their everyday experience of the places in which they live and work constitutes essential knowledge for planning and urban development. 'For policymakers, urban planners, architects and real-estate developers, accessing this knowledge is the best possible way to enhance the quality and impact of their work', they say.

The chances of success are accordingly heightened, because local stakeholders and players can be identified, and multiple communication channels opened up. The situation 'on the ground' is given a deep assessment, and new solutions and ideas can be generated. In the process the social impact and environmental sustainability are improved; in addition, the profile of the project is raised, thereby increasing the possibility of further ongoing support through a feedback loop of research, communication, design and development.

URBZ has developed various web-based tools to produce and share information from residents and stakeholders: mashup sites, including wikis, blogs, interactive maps, photos, video albums and dynamic web pages. 'Notwithstanding the digital divide, the web remains the best medium to archive and spread knowledge and information on localities', the group maintains. Not only is the web 'cheaper than print media', but also it 'allows many people to contribute over time'. URBZ stages regular participatory workshops of two to seven days with small →

Left:
Two participants at URBZ's Handstorm workshop work with recycled materials, Shivaji Nagar, Govandi, Mumbai, 2014.

Below:
Rooftop discussions at the Handstorm workshop organised by URBZ at Shivaji Nagar, 2014.

Left:
Public discussion in the street, Shivaji Nagar, about useful plants that can be grown at home, even with limited space. Handstorm workshop organised by URBZ, 2014.

groups of local residents and guests from different fields. The material developed – surveys, designs, multimedia products and documentation of activities – is uploaded on to a website accessible by all participants; this is edited, organised and summarised to maximise its value to them and all interested parties.

During the Handstorm workshop, dual-use furniture that was 'handstormed' included a bookshelf-staircase designed by architect Cecila Tramontano and local carpenter Ganga K Sharma. There were water-drain covers, designed by sanitation and water system specialist Julia King with collaborators, that could adapt to any contour in the tiny lanes and allowed water to seep in but blocked rubbish; adaptations to homes; neighbourhood greening; and a mobile plant shop. Facilities were forged – such as a local nursery-cum-gardening school – leading to other hybrid designs including a window grille in which to grow plants but also providing ventilation, security and space to dry clothes and store objects.

Some designs, like the drain cover, were presented as DIY temporary solutions; others, such as a steel-framed 'Jungle Gym' for children, could have a longer life. An ambitious shading project to keep the sun off street-level bazaars was prototyped. On the terrace of a two-storey building, team members assembled a machine to shape lightweight material elements – an idea given to URBZ by POPLab at the Massachusetts Institute of Technology – to create an igloo-like terrace room that went on to become the URBZ office, a location from which 'storming' activities were kept going. The Handstorm workshop led to the first, three-month phase of the ongoing Homegrown Things project, involving young local product designers Ramandeep Saini and Shweta Hiremath, interior designer Minakshi Jambalkar, and Rafique Bhatkar, an engineer. They worked with local welders,

Above:
'Jungle gym' built in less than a week during the Handstorm workshop, Shivaji Nagar, 2014. The area lacked a playground and the children could not wait to play on it!

Left:
Street in Shivaji Nagar, Mumbai. The informal settlement is next to the city's biggest dumping ground.

carpenters, plumbers and builders to make on-the-spot commissions for families in Shivaji Nagar.

Land use at Dharavi, the largest slum in Mumbai, where URBZ's office is based, has been threatened by a regional-government redevelopment plan first announced in 2004 but dropped in 2011. In 2014 a new comprehensive plan for the entire slum area was advanced by the Dharavi Redevelopment Authority (DRA), once again putting the area's future into question.

URBZ nonetheless operates in the face of these threats. In 2007, it staged Urban Typhoon, a week-long workshop with residents of the Koliwada area of Dharavi. Koliwada is a traditional artisanal manufacturing base for clothes, leather goods, pottery and the like, and is increasingly becoming co-dependently diverse as formal industrial manufacture has declined. Drawing on Mumbai's historic activist temperament, the group, together with invited artists, architects, activists and academics from all over the world, collectively generated ideas and plans for the area. Multicultural, multidisciplinary and multimedia, the workshop's aim was to create alternatives for the future, as well as to make a multimedia testimony to Koliwada's 'unique spirit'. The material was uploaded onto dharavi.org, a wiki-based website maintained by URBZ and young residents of Dharavi who took part.

The impetus of URBZ's workshops helps to galvanise further initiatives. The group is a strong advocate for incrementally developed, mixed-use, high-density, low-rise, pedestrian-friendly neighbourhoods with affordable housing in emerging countries – in China and Brazil, for example. Its commitments to local improvements have more recently been applied to an initiative for affordable housing called Homegrown Cities, developed with social entrepreneur Aaron Pereira and launched through a crowdfunding on Indiegogo.

The premise is that neighbourhood habitats have the ability to improve on their own over time. But these communities 'need as much support as they can get to improve infrastructure and amenities', says URBZ. The group is keen to advance a larger vision of their planning, and to fund repairs and upgrading, boost employment and improve the organisation of public space. This also helps to most productively open up collaborations with local construction artisans.

The next step for Homegrown Cities is to build an initial pilot house locally. With legal protection, this would also support URBZ's intention to operate within the local construction market, rather than to provide free houses. At the same time, this will leave the team free to do not-for-profit work creating affordable houses in different neighbourhoods, for example. URBZ hopes the Tata Institute of Social Sciences will evaluate its projects, and plans to set up a workshop on the financial aspects of the pilot house (a collaboration with local architect Sameep Padora and Arup), to brainstorm ideas for adapting its design and construction as a mainstream approach to affordable housing.

URBZ is also completing its own office in Shivaji Nagar. In Bhandup – a more economically diverse and older neighbourhood of Bombay – it has begun work with a local contractor, Pankaj Gupta, to repair a decrepit old house. In both these cases, the team has the freedom of not working with a client, creating immediately inhabitable shells that, each in its own way, can become showcases of new materials and technologies of construction (the office in particular). They also represent pilots of design and construction processes involving end users.

URBZ is advancing on its own strategy for an overall urban improvement plan for Shivaji Nagar. This involves documenting not only its physical structures, but also all its local institutions and the skills of local artisans in the field of construction and other community initiatives. From the very beginning, the group has held on to its hugely common-sense premise to 'avoid proposing a wholesale "redevelopment" plan but work on something that comes closest to the existing principles of home-grown settlements'. URBZ will not let it go now.

Vancouver Public Space Network

Vancouver, on the Pacific Coast of British Columbia, Canada, is one of the country's most popular places in which to live, admired for the quality of its planning and such initiatives as the Greenest City 2020 stewardship programme. But, like the vast majority of world cities, it is also rife with corporatisation and privatisation affecting the amenities and identity of its public spaces. 'Ad creep' – in the form of billboards, large adverts and other corporate signage – is now gaining ground as a result of industry lobbying and regulatory loopholes, which in some cases violate city bylaws. Ad creep impinges on the sense of enjoyment and public ease that residents of Vancouver (which hosts some of the largest democratic gatherings and protests in North America) would like to maintain.

VPSN creates socially inclusive spaces and street art, strengthening 'place capital'

Right:
Upcycled Urbanism, Vancouver, 2013. Salvaged styrofoam blocks recreated as modular design components, which the public could assemble as they wished. VPSN, MOV and UBC SALA.

There are other aspects to this amenity and access issue, to do with fair distribution of types of public spaces, the need for a balanced urban environment, and democratic access to public space – which, in today's corporatised urban environments, is often very hard to differentiate from private space. From the 1930s to the 1960s, large gatherings were typically broken up swiftly and often violently, but in the 1970s official attitudes changed, and public events became seen as 'manageable' rather than activities to prevent. The boundary between questions of critical planning and those of access is a blurred one, and this calls for all stakeholders to come to the table in dialogue about the identity of local urban environments and their futures.

The Vancouver Public Space Network (VPSN) places these interconnected issues of public space democracy at the

Right:
Upcycled Urbanism, Vancouver, 2013. The public made a mix of intended and unexpected street furniture and sculpture from the modular design components.

Below:
Lunch Meet, Vancouver, 2012. A downtown block was closed to traffic during the lunch hour, and a long table installed at which residents and workers could meet.

heart of its activities, in a way that the city arguably could not do on its own. Since its founding in 2006 as a small, grassroots collective by Andrew Pask (a planner with the City of Vancouver) and around 12 other collaborators at a kitchen table, VPSN has grown into a registered non-profit organisation with some 2,000 members.

VPSN's huge array of public events are aimed at raising awareness of both the issues and opportunities associated with Vancouver's public realm. These range from interventions and activations, research, policy analysis, workshops and community events, to more conventional forms of advocacy, such as letter-writing campaigns, petitions and presentations to local government officials.

VPSN is busy challenging attempts to privatise public space – parks and plazas, streets, sidewalks and laneways, as well as libraries, community centres and other civic buildings. It works at creating socially inclusive spaces and enabling street art, all of which strengthens 'place capital', supporting local democracy, public health, lower crime rates and urban democracy. Ethan Kent, director of Project for Public Spaces (see page 232) defines place capital as 'the shared wealth (built and natural) of the public realm'. He believes it is 'increasingly becoming society's most important means of generating sustainable economic growth for communities', and that without it, participation, creative processes and resources become diminished.[1]

VPSN has been successful in its adoption of a solution-based approach, advancing ideas to improve Vancouver's public life and spaces by focusing on assets and opportunities. This way it can 'create a constructive, inclusive dialogue that skirts the sort of cynicism that often accompanies city-building discussions.'[2] The organisation is a proactive connector of citizens, non-profit groups, academic bodies, local government and other entities working on public-space issues. Its meetings are open to all, and the materials it produces are open-source.

Vancouver's planning department, where Pask has his day job, engages with community concerns as part of consultation processes for the development of neighbourhoods. One such neighbourhood is Grandview-Woodland with its shops and restaurants on 'the 'Drive', which has a Community Plan for its →

↓ future growth over the next 30 years; Pask is a Community Planner there. Many locals felt that their views were not being listened to, in spite of there being a Citizens' Assembly of 48 local people (from 504 wishing to volunteer). Mayor Gregor Robertson, who has led the Vision Vancouver platform (for better public transport, affordable housing, and support for families and neighbourhoods), won a third term in 2014 after apologising for that shortcoming.[3]

What defines 'place-based planning' is a vital issue needing wider discussion. Vancouver is a leader in its focus on pedestrians and cyclists over cars, but it still has plenty of disused or drab, featureless spots. In its Public Space Manifesto in 2014, VPSN listed 50 ideas for improvements, ranging from a city-wide land-use plan, to small, socially inclusive spaces. 'In all of the good cities that people think of around the world,

We see the city as a laboratory, not static, dull and boring. The Day of Play made people realise that the city is changing, and that they can play a role in it

almost all of [the] places they think of are places in the public realm', says Pask.[4]

For the 2011 municipal election VPSN created a Public Space Route Map, a manifesto of policy ideas along with a summary of their own advocacy work, and organised the Last Candidate Standing election debate – featuring no fewer than 27 of the 49 candidates standing for mayor. The five rounds of competitive debate were won by Andrea Reimber, who had been elected to the city council in 2008 as part of Vision Vancouver's team. VPSN has also produced a guide to holding a neighbourhood block party, the spirit of which it called on for its 2013 Polka Dot Piano – Keys to the Streets initiative with City Studio, a post-secondary collective linking undergraduate students to local government employees. Pianos were left, guerrilla-style, in public places around the city for anyone to play. Locations included Robson

Above:
Vancouver Mayor Gregor Robertson plays the Polka Dot Piano installed, guerrilla-style, on Robson Square, a popular downtown gathering area, 2013.

Right:
A Block Talk workshop led by VPSN and the Museum of Vancouver as part of Upcycled Urbanism, 2012.

Square, a major downtown space in which VPSN has worked many times before; Mayor Robertson was among the many who played a piano in the streets.

Projects can reveal some potentially hard-hitting findings. In the lead-up to the 2010 Vancouver Winter Olympics, VPSN was joined by students from Simon Fraser University's School of Communication and 40 community volunteers to tally through the use of Geographic Information Systems (GIS) the distribution of more than 2,000 CCTV security cameras identified over the course of one day, mostly attached to the facades of shops, offices and apartment buildings. The group found that the cameras were the latest models, capable of recognising faces and vehicle number plates. Alternatively, new bonds can be forged through the experience of coming together, as in the case of Lunch Meet (2012), staged with the City of Vancouver and Space2Space. The four-day lunchtime long-table event occupied the whole of a downtown street, which had been closed to traffic for the Meet, and featured a DJ and street-food vendors.

One of the larger VPSN projects has been the Upcycled Urbanism participatory scheme, begun in 2012 and realised with the Museum of Vancouver (MOV), *Spacing Vancouver* magazine, the local Maker Faire and UBC School of Architecture and Landscape Architecture. Charles Montgomery, author of *Happy City: Transforming Our Lives Through Urban Design*, urbanist and Curatorial Associate at Museum of Vancouver, explains that they invited 'students, artists, designers, makers, and anyone with even a smidgen of creativity to reimagine and rebuild parts of Vancouver's public realm'.[5]

The students designed reconfigurable modules, and during a series of workshops at MOV ideas for redesigning the city were brainstormed based on these. The prototype art and street amenities were then scaled up during a Day of Play using old polystyrene blocks salvaged from the construction of the nearby Port Mann Bridge. 'We see the city as a laboratory, not as static, dull and boring', says Montgomery. 'The Day of Play helped people realise, not just that the city is changing, but that they play a role in it, and they can play any role they want.'[6] In their eagerness to redesign the streets, people found themselves coming up with ideas they had never have thought of before – in some cases, individuals had more than 30 ideas for the city.

While a programme of pleasurable street parties alone could lose sight of certain campaigning goals, VPSN's agenda brings about a carefully calibrated mix of endeavours on the ground, with an enhanced notion of culture that includes adaptive reuse. Its ongoing discussions focus especially on the notion of the preservation of the commons through various means.

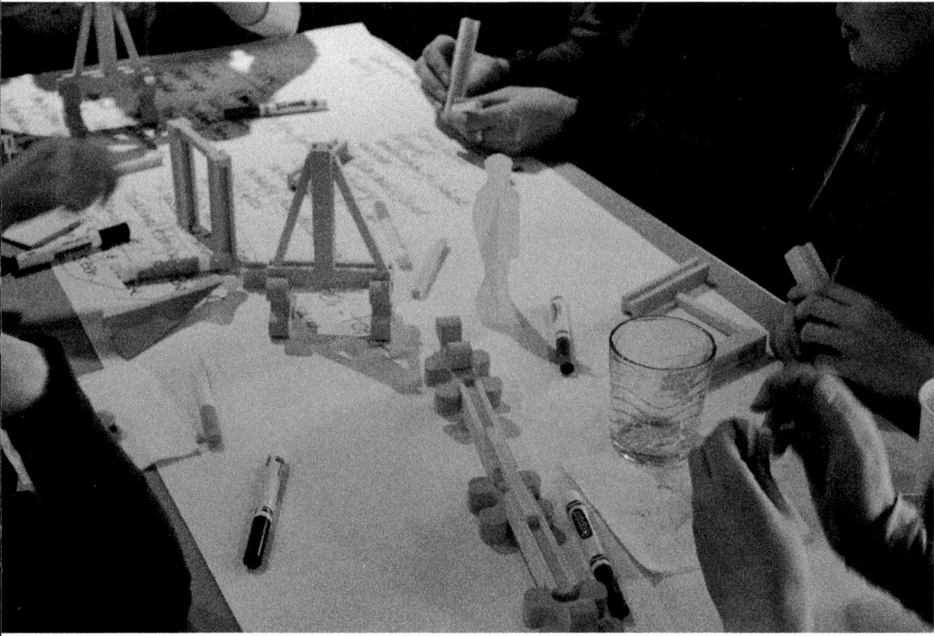

One of its projects demonstrating this ambition is Where's the Square, a design ideas competition held in 2008-9 for a central public square – Vancouver lacks this kind of grand gathering space that many cities have. The competition was opened up to the non-designer, and many community groups entered alongside architects and designers.

Vancouver citizens are active – the turnout at the 2014 municipal election was higher than for more than a decade. VPSN's own cumulative success may not be easily statistically verified beyond the sheer numbers of citizens involved and attending its programme of events. But with its passion and skilful advocacy it has helped to engage local people in the broader role of placemaking and enhancing public spaces throughout the city, through a broad but closely linked cultural platform. It serves as a role model of growth in participatory public space issues for other bodies around the world.

WikiHouse

The status of open source is building rapidly. One group that has done more than anybody to incubate its cultural potential and move it upstream have been 'fusing the culture of Web 2.0 with civic purpose' for quite a while.[1] Architecture 00:/ ('zero zero'), the practice-cum-platform specialise in action-led research, urban design strategy, architecture and place making was founded by Indy Johar and David Saxby in 2012. They are changing the economy for design, and that means going beyond the democratization of consumption to the democratization of production to help empower the user, says Alastair Parvin2, who joined 00:/ soon after its foundation.[2]

00 fast morphed from a design studio into a bigger platform for turning out new civic enterprises – system projects like Open Desk, a commercial firm, and the Civic Systems Lab. Parvin had already co-designed WikiHouse (wiki means 'quick' in Hawaiian, but has been adopted as a generic term for web content that can be collaboratively edited and improved) in 2011 with Nick Ierodiaconou. This open-source project aims to develop a construction system that uses digital manufacturing to massively simplify the process of designing and building high-performance, low-cost homes using widely available materials.

How WikiHouse works is that you take a model, print out the pieces of the house in 3D and build it. The premise is that an open-source construction system can develop 3D models using manufacturing information. People can use the coding languages to print out parts of a house, and already Google Nest's Learning thermostats are among the emerging open-source products, an area WikiHouse is now moving into. Parvin likes to quote John Maynard Keynes's quip that 'it is easier to ship recipes than cakes and biscuits' – an essential mentality for the maker revolution, and for sharing knowledge and software tools globally. It challenges the traditional financial business model of design.

The first open-source hardware start-up was set up at the Massachusetts Institute of Technology's Center for Bits and Atoms in 2001. Judging by the proliferation and proactivity globally of fabrication laboratories (fab labs) since then, in the past few years they have been driving new, scaleable solutions. However, it was about time that self-starting individuals created advanced tools and technologies re-engaging with socially advantageous economics. The challenge, as Parvin sees it, is to radically democratise the production of architecture and urban design. This means moving away first from the idea that architecture is only about making buildings, and secondly from debt-driven speculative development to design and development led by the end users of the homes, creating neighbourhoods as places in which to live, not just as arrays of assets to sell. This change in values calls for architecture to move towards an open economy: beyond the 20th century's industrial culture and the related assumption that development is something 'done to', not 'done by' citizens.

WikiHouse builds tools for the social economy, a field that needs appropriate institutions. Parvin sees the fastest-

Below:
WikiHouse design knowledge is shared under an open source Creative Commons licence, so anyone is free to take it, adapt it and improve it.

Bottom right:
Eight members of the Space Craft Systems team, a New Zealand-based social enterprise, developing the WikiHouse open source building system, 2015.

Left:
A-Barn, Scotland, 2015. Parts are cut from standard 4x8 sheets using a CNC machine. The joints are a hybrid of vernacular joinery and digital technology.

growing cities as the self-made ones; solutions to their ills arising from urbanisation, climate change and inequality lie in off-grid sustainable infrastructure, situated in a democratic commons. A number of factors have made WikiHouse's breakthrough possible. The rise of the web and open-source proprietary licences has brought down the marginal costs of producing information to zero. Increased automation has hugely affected what people can earn, while the evolution of more sophisticated parametric-driven automation tools means that the supermarket chain Tesco, for example, can go into producing housing. Above all, the rise of digital manufacturing using computer numerical control (CNC) machines means that the factory can be anywhere. This has brought the 'ability to think and share knowledge globally and solve [problems] locally', says Parvin.

WikiHouse's new suite of technologies developed for the home includes thermal energy and energy generation, waste treatment, electricity, data units and kitchens with Arduino sensors (open protocol and standard interfaces). It also includes solar-powered air-conditioning solutions, a necessary shift in order to move away from energy dependency. These were part of the 1:1-scale, two-storey, low-energy WikiHouse 4.0 built with the Building Centre for the London Design Festival in 2014. After it was dismantled, it was transferred to Liverpool for inclusion in Friends of the Flyover, a social enterprise scheme to convert a disused flyover →

It's easier to ship recipes than cakes and biscuits

into a community promenade.

The first WikiHouse was hacked (programmed quickly and roughly) with open-source electronics, says Francesco Anselmo, a lighting designer and environmental physicist at Arup who collaborated on this project. The scheme enables a shift to low-voltage direct current (DC) power – which most of WikiHouse's devices now use anyway – and to reduce energy consumption. But it also becomes safe for users to plug and play services, 'taking sustainable technology out of its proprietary "haut-tech" economy, and allowing users to design, maintain, and control their homes and their data', Parvin explains.

With DMX open protocols controlling the home, Anselmo sees scope to 'build on 20 years or so of work in open-source. The Internet brings power and data, creating an Internet of things in the house.'[3] A multi-sensor node with a plug-in system could 'evolve to have an element of 3D printing'. Through open hardware, which people could build themselves, they can scan the node with a phone and get to the

WikiHouse's open-source technologies change not only the identity of housing but also who builds it

interface of the house, which becomes a system. 'Any web developer could enter and play with it and create better interfaces.' This 'intranet of things' inside the house is helping to transform the ways in which houses can be created. As digital fabrication comes to the field of architecture, 'do we want it to be black box or open source?' asks Anselmo.

The rise of custom-build housing in the UK, which these ideas promote, has been prevented by high land prices and a problematic procurement model. WikiHouse has created its first houses and is now looking at neighbourhood-scale models, hoping that WikiHouse can become a 'new normal', as Parvin describes it, 'not being dependent on debt and finance capital', as most home owners currently are.

In essence, WikiHouse's open-source technologies will change not just what kinds of homes can be built and how they are built, but also who builds them – in other words, they will bring about new forms of social organisation. Parvin envisages support for groups to co-develop neighbourhoods, empowered by the capacity to make such a process less daunting, and making it more appealing to various types of public-sector institutions to play a genuinely supporting role. The WikiHouse catalogue will also expand to include a continually growing variety of technologies, and typologies adapted to particular problems, for example densification by building structures on unused rooftops.

WikiHouse has now become a global community with four chapters around the world and an increasing number of partners; it is developing a whole range of technologies, and setting up a WikiHouse Foundation. The first downloadable kit –

Left:
The parts of the first WikiHouse system, customised and digitally manufactured like a 'flat pack' to be slotted together in rapid assembly.

Right:
A three bedroom WikiHouse farmhouse being built by a family with their friends in a small rural community in the UK, 2015.

Left:
A-Barn, Scotland, 2015, made with a WikiHouse frame, which is raised by a traditional 'barn raising' process, requiring only conventional DIY tools.

a garden studio that others can also sell on – will be available in the near future. Before WikiHouse Parvin did research on land use, procurement and the housing crisis in the UK. Local governments told him that alternatives to the norm were 'too damn difficult'. But here to stay is the vision behind the research, embodied within 'Right to Build', an ongoing project with Architecture 00 begun with the University of Sheffield's Department of Architecture (made possible through the University's Knowledge Transfer Fund).[4] Right to Build addresses the economics of the housing crisis through self-provided and self-build housing (securing the land and planning permission, and managing the project oneself), as well as the future of democratic city planning and citizen-led development for resilient housing, infrastructure, neighbourhoods and cities.

One of the core proposals of Right to Build is a new land use category for the UK planning system, C5, which, if introduced, would effectively create a 'parallel' land market for homes not built primarily as financial assets, but as places to live. On top of the notional C5, explains Parvin, WikiHouse 'needs to establish a growing economy of professionals, manufacturers, and peer-to-peer support mechanisms for self-builders and custom-builders, thereby demystifying the process and making it faster and easier for everyone'.

Parvin stresses that WikiHouse is not new, as the machines have 'been around for ages', 14th-century Japanese wooden construction joints were made in a not dissimilar way, and 'vernacular is a web connection'. For him, 'usefulness is more useful than newness. Can we make it? There is a whole social economy around making.' Parvin acknowledges that open source does not solve all problems. But with it no problem needs to be solved twice, making open source very efficient – and disruptive of the status quo: 'WikiHouse has no destination, it is only a direction of travel. Our technology is very disruptive.'

WORKSHOP architecture

Every summer at Britain's WOMAD (World Festival of Music, Arts and Dance), in the grounds of Charlton Park, Wiltshire, artists from around the globe gather, their presence epitomising the event's commitment to cross-cultural awareness and tolerance. In 2012 WOMAD invited various architectural groups to make a structure using salvaged materials. One of these groups was the British-Norwegian team of WORKSHOP architecture (or WS, as on its logo). Not only did everyone work collaboratively, using their teamwork and design skills, but they also took time to debate 'the rights and wrongs of "aid architecture" and how best to design and build communities', says WS. 'Engagement makes the process an even playing field, where each party understands the value of what they can bring to the table.'[1]

Judging by the way WS engages and just two stories of its projects, the team knows what it is talking about. 'We focus on collaboration, learning by doing and cultivating a deep sense of place', and on building the capacity of threatened communities, declares the student-led non-profit design/make studio, which was registered as a UK charity in 2012.[2] The studio was founded by architects Clementine Blakemore (at time of writing, completing her Masters in architecture at London's Royal College of Art), Alexander Furunes (a recent graduate of the Architectural Association, also in London) and Ivar Tutturen (a graduate of the Norwegian University of Science and Technology/ NTNU who now works for Haworth Tompkins architects in London). They make a point of living temporarily with the communities they work with, as a way to get to know and harness the qualities of local people and their building crafts and materials.

While Tutturen was studying in Norway, with fellow students Furunes and Trond Hegvold he founded the non-profit Studio Tacloban to design and build a study centre in Tacloban, a coastal city of 220,000 in the Philippines. From autumn 2010 to summer 2011, they worked with a local informal settlement to create a centre that would help to get local children off the street. The project was accomplished in partnership with the Streetlight NGO, the Seawall Community and local engineers and suppliers, and constructed in locally available timber and bamboo. 'The aim was to use architecture as a tool to empower the parents to improve the learning conditions for their own children', WS explains.

At weekly community workshops the team worked on the centre with the mothers of the children who would be using it, with everyone exchanging their knowledge and passion. They collaboratively decided on the centre's location and siting to make the most of natural ventilation by the cool ocean breeze, as well as on its programme and design, and staged more workshops to design and build the furniture and interior fittings. The children themselves

→ **Right:** Chander Nagar classroom and craft space, enclosed by timber slats allowing ventilation and views, Dehradrum, India, 2012, WS.

↘ **Bottom right:** Hariharpur modelmaking workshop with the mothers and fathers of the schoolchildren attending the new school, 2013, WS.

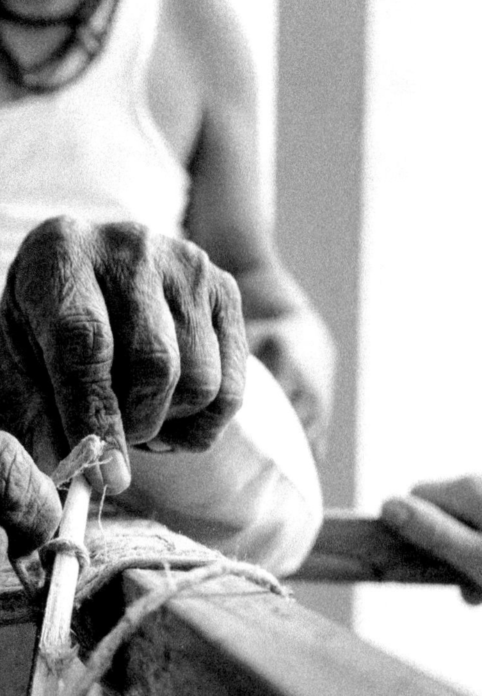

helped to design the roof truss, which incorporates a hidden mezzanine study space. The fathers, together with carpenters from within the community, worked on the construction, initially building a mock-up of the centre to test out the design ideas and develop their skills together. All the materials were sourced locally, as was the skilled labour, which helped to strengthen local businesses, knowledge and craft skills.

The visiting students worked on the first half of the construction, and the parents took over full responsibility for completing the centre; several of them have continued working in construction, using the centre as a reference to get better jobs. The locals called the process 'bayanihan', a traditional Filipino term describing a collective effort to achieve a particular objective, in which everyone can feel the spirit of participation and collaboration.

Left:
Nathai, a local farmer, learns jute weaving techniques at a design workshop run by Leika Aruga, Hariharpur Village, Uttar Pradesh, India, 2013, where WS is building a school.

Before the team could start building the second of the three buildings planned, in November 2013 Tacloban was devastated by Typhoon Haiyan, one of the strongest cyclones on record. Entire neighbourhoods were reduced to debris and up to 7,000 people were killed; thousands more were left to struggle as best they could. The centre survived the peak of the typhoon, but was destroyed in the subsequent storm surge. But the vivid memories and emotional association to the place spurred the families to start up workshops again and begin a rebuilding process, this time with an immense amount of experience.

Furunes returned to Tacloban in June 2014 to lead WS's support to reconstruct the centre, once again with Streetlight staff (all of whom had survived, along with all the children they support). This time a new, 4 hectare site located on higher ground was bought. Buildings can be rebuilt, and on higher land they may be safer from flooding, but while reconstruction was getting going, another powerful typhoon, Hagupit, brought chaos with flying roofs and other damage. This time the unsettled population, with no choice but to be resilient, evacuated in good time. Now the architects' orphanages, schools, clinics and offices will be ready in 2015.

For each project it undertakes, WS partners with NGOs and builds a team of collaborators, including community organisers and representatives, local architects, engineers, artisans and graphic designers. For a classroom and craft space in the Chander Nagar district of Dehradun, northern India, constructed over four months in 2012, the group got sponsorship from the Norwegian firm Lund+Slaatto, 'in kind' support from the engineers Ramboll, Tutteren's alma mater →

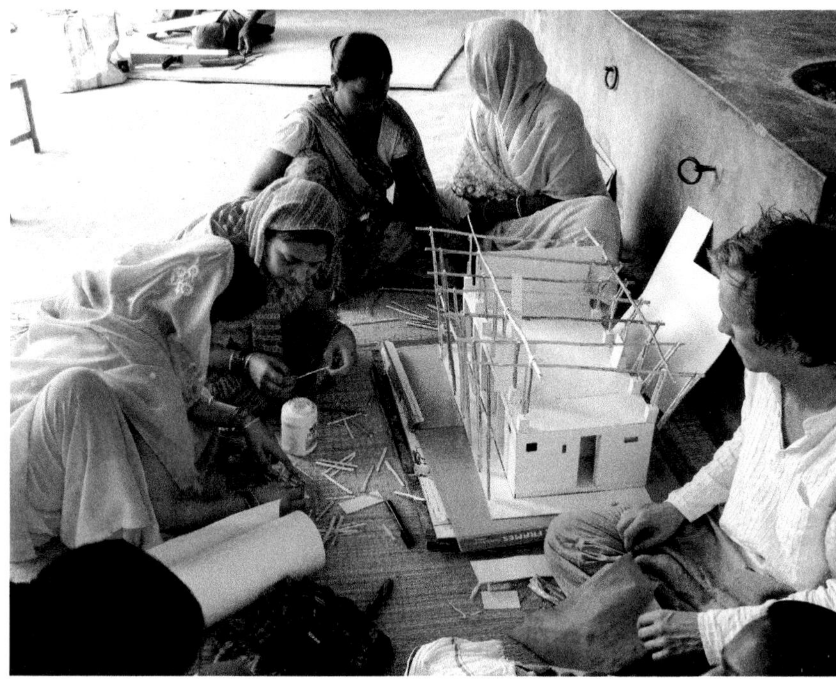

Below:
Study centre, Tacloban, Philippines, 2010-11. Fathers and carpenters from the informal settlement build a mock-up to develop skills and test design ideas.

Right:
The study centre at Tacloban, Philippines, seen from the park, 2010-11. WORKSHOP architecture.

NTNU and the Architectural Association, London, with both architectural schools collaborating on a joint Visiting School to the site.

At Chander Nagar the team made a collaboration with the Indian charity Nanhi Duniya International Movement for Children and their Friends. Nanhi Duniya runs 12 schools here for children from deprived backgrounds, including those with special needs. The team's plan was to renovate one of the schools, in order that the design strategy could be applied to others in future, to help build Chander Nagar's sustainability.

The resulting 'Rangshala' – a Hindi term joining the words for 'colour' (*rang*) and 'school' (*shala*) – is a lightweight multifunctional classroom for crafts and other making activities, open to the whole community as well as to the school children. Well ventilated and open to the playground, it was designed and built collaboratively with the local community, skilled craftsmen, a local contractor, three UK engineers from Ramboll and a team of students from the NTNU/Architectural Association Visiting School. Parents contributed to the construction and brought fruit and vegetables during the Visiting School. As part of the project, three of the mothers took part in a woodblock training programme with a local NGO. They then shared their knowledge with the teachers, who were able to add woodcut printing to the curriculum.

The following year, from March to August 2013, WS realised its second project in India at Hariharpur village; the masterplan included a health centre, a theatre and an exhibition space, but the first stage was to build primary school building. Hariharpur, which has a population of 2,000 people, is in rural Uttar Pradesh, a predominantly agrarian society with a strong cultural heritage. This time WS collaborated with the Indian Trust for Rural Heritage and Development (ITRHD), which works to promote the area's tradition of classical music through the realisation of resources in the areas of health, education and sanitation; the project was supported by a grant from the British Council, which supports WS's belief that architecture can be a tool to promote positive social change. The idea was to create a structure that would serve 'as a prototype for contemporary rural architecture in India'.

The team moved to the village to work as part of an expanded group with architect Kritika Dhanda, local artisans and craftspeople, the schoolteachers and the community organiser Leika Aruga. Workshops in design, model-making

and traditional jute weaving were staged for the parents of the schoolchildren (who included the school's construction supervisor). The team discussed siting, orientation, window frames and interior finishes. 'The design and construction of the school was an opportunity to learn from vernacular building methods, reinterpreting and evolving them to create a building which addresses today's needs and aspirations', says WS. 'Our research and design began with a series of 1:1 mock-ups and materials testing', the architects explain, and they put their first designs on display in the 'Building Community' and 'Not What, But How' exhibitions at the British Council in New Delhi in 2013 as part of the second Visiting School workshop for the NTNU/ Architectural Association in India.

'Exhibitions are important to us, not so much as vehicles to showcase our work, but as public platforms for debate and exchange', says WS, which also created a daily blog diary with contributors from the team, documented in their extensive publication released in 2013 (see endnote 1). 'We used [the exhibitions] as tools to [open] illicit conversations and collaborations with experts and practitioners both locally and internationally.' The whole process of making the project at Hariharpur village was live on site and in the public realm from start to finish. For example, in February 2013, before they began, the WS team staged a discussion about their work at the UnBox Festival in New Delhi, an event focused on 'hands-on, minds on' approaches to construction of prototypes and artefacts, breaking down traditional notions of work and play.

At Hariharpur they created the new school masterplan as a collaborative learning process, including weekly design workshops run by the teachers with guidance from Aruga, reflecting in their work the principles of the traditional Hindu construction manuals, *Vastu Shastra*, and local beliefs. The parents were also given the opportunity to learn how to make traditional brick barrel vaults by watching local construction workers (who had been given three weeks of tuition by a master mason) apply the techniques to the roof – leading to 'the resurgence of skills that had been lost in the local area', says WS. Mothers and grandmothers mud-plastered the walls of the brick structure, then decorated them with rice paint. In August 2013 the school, consisting of a two-storey building and ten toilets, was handed over to ITRHD and the local community; four more classrooms are now being built by the community.

The British Council grant enabled WS to put its ideas into action through an exemplary project of great social value, that serves as a model for others to study and take inspiration from. 'Being in some way "accountable" to people one step removed from the project can be very productive, and allows the local dialogues taking place on site to join a wider international discussion', say the architects. That wider discussion is about the mindsets of practitioners approaching a specific context, wherever it is. 'We believe that architecture should be deeply embedded in the social, economic, cultural and climatic context of the site', and 'never implant something new but rather to build upon what is already there.'

We believe that you should never implant something new, but build on what is already there

Left:
Leika Aruga, the community organiser, running the design workshop for Hariharpur village, Uttar Pradesh, India, 2013, WORKSHOP architecture.

How can plans for threatened urban waterfronts enable resiliency and liveability to go hand in hand? How can you reconnect citizens to the waterfront but protect it at the same time? Storm surges threaten coastal parkland; yet it is a relatively new concept to develop waterfront areas that are accessible and have infrastructure and amenity enhancements, while also attenuating those surges and managing storm water.

WXY Studio

In New York, climate change had been a key subject of discussions for some time, but after the devastating Hurricane Sandy of 2012, talks were held with various international experts on approaches taken to flooding in the similarly low-lying Netherlands and Venice. The impact of Sandy also resulted in long-awaited renovations to the East River Greenway cycling and walking lanes, from Brooklyn Bridge to East 38th Street. The East River Blueway Plan for the Greenway, designed by WXY Studio, brought waterfront access, new public spaces and storm- and flood-water management to the existing lanes.

Drawing up the plan involved WXY in many public meetings with numerous community groups, and consultations with seven different city and state agencies. Adam Lubinsky, the architect, urban designer and managing principal (since 2011) with founding partner architect Clare Weisz of WXY Studio (established in New York in 1998), describes the discussions as very transactive: 'Where are all the street crossings? What are they, what are the big goals that you want to achieve with this?' It was a matter of 'capturing all of that local knowledge, being able to deal with smaller issues but also able to essentialise big goals, with big ideas that were not at all on the radar with people there at all.'[1]

Lubinsky feels that participatory placemaking in the US has entered an exciting stage in its development. Technology is now a strong tool, but also 'the nature of funding and delivering different kinds of projects has changed the nature of people participating'. There is 'a real pedagogical side to this work in how you approach the shared learning of these things', because today the planning profession, and the architecture and design professions, each with their separate legacies, are 'now in the same moshpit together'.

WXY Studio is known for its high-quality design and its understanding of the technical side of planning, and it bridges these with community-based planning. Lubinsky says that he and Weisz 'have a transactive process and a design process. There are two very separate, different traditions with planners and designers, and they're both meeting in this arena of public participation, both

Bottom left:
Existing esplanade along South Street underneath the FDR Drive, with downspurts emptying into the East River, East River Blueway Plan, WXY Studio, 2011-ongoing.

Left:
Render of WXY's proposed East River Esplanade, New York City, from the Brooklyn Bridge to East 38th Street, 2011.

Below:
Workshop table at one of the six community meetings held for the East River Blueway Plan, WXY Design, 2011-2013.

reacting to different professional issues. Getting it right is tricky.'

From his time working for the Department of Environmental Protection in the Bronx, Lubinsky learned that the activities of local community-based organisations (CBOs) and grassroots groups created an interesting dynamic. In New York 'the politics of participation are unique. There is an amazing opportunity for CBOs and grassroots groups to get involved. They are very intertwined with local politicians, and there's a real feedback there. It's not all good. Some of it's great, and the CBOs carry a lot of power. They can force issues to the attention of politicians and Congress people because they can be seen as validating.'

Context is all. When WXY Studio carried out an adaptive reuse of the Bronx Charter School for the Arts (2004-6), Lubinsky 'led a participatory design process trying to build in pedagogical ideas about how to create spaces for a school with arts-based individualised learning'. It was a different matter with a design mediation for a bulkhead that began collapsing at Manhattan's Pier 40 near the Meatpacking District, where land is looked after by the Hudson River Park Trust. A private conservancy funded by private donations accepted responsibility for maintaining everything, and the situation called for 'very specific design input on what the desires were' – especially as the team had briefs that were in conflict with one another. 'Particularly in a place like NYC, it's very hard to find consensus. So the point is for architects and designers to be not controlling but to do what they do, and find the right way to get feedback and input. Even within one project, you can have a spectrum range of approaches.'

The team 'did a series of designs, showed them to people, got some reactions, and then eventually presented what we thought was a great option that met all sorts of complicating requirements by stakeholders'. There was a 'need for a strong hand on the design side to step in and say, "right, there's no potential for a communitarian design, there are way too many conflicts to reach agreements." What designers like to do is to use their skills and imagination and come up with something that attempts to mediate.'

'The whole principle of advocacy planning [a term coined by planning theorist Paul Davidoff in the 1960s] was essentially sharing knowledge', Lubinsky explains. 'The local community has knowledge, →

Right:
Potential issues at Brooklyn Bridge Beach identified at a community meeting, 2011, WXY Studio.

Below:
Existing Brooklyn Bridge Beach, New York City, 2011, WXY Studio.

planners have knowledge – let's work together to share our knowledge. This is really different from the way architects enter a job. They have a brief, and they may want to interview the client, whether one person or many, go away and work things out, understand their goals, learn how it informs the brief, and then they have a design process. It's about working towards those goals, but not necessarily having the direct things that they want to have come out of it.'

WXY's QueenWay plan in Queens – 'a kind of High Line' – will 'be very different, very local and responsive to the local communities and the diversity there… it has citywide biking advocates; in the Blueway a lot of citywide boating advocates'. Mining social media for feedback, especially from those people who cannot get to meetings, WXY feel online tools are 'really good for pulling in people who are like that, and who have these big interests, but don't live in this community. Sometimes you do community events, and there's real tension between people who just want to find a launching place for their kayak versus someone who lives in social housing, and they're like, I'm not going to go kayaking.'

Social media 'is useful more and more as the projects have both a city-wide and a local potential', Lubinsky adds. 'They become ways for us, not to segment it, but to reduce some of the tension if we advertise a meeting in the Lower East Side that was to bring in the whole boating community, it could be a big disaster. So there are a number of reasons why technology is useful.' What is unique about both the Blueway and the Queens Way, he feels, is that they're 'embedded in communities that are generally underserved'.

Finding a way for people to understand trade-offs is important. 'If there's a mixed-use development here, and you consider some height, then you might get a community space or open space out of this. So using physical tiles and cubes to stack and piles of different land use tabs, and getting people to understand, well, if we do this, we might get some of those and trying to build a game out of it, like the Bronx School for the Arts, where we had square footage room sizes, and adaptive reuse, so we had icons and

means for different kinds of programmes and activities, from stickers and to simply drawing.'

There are certain meetings, and certain groups, stakeholders and certain client types, 'that you will gear certain tools for, like these area action plans I was doing in London (where he worked and did his PhD in planning over eight years), where the idea of density was really on people's minds. How do you communicate its positive benefits? By contrast in the early stage of the Bronx project was about 'gathering ideas - some of that is quite traditional listmaking. There's generally many tools that apply to particular situations.' For workshops 'we close the office and get our entire staff to come facilitate, so we'll always have two people working hands-on at a table, one moderating, and one helping people apply stickers'.

At the 2014 Atlanta APA National Planning Conference, WXY showed how its DIAS-Platform (Defining Issues Aligning Stakeholders) with Tygron gaming software uses technology, planning research and charrette techniques to create a new model providing live feedback on the impacts on development scenarios. 'The process allows stakeholders to interrogate, in an integrated way, urban design approaches, planning policies, infrastructure needs and financial viability, making charrettes more useful, reducing lengthy permitting processes and benefiting all stakeholders.'

Managing expectations in participatory processes is 'tough, because you get disappointment and then you get disillusionment, but the thing that I've got since I've been back in NYC, which I didn't get before, is if we help you with this, and we participate, are we are going to be able to live here when all of this stuff happens?', Lubinsky explains. 'That's a harder question to handle, and there is disillusionment when you say, "there's $20 million and this is the limit of what we can do. There's participation, and not everything gets done or not the way you want it."'

Lubinsky elaborates: 'Part of it is, well, if you participate in this, we will look at some of the affordability issues, which comes full circle to some of your questions about the role of urban design and non-physical and physical. The more we get into these projects, the less it's just about design and the more it's about economic development, affordable housing, job creation, and it's really a much bigger picture at work here – and resilience. And some of this is really limited by the client, [by] who your client is; making your case, whether [the scheme] will be affordable at the end of the day, is hard.'

Left:
Proposed Brooklyn Bridge Beach, render, part of the East River Blueway Plan, WXY Studio, 2011.

> **Lubinsky feels that participatory placemaking in the US has reached an exciting stage in its development**

ENGAGEMENT
REPLICABILITY
DESIGN DRIVEN
SCALE
IMPACT

IDENTIFY → ENQUIRE → DEVELOP → CO-DESIGN → CO-CONSTRUCT → HAND-OVER

Voices

These six essays, from thought leaders in the field of architecture, urban design and applied social innovation, evaluate participatory placemaking in relation to a variety of topical themes.

Eva Franch i Gilabert
Andy Lipkis
Josiah Mugambi
Michael Norton
Edgar Pieterse
Ute Weiland

Eva Franch i Gilabert Articulating the multiple voices of society

Architecture today needs to return to a certain notion of civic body. We often forget that it is the very mandate and duty of the architect to articulate the multiple voices of society. This role can bring those who do not have voices or power to sit on the decision-making table. This aspiration for new forms of collectivity is the essence and the core of the definition of what an architect's role is. I would therefore argue that participatory placemaking is not a new discipline. However there has been a double-sided loss: on one hand architects have stopped embodying this collective responsibility, and on the other hand – and perhaps as a consequence – society has a misperception of the architect's role within society.

I differentiate between three types of architects. The first is the enabler, the facilitator, the person who allows all the different voices to be brought to the table. The enabler is similar to the dictator, perpetuating existing ideologies simply because he is not, in fact, questioning the values and the ideas that are being brought into the space of conversion. I think that, occasionally, the problem with participatory projects is that they are in fact just collecting the minimum common denominator, and as a result, sadly, just end up compiling the most mediocre and average ideas about place.

The second is the iconographer. These are architects who try to produce spaces of representation, use metaphors and structures of signification to resonate with a collective imaginary. The iconographers argue that society tends to accept a new building as an icon when they successfully create meaning to gather in and around. Icons that dwell on symbolic and metaphorical structures are a way to produce collective readings – one could argue – participatory readings. The drawback of icons within collective forms is that it lends itself rapidly to banality and superfluous readings.

The third is the agitator - the one who can be seen as against everything and all and constantly trying to question, reconfigure and reconstitute the power structures and formal ideals in place.

I am most interested in architects that unite these three types. Those who do their best to ask the right questions, facilitate current desires and also channel new ones while challenging form and function, both aesthetically, politically and methodologically. Participative processes are often carried out by enablers. Where I would stress a difference is that to really innovate one needs to agitate as well, and not only that, one needs to strive to understand the new aesthetic forms that are able to come together in the renewed spaces of collectivity.

We can create social equity through architectural design, but it requires that we break free from spatial protocols inherited from economic and political systems which have historically always tried to empower those at the top. In my opinion, the potent social movements we see today are the result of a lack of active scrutiny of the establishment over the last 20 years, and that lack is also expressed in the form of the city today. The inadequacy of the current models of politics and practice is one of the biggest challenges we have, and it explains the increasingly loud protests around the world. It has less to do with economic crises and mistrust of politics, and more to do with a cultural misperception of who we are as a society.

Recently at Storefront for Art and Architecture, for a project called Letters to the Mayor, we commissioned different architects around the world to speak on behalf of architecture – not of themselves – to their mayors explaining the role and relevance of architecture and design in the making of cities and territories.

I am still not sure how we qualify good designs, because 'good' is always defined in relationship to values acquired from our sense of understanding which belong to the past. The idea of new is definitely too easy and already obsolete. I would prioritise the ways in which you enable other designs and other forms of understanding of spaces that allow us to come together in different ways, that make us feel less organised, less civilised, less politically ordered, less economically separated.

Recoded City includes a lot of stories to express the different styles and edges of participatory placemaking Another good example is Packman, an architecture group based in Madrid, who define themselves loosely as a collective, and are constantly evolving and embracing the talents of new individuals on projects that have to do with civic empowerment. By creating events that transform the city fully and totally, in which one totally abandons any preconceptions of what a city is, one can sense new potentialities. To create moments of exception is easy in events, performances and festivals, but is harder in architecture defined in its long-lasting temporal sense. However, one must also consider that temporary architecture has been recuperated and appropriated by the status quo, leaving us without a clear space or time for radical action. It seems as if suddenly the field of practice and alternative action is more open than ever.

Text based on a phone conversation between Eva Franch and Thomas Ermacora.

Eva Franch i Gilabert is an architect and the executive director and chief curator of Storefront for Art and Architecture in New York since 2010. In 2004 she founded her practice OOAA (Office Of Architectural Affairs). She studied at TU Delft and earned an M. Arch from ETSA Barcelona-UPC, and an M. Arch. II from Princeton University, New Jersey. She has since taught at Columbia University, New York, the University of Venice, SUNY Buffalo and Rice University, Texas, and has lectured at various institutions on art, architecture and the importance of alternative practices in the construction and understanding of public life. Her work has received numerous accolades and has been exhibited at FAD Barcelona and at the Shenzhen Biennale of Architecture and Urbanism. In 2013 the US State Department selected Storefront and Franch, jointly with a curatorial and design team, to represent the US Pavilion at the 2014 Venice Architecture Biennale.

Andy Lipkis TreePeople and citizen forestry

I began the work of TreePeople in 1970 when I was 15 years old. Born and raised in Los Angeles, the city with the worst air quality in the United States, I found strength and motivation in organising people to join me in planting smog-resistant trees to replace the forests that were being killed by air pollution.

Growing up with the smog burning my lungs and making it hard to play in the city, I fell in love with the forest 100 miles east of Los Angeles because of the beauty, clean air and freedom to play without coughing and pain. On learning that the smog was killing the trees and the forest, my first reaction was anger. But while we felt powerless to clean up the pollution, I found that planting trees, working with others and seeing real change take place as we restored damaged portions of the forest, built my strength and knowledge and fuelled my dreams and conviction to do more.

I was as motivated by planting the trees as I was by seeing other people, especially teenagers, get inspired and energised from the work, gaining a sense of their power to make change in the face of an overwhelming problem. Research from the US Forest Service and the University of California, Riverside showed that smog was killing the trees, and that this could ultimately lead to the collapse or disappearance of the pine forest ecosystem of southern California. Restoring the forest was not viewed as a priority by the US Congress, which was engaged in cutting the Forest Service budget, so the Forest Service was not in a position to take on the restoration efforts.

In the beginning people joined our work both because they could see trees dying and because large numbers were being logged from public recreation areas in the national forest. Also there was wide-spread public awareness after the first Earth Day in 1970, that forests were in decline and needed help. We made the volunteer work attractive and compelling by sharing information about the impact of forest decline on human and wildlife health.

We knew that simply planting smog-resistant trees was equivalent to putting a plaster on the symptom, and we sought to go further to actually move people to solve the air pollution problem. We found that getting people physically involved built both awareness and deeper caring about the connected issues of the trees, the forest, the animals and the city's air quality, and thereby deepened people's commitment to solving the larger air pollution problem. We increased the scope of our work from simply replanting the forests, to engaging people in planting trees in the city to improve the quality of life in their neighbourhoods, schools and parks. The work itself – connecting with neighbours, sharing and implementing dreams, changing their streets and the city – provided sufficient self-evident results to motivate people to get involved.

We learned over time that it was vital to support local people in crafting a response and a dream of their own to address the issues that threatened their quality of life in the city. Instead of TreePeople simply planting trees for them, we guided them to discover the challenges and to build a project that represented their dreams and ideas. We found that when we took this approach, people really 'owned' the trees and took much better care of them and protected them. The difference in results was stunning: up to 95% of the trees survived after five years, whereas nationwide the survival rate of urban trees was around 10%.

We named this whole approach 'citizen forestry', and reformatted our strategy on urban greening based on this. We formalised a training and support system that became the primary way TreePeople implemented urban greening. This approach of training and supporting citizens in organising their neighbourhoods to craft a shared vision and implement it together (including raising an initial portion of the funding for their project) not only resulted in higher tree survival rates, but also led to increased community cohesion, communication and strength. When neighbourhoods saw that they could raise funds and make things happen, and change the look of their neighbourhood overnight, then they had a basis on which to take on other issues. Some organised neighbourhood watch groups, others day-care centres.

A great and extraordinary example of our Citizen Forester programme is the planting of Martin Luther King Jr Boulevard in Los Angeles. One of our Citizen Foresters, retired high-school teacher Eudora Russell, took our training and then implemented her first project, a planting of 22 trees in a particularly challenging neighbourhood in south-west Los Angeles. The project took several years to plan, organise and execute, but she succeeded in bringing a large and diverse team together, who then raised initial funds, planted, cared for the trees, installed irrigation systems and built an ongoing team of volunteers that ensured the trees survived. After several years of managing this and witnessing its success, Eudora dreamed a bigger dream: creating the largest living monument to Dr King by planting all 7 miles of the boulevard to honour him.

Eudora talked to the mayor and other city officials, who thought it was a good idea but said it would take millions of dollars and many years to make it happen, and that the city wasn't in a position to fund the project. She told me of her dream and the disappointing official response. I validated her dream and suggested that we should show the power of dreams and community action, and honour Dr King, by inviting the community to plant the boulevard in one single day.

Eudora was willing to go for it. Ultimately TreePeople hired another Citizen Forester, Fred Anderson, to be the project manager, and he worked with Eudora, me, TreePeople staff and the community to organise and fundraise for it. It took six months of organising, enrolling churches and schools and the support of four city council members, canvassing the homes and businesses along all 7 miles of the boulevard, and training 1,000 volunteers in advance of the main event.

The boulevard was comprised of 52 blocks, which we divided into 26 two-block long 'neighbourhoods' each with a captain, a trained logistics team, tools, a portable toilet – and a birthday cake. On 15 January 1990, the anniversary of Martin Luther King's birth, some 3,000 volunteers turned out to plant trees; in about four hours, 300 trees had been planted. Each tree was named and dedicated by its volunteer planting team, and a local resident living within a few hundred feet of the tree was assigned as its caregiver. During the planting process, each of the planters placed a small clump of their hair or another personal object into the tree pit so the new tree could 'eat' it and make the gift part of itself. This created a very special bonding with the tree, and resulted in that much more 'ownership' and protection of the tree.

In order to guard public health and safety from floods, and to prevent both disease and destruction of the built environment from stagnant water, 'modern'

cities have been designed to 'shed' rainwater: it is sent away as soon as possible, via storm drains or sewers, either treated or untreated, to rivers or oceans. While meeting the protective goals, in Los Angeles and elsewhere this practice also unwittingly wiped out fish habitat and polluted the rivers and oceans. In many cases it also created local water shortages as abundant local rainwater was being 'thrown away' and replaced with expensive water, often transferred by aqueduct from remote sources at great energy expense and damage to the source ecosystem. This approach breaks the natural water cycle, resulting in multiple problems and expenses, and is inherently unsustainable.

Our work involves bio-mimicking the functions of a natural forest ecosystem or watershed/catchment to design green infrastructure retrofits for cities. In Seattle, Los Angeles, Santa Monica and other cities, NGOs and engineers have been piloting and incorporating this approach to restore fish spawning habitat, and to prevent pollution, drought and flooding. Aside from catching rain on individual residential, commercial and industrial properties, a huge opportunity exists to convert green highway strip; and nature strip along streets can be adapted to function like a creek or natural wetland. In this case, the nature strip is re-engineered to look like a creek and function as a treatment wetland, as the water flows slowly through it. Holes are cut in the kerb, allowing water to safely flow off the street and kerb and into the adjacent 'creek' bed; there, the water flows through mulch and living plants that can filter and treat the pollutants and allow the cleaned water to soak into the ground or local aquifers.

I saw there was a huge need to capture, treat, store and use the abundance of rainwater, and figured out a way to engage with government agencies and infrastructure issues that were not usually of interest to the public. We had to engage with the agencies on terms they understood, and then, using their engineering approaches and economic styles, we conducted studies, built demonstration projects and piloted programmes to show that the 'green infrastructure' approach was technically, economically and socially feasible. We also had to show them that they could do a better job using a multi-agency collaborative approach to create multi-purpose infrastructure that could supply water, and prevent flooding and water pollution. The key to this was to move from centralised, vulnerable and massive infrastructure facilities such as storm drains or artificial lakes, to decentralised and distributed green infrastructure systems that can catch rain on every land-use parcel, clean it and then re-inject it into the aquifer via permeable soils and rainwater catchment systems like cisterns, rain gardens and bioswales.

Over 40 years of work, we've become expert in engaging citizens to become active participants in improving the water, flood protection, and so on. One example is our Citizen Forester training and support programme cited at the beginning of this piece. When it comes to the future development of participatory placemaking, with new technologies and increased acceptance as the cases to support it grow, there are a number of key points to remember. Increasingly, people are wanting to make a difference, especially in making their home, neighbourhood or city become climate resilient. Everyone in a city is a co-manager of the ecosystem. They are managers of the water, rubbish or waste, energy use and air quality. If people aren't consciously managing the resources, then they're mismanaging them.

When it comes to funding and value to the community, our work has been carried out in the context of public infrastructure budgets, which are generally available on the public record. We have consistently sought to show that our approach makes financial sense and could save local governments money, if they coordinate proportional investments in the project with each respective agency paying for their share the green infrastructure services and outcomes.

With the advent of mobile phone apps and gamification, it is possible to provide people with expert guidance, feedback and incentives so as to encourage them and ensure their contribution succeeds. Today's generation is increasingly focused on engagement and feedback to their actions, including monitoring exercise and health, with devices such as the Fitbit decorative accessory or bracelet, that reports data to the user's mobile phone. Through this method, it is possible to provide information and incentives to expertly guide, ease, and reward action (for example, to design and installation of a rainwater harvesting landscape), and monitor whether the green infrastructure system is properly functioning, being maintained or cared for. This approach can attract and enable thousands or even millions of people to participate in actions and remain engaged over the long haul.

After 44 years of doing this work, mobilising volunteers to replant forests after fires, to dream and recreate their neighbourhoods, or to respond to flood emergencies by helping to rescue people and save homes, I have come to believe that humans have a strong innate need to participate in helping heal one another, other critters and the ecosystem more widely. For the most part, people are not consciously aware that there is damage being done to nature, but they can sense it, just like when there is physical danger or threat. Most need to experience a drip or shot of adrenaline to wake them up and move them into action.

Scientists and doctors report that people who volunteer to serve others have stronger immune systems and higher T-cell counts to protect them. Throughout TreePeople's history I have observed how people who volunteer with us, report having more energy after a weekend of exhausting volunteer work than they did when their weekend began.

Text based on conversations between Andy Lipkis and Thomas Ermacora.

Andy Lipkis is President of TreePeople, the California-based, non-profit environmental advocacy group promoting sustainable urban ecosystems in the Greater Los Angeles area. He founded TreePeople in 1973, at the age of 18, and parallel with this invented the concept of 'citizen forestry'. TreePeople supports people in planting and caring for trees in their residential contexts, schoolyards and neighbourhoods, and promotes urban watershed management, using green infrastructure to address critical urban water issues. The organisation has more than 50 staff members based at its bespoke eco-centre at the 45-acre Coldwater Canyon Park, and collaborates with thousands of members and volunteers. Lipkis's pioneering work in this field has been recognised by numerous distinctions including the United Nations Environmental Program global roll of honour and the prestigious Ashoka Fellowship.

Josiah Mugambi Nairobi's iHub for open-source innovation

In Kenya, the rise of the idea of open-source development has arguably been instrumental in growing the tech community to what it is now. In the last decade of the 20th century, there was limited, if any, use of open-source software in software development. At that time, few people in the country grasped the concept of developing software that was open and could be reviewed by anyone else. In the wider world, most open-source software (there was nothing much else that could be called 'open' then anyway) was still the stuff of geeks, but it was becoming increasingly apparent that the open and collaborative mindset behind the open-source movement has a major role in innovation.

The now burgeoning tech community in Kenya started in the late 1990s and early 2000s with the beginning of the Kenya Linux User Group, of which I was privileged to have been an early member. Back then, the tech community was much smaller than it is now, by several orders of magnitude. Communication was frequent however, on a mailing list, with regular physical meetings augmenting the online interactions.

When Silicon Bazaar opened an office in Kenya, a milestone of sorts was reached, as very few, if any, software companies at that time had set up shop in Kenya with products based purely on open-source software. The proprietor of Silicon Bazaar, Githogori wa Nyangara-Murage, a fierce advocate of open source, said at the time: 'The free software model makes sense for Africa. It puts Africa and the rest of the world on an equal level.'

The Silicon Bazaar offices at that time formed a nexus point for a small but vibrant technology community (primarily open-source enthusiasts) to physically meet, every Friday afternoon. I had an opportunity to intern there over school holidays hacking all sorts of things, but more importantly, the regular meet ups and interactions were significant in growing the community.

In 2006, this community had grown considerably, and was largely composed of people from the Internet service provider (ISP) industry and the few software houses around. During a chat with the technologist Erik Hersman (I think that was the first time we met), the founder of Ushahidi (see page 53), and Riyaz Bachani (then at Kenya Data Networks, and the founder in 2004 of cloud services firm Angani), the idea behind the Skunkworks techies mailing list was born, and in

February 2007 we held our first meeting at Nairobi's Steers Muindi Mbingu restaurant – about 25 people talking ideas tech over chicken and burgers. It was an open, collaborative exchange of ideas and information, pretty much in the open-source tradition.

A local ISP, Wananchi, hosted subsequent weekly meetings and the group grew exponentially. Lots of learning took place, lots of connections were made. The first BarCamp – an 'unconference' – where content is user-generated, and is open and participatory) was held a couple of months later; 23 people attended this event, which pales in comparison to the 400+ for the 2014 Nairobi edition. However, this early community and the events happening then were the start of something bigger.

At an informal chat as the third BarCamp was winding down in early 2008, the idea behind the iHub was first born; a place where such interactions, connections, learning and conversations could take place, but on a continuous basis. March 2010 was the culmination of that dream when, the iHub opened its doors to the tech community in Nairobi, in a space funded by the Omidvar Network and Hivos.

The open-source community is obviously much larger now. More importantly, many of the core elements that drive this community forward are spread across the tech community. Openness and collaboration are vital in a tech ecosystem, and foster the exchange of ideas and knowledge, which builds the community. A lot of such communication does take place in an online platform. However, when augmented with physical interactions, much more can happen, as has been seen at the iHub over the years, with people meeting and co-founding companies.

In being part of this tech community, one of the key elements in fostering collaboration, is nurturing an environment where individuals from diverse backgrounds and cultures are able to think creatively and innovatively without the fear of being unfairly put down. An environment where failure is considered to be part of the path towards success is very important in encouraging innovation. Of course entrepreneurs must take whatever steps they need to mitigate failure as they work on their start-up ideas or businesses, and avoid carelessness that leads to failure, but they must not be afraid to take risks on their path to success.

Innovation and entrepreneurship must be 'ground up', not a top-down hierarchical activity but rather a network: something that originates from individuals and groups of people, working collaboratively and openly. This means that anyone in a community is capable of coming up with a solution to a problem that affects all. No one should be looked down upon for whatever reason. A culture that encourages mutual respect, participation and collaboration allows this to happen.

In the five years since its inception the iHub's creative co-working culture, supported by technology giants such as Google, has grown, and boosted the wider ecology of the Kenyan innovative tech scene. Today the iHub also has the potential to be a valuable placemaking hub, helping to foster the innovative ideas of local collaborators investigating how both Kenyans and other citizens further afield can use technology and data related solutions to improve their living spaces. This could perhaps even impact on their infrastructures, given a growing focus in Kenya on innovative collaborations using design to solve local developmental problems (for example, PITCHAfrica, see page 228).

African cities, both the slums as well as formalized urban centres need new technological tools, resources and concepts to help leapfrog the relative lack of planning and building controls, but also to allow new dialogues to take place between citizens. By facilitating participation and collaboration through technological means, communities in Nairobi and other centres will benefit incrementally, and, with time, the impact of the iHub will be felt, well beyond its walls.

Josiah Mugambi is an ICT expert and entrepreneur appointed Executive Director in 2013 of the Kenyan iHub, taking over from founder Erik Hersman, the leading community catalyst for technology in east Africa, supporting new digital platforms, tools, placemaking and economic development. Mugambi has several years' experience in ICT, including software solutions development and networking, and spent nine years working in the telecommunications space with NSN and Huawei before taking the helm at iHub.

Michael Norton
Cities are for people

Most of the world's population now lives in cities, some of which are becoming megacities of an unprecedented scale. These cities and megacities are for people – and it is people who make the city, not architects and planners. The built environment is the backdrop against which the city comes to life. Traffic is a big enemy. Its incompatibility with people was noted by Le Corbusier in his 1920s Ville Radieuse ('Radiant City') proposal, although his proffered solution was a city of tower blocks, urban freeways and publicly managed green spaces in between, which is hardly a good recipe for a liveable city.

Cities are being brought to life in all sorts of ways, all of them people-powered. Here are some examples:

Guerrilla gardening: As I cycle into central London from my home in Hampstead, I pass a traffic island where the local council has planted a tree. Around its base, somebody has lovingly planted a circle of flowers. It makes me smile; and smiling is good for me, and good for my city.

Talking statues: Once-notable public personalities, geniuses and military heroes stare down at us imposingly. We have almost certainly forgotten who they are or why they were famous. They may have a story to tell us, but their lips are sealed (literally). Talking statues brings the statues in the city to life. You download an app, and as you pass a statue it texts or phones you to tell you that it would like to speak to you. Well-known writers and actors have scripted the conversation, which is full not of dreary historical facts but of gossip and intimacies, bringing these dead people (and the city) back to life.

The smoking ban: In Britain, smoking is now banned in all enclosed public places, except in designated smoking areas. This is great for all of us non-smokers, who now do not suffer the discomfort of passive inhalation. But at the same time it has created a party atmosphere in the street outside pubs and offices. Even in the rain, smokers are now forced to smoke in the company of other smokers, and assert their right to do this by having fun.

Mural painting: Grey walls and boring buildings can be brought to life with a mural, painted by artists, graffiti writers or communities who wish to express themselves in colour. That once-despised scribble might be a Banksy, and worth millions.

The World Naked Bike Ride: This happens once a year in summer, when cyclists in many cities all over the world ride as bare as they dare to promote the idea of cycling and have a bit of in-your-face fun. It's not as embarrassing as you might think, but much more uncomfortable!

Reclaim the Beach: Paris may have its Paris Plages, but the Thames has real beaches which appear at low tide. Reclaim the Beach used to organise flashmob London beach parties with music, entertainment and bring-your-own refreshments. The police tended to turn a blind eye, as they knew that the party would have to stop when the water level rose again.

The Big Lunch: An annual event in the UK for which people invite their neighbours to join them for lunch out in the street. In 2014, an amazing 4.8 million people had lunch together.

Busking: You don't have to give, but you can. And buskers are a healthy antidote to chuggers, those charity fundraisers who 'mug' you in the street. From playing music to being a living statue, buskers bring life into the streets and on the Underground (or metro, or subway). If you enjoy what they are doing, thank them.

Big Issue sellers: And then there are of course the homeless on the streets, having a hard time. Buy a *Big Issue* magazine from them, or just chat to them. Their pain could become your pleasure.

The Laboratory of Experimental Tourism: This proposal provides you with around 30 unexpected ways to enjoy the city, from trying to find your loved one without the aid of a mobile phone or a satnav, to flipping a coin at each corner to determine which way to go.

The Society for the Deceleration of Time: We rush around the city taking care of our own business, not looking to the right or to the left. But what if we tried to live our life more slowly, savouring the moments and enjoying just being where we are? Members of this society would set up speed traps for pedestrians, and if they were walking too fast would stop them to ask if they would like to live their life at a slower pace and enjoy it more. And of course there are slow cities, with slow food and even slow sex as part of the Slow Movement.

'Green drinks', knit-in-public events, treasure hunts and many more ideas spring up because people want to add their creativity to the fabric of the city. These are what make a city what it should be.

You could collect hundreds of these ideas, and write a book on how people are bringing cities to life. My book *365 Ways to Change the World* provided for each day of the year a single big issue that needed addressing, from the environment to human rights and everything in between, plus some little actions that you could take that would make a difference in lots of fun and unexpected ways.[1]

What we need are planners who understand this and plan the city, not Le Corbusier-like with everything looking good on a drawing board, but as a canvas on which people can express themselves, meet and share with others, and animate their environment to make it human and enjoyable.

Michael Norton OBE is the honorary director and a trustee of the Centre for Innovation in Voluntary Action (CIVA). He is the founder of many innovative projects in the UK social enterprise sector, including the Directory of Social Change (1975), Changemakers (1994) and YouthBank UK (1998); and co-founder of UnLtd, supporting social entrepreneurs and recipient of the £100 million Millennium Legacy endowment. His books on fundraising and charitable status include *The WorldWide Fundraiser's Handbook* (2009), *Writing Better Fundraising Applications: A Practical Guide,* with Mike Eastwood (2010), and *The Complete Fundraising Handbook,* with Nina Botting Herbst (2012), all published by Directory of Social Change.

Edgar Pieterse
Participatory placemaking amidst slum urbanism

Urbanisation in Africa is distinctive. More than 60% of urban dwellers live in makeshift structures, which is twice the proportion of South Asia (35%), the other very poor region in the world. Furthermore, only 28% of the labour force is in stable employment, which denotes being a salaried employee or business owner. Unsurprisingly, informal economic activities contribute 55% to the GDP of Africa. Looking beyond settlement and economic patterns, most households rely on para-state systems of delivery in order to secure water, energy, waste collection and transport services. Informality is the predominant mode of urbanisation and social exchange across most sub-Saharan African cities.

For these systems of urban life to be interlocking and effective, they require vast social infrastructures of mutual support, collaboration, exchange, sharing and communication. In this sense, through sheer necessity most of everyday life in Africa is mediated by dense systems of collaborative placemaking. There is simply no other way of getting by or surviving. However, it would be a profound error to celebrate this situation or to project it as something innately positive. Africa remains mired in extreme levels of poverty. Narrow income-based indicators of poverty demonstrate that 70% of the population in sub-Saharan African eke out a living below $2 per day!

In conditions of such severe and widespread poverty, it can be expected that the informal systems of rule and service provision that dominate slum areas are predatory, exploitative and frequently laced with violence or the threat of it. In the vacuum left by the state, informalised organisations of provision and coordination emerge to establish under-regulated markets that ensure a measure of provision. However, this means that the unit costs for basic resources like water or energy are much higher than those paid by middle-class residents connected to the public grid operated by the state or the utilities. Since most households do not have a regular or sufficient cash income, people consume services in micro units and only when they can afford to. These same households are prone to become victims of predatory credit systems – loan sharks – that proliferate in popular neighbourhoods.

These patterns point to the imperative to fundamentally rethink the paradigm of urban development in Africa. However, a new approach must be realistic about the low levels of economic development, small tax base, limited state capability and scale of the need. Participatory placemaking is at the core of this new agenda. The overall approach is best described and understood as adaptive urbanism. At its core is a specific hierarchy of investments that should be pursued by developing states and ensured through active civil society mobilisation that combines advocacy and illustrative interventions to forge these alternatives in practice. The hierarchy is premised on the realisation of socio-economic rights, which suggests simultaneous investments in:

- Essential basic services such as water, sanitation and energy;
- Human development drivers: education and health care;
- Public infrastructure – especially affordable and safe public transport – to enhance livelihoods, security and mobility;
- Economic infrastructure calibrated to enhance the informal survival practices of slum dwellers especially, instead of huge 'smart city' projects designed to lure footloose international capital;
- Ecosystem restoration to enhance well-being and to create liveable neighbourhoods that are optimised for vibrant public life;
- Shelter improvements that should predominantly take the form of tenure security combined with incremental people-driven upgrading.

It is impossible to address these imperatives without planning and coordinating a variety of sectorial or discrete investments. Through the lens of participatory placemaking it is possible to envisage a variety of public pedagogies that can empower ordinary people to figure out how best they want to harness, sequence and balance public investments so that they can control and direct the transformation of their communities over time. In this process, they can also figure out how to connect the emerging strategies that have grown organically with more systematic public sector-driven processes, but this will require active dialogue and co-production. Participatory placemaking techniques also provide the ideal technologies for such processes of channelling adaptive urbanism.

For this to work it is important that the rich global learning about participatory placemaking showcased in this groundbreaking volume, *Recoded City*, informs the work of strategic intermediaries in African cities. These bodies are a layer of public-interest organisations that work with grassroots formations to instil literacy in terms of spatial design and relating budgeting without imposing external values or priorities on these groups. Strategic intermediaries can also move between the interests, perspectives and logics of the state and grassroots organisations, fulfilling a vital translation service. One of the critical priorities over the next decade is to nurture and grow this underdeveloped sector in African cities.

Professor Edgar Pieterse is holder of the South African Research Chair in Urban Policy and founding director of the African Centre for Cities (ACC) at the University of Cape Town. He is currently leading a team of experts working on an Urban Development Framework for South Africa. Pieterse is co-editor with Ntone Edjabe of *Cityscapes*, the international biannual magazine on emerging urbanism in the global South. His books include *Africa's Urban Revolution* (ed. with Susan Purnell, Zed Books, 2014); *Rogue Urbanism: Emergent African Cities* (ed. with Abdoumaliq Simone, Jacana Media, 2013); *African Cities Reader II: Mobilities & Fixtures* (ed. with Ntone Edjabe, Chimurenga Press and African Centre for Cities, 2011).

Ute Weiland
Making the invisible visible

Cities – particularly megacities – have become too complex to be governed with a top-down approach. Accordingly, and more in line with one that is bottom-up, successful urban politics are nowadays largely based on temporary alliances, created for the solution of concrete challenges. Moreover, in the ever-expanding cities of our modern age it has become doubly important to foster and nurture urban grassroots projects that seek to improve the livelihood of the inhabitants of certain areas. Evidence indicates that such small schemes can serve as blueprints for other, far-reaching initiatives guided by influential public personas or entities that foster, expand or slightly alter the fundamental concepts of these grassroots projects in an effort to address the challenges of urban life in rapidly growing megacities.

It was this realisation that served as the impetus for the initiation in 2007 of the Deutsche Bank Urban Age Award which annually recognises exemplary, locally organised projects designed to improve people's quality of life as well as the urban environment. As such the award can be viewed as means to facilitating those grassroots projects that creatively seek to solve the problems with which a large share of our city dwelling global population is confronted on a daily basis. Thus the aim of the award is to make the 'invisible' visible.

Among the number of projects that have received this award over these years is one – Triratna Prerana Mandal (TPM), a community toilet in a slum in Mumbai, India – that underlines my key argument: projects that are initiated on a localised level by locals and for locals have the potential to improve the livelihood not only of those living in its immediate vicinity but also of those living at a greater distance – provided that a project can be used as a blueprint for a similar initiative in a different city but under similar circumstances. This is exactly what took place in the case of TPM.

The TPM community toilet project started out in the late 1990s in the Khotwadi informal settlement in Mumbai's Santacruz district. The essence of the project was the construction by a municipal corporation of public toilets that would then be maintained by a local community-body organisation. However, as far as TPM was concerned, this was only the first step. The project slowly evolved to include a computer lab on the first floor of the toilet complex, as well as a childcare centre. In addition, part of the facility now serves as a kitchen where women are employed to cook food under the government's mid-day meal scheme. It even helps the local government with waste management through waste collection, classification and composting. Moreover, as part of TPM a local building in the area now serves as meeting place for local women's self-help groups as well as a gathering point for gym and yoga classes. TPM thereby improved the local inhabitants' daily lives by means of initially providing clean and well-maintained sanitary facilities. The fact that those facilities subsequently morphed into a hub for the provision of a wide range of local community services only served to further improve the quality of urban life in that select neighbourhood. Additionally, it is striking that in an area that would normally be classified by most as a slum, the local community proved this ingenious and resourceful in setting up a project that improves the local environment to a substantial degree.

Furthermore, TPM in fact proved so successful that the influential architect, professor and chair of the Department of Urban Planning and Design at Harvard University, Rahul Mehrotra adopted TPM's concept as a blueprint and expanded on it for the purposes of altering a similar public sanitation initiative in another Mumbai slum, Saki Naka. Mehrotra approached those entities responsible for the construction and the maintenance of the facilities and encouraged a more aesthetically pleasing design, as this would contribute to improving the infrastructure of the neighbourhood. Subsequently, that project – similar to TPM – was evolved intentionally and became something akin to a community centre for the inhabitants of the slum.

It is my firm belief that in light of this evidence one can make a sufficiently strong case for the fact that grassroots projects – if executed properly and carefully – have the potential to fundamentally impact, alter and improve the quality of life not just in the neighbourhood they were instigated in but also in other environments – of course provided that they are recognised for their immense societal value and subsequently utilised as a blueprint for similar initiatives. Moreover, I staunchly believe that these grassroots projects have a vast and untapped potential. One only has to think of the impact that jumpstarting similar developments by initiatives such as the Deutsche Bank Urban Age Award, or individuals like Rahul Mehrotra, could have on urban life in other cities in Asia facing similar societal challenges as Mumbai. The possibilities are unlimited.

Ute Weiland has been the Deputy Director of the Alfred Herrhausen Society, Deutsche Bank's international forum, since 2007, and a member of the Executive Board of the Urban Age conference programme, jointly organised by the London School of Economics and the Alfred Herrhausen Society since 2004. With Marcos L Rosa (Stories, page 200), she is the editor of *Handmade Urbanism: From Community Initiatives to Participatory Models*, Jovis, 2013. In 1997 she co-founded the Erich Pommer Institute for Media Law and Media Management at the University of Potsdam and was its deputy managing director until 2003.

Photo Credits

pp 20–21, 48–49, 66, 72–75, 80–81, 116, 138–39(b), 151, 154–55, 162, 166–67, 177, 198, 202, 206–07, 231, 251, 255, 268 © The Design Surgery.

pp 22–23 © FLC/ADAGP, Paris and DACS, London 2015.

p 24 © Photo by Fred W McDarrah/Getty Images.

p 25 © Sandra Hennigson.

pp 26–27 © Mihai-Bogdan Lazar/Shutterstock.com.

pp 27, 282–83, 284(t), 285 © Workshop.

pp 28–29 © dabidy/Shutterstock.com.

pp 32–33, 115, 117 © aaa.

p 35 © Photo by Lidove noviny/Ondrej Nemec/isifa/Getty Images.

p 37 © Photo By RDImages/Epics/Getty Images.

pp 38–39 © Jana Chiellino.

pp 40–41, 278(t), 279(t), 280–81 Courtesy of Wikihouse Foundation. Creative Commons Attribution 4.0 International Licence: https://creativecommons.org/licenses/by/4.0/.

pp 42, 99 © Photographs by Ruth Ben-Tovim, Encounters Arts.

pp 44–45 © Photo by Quinn Comendant. Creative Commons Attribution-ShareAlike 2.0 Generic: https://creativecommons.org/licenses/by-sa/2.0/.

p 47 © Photo by Sean Mathis/WireImage/Getty Images.

pp 50–51 © Photos by Michael Kirkham Photography.

pp 52–53 © AP Photo/Pablo Martinez Monsivais.

pp 56–57, 266(t), 266–67(b), 269 © Photograph by Daniel Schwartz/U-TT at ETH 2013.

p 59 © jejim/Shutterstock.com.

p 60 © Getty Images.

p 61 © Kevin Scott.

pp 62–63 © Photograph by Daniel Schwartz/U-TT at ETH 2012.

pp 64–65 © Dona_Bozzi/Shutterstock.com.

p 65 © Grant Smith.

pp 76–77, 129(t) © Per Morten Abrahamsen.

pp 78, 128, 128–29(b), 130(b), 131(b), 132–35 © Clear Village.

p 84 © Gemma Thorpe/Spacemakers.

p 87 © Spacemakers, photo Ash Finch.

p 89 Creative Commons Attribution-ShareAlike 2.0 Generic: https://creativecommons.org/licenses/by-sa/2.0/.

p 90 © coloursinmylife/Shutterstock.com.

p 91 © Daryl Lang/Shutterstock.com.

pp 92, 178–79 Courtesy of Herkes İçin Mimarlık (Architecture for All).

p 93 © EvrenKalinbacak/Shutterstock.com.

pp 94–96, 164–65 © Elemental.

p 98 © Camilo Calderon.

pp 100–01, 228–30 © PITCHAfrica.

p 102 © giulio napolitano/Shutterstock.com.

p 103 © ecosistema urbano, photo Santiago Carneri.

pp 108–09, 111, 112–13 © Nathaniel Corum.

pp 110(t), 110–11(b) © Architecture for Humanity.

pp 114-117 © aaa.

pp 118, 119(t) © Miguel Souto.

p 119(b), 121 © Caranerai Team, photos Cany Ash.

p 120 © Caravanserai Team, photo Robert Sakula/Ash Sakula.

p 122(b) © Kevin Noble.

pp 122(t), 123–27 © The Center for Urban Pedagogy.

pp 130–31(t), 316 © Thomas Ermacora.

pp 136–37, 138–39(b), 140–41 © Collectif Etc.

pp 142–47 © urbam EAFIT, photos Luigi Baquero 2014.

pp 148–50 © Teddy Cruz.

pp 152–52 © Collective Heritage Institute/Bioneers.

pp 156–59 © Travis Watson/Dudley Street Neighborhood Initiative.

p 160 © ecosistema urbano, photo Christoffer Horsfjord Nilsen.

p 161(t) © ecosistema urbano, photos Christoffer Horsfjord Nilsen and Emilio P Doiztua.

pp 161(b), 163 © Emilio P Doiztua.

pp 168–69, 170(t), 171(t) © Courtesy of Friends of the High Line.

pp 170–71(b), 172–73 © Rowa Lee, courtesy of Friends of the High Line.

p 173 © Photo by Dimitrios Kambouris/Getty Images for Coach.

p 174(b) © Gap Filler.

pp 174–75 © BeckerFraserPhotos.

p 175(t) © Tim Church.

p 176(t) © Gap Filler, photo Trent Hiles.

p 176(b) © Fairfax NZ/The Press.

pp 180(t), 181(b) Courtesy of the construction team.

pp 180–81 Courtesy of PMK/Bauerndick.

p 182(b) © Ian Lockwood PE, Toole Design Group.

pp 182–83, 188(t), 188–89(b), 208–09, 210–11(t) © Iwan Baan.

pp 184–85 © Toyo Ito & Associates, Architects.

p 186(b) © Kai Nakamura.

pp 186–87(t), 187(b) © Klein Dytham architecture.

pp 189(t) © Kéré Architecture.

p 190(l) © Kére Architecture, photos Erik Jan Ouwerkerk.

pp 190–91, 191(b) © Kéré Architecture, photos Siméon Duchoud.

pp 192–93, 194–95(t&b) © Jhono Bennett.

p 195(t) © 1to1 – Agency of Engagement.

pp 196–97 © ORLI/IMixed Paper Design Collaborative.

p 199 © ORLI/Daniel Horn.

pp 200–01(t) © Marcos L Rosa and Kristine Stiphany.

pp 201(b) © Karyn Hochleitner, Marcos L. Rosa.

p 203 © Marcos L Rosa.

pp 204–05(t) © Marko&Placemakers.

p 205 © Francis Moss.

p 210(b) © MASS Design Group.

pp 212–14 © MIT Senseable City Lab.

p 215 © MIT Senseable City Lab senseable.mit.edu/copenhagenwheel/. Photo by Max Tomasinelli www.maxtomasinelli.com.

pp 216-17(t) © Making Space in Dalston design team: muf architecture art, J+L Gibbons, Objectif and Appleyards.

p 217(b), 218–19 © J & L Gibbons/Sarah Blee.

pp 220–23 © Neighborland, Inc with a Creative Commons CC BY-NC-SA 4.0 License.

pp 224–05, 227(b) © Partizaning.

pp 224–05(b) © Anna Peshkova.

pp 226–27(t) © Alex Melnikoff.

pp 232, 234–35(t) © Project for Public Spaces, Inc.

p 233 © Campus Martius Park.

p 235 © Photo Ara Howrani. Courtesy of Campus Martius Park.

pp 236–37 © Project H Design.

pp 238–41 © Rural Urban Framework: Joshua Bolchover and John Lin, The Department of Architecture, The University of Hong Kong.

pp 242–43, 244(l), 247 © SERA Architects.

pp 244–45(t), 245(b), 246 © SERA Architects, photos Timothy Smith.

pp 249–49 © LOWaste for Action.

p 250 © CO/Auletta.

p 252(l) © Soundings, photo Oran Blackwood.

pp 252–53(t) © Image by Visualisation One.

pp 253(b), 254(r) © Soundings, photo John McGovern.

p 254(l) © Soundings.

pp 256–58, 259(b) © La 27e Région - programme Transfo Bourgogne.

p 259(t) © La 27e Région - programme Transfo PACA.

pp 260–61 © Studio Mumbai Architects.

pp 262–63, 264(l), 264–65(t) © TYIN tegnestue Architects.

pp 264–65(b) © TYIN tegnestue Architects, photo Andreas Skeide.

p 267(t) © Photograph by Mirko Gatti/U-TT at ETH 2013.

pp 270, 272–73(t) © urbz.net.

pp 271, 272(b) © urbz.net, photos by Florence Moreau.

pp 274, 275(t), 277 © Photos/Images by VPSN/Zanny Venner.

p 275(b) © Photo/Image by VPSN/Space2Place.

p 276 © Gian-Paolo Mendoza.

pp 278–81WikiHouse Foundation. Creative Commons Attribution 4.0 International Licence: https://creativecommons.org/licenses/by/4.0/.

p 284(b) © Workshop, photo by Nerren Homeres; pp 286–87, 288(r), 289 © WXY architecture + urban design; p 288(l) © Albert Vecerka/ESTO

p 316 © Jana Chiellino

p 317 © David Vintiner

Endnotes

Preface

1 Pimbert, M, *Towards Food Sovereignty: Reclaiming Autonomous Food Systems*, International Institute for Environment and Development, London, 2009.

Introduction

[1] 'Natural capital' is defined by the Natural Capital Committee, an independent advisory body set up in 2012 to advise the UK government, as 'the elements of nature that produce value (directly and indirectly) to people, such as the stock of forests, rivers, land, minerals and oceans. It includes the living aspects of nature (such as fish stocks) as well as the non-living aspects (such as minerals and energy resources)'. It 'underpins all other types of capital... and is the foundation on which our economy, society and prosperity is built', www.gov.uk. That relationship was affirmed by Hawken, P, Lovins, H and Hunter, L, in *Natural Capitalism: Creating the Next Industrial Revolution*, Back Bay Books, 2000. The term was first used by by EF Schumacher in his book *Small is Beautiful: A Study of Economics as if People Mattered*, Harper & Row, 1973.

[2] Piketty, T, *Capital in the Twenty-first Century*, The Belknap Press of Harvard University Press, 2014.

[3] Robert F Kennedy, University of Kansas, 18 March 1968, transcript from recording, John F Kennedy Presidential Library and Museum, http://www.jfklibrary.org, accessed 12 May 2013. The term Gross National Happiness (GNH) was coined by Bhutan's fourth Dragon King, Jigme Singye Wanchuck in 1972. GNH consists of fair socio-economic development, conservation and promotion of a vibrant culture, environmental protection and good governance, GNH Centre, www.gnhbhutan.org

[4] Florida, R, *The Rise of the Creative Class: And How It's Transforming Work, Leisure, Community and Everyday Life*, Basic Books, 2002; its updated version *Revisited*, Basic Books, 2014; Landry, C and Bianchini, F, *The Creative City*, Demos, 1995; Landry, C, *The Creative City: A Toolkit for Urban Innovators*, Routledge, 2008.

[5] McGuirk, J, *Radical Cities: Across Latin America in Search of a New Architecture*, Verso Books, 2014. *Uneven Growth: Tactical Urbanisms for Expanding Megacities, exhibition, Museum of Modern Art*, New York (MoMA), 22 November 2014-25 May 2015, and book, Gadanho, P, with essays by Burdett, R, Cruz, T, Harvey, D, Sassen, S and Tehrani, N, MoMA, 2014.

[6] Bullivant, L, *Masterplanning Futures*, Routledge, 2012; Bullivant, L (ed.), *4dsocial: Interactive Design Environments*, AD, July/August 2007, John Wiley & Sons, 2007.

[7] Banham, R, *The Age of the Masters: A Personal View of Modern Architecture*, Architectural Press, 1962.

[8] Jacobs, J, *The Death and Life of Great American Cities*, Jonathan Cape, 1961.

[9] Neil Gershenfeld, 'The State of Fab Labs', keynote, Fab10: From Fab Labs to Fab Cities, Disseny Hub Barcelona, 7 July 2014.

[10] Callon, M, Lascoumes, P and Barthe, Y, *Acting in an Uncertain World: An Essay on Technical Democracy*, MIT Press, 2011.

Chapters

The rise of bottom-up placemaking

[1] Virgil, *Aeneid*, revised edition, trans. David West, Penguin Classics, 2003.

[2] Ulrich, W, 'Reflections on Reflective Practice' (5/7), *Practical Reason and Rational Ethics: Kant*, March-April 2009, wulrich.com/bimonthly_march2009, accessed 30 August 2014.

[3] Smith, A, *An Inquiry of the Nature and Causes of the Wealth of Nations*, Book II: *Of the Nature, Accumulation and Employment of Stock*, chapter 1, Methuen & Co, 1904.

[4] Porritt, J, *Capitalism as if the World Matters*, Routledge, 2007.

[5] Sandercock, L, *Towards Cosmopolis: Planning for Multicultural Cities*, John Wiley & Sons, 1997.

[6] Quoted in 'Out of the Ashes: A New Look at Germany's Postwar Reconstruction', Leick, R, Schreiber, M and Stoldt, H-U, Spiegel Online, Spiegel.de, accessed 18 August 2014.

[7] 'Root shock' is a term coined by Dr Mindy Fullilove, author of *Root Shock: How Tearing up City Neighborhoods Hurts America, and What We Can Do about It*, One World, 2004.

[8] Banham, R, *Age of the Masters: A Personal View of Modern Architecture*, Architectural Press, 1962.

[9] Perlman, J, *The Myth of Marginality: Urban Poverty and Politics in Rio de Janeiro*, University of California Press, 1980.

[10] Platt, H, *Building the Urban Environment: Visions of the Organic City in the United States, Europe, and Latin America*, Temple University Press, 2015.

[11] McLuhan, M and Fiore, Q, *The Medium is the Message: An Inventory of Effects*, Penguin Books, 1967.

[12] Chomsky, N and Herman, ES, *Manufacturing Consent: The Political Economy of the Mass Media*, Vintage, 1988.

[13] Jacobs, J, *The Death and Life of Great American Cities*, Jonathan Cape, 1961.

[14] Davidoff, P, 'Advocacy and Pluralism in Planning', *Journal of the American Institute of Planners*, 1965.

[15] Ratti, C and Claudel, M, *Life in the Uber City*, Project Syndicate, 14 June 2014, project-syndicate.org, accessed 30 August 2014.

[16] Gehl, Jan, *Cities for People*, Island Press, 2010.

[17] Anderson-Oliver, M, *Cities for People: Jan Gehl*, Assemble Papers, 13 June 2013, assemblepapers.com.au, accessed 30 August 2014.

[18] Quoted from Lisa Scafuro's film *The Vision of Paolo Soleri: Prophet in the Desert* (2013).

[19] The 'Big Society' concept was originated by Steve Hilton, then director of strategy of the Conservative Party, in 2010.

[20] Richard Rogers, quoted in 'Cuts in council planning could "let developers command agenda"', Robert Booth, *The Guardian*, 26 March 2013, accessed 26 March 2013.

[21] The phrase 'build it and they will come' paraphrases both Noah's mandate in The Old Testament and a line of dialogue in the film *Field of Dreams* (1989).

Wiki culture

[1] Bauman, Z, 'The Demons of an Open Society', lecture, LSE, London, Ralph Miliband programme, 20 October 2005. All subsequent unreferenced quotations of Bauman are from the same source.

[2] Wolf, N, 'Ten Steps to Close Down an Open Society', in *The End of America: A letter of Warning to a Young Patriot*, Chelsea Green Publishing, 2007.

Endnotes

[3] The wiki is named after the Hawaiian word *wiki*, meaning 'quick', and was added to the Oxford English Dictionary in 2007.

[4] The Internet of Things: the extension and interconnectivity of the Internet with smart, embedded devices and machines, in rapid development due to the growth in analytics and cloud computing, enabling data to be dynamically generated, analysed and communicated in a semantic web. The Internet of Things is advancing the rise in automation, with advanced applications such as smart grids for smart cities such as Songdu, South Korea, and many other forms of environmental monitoring and infrastructure and energy management.

[5] Wikipedia entry on itself, en.wikipedia.org, accessed 8 December 2014.

[6] Hine, D and Kahn-Harris, K, *Despatches from the Invisible Revolution: New Public Thinking, Reflections on 2011*, #1, Pedia Press, 2012.

[7] Charny, D, *Power of Making: the Case for Making and Skills*, V&A Publishing, 2011.

[8] Pathos is a communication technique used most often in rhetoric (where it is considered one of the three modes of persuasion, alongside ethos and logos), and in literature, film and other narrative art. Emotional appeal can be accomplished in a multitude of ways.

[9] Fab International, http://wiki.fablab.is/wiki/Portal:Labs; en.wikipedia.org/wiki/Hackerspace.

[10] Joi Ito, '9 Principles of the Media Lab', lecture, 'The Open Internet...and Everything After', 2014 MIT-Knight Civic Media Conference, 22-24 June 2014. Subsequent unreferenced quotations of Ito are from the same source.

[11] Castells, M, *The Rise of the Network Society: Economy, Society and Culture*, volume 1, Wiley-Blackwell, 2009, 2nd edition.

[12] Castells, M, 'Networks of Outrage and Hope', lecture, Royal Society of Arts, London, 20 March 2013.

[13] Upcycling: optimising the materials, ingredients and processes of architecture in such a way that waste is converted to raw materials for nature or some other industry.

[14] Rifkin, J, *The Zero Marginal Cost Society: The Internet of Things, the Collaborative Commons, and the Eclipse of Capitalism*, Palgrave Macmillan, 2014.

[15] Bauwens, M, P2P Foundation, Mission and Objectives, 29 November 2005, p2pfoundation.net, accessed 16 December 2014.

[16] Gansky, S, *The Mesh: The Future of Business is Sharing*, Portfolio, 2012.

[17] Godin, S, *Tribes: We Need You to Lead Us*, Piatkus, 2008.

Fast forward now

[1] Moore's law was named after Gordon E Moore, co-founder of the Intel Corporation.

[2] The Singularity University was founded in 2008 by Dr Peter Diamandis and Dr Ray Kurzweil.

[3] See Edwards, S A, *The Nanotech Pioneers: Where Are They Taking Us?*, Wiley, 2008.

[4] Kurzweil, R, *The Singularity Is Near: When Humans Transcend Biology*, Penguin, 2006.

[5] *Ibid.*

[6] Crowdfunding Industry Report, crowdsourcing.org, May 2012, accessed 1 June 2012.

[7] Chris Gourlay, Spacehive media statement, 7 November 2014.

[8] Chris Gourlay, interviewed by Lucy Bullivant, 15 April 2013.

[9] Rifkin, J, 'Capitalism is making way for the age of free', *The Guardian*, 31 March 2014, theguardian.com, accessed 31 March 2014.

[10] Rifkin, J, *The Zero Marginal Cost Society: The Internet of Things, the Collaborative Commons, and the Eclipse of Capitalism*, Palgrave Macmillan, 2014.

[11] Jenkins, H, *Convergence Culture: Where Old and New Media Collide*, New York University Press, 2008. See also Jenkins, H, with Purishotma, R, Weigel, M, Clinton, K and Robison, A J, *Confronting the Challenging of Participatory Culture: Media Education for the 21st Century*, MIT Press, 2009.

Reframing placemaking

[1] Bauman, I, *Retrofitting Neighbourhoods*, RIBA Publishing, September 2015.

[2] IPCC: Intergovernmental Panel on Climate Change.

[3] *Climate Indicator Bulletin*, World Meteorological Organisation (WMO), Regional Climate Centre – Network for Europe, reported by the WMO, 17 December 2014, wmo.int, accessed 17 December 2014.

[4] participatorybudgeting.org

[5] budgetparticipatif.paris.fr/

[6] Callon, M, Lascoumes, P and Barthe, Y, *Acting in an Uncertain World: An Essay on Technical Democracy*, MIT Press, 2011.

[7] Richard Rogers, speaking at 'Designing liveable cities', a Guardian Cities event, 9 December 2014, Arup, London, quoted by Oliver Wainwright in '50 Years of Gentrification: will all our cities turn into "deathly" Canberra?', *The Guardian*, 12 December 2014, theguardian.com, accessed 12 December 2014.

[8] Sennett, R, *Together: The Rituals, Pleasures, and Politics of Cooperation*, Yale University Press, 2012.

[9] Sennett, R, *Corrosion of Character: the Consequences of Work in the New Capitalism*, WW Norton, 1999.

[10] Sennett, R, Open City lecture, Harvard Graduate School of Design, 19 September 2013, richardsennett.com, accessed 1 October 2013.

[11] Refugee camps, which appeared with the fall of the Ottoman Empire in the 1920s, have had a nebulous status, being neither informal nor formal, but temporary. They are now apparently being replaced, in the Middle East, Asia and Africa, by the 'solution' of spontaneous camps.

[12] UNISDR, 130th Assembly of the Inter-Parliamentary Union, Geneva, 19 March 2014, unisdr.org.

[13] Rebuild by Design is sponsored by the US Department of Housing and Urban Development; the Rethink Relief workshops are organised by D-Lab, Massachusetts Institute of Technology and the Faculty of Industrial Design Engineering, TU Delft, the Netherlands.

[14] Charlesworth, E, *Humanitarian Architecture: 15 Stories of Architects Working After Disaster*, Routledge, 2014.

[15] Design4Disaster was founded by the firms Econcept and Ecosense.

[16] Sorensen, A, 'Towards Liveable Communities in Japan', *Japan Focus*, 31 January 2008, and Sorensen, A and Funck, C, *Living Cities in Japan: Citizens' Movements, Machizukuri and Local Environments*, Nissan Institute/Routledge Japanese Studies Series, Routledge, 2007.

[17] Solnit, R, 'Why Imperfect Occupy Still Had Lasting Effects', Introduction to Schneider, N, *Thank You, Anarchy: Notes from the Occupy Apocalypse*, University of California Press, 2013, and published in TomDispatch, 16 September 2013, http://www.tomdispatch.com, accessed 18 September 2013.

[18] Relational Urbanism, relationalurbanism.com, accessed 2 January 2012.

[19] Hennig, B D, *Rediscovering the World: Map Transformations of Human and Physical Space*, Springer Verlag, 2013.

[20] Marco Lampugnani, quoted in documentation made available to the authors by Marco Lampugnani of snark, February 2014.

Recoding: the art of participatory placemaking

[1] Gehl, J, *Cities for People*, Island Press, 2010.

[2] Nye, J S, *Soft Power: The Means to Success in World Politics*, Public Affairs, US, 2005.

[3] Gladwell, M, *Outliers: The Story of Success*, Back Bay Books, 2011.

[4] Paul Stamets, 'Solutions from the Underground: How Mushrooms Can Help Save the World', Bioneers conference plenary lecture, 2011.

[5] 'Slime design mimics Tokyo's rail system: efficient methods of a slime mold could inform human engineers', *Science Daily*, 22 January 2010, sciencedaily.com, accessed 20 February 2014.

[6] Benjamin, W, 'The Storyteller', in *Illuminations: Essays and Reflections*, Schocken, 1969.

[7] Makerhood, makerhood.com.

[8] Robert F Kennedy, University of Kansas, 18 March 1968, transcript from recording, John F Kennedy Presidential Library and Museum, jfklibrary.org, accessed 12 May 2013.

[9] *The Analects of Confucius* (part 13), china.usc.edu/confucius-analects-13.

Open society, inequality and the post-individualist spirit

[1] 'Redlining' is a term deriving from John McKnight, an American sociologist and community activist in the late 1960s, referring to the marking of a red line on a map to delineate the area where banks would not invest. More recently it has been applied to discriminatory 'redlining' practices against groups of people on the basis of race and gender. These either deny locals home and business loans, insurance, health care and other essentials, or offer them solely at exorbitant rates.

[2] In Italy, for example, the Gini coefficient, 'the most common measure of economic inequality, has returned to the same levels of the 1970s. In 2012 it averaged out at 34.9 per cent, a level as high as in 1979.' Quoted in '"An injury to all': the class struggle is back in Italy', Alfredo Mazzamauro, *ROAR*, 24 November 2014, www.roar.org, accessed 24 November 2014.

[3] Ban Ki-Moon, UN Secretary General, opening the UN's General Assembly debate, 25 September 2014.

[4] Solnit, R, 'Why Imperfect Occupy Still Had Lasting Effects', Introduction to Schneidler, N, *Thank You, Anarchy: Notes from the Occupy Apocalypse*, University of California Press, 2013, and published in TomDispatch, 16 September 2013, tomdispatch.com, accessed 18 September 2013.

[5] Acemoglu, D, 'Development Won't Ensure Democracy in Turkey', *New York Times*, nytimes.com, 5 June 2013, accessed 6 June 2013.

[6] Callon, M, Lascoumes, P and Barthe, Y, *Acting in an Uncertain World: An Essay on Technical Democracy*, MIT Press, 2011.

Futures

[1] LSE Cities, 'Innovation in Europe's Cities: Bloomberg Philanthropies' 2014 Mayors Challenge', a report, LSE Cities, 2015.

[2] Global Health Observatory (GHO) data, 2014, quoted by the World Health Organisation, who.int, accessed 14 November 2014.

[3] UN-Habitat, State of the World's Cities Report, 2012/13, *Prosperity of Cities*, Routledge, 2013.

[4] UN World Economic and Social Survey 2013, un.org, accessed 14 November 2014.

[5] Calderon, C, *Politicising Participation: Towards a New Theoretical Approach to Participation In the Planning and Design of Public Spaces*, Faculty of Natural Resources and Agricultural Sciences, Department of Urban and Rural Development, Swedish University of Agricultural Sciences, Uppsala, 2013.

[6] Virilio, P and Depardon, R (eds), *Native Land: Stop Eject*, Actes Sud, 2009.

[7] Mehaffy, M and Salingaros, N A, *Design for a Living Planet: Settlement, Science and the Human Future*, Sustasis Foundation, 2015. Salingaros was quoted in Mehaffy, M, 'Networks of Tradition', *Traditional Building*, October 2012, traditional-building.com, accessed 19 February 2015.

[8] Professor David Orr, 'Resilience in a Black Swan World', lecture, Bioneers Chicago conference, Roosevelt University, Chicago, 1 November 2013, frequency.com, accessed 2 January 2014.

[9] Kunstler, J H, *The Geography of Nowhere: the Rise and Decline of America's Man-Made Landscape*, Touchstone, 1993.

[10] Hawken, P, *Blessed Unrest: How the Largest Social Movement in History is Restoring Grace, Justice and Beauty to the World*, Penguin Books, 2008.

[11] Paul Hawken, 'Blessed Unrest', lecture, Bioneers conference, 2006, www.blessedunrest.com, accessed 2 May 2013.

[12] Paul Hawken, quoted in 'First Look: environmental entrepreneur Paul Hawken's long-awaited book', Marc Gunther, *The Guardian*, 22 October 2014, theguardian.com, accessed 22 October 2014.

[13] The word 'Anthropocene' was coined in the 1980s by ecologist Eugene F Stoermer and Nobel Prize-winning chemist Paul Crutzen to describe the current era in which humans have caused mass extinctions of plant and animal species, polluted the oceans and the earth's atmosphere. While environmentalists and geologists do not agree on the most suitable term for the contemporary era, the anthropo ('man')-'cene' (new) age arguably began with the Industrial Revolution in the early 1800s or the atomic age in the 1950s.

[14] From a statement issued on 12 May 2014 following the Vatican's Pontifical Academies of Science and Social Science (PASS) Joint PAS/PASS Workshop on Sustainable Humanity, Sustainable Nature: Our Responsibility, Rome, 2-6 May 2014.

[15] Bonaiuti, M, *The Great Transition*, Routledge Studies in Ecological Economics, 2014.

[16] Wainwright, O, 'The truth about property developers: how they are exploiting planning authorities and ruining our cities', *The Guardian*, 17 September 2014, theguardian.com, accessed 17 September 2014.

[17] Calderon, *Politicising Participation*.

[18] appropedia.org.

[19] Rory Sutherland, 'Life Lessons from an Ad Man', TED talk, July 2009, ted.com/talks

[20] Naughton, J, '2014: the year the internet finally came of age', *The Observer*, 28 December 2014, observer.theguardian.com, accessed 28 December 2014.

[21] Jeffrey Sachs at the Vatican's Pontifical Academies of Science and Social Science (PASS) Joint PAS/PASS Workshop on Sustainable Humanity, Sustainable Nature: Our Responsibility, Rome, 2-6 May 2014.

Stories

Architecture for Humanity

[1] Nathaniel Corum, interviewed by Lucy Bullivant, 28 April 2013. All subsequent unreferenced quotations are from the same source.

[3] Acupuncture, or the concept of punctually applied urban design, as applied by architect and urban planner Manuel de Sola Morales. It was developed further by Casagrande, M and Lerner, J in *Urban Acupuncture: Celebrating Pinpricks of Change that Enrich City Life*, Island Press, 2014.

[3] LEED stands for Leadership in Energy and Environmental Design, the green building certification programme of the US Green Building Council, usgbc.org.

[4] Corum, N, *Building a Straw Bale House*, Princeton Architectural Press, 2005.

atelier d'architecture autogérée

[1] Petcou, C and Petrescu, D, 'R-Urban: Resilient Agencies, Short Circuits, and Civic Practices in Metropolitan Suburbs', *Harvard Design Magazine*, no.37, 'Urbanism's Core', Harvard University Graduate School of Design, Winter 2014. All subsequent quotations are from the same source.

Canning Town Caravanserai

[1] Cany Ash, interviewed by Lucy Bullivant, 25 August 2014. All subsequent unreferenced quotations are from the same source.

[2] From material supplied to Lucy Bullivant by Cany Ash of Ash Sakula.

[3]Valerie Segree, interviewed by Lucy Bullivant, 25 August 2014.

[4]The term 'third space' was coined by the urban sociologist Ray Oldenburg; see *The Great Good Space*, 3rd edition, Marlowe & Co, 1999.

Center for Urban Pedagogy

[1]Christine Gaspar, interviewed by Lucy Bullivant and Thomas Ermacora, 3 May 2013. All subsequent quotations are from the same source unless otherwise specified.

[2]Christine Gaspar, 'Engaging Design', lecture at Taubman College of Architecture + Urban Planning, University of Michigan, 4 February 2013.

[3]*Ibid.*

[4]*Ibid.*

[5]'Redistricting' is the American term for adjusting districts boundaries in the USA in a way that determines elected legislators. See: redistricting.lls.edu/what.php

Clear Village

[1]Thomas Ermacora, interviewed by Lucy Bullivant, various dates, 2013-14. All subsequent quotations are from the same source unless otherwise stated.

[2]Ermacora quoted in 'The only way is Essex: the community breathing new life into a disused country estate', Laura Sevier, *The Ecologist*, 11 November 2011, theecologist.org, accessed 13 February 2013.

[3]Quoted from feedback documentation compiled by Clear Village.

[4]Ibid.

Collectif Etc

[1]Victor Mahé, interviewed by Thomas Ermacora and Lucy Bullivant, December 2012, and by Lucy Bullivant, January 2013. All subsequent unreferenced quotations are from the same source.

[2]Interview with Victor Mahé, Nathan John, November 2012, spacehacking//citytactics blog, accessed 1 December 2012.

Alejandro Echeverri, Sergio Fajardo, Municipio de Medellín

[1]'Transforming Medellín and Antioquia through Social Urbanism and Education', lecture by Sergio Fajardo, Embassy of Colombia to the UK, July 2013, wn.com, accessed 4 September 2013.

[2]Fajardo, quoted by Alejandro Echeverri, presentation, Urban Age South America: securing an Urban Future, São Paulo, 2008.

[3]Fajardo, speaking in a film about Medellín, winner of the Grand Prize for Transformative Public Works, Curry Stone Design Awards, Curry Stone Foundation, 2009.

[4]Alejandro Echeverri, speaking in a film about Medellín, as above.

[5]Fajardo, speaking in a film about Medellín, as above.

[6]Medellín lecture by Alejandro Echeverri, 'Urban Colloquium II: Inescapable Ecologies', Parsons, the New School for Design, 14 February 2013.

[7]*Ibid.*

[8]UN-Habitat, Urban Equity in Development – Cities for Life, concept paper produced for the 7th World Urban Forum, Medellín, 5-11 April 2014.

[9]*Ibid.*

[10] Fajardo, in a film about Medellín, as above.

[11] Interview with Sergio Fajardo by Harley Shaiker, Chair, Center for Latin American Studies (CLAS), UC Berkeley, April 2014, wn.com, accessed 2 February 2013.

Estudio Teddy Cruz

[1]Cruz, T, 'The Political Equator: Conversations on Co-Existence: Border-Drain-Crossing', unpublished text, 2014. All subsequent quotations are from the same source.

Dreaming New Mexico

[1]Peter Warshall, 'Dreaming New Mexico: An Age of Local Foods and a Fair Trade State', lecture at the Bioneers Conference, 15 October 2010, San Rafael, California, media.bioneers.org, accessed 3 February 2014. Warshall died in April 2013.

[2]*Ibid.*

[3]Peter Warshall, interviewed by Kenny Ausubel, Bioneers Conference, 15 October 2010, San Rafael, California, media.bioneers.org, accessed 3 February 2014.

[4]*Ibid*, and all subsequent quotations.

Dudley Street Neighborhood Initiative

[1]*Holding Ground: The Rebirth of Dudley Street*, directed by Leah Mahan and Mark Lipman, New Day Films, 2006.

[2]Sklar, H, 'Sustainable Happiness', *YES! Magazine*, Winter 2009, yesmagazine.org, accessed 13 March 2013. Sklar, H and Medoff, P, *Streets of Hope: The Fall and Rise of an Urban Neighborhood*, South End Press, 1994.

[3]DSNI, 'Declaration of Community Rights', 1993, www.dsni.org, accessed 14 September 2014.

[4]Quoted by Sklar, H, 'Sustainable Happiness', *YES! Magazine*, Winter 2009, www.yesmagazine.org, accessed 13 March 2013.

[5]Sheena Collier, Dudley Street Neighborhood Initiative, TV programme, BNN News, 1 August 2012.

[6]DSNI's Facebook page, 22 January 2015.

[7]*Gaining Ground: Building Community on Dudley Street*, directed by Llewellyn Smith, Holding Ground Productions, 2014.

[8]'Common Ground', TV programme, 8 October 2014, Suffolk County Sheriff's Department.

Ecosistema Urbano

[1]Tato, B and Vallejo, J.L. (Ecosistema Urbano), 'Negotiating at all levels', *a+t*, a+t Architecture Publishers, 30, Vitoria-Gasteiz (Álava), 2011. All subsequent quotations from the pair are from the same source.

[2]exumadreams.org.

Elemental

[1]GDP = Gross domestic product.

[2]Alejandro Aravena of Elemental, speaking in the short film Elemental made about the project, *The Magnet and The Bomb – Calama PLUS*, 2012, elementalchile.cl. All subsequent quotations are from the same source.

Friends of the High Line

[1]Robert Hammond, interviewed by Lucy Bullivant and Thomas Ermacora, 4 May 2013. All subsequent unreferenced quotations are from the same source.

[2]Whyte, WH, *The Social Life of Small Urban Spaces*, Project for Public Spaces, 1980.

[3]David, J and Hammond, R, *High Line: The Inside Story of New York City's Park in the Sky*, Farrar Straus Giroux, 2011.

Gap Filler

[1]Reynolds, R, 'Performance and Temporality', paper presented at Performance Studies International (PSi) conference, Stanford University, 26-30 June 2013, published as 'Unexpected Urban Narratives', PSi, Stanford University, 2013.

[2]Reynolds, R, 'Performance Invitations', unpublished essay for Australasian Drama Studies, 2013.

[3]Reynolds, R, 'Performance and Temporality'.

[4]*Ibid.*

[5]*Ibid.*

[6]Reynolds, R, 'Performance Invitations'.

[7]Reynolds, R, 'Performance and Temporality'.

[8]Newman-Storen, R and Reynolds, R, 'Conversations over the Gap', *Performance Research: a journal of the performing arts*, 18(3), 2013.

[9]Email from Reneé Newman-Storen to Ryan Reynolds, 19 July 2012, provided to the authors by Reynolds.

[10] Email from Ryan Reynolds to Reneé Newman-Storen, 19 July 2012, provided to the authors by Reynolds.

[11] Email from Reneé Newman-Storen to Ryan Reynolds, 19 July 2012, provided to the authors by Reynolds.

[12] Newman-Storen, R and Reynolds, R, 'Conversations over the Gap'.

Herkes için Mimarlik

[1]Lefebvre, H, 'Le Droit à la ville', 1968, republished in English in *Writings on Cities*, translated and edited by Eleonore Kofman and Elizabeth Lebas, Wiley-Blackwell, 1995.

[2]Quoted in material supplied to the authors by HiM. All subsequent quotations are from the same source unless specified.

[3]Workshop participant, quoted by HiM in material supplied to the authors.

Anna Heringer

[1]Anna Heringer, quoted by Chilkoti, A, 'Mud World', *Financial Times*, 19 October 2012, ft.com, accessed 19 October 2012.

[2]Anna Heringer, quoted in 'Handmade architecture as a catalyst for development', video, UN-Habitat, 22 April 2014.

[3]Saffron, I, 'Dirt is Making a Comeback', Philly.com, 6 April 2012, articles.philly.com, accessed 13 May 2013.

[4]Anna Heringer, quoted in *MudWorks*, video by Maggie Janik, Harvard GSD, 5 July 2012.

[5]Anna Heringer, quoted in *Handmade Architecture as a Catalyst for Development*, video, UN-Habitat, 22 April 2014.

[6]*Ibid.*

[7]*Ibid.*

Home for All

[1]Quoted in unpublished Home for All promotional documentation supplied to the authors by Klein Dytham architecture (KDa), 2013.

[2]Toyo Ito, 'Architecture's Direction post-March 11', lecture, Japan Society, New York, 15 October 2012.

[3]NPO: non-profit organisation.

[4]Toyo Ito, 'Architecture's Direction post-March 11'.

[5]Home for All documentation provided to the authors by KDa, March 2014.

Kéré Architecture

[1]UNICEF statistics for Burkino Faso, 2007-2011, based on the international poverty line of US$1.25 per day, 18 December 2013, unicef.org.

[2]Francis Kéré, quoted in *Architecture Is a Wake-up Call*, video interview by Marc-Christoph Wagner, Louisiana Channel, Louisiana Museum of Modern Art, Copenhagen, 2014.

[3]Francis Kéré, Harvard Graduate School of Design, Dean's Diversity Lecture, 10 November 2011.

[4]Francis Kéré, quoted in *Architecture Is a Wake-up Call.*

[5]Francis Kéré, quoted in video for 'Sensing Spaces: Architecture Reimagined' exhibition, Royal Academy of Arts, directed by Candida Richardson, 2014.

[6]Francis Kéré, lecturing at Design Indaba, 2011. designindaba.com/profiles/francis-kéré.

1tol Agency of Engagement

[1]The total households who live in informal residential areas or in shacks not in a backyard = 1,660,380, 11% of all households, quoted in *South Africa: Informal settlements status 2013*, research report, Housing Development Agency, South Africa, 2013.

[2]Jhono Bennett, 'Critical engagement in South African Architecture as a Means Beyond Redevelopment', lecture as part of the panel, 'The role of alternative architecture education platforms', at the 3rd International Architectural Education Summit, ANCB The Metropolitan Laboratory, Berlin, 13-14 September 2013. ancb.de.

[3]*Ibid.*

[4]Bennett, J, *Platforms of Engagement: A Process of Critical Engagement Within a Development Context*, MArch (Prof) dissertation, Faculty of Engineering, Built Environment and Information Technology, University of Pretoria, Pretoria, South Africa, 2011.

Operation Resilient Long Island

[1]Taken from material provided on ORLI's activities to the authors by Daniel Horn, November 2013. All subsequent quotations are taken from the same source unless otherwise stated.

[2]ORLI, 3C – Comprehensive Coastal Communities Playbook, 2013.

Marcos L. Rosa

[1]World Urbanization Prospects, United Nations, 2014.

[2]Marcos L Rosa, in conversation with Lucy Bullivant during the Urban Age Conference, Rio de Janeiro, December 2013.

[3]'Handmade Urbanism', lecture by Marcos Rosa, Metropolis Nonformal – Anticipation. Launching the UN-Habitat Hub on Informal Urbanism, conference, 20-23 November 2013.

[4]Rosa, ML, *Microplanning: Urban Creative Practices*, Editora de Cultura, 2011.

[5]Rosa, M L and Weiland, U E (eds), *Handmade Urbanism: From Community Initiatives to Participatory Models*, Jovis, 2013. LSE Cities, the international centre at the London School of Economics, is co-organiser of the Urban Age series of conferences with the Alfred Herrhausen Society.

[6]Rosa, M L, panel discussion at 'LADA encounters', Laboratory of design and anthropology (LADA), ESDI (Superior School of Industrial Design), Rio de Janeiro, 31 October 2013. Organised by Zoy Anastassakis.

[7]Rosa, M L, 'Urban challenges: Projetos comunitários devem servir como norte para atuação do poder público', interviewed by Thalita Pires, *Rede Brasil Atual*, 9 April 2013, redebrasilatual.com.br/blogs.

[8]Lefebvre, H, discussed in *La Somme et le Reste*, La Nef de Paris Editions, 1959.

[9]Rosa, M L, 'Nós Brasil! We Brazil!' Weltstadt newspaper produced to accompany the German contribution to the Bienal de Arquitectura de São Paulo, 'Modos de Fazer, Modos de Usar' (Ways of Making, Ways of Using), 12 Oct-1 Dec 2013.

[10]Agência de Redes para a Juventude, agenciarj.org.

[11]Rosa, ML, quoted in Deutsche Bank Urban Age Award 2013 Rio, Alfred Herrhausen Society in association with LSE Cities, 2013, digital PDF, dbuaaward.com, accessed 1 June 2014.

[12]*Ibid.*

[13]*Ibid.*

Marko and Placemakers

[1]From material supplied by Marko and Placemakers to the authors.

[2]Project credits: Markoandplacemakers (FoRM Associates), AECOM, LDA Design and Peter Neal.

[3]Interview with Igor Marko published in *BOND* magazine, May 2012.

[4]Petra Havelska of Marko and Placemakers, interviewed by Lucy Bullivant, 5 May 2013 and 10 February 2015.

[5]Igor Marko, interviewed by Lucy Bullivant, 4 June 2014.

MASS Design Group

[1]Adjaye, D, *Adjaye Africa Architecture*, Thames & Hudson, 2011.

[2]Buchan, K, 'Rwanda Reborn: Kigali's culture, heart and soul', *The Guardian*, 11 April 2014, accessed 11 April 2014.

[3]Statistic quoted by Sharma, M, in 'Remaking Kigali: a 21st-century Rwanda built by Rwandans', Matador Network, 9 May 2012, accessed 15 July 2013.

[4]Quotation and subsequent quotations of MASS staff taken from MASS Design Group-directed Beyond the Building series of videos, available online, massdesigngroup.org.

[5]*Ibid.*

SENSEable City Laboratory, MIT

[1]Ratti, C and Claudel, M, 'Life in the Uber City', Project Syndicate [Online], 16 June 2014. project-syndicate.org/commentary, accessed 25 August 2014.

[2]Dietmar Offenhuber, interviewed by Lucy Bullivant, 9 June 2013. All subsequent unreferenced quotations are from the same source.

Endnotes

[3] Quoted in documentation provided to the authors by SENSEable City Lab, MIT, 2013.

[4] Trash Track press release, SENSEable City Lab, MIT, 2009.

Muf Architecture/Art, J&L Gibbons

[1] Florida, R, Matheson, Z, Adler, P and Brydges, T, *The Divided City and the Shape of the New Metropolis,* The Martin Prosperity Institute (MPI), Rotman School of Management, University of Toronto, September 2014.

[2] *A Profile of Hackney, its People and Place,* London Borough of Hackney Policy Team, September 2014.

[3] Hackney Co-operative Developments, website, hced.co.uk, 2015.

[4] Liza Fior, quoted in Bullivant, L, 'How are women changing our cities?', *The Guardian Cities,* 5 March 2015.

[5] *Ibid.*

[6] Stern, M J, Seifert, S C, *Cultivating 'Natural' Cultural Districts,* University of Pennsylvania, School of Social Policy and Practice, 2007.

[7] 'Dalston Scheme wins UK's Top Landscape Award', London Parks & Gardens Trust, 12 December 2011, londongardenstrust.org, accessed 15 January 2012.

[8] Johanna Gibbons, in *Creating Healthy Places: Dalston Eastern Curve Garden,* Landscape Institute film, 13 November 2013.

[9] Bill Parry-Davies of Open Dalston, quoted in 'Out with the Old? "Outdated" Kingsland Shopping Centre could be bulldozed to make way for towers', *Hackney Citizen,* 11 July 2013, hackneycitizen.co.uk, accessed 1 March 2015.

[10] Brian Cumming of GrowCookEat, quoted in 'Path through Dalston Eastern Curve Garden is not negotiable say developers', Syma Mohammed, *Hackney Gazette,* 26 February 2014.

[11] Liza Fior, quoted in Bullivant, L, 'How are women changing our cities?'.

Neighborland

[1] Candy Chang, interviewed in *Urbanized,* film by Gary Hustwit, 2011.

[2] *Ibid.*

[3] *Ibid.*

[4] Source: National Restaurant Association (USA), quoted by Gan, V, 'Cities can't ignore that Food Trucks have Grown Up', *Next City,* 25 August 2012, nextcity.org, accessed 3 September 2014.

[5] Quoted in *GOOD Ideas for New Orleans,* Neighborland, video, 2013.

[6] *Ibid.*

Partizaning

[1] Malhotra, S, 'Partizaning: participatory art, research and creative urban activism', *Urbanista,* issue 2, 2013, www.urbanista.org, accessed 12 July 2013. Quotations in the next three paragraphs are from the same source.

[2] Polsky, A, 'Sobyanin, Baby, C'mon!', eng. partizaning.org, 3 January 2013, accessed 5 January 2013.

[3] Shriya Malhotra and Igor Ponosof, interviewed by Lucy Bullivant, 21 November 2014. All subsequent quotations are from the same source.

PITCHAfrica

[1] Jane Harrison and David Turnbull, interviewed by Lucy Bullivant, 4 April 2013 and subsequent dates. All subsequent unreferenced quotations are from the same source.

[2] Statistics from PITCHAfrica, 2013.

[3] Actor-Network-Theory (ANT), a sociological theory about the social and the associative capacities of human 'actors' for 'making their own theories, contexts, frames, metaphysics, even their own ontologies', as unique events. It places emphasis on the actions of mediators, rather than on media or tools. Latour, B, *Reassembling the Social: An Introduction to Actor-Network-Theory,* Oxford University Press, 2005. ANT was first developed in the early 1980s by sociologists Michel Callon and Bruno Latour, and John Law, when Callon and Latour were members of staff at the Centre de Sociologie de l'Innovation (CSI), Ecole nationale supérieure des Mines de Paris.

Project for Public Spaces

[1] Ethan Kent, interviewed by Lucy Bullivant and Thomas Ermacora, 4 May 2013. All subsequent quotations of Ethan Kent are from the same source unless otherwise stated.

[2] Whyte, William H, *The Social Life of Small Urban Spaces,* Conservation Foundation, 1980. An accompanying, eponymous documentary supported by the Municipal Art Society, New York, was released in 1988.

[3] Ethan Kent, presentation, 'Future of Places' conference, Norra Latin, Stockholm, 24-26 June 2013.

[4] Quoted from documentation provided by PPS to the authors during the book's research process.

[5] Statistics included in 'The Rise and Fall of Detroit: A timeline', Peter Weber, *The Week,* 19 July 2013, www.week.com, accessed 23 January 2015.

[6] *Ibid.*

[7] 'What British cities can learn from Detroit: Motor City's turnaround should be a model for regeneration', Jonathan Brown, *The Independent,* 18 June 2014, independent.co.uk, accessed 19 June 2014.

[8] Quoted in 'Detroiters Work: The Lighter, Quicker, Cheaper Regeneration of a Great American City', Project for Public Spaces, 10 November 2013, pps.org, accessed 2 February 2014.

[9] *Ibid.*

[10] *Ibid.*

[11] 'Rapson: Detroit is on track for a positive future', *Detroit News,* 12 November 2014, detroitnews.com, accessed 2 February 2015.

[12] Placemaking Leadership Council, PPS website, pps.org.

[13] Quoted from documentation provided by PPS to the authors.

Project H Design

[1] Pilloton, E, *Design Revolution: 100 Products that Empower People,* Metropolis Books, 2009.

[2] Pilloton, E, 'Teaching Design for Change', TEDGlobal talk, Oxford, UK, July 2010, www.ted.com.

[3] *If You Build It,* directed by Patrick Creadon, ifyoubuilditmovie.com, 2013.

[4] Pilloton, E, *Tell Them I Built This: Transforming Schools, Communities and Lives with Design-Based Education* , TED e-Book, 2012.

[5] Pilloton, E, 'Teaching Design for Change'.

Rural Urban Framework

[1] Bolchover, J and Lin, J, *Rural Urban Framework: Transforming the Chinese Countryside,* Birkhäuser Verlag, 2014. All subsequent quotations are taken from the same source.

SERA Architects

[1] Smith, T, 'Civic Ecology: a Citizen-Driven Framework for Transforming Suburban Communities', paper given at the 50th International Making Cities Liveable Conference, Portland, Oregon, 26 June 2013. All subsequent quotations are from the same source unless otherwise stated.

[2] Glaeser, E, *Triumph of the City: How Our Greatest Invention Makes Us Richer, Smarter, Greener, Healthier, and Happier,* Penguin Press, 2011.

[3] Urban Land Institute, *Shifting Suburbs: Reinventing Infrastructure for Compact Development,* Urban Land Institute, 2012, uli.org, downloaded 2 March 2014.

[4] Seltzer, E, Smith, T, Cortright, J, Bassett, E M, Shandas, V, 'Making EcoDistricts', September 2010, serapdx.com, accessed 2 April 2014.

[5] Putnam, R D, Leonardi, R and Nanetti, R, *Making Democracy Work: Civic Traditions in Modern Italy,* Princeton University Press, 1994.

[6] Putnam, R D, *Bowling Alone: The Collapse and Revival of American Community,* Simon & Schuster, 2000.

[7] Barber, B, *Strong Democracy: Participatory Politics for a New Age,* University of California Press, 2003.

snark space making

[1] Quotation taken from documentation made available by Marco Lampugnani of snark to the authors, February 2014. All subsequent quotations are from the same source.

Soundings

[1] Quotation taken from material supplied by Christina Norton and Steve McAdam to the authors. All subsequent quotations are from the same source.

[2] PechaKucha is a simple public presentation format with 20 images, each shown for 20 seconds. It was devised by Astrid Klein and Mark Dytham, Klein Dytham architecture (see Home for All, page 184) for their club Superdeluxe, Tokyo, in February 2003, and they continue to organise and support the global PechaKucha Night network and to organise PechaKucha Night Tokyo.

Strategic Design Scenarios and La 27e Région

[1] François Jégou, quoted in Tiesinga, H, Berkhout, R, Jezierski, E, Harvey, J, Hansen, L, Takeuchi, M, Sinha, R, Moerbeek, K, Kieboom, M, Lochard, A, Marlin, M, *Labcraft: How Innovation Labs Cultivate Change Through Experimentation and Collaboration*, Labcraft Publishing, 2014.

[2] François Jégou, 'From the Design of Public Services to the Design of Public Policies', lecture, Parsons Desis Lab/The New School, 24 April 2012.

[3] Quoted in a film made by La 27e Région about its work, la27region.fr, accessed 2 March 2014.

[4] Jégou, F, Vincent, S, Thoresen, V, 'My College Tomorrow: Innovation Labs to Enable Collective Public Action on Education Environments', Enabling Responsible Living Conference, PERL, Istanbul, 2011.

[5] La 27e Région, Design des politiques publiques, la Documentation française, 2010.

[6] Jégou, F, Vincent, S, Thévenet, R and Lochard, A, 'Friendly hacking into the public sector: co-creating public policies within regional governments', Co-Create 2013 document, La 27e Region, la27region.fr, accessed 3 January 2013.

[7] Ibid.

[8] Jégou, F, Seyrig, A and Scholl, G, *Sustainable Street 2030: Corpus Toolkit for Collaborative Scenario Building*, Corpus Project/Institute for Ecological Economy Research (IOW), 2012, issuu.com.

Studio Mumbai

[1] Bullivant, L, *Architecture As a Community*, Domus digital edition, 30 November 2012, domusweb.it, accessed 14 November 2014. Bijoy Jain was speaking at a roundtable organised by the BSI Swiss Architectural Award 2012 (won by Studio Mumbai), Fondazione Querini Stampalia, Venice, 22 September 2012. All subsequent quotations are taken from the same source unless otherwise indicated.

[2] Quoted in documentation provided by Studio Mumbai.

[3] Serrazanetti, F and Schubert, M (eds), *Studio Mumbai: Inspiration and Process in Architecture*, Moleskine SpA, 2013.

TYIN tegnestue Architects

[1] This and all subsequent quoted statements taken from documentation made available by TYIN to the authors, November 2013.

[2] Thailand national census, 2010, Thai Ministry of Foreign Affairs, quoted in World Population Review, worldpopulationreview.com and Millennium Development Goals Indicators, United Nations, 2009, un.org.

Urban-Think Tank

[1] SDI South African Alliance, 'Annual Report 2012/2013: Upgrading Lives, Building the Nation', SDI South African Alliance, 2013.

[2] Bolnick, A, 'Transforming Minds and Setting Precedents: Blocking out at Ruimsig Informal Settlement', Slum Dwellers International (SDI), sdinet.org

[3] Brillembourg, A, Klumpner, H, 'From Casablanca to Cape Town: reimagining urban possibilities', *S.L.U.M. Lab Magazine*, ETH Zurich, February 2014.

[4] Brillembourg, A, Klumpner, H (eds), Kalagas, A (Guest Ed.), 'Made in Africa', *S.L.U.M. Lab Magazine*, ETH Zurich, February 2014. All subsequent quotations are taken from the same source.

[5] The total number of households who live in informal residential areas or in shacks not in a backyard = 1,660,380, 11% of all households, quoted in South Africa: Informal settlements status 2013, research report, Housing Development Agency, South Africa, 2013.

URBZ

[1] This and all subsequent quotations taken from documentation provided by URBZ to the authors, 2013-14.

Vancouver Public Space Network

[1] Kent, E, 'Place Capital: The Shared Wealth that Drives Thriving Communities', Project for Public Spaces (PPS), online article, ppp.org, accessed 12 September 2013.

[2] Pask, A, Vancouver Public Space Network, website, vancouverpublicspace.ca, accessed 3 December 2014.

[3] Stueck, W, 'A passion for planning Vancouver's public spaces', *Globe and Mail* (Vancouver), 30 December 2014.

[4] *Ibid.*

[5] Montgomery, C, *Happy City: Transforming Our Lives Through Urban Design*, Penguin, 2013.

[6] Quoted in *Upcycled Urbanism*, video by the Museum of Vancouver, 16 September 2013.

WikiHouse

[1] *Compendium for the Civic Economy: What Our Cities, Towns and Neighbourhoods Should Learn from 25 Trailblazers*, 00:/, Trancity*Valiz and Nesta, 2012.

[2] Alastair Parvin, interviewed by Lucy Bullivant, 26 September 2014. All subsequent unreferenced quotations of Parvin are from the same source.

[3] Francesco Anselmo, speaking at the 'Building on Open Source Design' event, Building Centre, London, 19 September 2014.

[4] Parvin, A, Saxby, D, Cerulli, C, Schneidler, T, *Right to Build: the next mass-house building industry*, University of Sheffield School of Architecture and Architecture 00:/, 2011, issuu.com/alastairparvin.

WORKSHOP architecture

[1] WORKSHOP, Project Hariharpur, Uttar Pradesh, India, 2013, issuu.com/aaschool/docs/13.11.05_project_hariharpur_book3; wrkshp.org/books.

[2] From information provided by WS to the authors. All other quotations are from the same source unless otherwise stated.

WXY Studio

[1] Adam Lubinsky, interviewed by Lucy Bullivant and Thomas Ermacora, 7 May 2013. All subsequent quotations are from the same source.

Voices

Michael Norton – Cities are for people

[1] Norton, M, *365 Ways to Change the World: How to Make a Difference One Day at a Time*, Free Press, 2007.

Acknowledgements

Looking out on the Venetian Lagoon while writing these last words before it all goes to print, and reflecting on the meaning of this mini odyssey, I dedicate this book to my little boy Arthur, because ultimately it is all about what we leave to the next generation. Arthur's curiosity, playful mind and storytelling talents will surely help him to navigate the exciting but complex future ahead. As it is possible that he may live to see mankind land life on Mars, converse with friendly cyborgs, or program nanobot colonies to rebuild our blue planet, I hope that his values and actions will keep the torch of humanism bright and that he pursues his dreams with grace. My thoughts are with my adored father, Roberto Ermacora, an inspiring, timeless and real man, who didn't always like the implications of the virtual world and departed prematurely thinking the world was becoming absurd. He gave me the sense of duty to challenge the often dominant techno-optimistic assumption that everything new is good.

My thanks go first to my beloved and brilliant wife, Princess Khaliya, who has sparred with me while seeing me work tirelessly to bring years of ideas and experiences into a concise format. Together we have many plans, including collaborating on radical innovation projects to leapfrog health care and education where it is the most needed, as a parallel road to the incrementalism implied in recoding... My thanks also go to my poetic and wise mother, Bente Skibsted, who gave me the aesthetic eye and creative gift, and who continues to believe in me and the importance of the missions I have set for myself.

It is obvious that without the intellectual tenacity and immense contribution of my co-author, Lucy Bullivant, it would have been a much longer and more strenuous journey to realise my project. Lucy truly has been instrumental in putting focus on delivering my ambition: to share a design philosophy that may scale up the impact of the efforts of pioneering peers to mend and balance cities.

I am grateful to have had the support and critique of esteemed colleagues and friends, such as Frank Van Hasselt and Paul Hughes. It has been a pleasure to collaborate with the Design Surgery, with whom I've co-directed the design of this book from cover to cover so as to help the visually minded to absorb some of the core concepts and key narrative elements in a flash. I also want to thank Marion Moisy and Caroline Ellerby's professionalism respectively to copy edit and assemble illustrations and caption data.

The list is always long when you want to thank everyone, and I cannot say how much it has meant to me that so many exceptional people have trusted Lucy and me to tell their story, and that many luminaries of our time have given us their written contributions and endorsements. I thank in particular John Thackara, Cameron Sinclair, William McDonough, Bjarke Ingels, Eva Franch i Gilbert, Edgar Pieterse, Michael Norton, Andy Lipkis, Josiah Mugambi, Ali Grehan and Ute Weiland.

I want to add a small list of close individuals, repeat collaborators, clients and encounters with notable figures who over the years have been part of shaping my choices and views: my brother Jens Martin Skibsted, Michael Nellemann, Jan Gehl, Imogen Heap, Alexandra Sauveplane, Simon Parkinson, Mireille Murat, Stephane Lelux, Yann Arthus Bertrand, Ed Burtinsky, Ken Yeang, Jean Marie Theodat, Ken Morse, Chris Anderson, Nathaniel Corum, Alex Haw, Indy Johar, Andy Groarke, Kevin Carmody, Shigeru Ban, Alex Steffen, Ginevra Elkann, Yves Behar, Ross Lovegrove, Richard Sennett, Andrew Zolli, Charles Melcher, Jonathan Robinson, Marcus Heal, Marc Fleury, Alexandre Delamarre, Ian Pont, Herve Quentel, Peter Clausen, Alex Fleetwood, Felix Bopp, Geoff Mulgan, Lucy McRae, Rachel Wingfield, Kigge Hvid, Tom Darden, Edwin Heathcote, Ilse Crawford, Colin Firth, Oliver Wainwright, David de Rothschild, Chris Gourlay, Tony Hsieh, Antoni Vives, Malcolm Smith, Niels-Peter Flint, Chris Luebkeman, Rachel Armstrong, Peter Rathje, Dougald Hine, Alastair Parvin, Marc Kushner, Ricky Burdett, Richard Branson and Al Gore.

Thomas Ermacora

'To you I am nothing more than a fox like a hundred thousand other foxes. But if you tame me, then we shall need each other. To me, you will be unique in all the world. To you, I shall be unique in all the world'
– Antoine de Saint-Exupéry, *The Little Prince*

I dedicate this book to the youngest members of the next generation of co-creators most personally significant to me: Edie and Lily Juniper, Aaron and Ben Bullivant-Norris, Charlotte Bullivant, Giacomo and Lulu Poletto-Pasquero. I hope that their courage, flair and nimble-mindedness, and knowing that 'if you touch one thing with deep awareness, you touch everything' (Thich Nhat Hanh), will bring them success in all their individual and collaborative endeavours. I thank my inspirational and tirelessly supportive parents: my father Dargan Bullivant, an always stimulating interlocutor on urban design and planning; my mother Patricia Bullivant, likewise, and for nurturing our mutual love of the natural world and keeping all my childhood drawings observing the world; and my dear siblings Helena, Victoria and Alexander, with whom I first practised the art of co-creating hideouts made out of recycled materials and furniture.

Thomas Ermacora, my co-author and creative sparring partner, for his motivation and ambition to initiate this unique book, his versatile *'explosante-fixe'*[1] approach to it, and appetite for the mountain-scaling efforts we made in combining our respective ideas and research.

A huge thanks for their generosity and insights to all the international practitioners we have featured (Stories), and who have contributed (Voices) and acted as endorsers of our book.

Marion Moisy for rigorous and meticulous copy editing; Caroline Ellerby for marshalling the book's picture research/rights programme with focus and energy; Design Surgery's Shane Mizon, Matthew Rowett, Adam Softley and Carrie-Ann James for their creativity and patience; and various friends, plus Frank Van Hasselt, Clear Village, for commenting on book drafts.

My professional collaborators for their support and stimulation during the last three years of researching and writing the book: Kristen Richards, Oculus/AIA NYC; Simona Finessi, Anna Masello and Luca Molinari, ArchMarathon; Lorraine Landels and Roger Nickells, Buro Happold; Michael Speaks, Dean, School of Architecture, Syracuse University; Gianpiero Venturini, New Generations; my PhD supervisor, Professor Peter Carl, CASS London Met, and examiners Professor Nick Bailey and Renata Tyszczuk; LSE Cities/Urban Age cohorts Ricky Burdett, Richard Sennett, Saskia Sassen, Ute Weiland, Sophie Body-Gendrot and Adam Kaasa (RCA); Dr Katharine S Willis, School of Architecture, Design and Environment, Plymouth University; Kristen Feireiss and Hans-Jurgen Cömmerell, ANCB, Berlin; Eva Woode, Roca London Gallery; Helen Castle, Wiley & Son; and a special thanks to John Thackara, who kindly wrote our preface.

My friends, cohorts and collaborators for wit and wisdom, inspiration and enthusiasm: Liza Fior, Alison Brooks, Alessandra Cianchetta, Johanna Gibbons, Irena Bauman, Claudia Pasquero, Marco Poletto, Susie Dawson, Christine Styrnau, Torsten Neeland, Renata Gatti, Gioia Meller Marcovicz, Januscz Podrazik, Alejandro Zaera-Polo, Ole Bouman, David Adjaye, Simon Brown, David Turnbull, Jane Harrison, Karim Badawi, Rod Tahoun, Alisa Andrasek, Raffaele Pé, Hubert Klumpner, Alfredo Brillembourg, Mark Dytham, Astrid Klein, Nico Macdonald, Eva Sopeoglou, Megumi Yamashita, John Hyatt, Julia Thayne, Marco Guarnieri, Rafael Lozano-Hemmer and my departed, ever treasured, friends Barbara Putt, Ed Annink, James Irvine and Greg Daville.

Finally, we would both like to extend our gratitude to Nicole Solano, Sadé Lee and Alex Hollingsworth at Routledge Taylor & Francis for their professional support of *Recoded City* as a major and unprecedented title in the publisher's international urbanism book list.

[1] Surrealist writer André Breton coined the term 'explosante-fixe' (exploding-fixed), in Nadja (1973); this was chosen by Pierre Boulez for the title of one of his finest musical compositions (1985/93), which demonstrates beautifully Breton's belief that works of art must be bursting with ideas, yet stabilised by predetermined logic.

Lucy Bullivant

'If you touch one thing with deep awareness, you touch everything' – Thich Nhat Hanh

Thomas Ermacora is a Danish-Italian regeneration architect, impact entrepreneur and futures thinker. He is the producer, design director and co-author of *Recoded City*. His career is marked by a passionate pursuit of scalable solutions for today's pressing social and environmental issues, and he has led pioneering projects in the fields of architecture, design, film, music, gastronomy and technology, frequently collaborating with leading iconoclasts.

A mostly self-taught creative polymath, Ermacora grew up in a family of industrial engineers and holds a 'Maitrise de Geographie' from the Panthéon-Sorbonne University in Paris with a specialism in Urban Design and Sustainable Development, as well as an International Affairs and Philosophy Bachelors degree from the American University of Paris; he has undertaken further studies at the Massachusetts Institute of Technology, Northwestern University, the University of Copenhagen and the IMD business school. His 'Virtual Centrality' thesis was the basis of his initial work as a digital-divide researcher and consultant for Tactis, France, predominantly on projects for the French prime minister's technology advisory organisation (CSTI), analysing ways of introducing broadband to help regenerate remote areas and villages.

In 2001, with his eco-living consultancy Etikstudio, Ermacora curated the first exhibition on urban cycling culture for the Danish House, Paris, depicting the bicycle as a Trojan horse for urban sustainability. The Mayor of Paris extended a written tribute to Ermacora's successful alternative advocacy platform for changing commuting attitudes, acknowledging its inspiration for the city's Velib bike-sharing programme. In 2004, when Ermacora rebranded the exhibition Dreams on Wheels for the Danish Design Museum the Danish Foreign Ministry selected it to be one of the 2 global exhibitions promoting the Copenhagen UN Summit COP15. During 2007-9 it toured to 15 countries including the UK, Russia, Japan, Mexico and Australia, showing at notable venues such as the Federation Square in Melbourne and London's City Hall. The exhibition, which won the NEXT award from Moscow's ARCH festival, was seen by over a million people, brought global attention to Gehl Architects' work, and became the launch platform for the Danish Cycling Embassy and Copenhagenize Consulting.

After carrying out eco-retrofits and contributing to low-carbon masterplans such as the Sonderborg Harbour Project Zero under Gehry Partners, Ermacora shifted his attention towards empowerment of citizens, and in 2008 he founded the tactical urban design non-profit Clear Village (Clear-Village.org). As chief creative and strategist he has delivered participatory initiatives across Europe for social landlords, local authorities, and clients such as World Design Capital 2012, UNESCO Design Cities and the Design Council (UK). The tools and processes he has invented and developed have received numerous peer accolades and been nominated for the INDEX award 2013 and Placemaking Awards 2014 and 2015.

In 2012 Ermacora founded the Limewharf (Limewharf.org), a hybrid cultural innovation hub including London's first fab lab (MachinesRoom.org) in Hackney, East London. Here he designed and renovated the 20,000 square feet Limewharf buildings from reclaimed objects and simple DIY materials custom-fitted in a workshop built in the basement. Limewharf has become a leading art and technology experimentation and incubation space in which Ermacora has curated groundbreaking shows such as Adhocracy with Joseph Grima, Global Feast with Alex Haw, Biological Kitchen with Lucy McRae and Loop.ph, and salons including the Recode Talks with Lucy Bullivant and the Urban Design Group. His incubatory focus has helped the success of Technology Will Save Us and other local initiatives, and the Machines Room has become a go-to place for institutions such as NESTA, the Crafts Council, the British Council's Maker Library Network, the Royal Society of Arts and various universities. To pave the way for expansion, Ermacora has co-designed an extension to the Limewharf with architects Carmody Groarke, with whom he is now developing other activities.

Ermacora's works and ventures have been featured in *The Ecologist, ArchDaily, Wired, Wallpaper*, London Design Festival, Epoch Times, Dezeen, Poptech* and many other publications. He has written for influential magazines including *Architectural Review, Arup Thoughts* and for *Inhabitat* as a contributing editor and co-owner (between 2008 and 2012).

Ermacora has spoken and lectured at TEDu Global, Forum for the Future, the Future Laboratory, Chinese Arts Academy (CAA), UIP ESARQ (Master's Programme in International Cooperation and Sustainable Emergency Architecture), Aarhus School of Architecture, Clerkenwell Design Week, Future Perfect, Club of Amsterdam, TEDxNYIT, TEDxHelsingborg, Netherlands Architecture Institute, 100% Design London, Edinburgh Science Festival, SummitSeries, YouAreInControl, DesignBoost, and the Moscow Douma. He was a member of the jury for the IAAC Digital Fabrications Master 2014 and the Dwell Reburbia competition 2009, has advised RIBA Building Futures, Worldchanging, Helsinki Design Week and Bioneers, and sits on the board of a number of ethical radical innovation start-ups.

Thomas Ermacora

Lucy Bullivant PhD Hon FRIBA is a cultural historian, award-winning author, consultant, curator, Adjunct Professor, Urban Design History and Theory at Syracuse University, the founder and editor-in-chief of Urbanista.org, a consultant and the co-author of *Recoded City*. She was elected an Honorary Fellow of the Royal Institute of British Architects (RIBA) for her services to architectural culture in 2010.

Since the early 1990s Bullivant has consistently investigated, evaluated and presented innovative synergies in contemporary architecture and urban design between theory and practice across cultures. Through her international exhibitions, conferences and publications, public speaking and consultancy work she advocates higher design standards and experimental multidisciplinary strategies to help counter the negative effects of globalisation and of other retrogressive practices.

Bullivant's focus on masterplanning and adaptive frameworks, relational urbanism and social equity in the formal and informal city and 'hyper-local' digital-physical strategies is complemented by her PhD by Prior Output, Sir John Cass Faculty of Art, Architecture and Design, London Metropolitan University, for *From Masterplanning to Adaptive Planning: Understanding the contemporary Tools and Processes for Civic Urban Order* (2015), and publications including *Masterplanning Futures* (Routledge, 2012; Book of the Year, Urban Design Awards, 2014) and *Responsive Environments: Architecture, Art and Design* (2006). Works such as *4dsocial* (AD, 2007) and *4dspace* (2005), guest-edited by Bullivant, were the first of their kind on the potential of interactive architecture for public space. *New Arcadians: Emerging UK Architects* (2012) and *Anglo Files: UK Architecture's Rising Generation* (2005) investigated the activities of new generations of architects.

Bullivant has curated many acclaimed international exhibitions including Urbanistas: Women Innovators in Architecture, Urban and Landscape Design, at the Roca London Gallery, 2015; Space Invaders, with Pedro Gadanho, for the British Council, which toured Europe, Japan and Brazil (2001-3); Kid Size: The Material World of Childhood, with Vitra Design Museum (global tour, 1997-2005) and The Near and the Far: Fixed and In Flux, the British exhibition, XIX Triennale di Milano (1996) supported by the UK government. Prior to that Bullivant was Heinz Curator of Architectural Programmes, Royal Academy of Arts, London, and a successful art curator.

Bullivant is a public speaker at venues including AIA NY Center for Architecture, Syracuse University, Cooper Union, New York Institute of Technology, Architectural League, University of California, Los Angeles, Institute for Advanced Architecture of Catalonia, TEDxVienna and across the UK. She has lectured at conferences on future urbanism including Territorial Encounters, Future Cities Lab, ETH Zurich (2012) and Second Nature, Institute of Malaysian Architects, Kuala Lumpur (2010). She chairs such events as Mediacity 5, Plymouth University (2015); ReWork (2014); 4dspace, ICA; Softspace, Tate Modern, London.

Bullivant writes for *The Guardian* and *The Plan* (as special correspondent) and has published features in *Volume, Harvard Design Magazine, Domus, Architectural Review, Architecture Today, A+U, AD, Uncube, The Plan, Indesign* and *Metropolis*. Her work has been profiled in *A+D+M* and *Arkitekten*. She is co-chair of ArchMarathon, Milan; a member of the Scientific Committee of the Institut pour la Ville en Mouvement, Paris; Comité Technique, FRAC, Orléans; Quality Review Panel for the London Legacy Development Corporation, 2011-13. Urbanista.org: www.urbanista.org; Lucy Bullivant & Associates: www.lucybullivant.net.

Lucy Bullivant

The Design Surgery is a creative agency based in central London specialising in graphic design, illustration, information design, animation, editorial, digital and branding. Founded in 2004 by Adam Softley and Shane Mizon, The Surgery draws on an emotionally and ethically driven approach to create visually inspiring, clear and strategic contemporary design. The Surgery team works with a wide range of prestigious clients spanning a range of audiences and sectors, including governmental organisations and commercial entities locally and internationally, such as Thomson Reuters, PA Consulting Group, AON, GfK, *The Times* and the *Sunday Times, Raconteur, Countrywide* and Turkish Airlines.

The Design Surgery

Index

This short index includes the names of individuals and organisations referred to in the core chapters, and the names of contributors to the book (Voices, Preface).

Authors
Thomas Ermacora
Lucy Bullivant

Producer/ Design Director
Thomas Ermacora

Art Direction
Shane Mizon

Infographic Strategist
Thomas Ermacora

Infographic Director
Matthew Rowett

Editorial Design
Carrie-ann James
Matthew Rowett

Copy Editor
Marion Moisy

Picture Research/ Rights Management
Caroline Ellerby